Shojo Beat

ORESAMA TEACHER

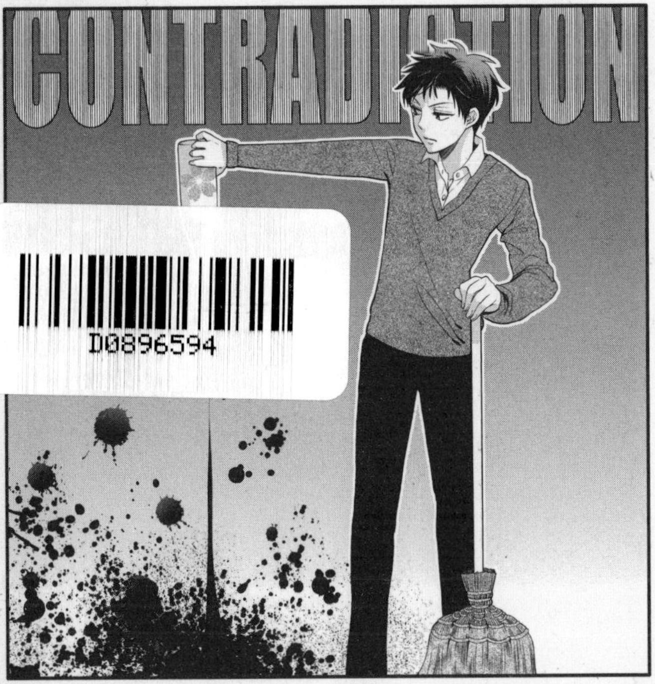
CONTRADICTION

Vol. 12

Story & Art by

Izumi Tsubaki

ORESAMA TEACHER

Volume 12
CONTENTS

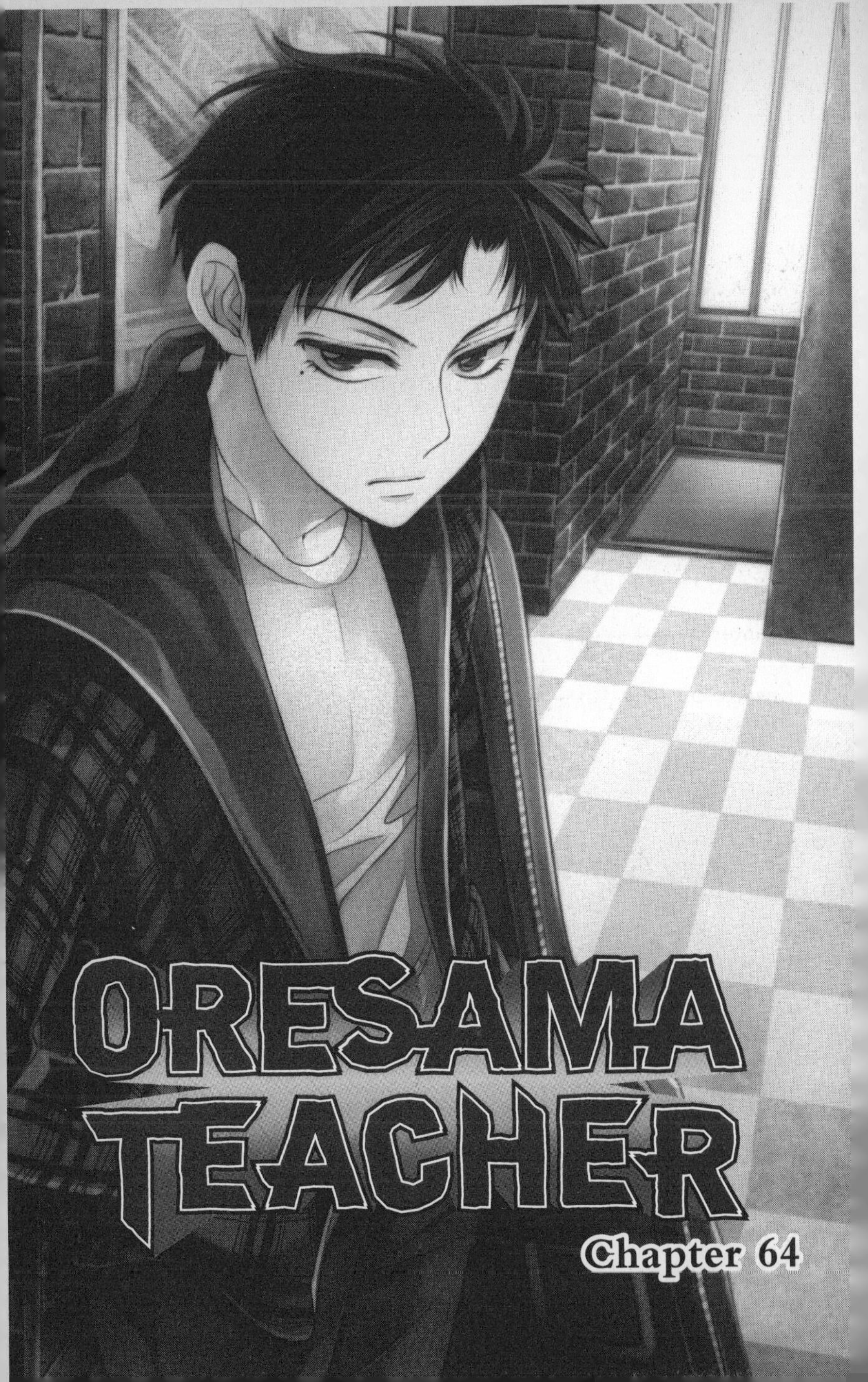
ORESAMA TEACHER
Chapter 64

THE STALKER AND US

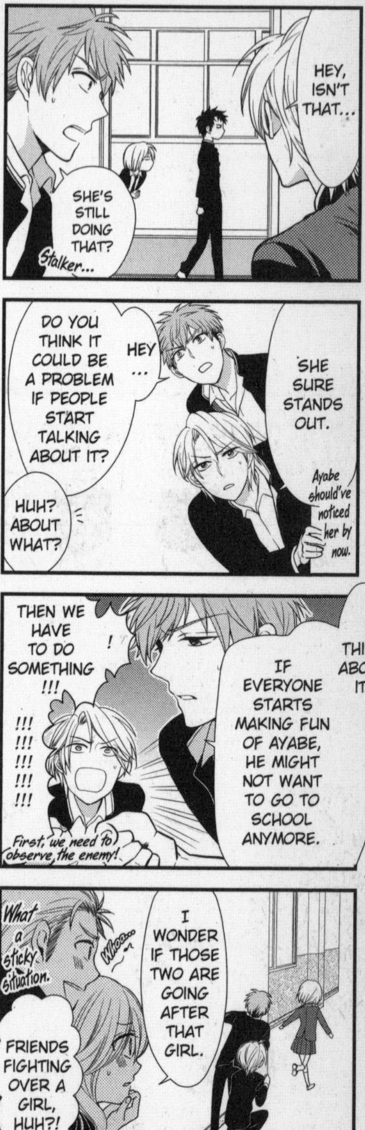
HEY, ISN'T THAT...
SHE'S STILL DOING THAT?
Stalker...
SHE SURE STANDS OUT.
Ayabe should've noticed her by now.
HEY ...
DO YOU THINK IT COULD BE A PROBLEM IF PEOPLE START TALKING ABOUT IT?
HUH? ABOUT WHAT?
THINK ABOUT IT.
IF EVERYONE STARTS MAKING FUN OF AYABE, HE MIGHT NOT WANT TO GO TO SCHOOL ANYMORE.
!
THEN WE HAVE TO DO SOMETHING !!!
!!! !!! !!! !!! !!!
First, we need to observe the enemy!
I WONDER IF THOSE TWO ARE GOING AFTER THAT GIRL.
Whoa...
What a sticky situation.
FRIENDS FIGHTING OVER A GIRL, HUH?!

A SCOOP

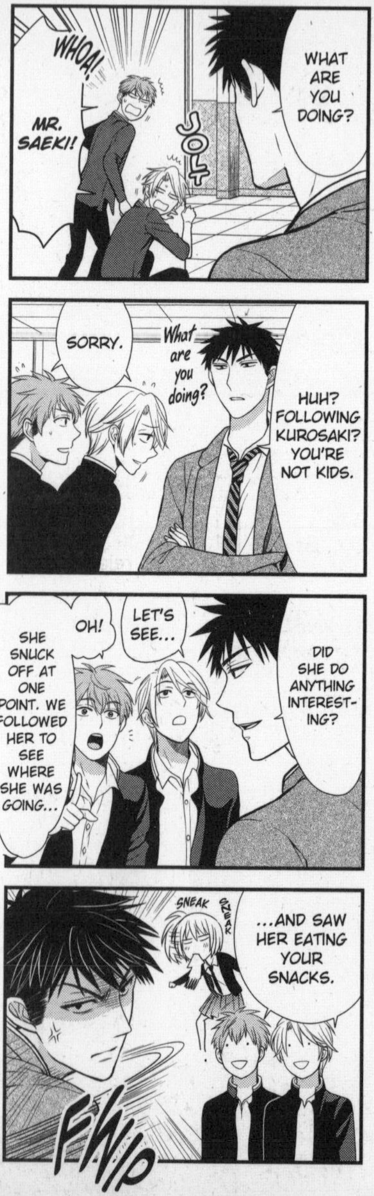
WHAT ARE YOU DOING?
JOLT
WHOA!
MR. SAEKI!
HUH? FOLLOWING KUROSAKI? YOU'RE NOT KIDS.
What are you doing?
SORRY.
DID SHE DO ANYTHING INTERESTING?
LET'S SEE...
OH!
SHE SNUCK OFF AT ONE POINT. WE FOLLOWED HER TO SEE WHERE SHE WAS GOING...
...AND SAW HER EATING YOUR SNACKS.
SNEAK SNEAK
FWIP

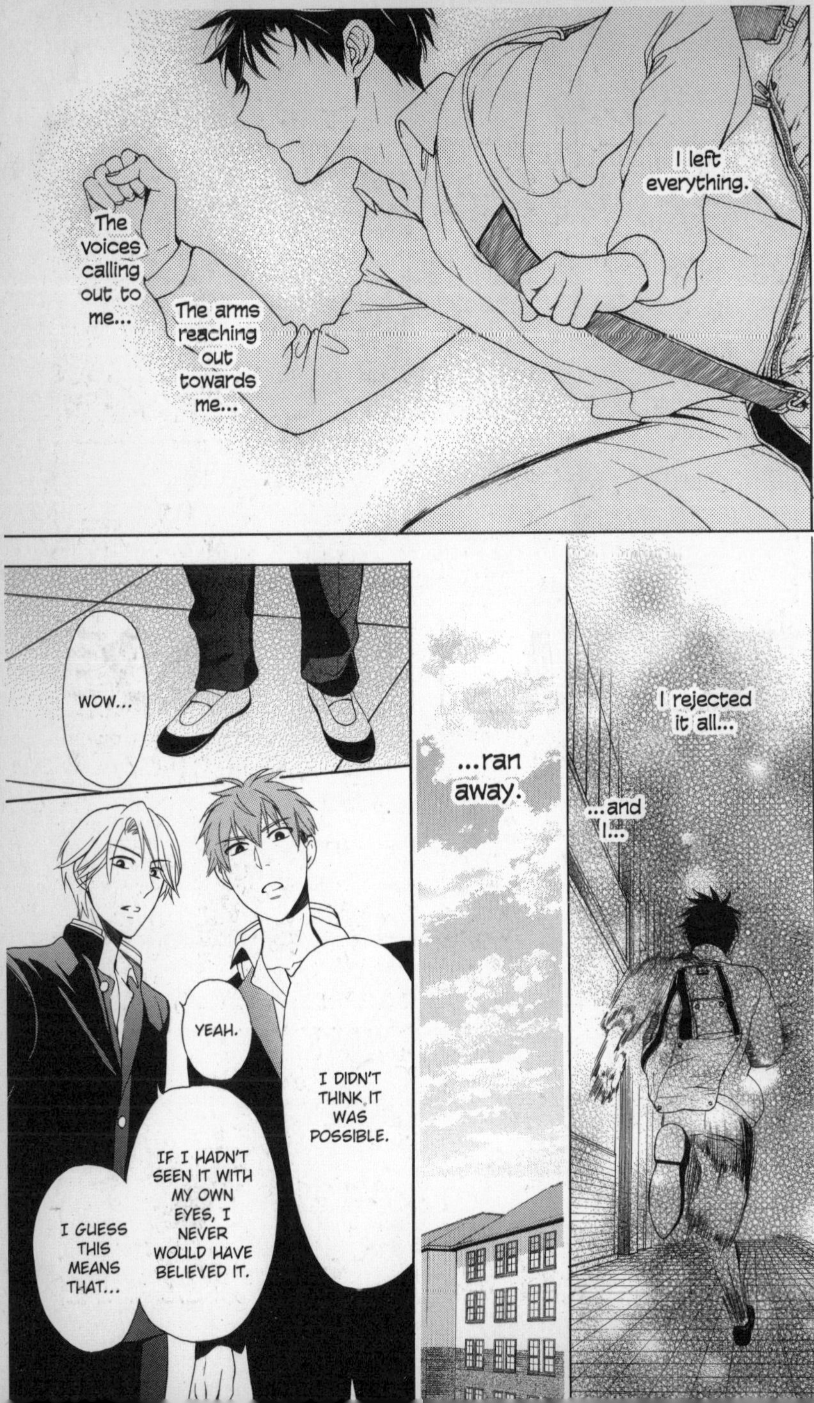
I left everything.
The voices calling out to me...
The arms reaching out towards me...
I rejected it all...
...and I...
...ran away.
WOW...
YEAH.
I DIDN'T THINK IT WAS POSSIBLE.
IF I HADN'T SEEN IT WITH MY OWN EYES, I NEVER WOULD HAVE BELIEVED IT.
I GUESS THIS MEANS THAT...

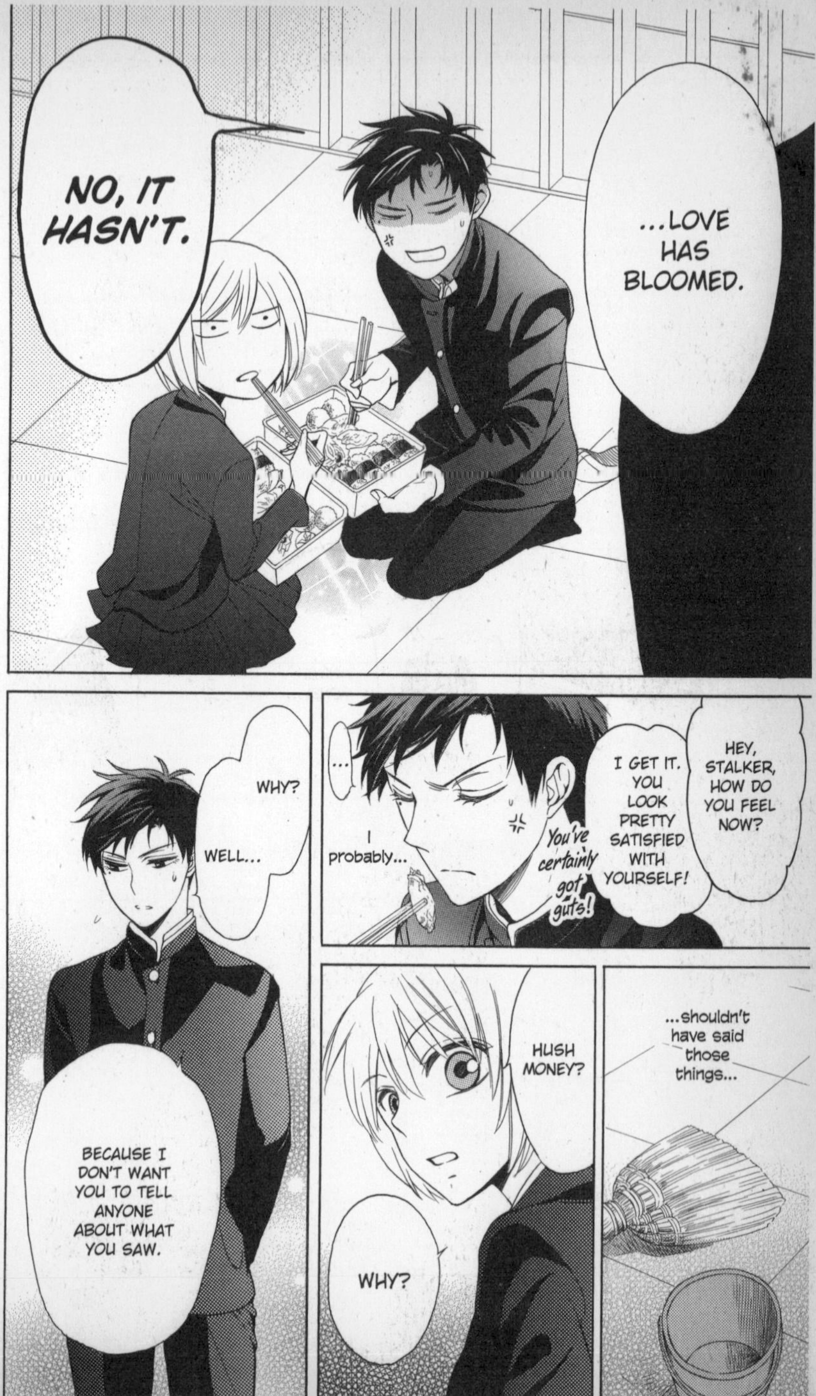
...LOVE HAS BLOOMED.
NO, IT HASN'T.
HEY, STALKER, HOW DO YOU FEEL NOW?
I GET IT. YOU LOOK PRETTY SATISFIED WITH YOURSELF!
You've certainly got guts!
...
I probably...
...shouldn't have said those things...
HUSH MONEY?
WHY?
WHY?
WELL...
BECAUSE I DON'T WANT YOU TO TELL ANYONE ABOUT WHAT YOU SAW.

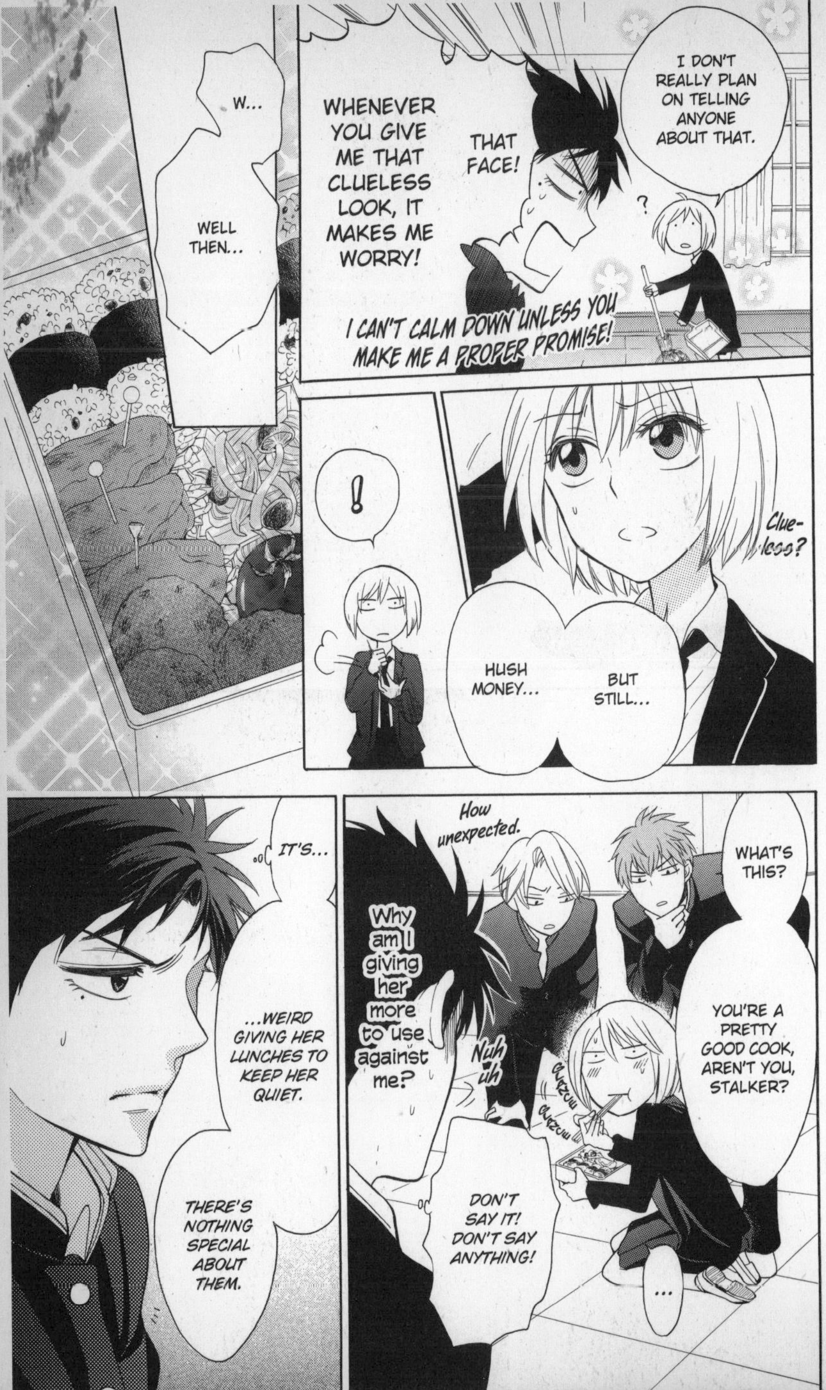
I DON'T REALLY PLAN ON TELLING ANYONE ABOUT THAT.
?
THAT FACE!
WHENEVER YOU GIVE ME THAT CLUELESS LOOK, IT MAKES ME WORRY!
I CAN'T CALM DOWN UNLESS YOU MAKE ME A PROPER PROMISE!
Clue-less?
HUSH MONEY...
BUT STILL...
!
W...
WELL THEN...
WHAT'S THIS?
How unexpected.
YOU'RE A PRETTY GOOD COOK, AREN'T YOU, STALKER?
Why am I giving her more to use against me?
Nuh uh
DON'T SAY IT! DON'T SAY ANYTHING!
...
IT'S...
...WEIRD GIVING HER LUNCHES TO KEEP HER QUIET.
THERE'S NOTHING SPECIAL ABOUT THEM.

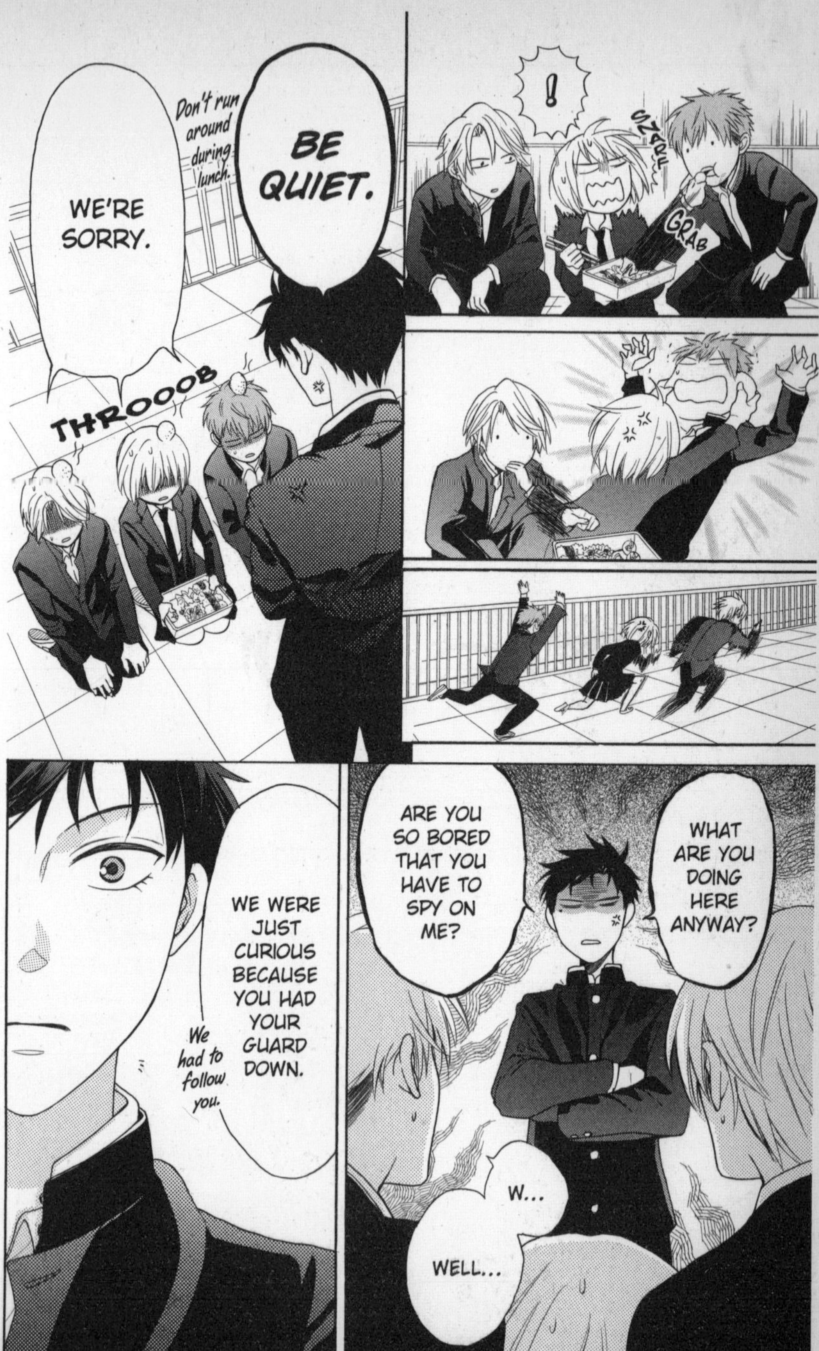
!
SNARF
GRAB
BE QUIET.
Don't run around during lunch.
WE'RE SORRY.
THROOOB
WHAT ARE YOU DOING HERE ANYWAY?
ARE YOU SO BORED THAT YOU HAVE TO SPY ON ME?
W...
WELL...
WE WERE JUST CURIOUS BECAUSE YOU HAD YOUR GUARD DOWN.
We had to follow you.

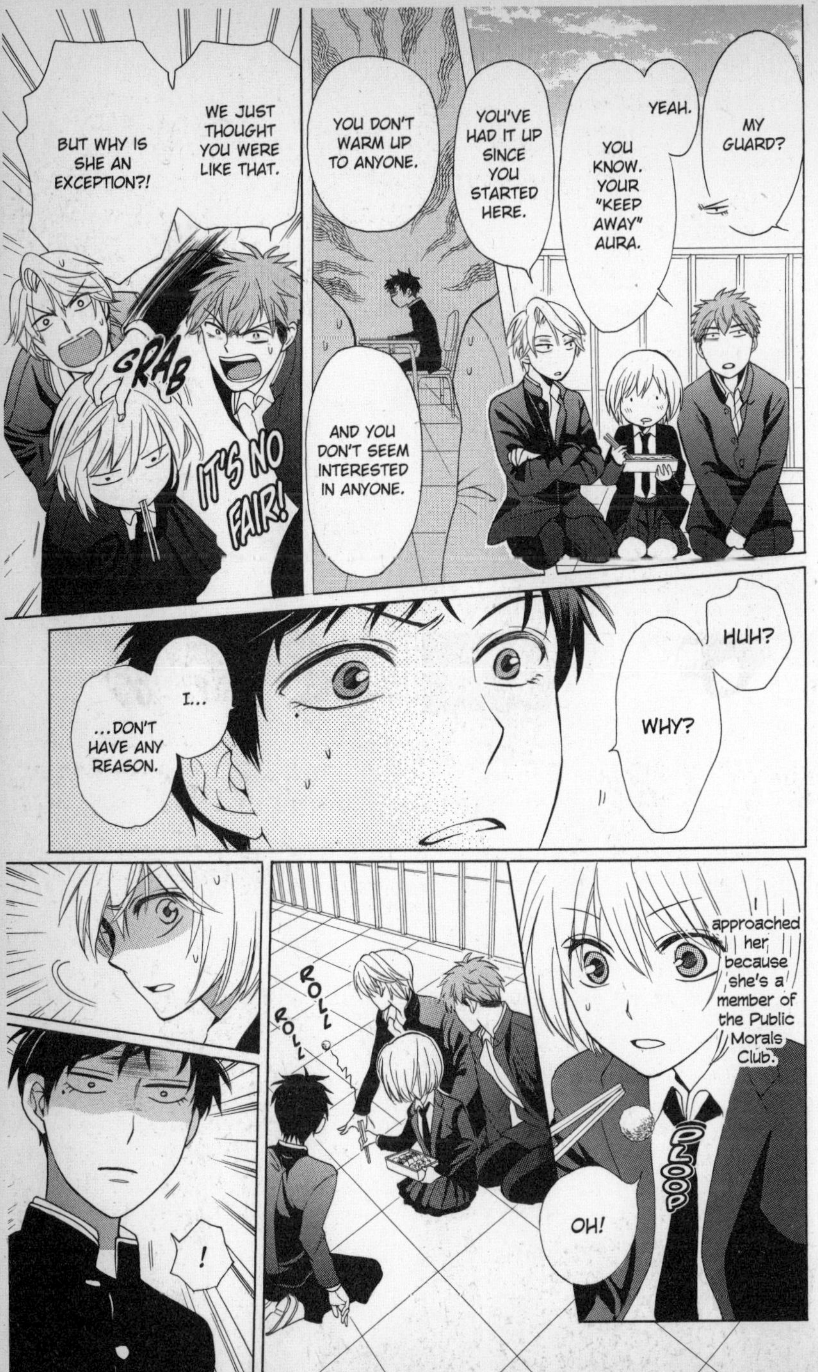
MY GUARD?
YEAH.
YOU KNOW. YOUR "KEEP AWAY" AURA.
YOU'VE HAD IT UP SINCE YOU STARTED HERE.
YOU DON'T WARM UP TO ANYONE.
AND YOU DON'T SEEM INTERESTED IN ANYONE.
WE JUST THOUGHT YOU WERE LIKE THAT.
BUT WHY IS SHE AN EXCEPTION?!
GRAB
IT'S NO FAIR!
HUH?
WHY?
I...
...DON'T HAVE ANY REASON.
I approached her because she's a member of the Public Morals Club.
PLOOP
OH!
ROLL
ROLL
!

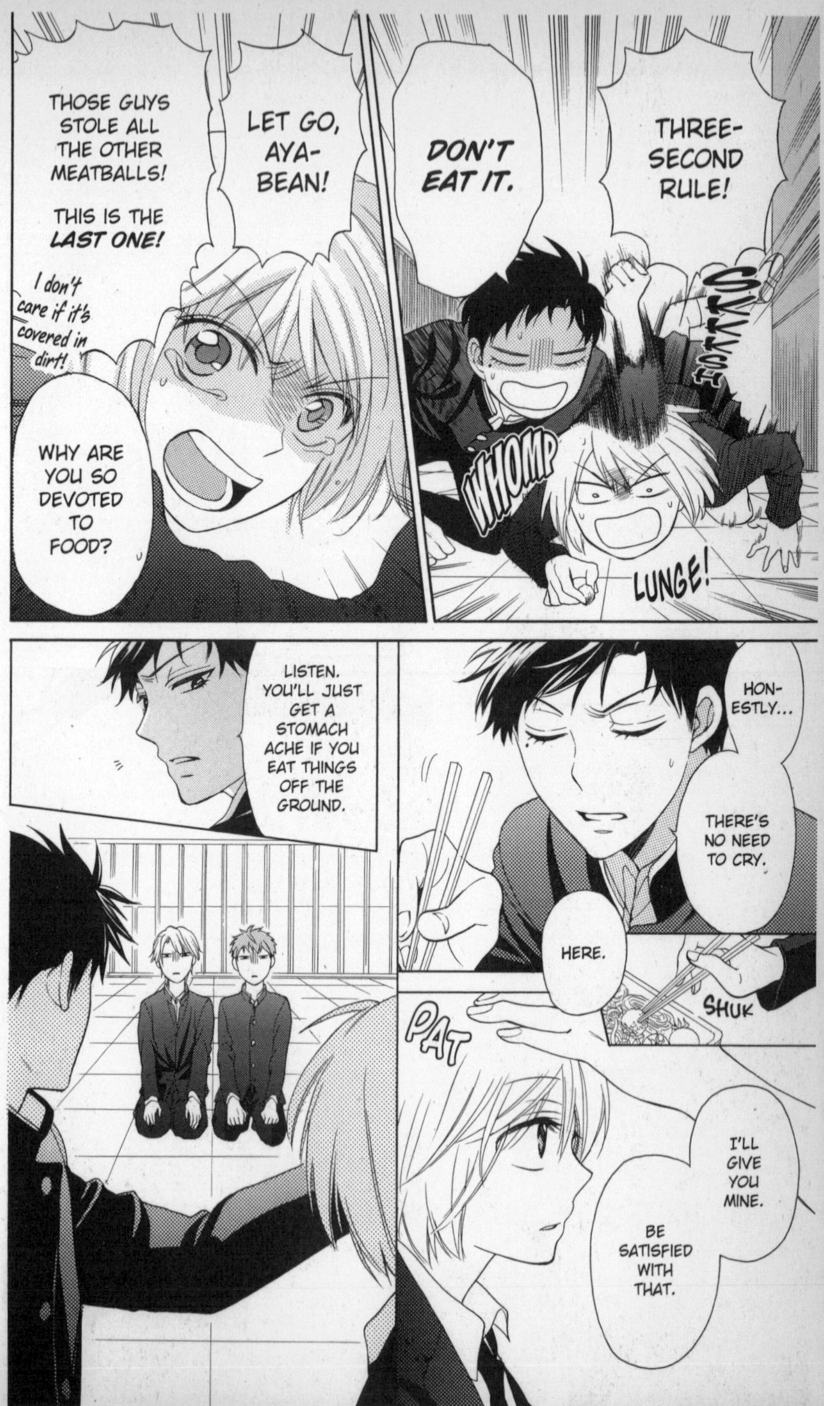
THREE-SECOND RULE!
DON'T EAT IT.
SKKKKSH
WHOMP
LUNGE!
LET GO, AYA-BEAN!
THOSE GUYS STOLE ALL THE OTHER MEATBALLS!
THIS IS THE LAST ONE!
I don't care if it's covered in dirt!
WHY ARE YOU SO DEVOTED TO FOOD?
HON-ESTLY...
THERE'S NO NEED TO CRY.
LISTEN. YOU'LL JUST GET A STOMACH ACHE IF YOU EAT THINGS OFF THE GROUND.
HERE.
SHUK
PAT
I'LL GIVE YOU MINE.
BE SATISFIED WITH THAT.

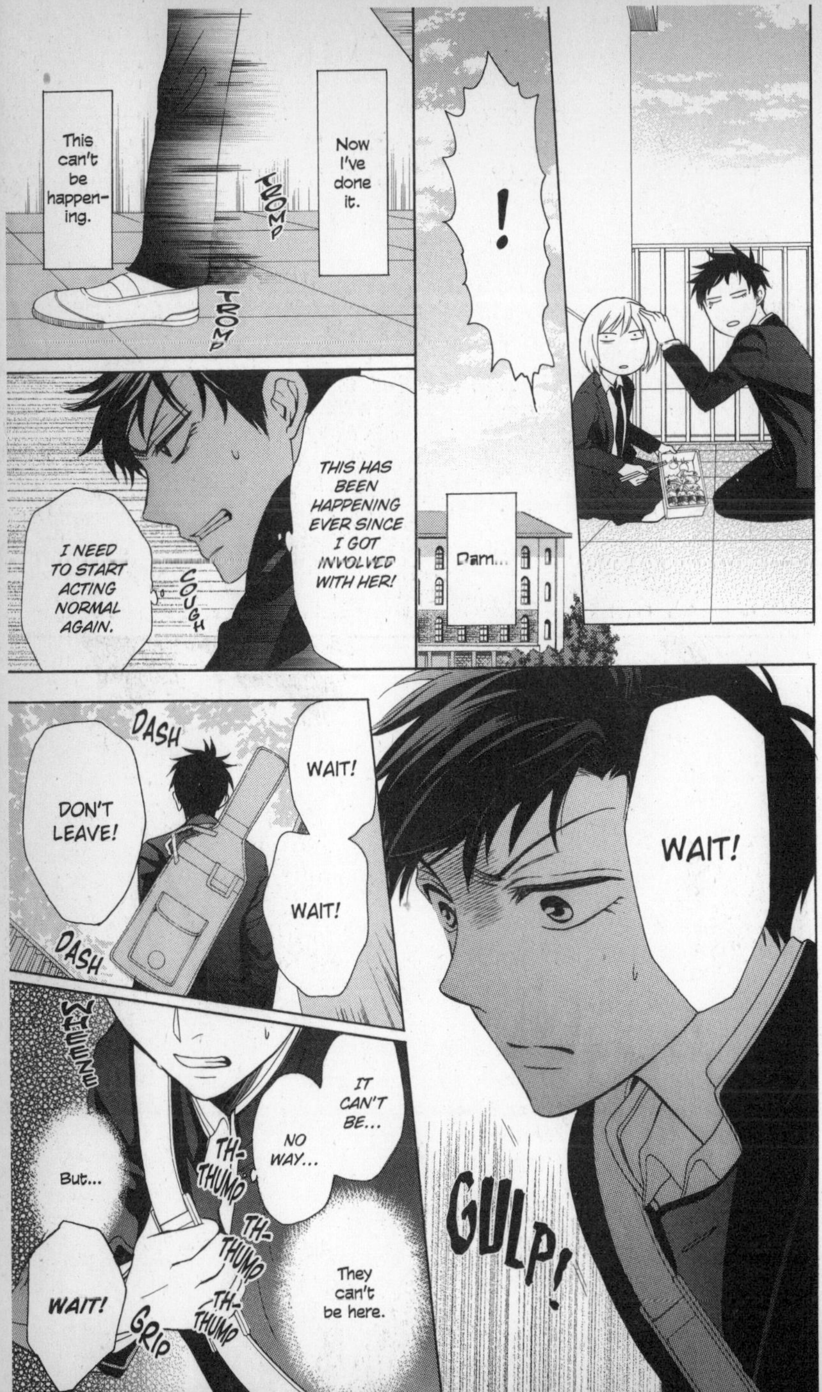
!
Dam...
Now I've done it.
This can't be happening.
TROMP
TROMP
THIS HAS BEEN HAPPENING EVER SINCE I GOT INVOLVED WITH HER!
COUGH
I NEED TO START ACTING NORMAL AGAIN.
WAIT!
GULP!
DASH
WAIT!
WAIT!
DON'T LEAVE!
DASH
IT CAN'T BE...
NO WAY...
They can't be here.
TH-THUMP
TH-THUMP
TH-THUMP
WHEEZE
But...
WAIT!
GRIP

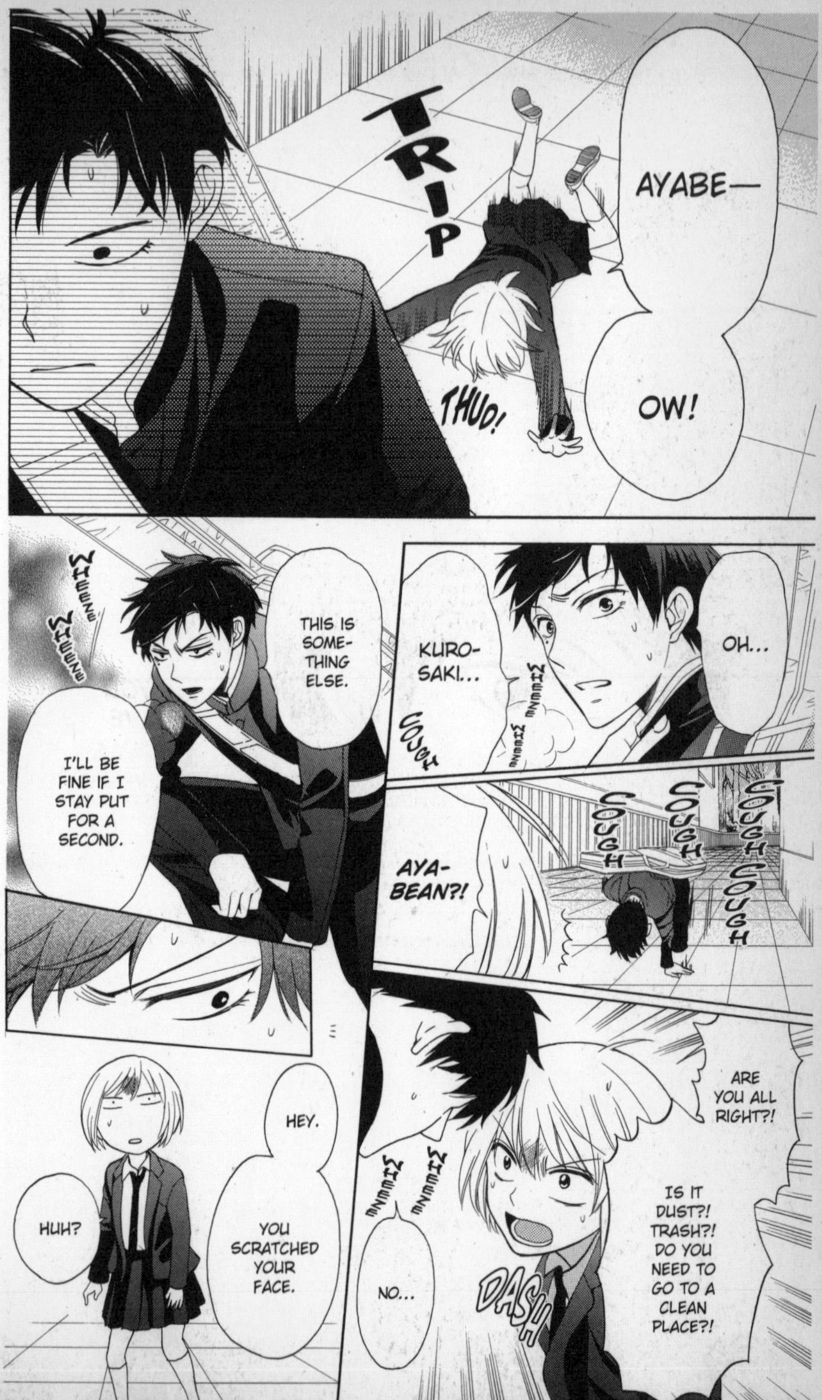
AYABE—
TRIP
OW!
THUD!
OH...
KURO-SAKI...
WHEEZE WHEEZE
COUGH
COUGH COUGH COUGH COUGH COUGH
AYA-BEAN?!
THIS IS SOME-THING ELSE.
WHEEZE WHEEZE
I'LL BE FINE IF I STAY PUT FOR A SECOND.
ARE YOU ALL RIGHT?!
IS IT DUST?! TRASH?! DO YOU NEED TO GO TO A CLEAN PLACE?!
DASH
WHEEZE WHEEZE
NO...
HEY.
YOU SCRATCHED YOUR FACE.
HUH?

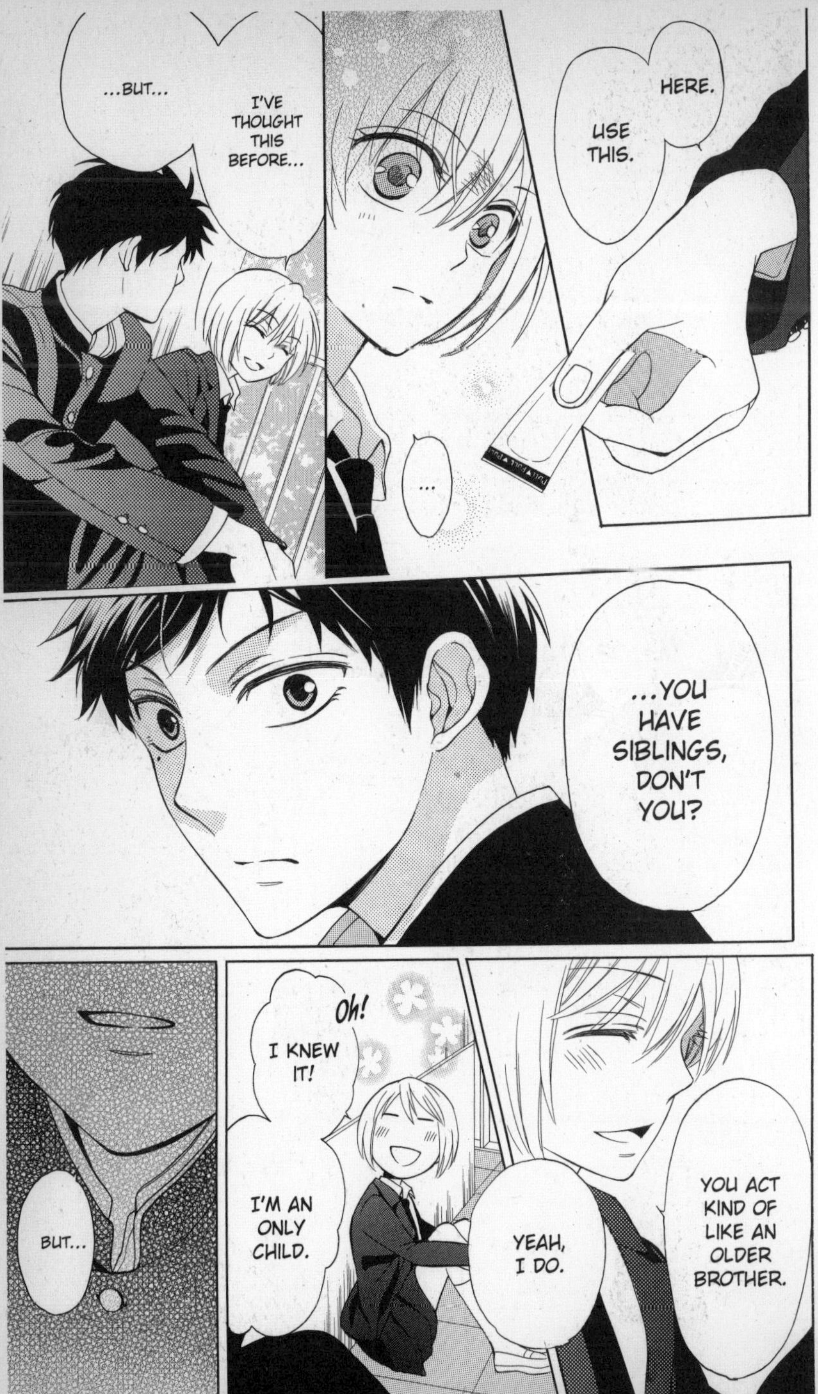
HERE.
USE THIS.
...
I'VE THOUGHT THIS BEFORE...
...BUT...
...YOU HAVE SIBLINGS, DON'T YOU?
YOU ACT KIND OF LIKE AN OLDER BROTHER.
YEAH, I DO.
Oh!
I KNEW IT!
I'M AN ONLY CHILD.
BUT...

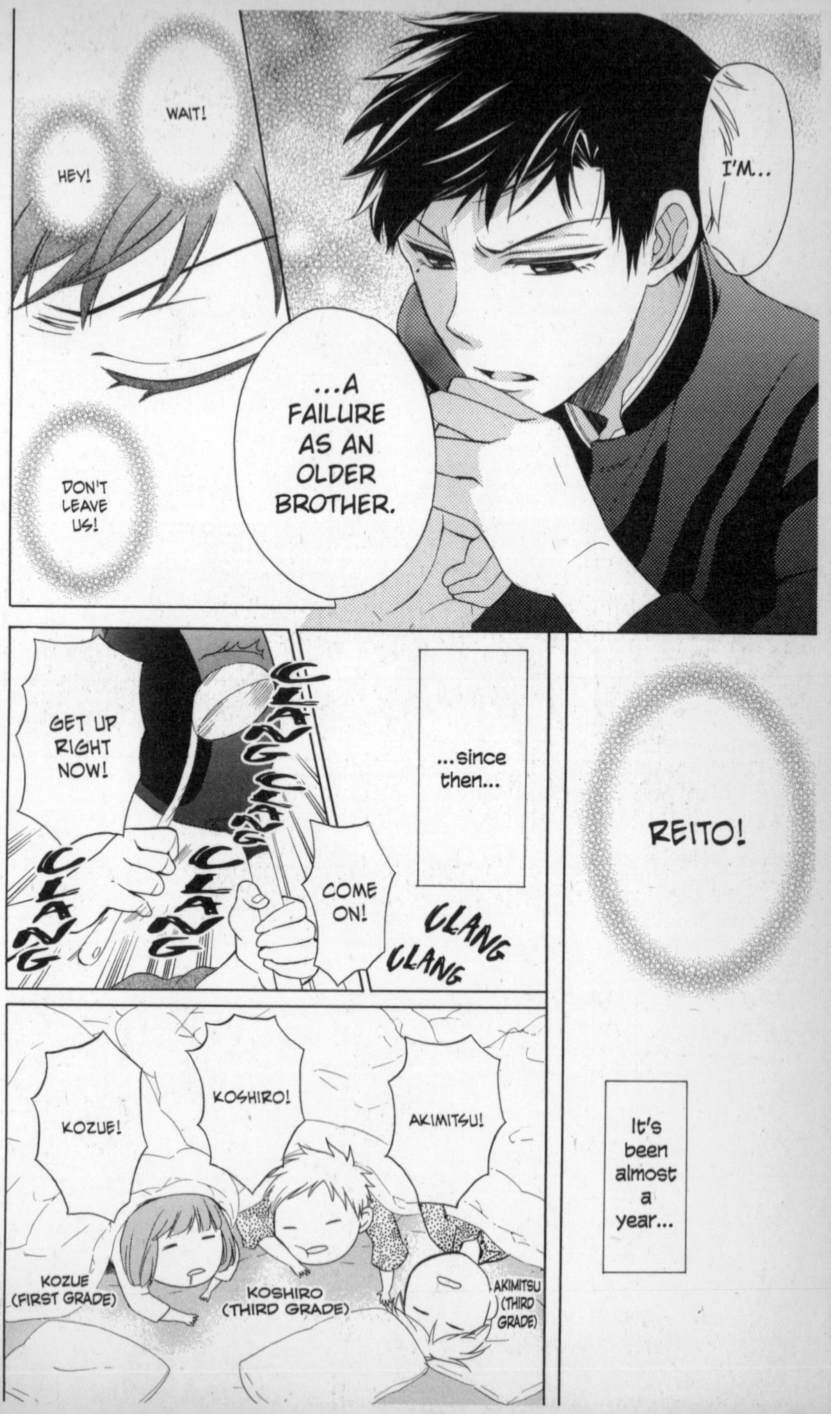
I'M..
...A FAILURE AS AN OLDER BROTHER.
WAIT!
HEY!
DON'T LEAVE US!
REITO!
It's been almost a year...
...since then...
CLANG CLANG
CLANG CLANG
COME ON!
GET UP RIGHT NOW!
CLANG
CLANG
AKIMITSU!
KOSHIRO!
KOZUE!
AKIMITSU (THIRD GRADE)
KOSHIRO (THIRD GRADE)
KOZUE (FIRST GRADE)

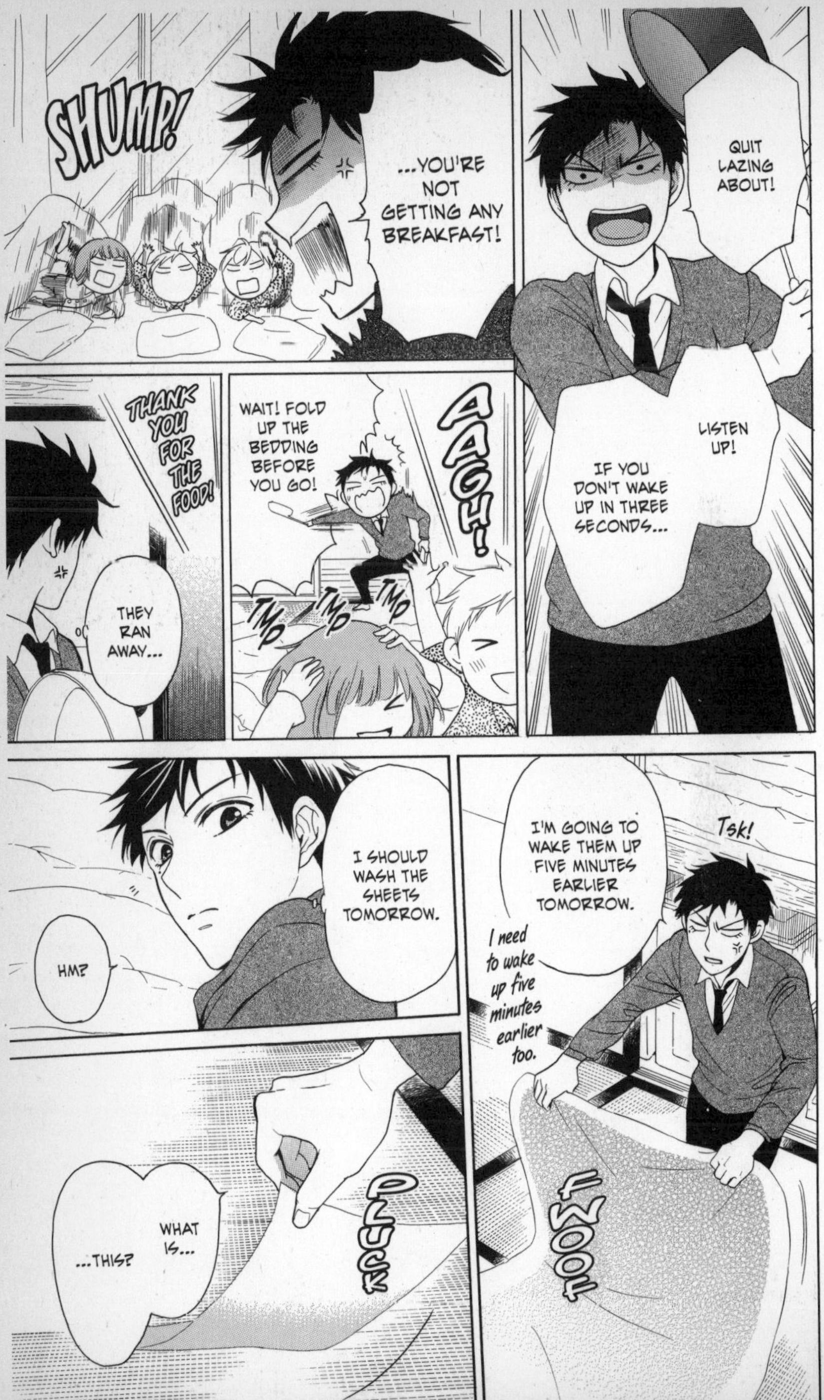
QUIT LAZING ABOUT!
LISTEN UP!
IF YOU DON'T WAKE UP IN THREE SECONDS...
...YOU'RE NOT GETTING ANY BREAKFAST!
SHUMP!
WAIT! FOLD UP THE BEDDING BEFORE YOU GO!
AAGH!
TMP
TMP
TMP
THANK YOU FOR THE FOOD!
THEY RAN AWAY...
Tsk!
I'M GOING TO WAKE THEM UP FIVE MINUTES EARLIER TOMORROW.
I need to wake up five minutes earlier too.
FWOOF
I SHOULD WASH THE SHEETS TOMORROW.
HM?
WHAT IS...
...THIS?
PLUCK

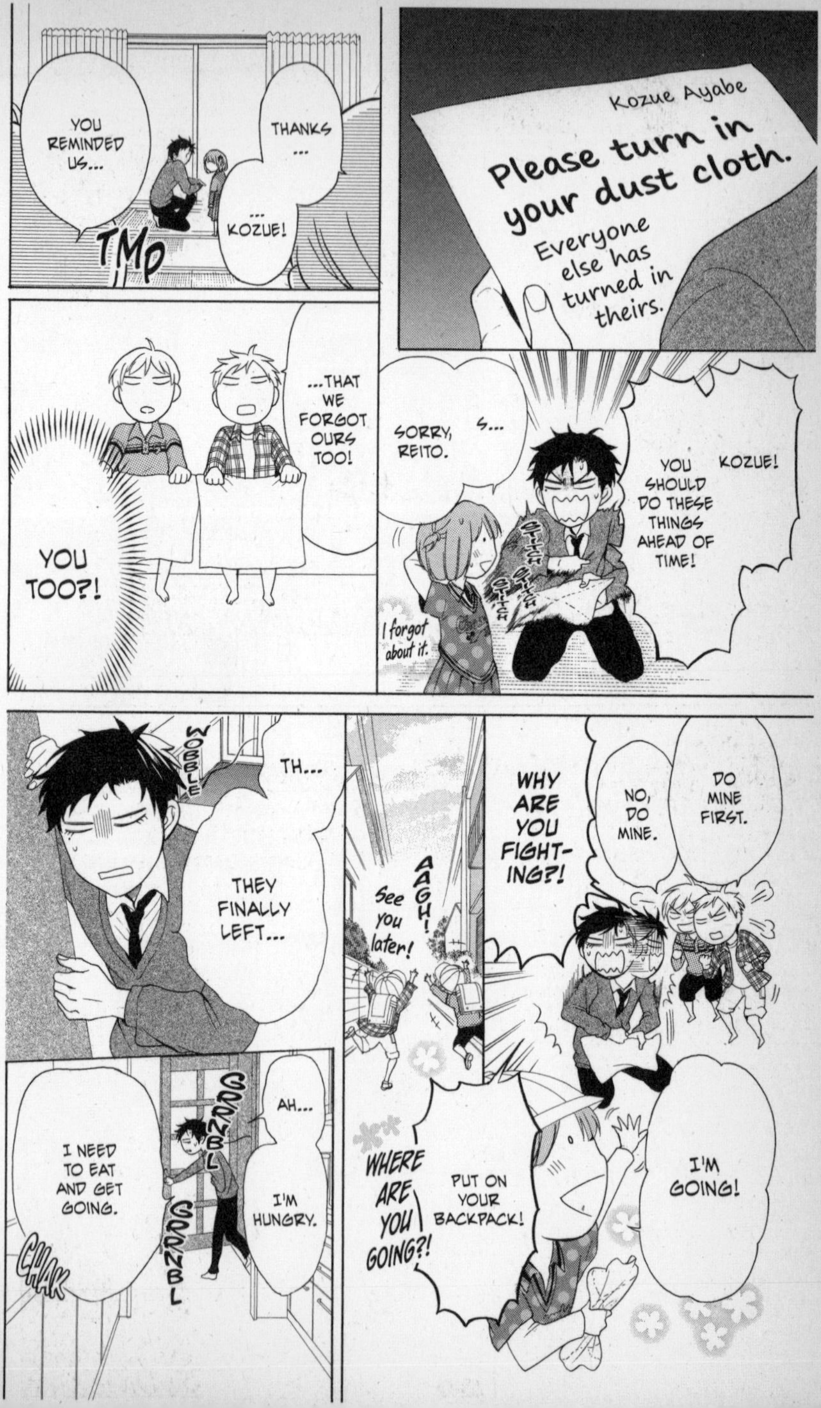
Kozue Ayabe
Please turn in your dust cloth.
Everyone else has turned in theirs.
THANKS...
...KOZUE!
YOU REMINDED US...
TMP
KOZUE!
YOU SHOULD DO THESE THINGS AHEAD OF TIME!
S...
SORRY, REITO.
STITCH STITCH STITCH
I forgot about it.
...THAT WE FORGOT OURS TOO!
YOU TOO?!
DO MINE FIRST.
NO, DO MINE.
WHY ARE YOU FIGHT-ING?!
AAGH!
See you later!
I'M GOING!
PUT ON YOUR BACKPACK!
WHERE ARE YOU GOING?!
TH...
THEY FINALLY LEFT...
WOBBLE
AH...
I'M HUNGRY.
GRRNBL
GRRNBL
I NEED TO EAT AND GET GOING.
CHAK

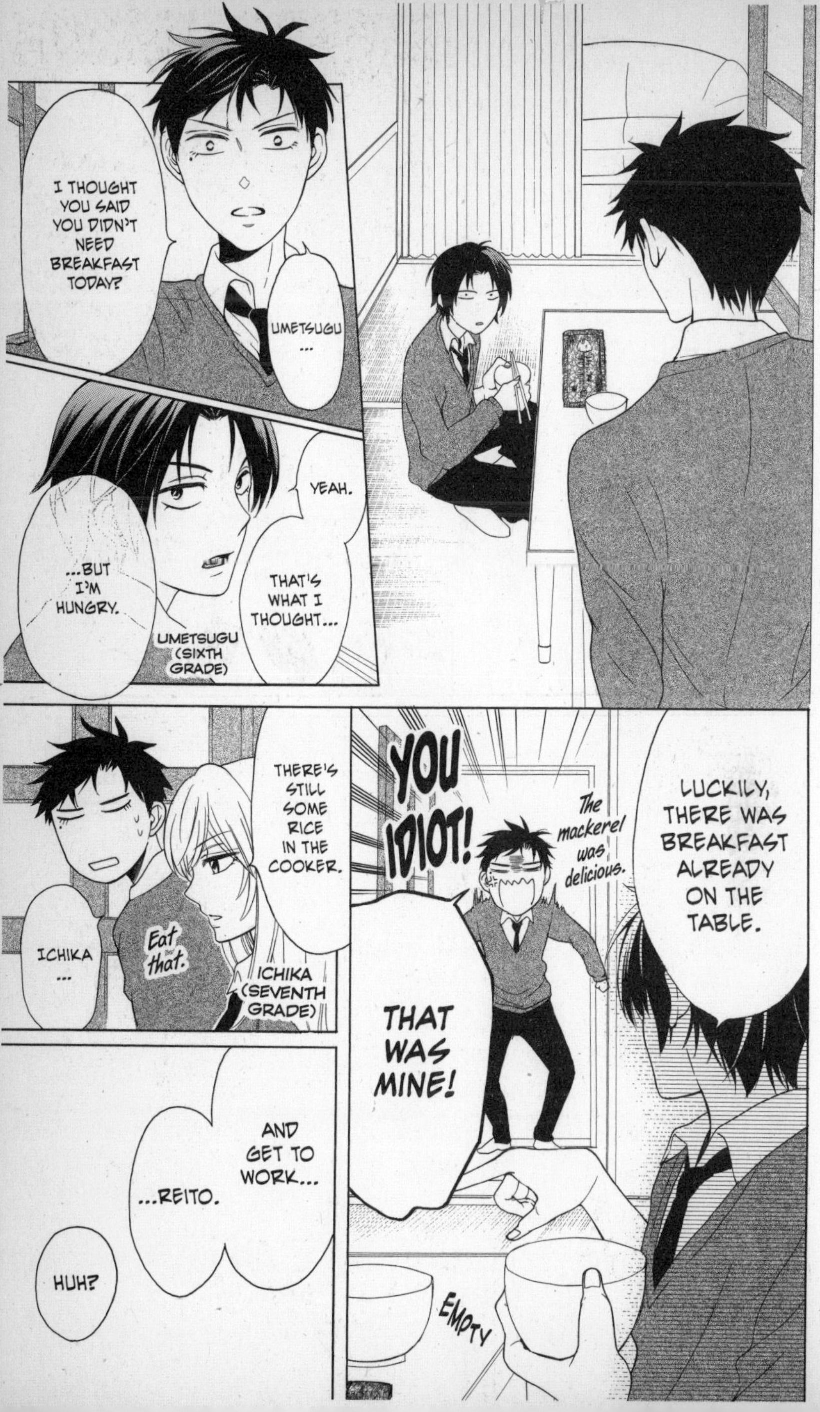
UMETSUGU ...
I THOUGHT YOU SAID YOU DIDN'T NEED BREAKFAST TODAY?
YEAH.
THAT'S WHAT I THOUGHT...
...BUT I'M HUNGRY.
UMETSUGU (SIXTH GRADE)
LUCKILY, THERE WAS BREAKFAST ALREADY ON THE TABLE.
YOU IDIOT!
The mackerel was delicious.
THAT WAS MINE!
EMPTY
THERE'S STILL SOME RICE IN THE COOKER.
Eat that.
ICHIKA (SEVENTH GRADE)
ICHIKA ...
AND GET TO WORK...
...REITO.
HUH?

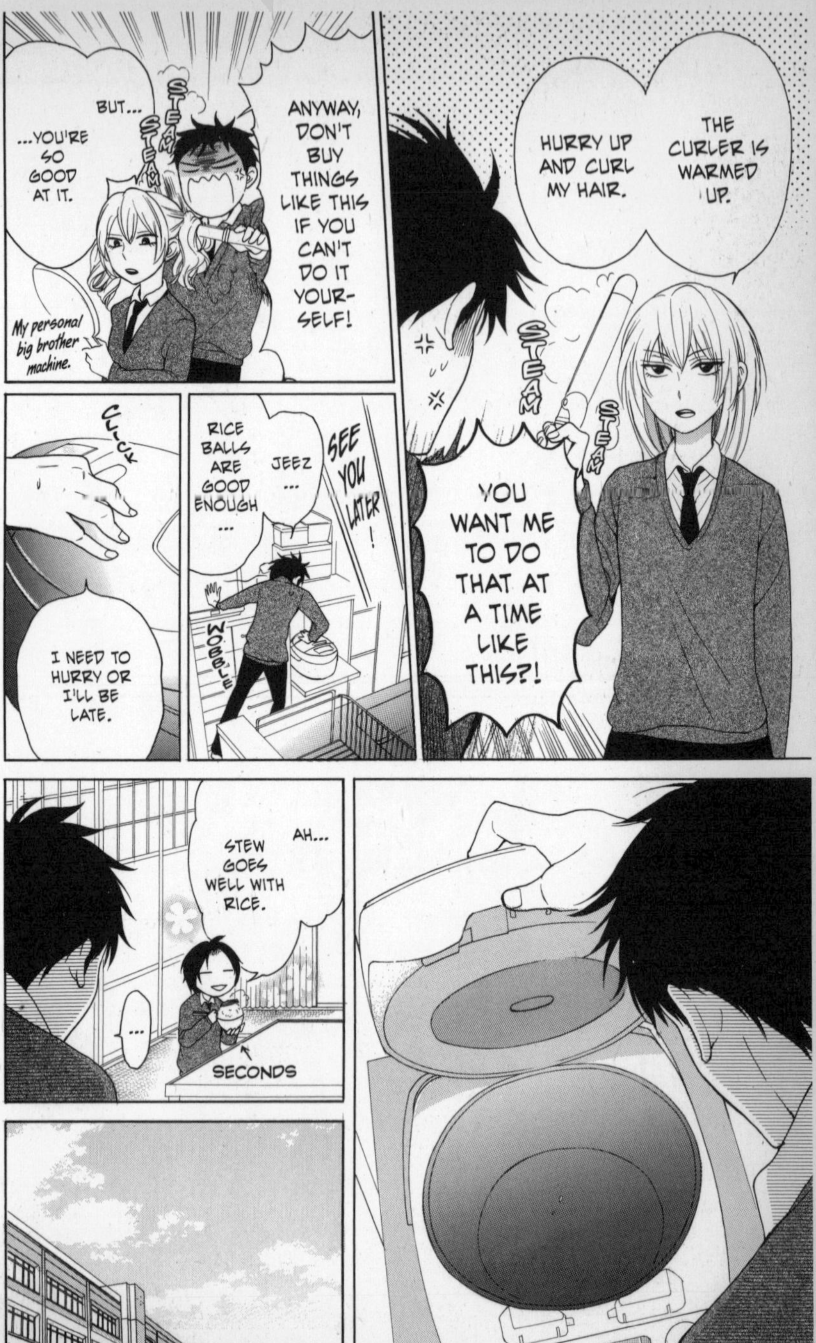
THE CURLER IS WARMED UP.
HURRY UP AND CURL MY HAIR.
STEAM
STEAM
YOU WANT ME TO DO THAT AT A TIME LIKE THIS?!
ANYWAY, DON'T BUY THINGS LIKE THIS IF YOU CAN'T DO IT YOUR-SELF!
STEAM
STEAM
BUT...
...YOU'RE SO GOOD AT IT.
My personal big brother machine.
SEE YOU LATER!
JEEZ...
RICE BALLS ARE GOOD ENOUGH...
WOBBLE
CLICK
I NEED TO HURRY OR I'LL BE LATE.
AH...
STEW GOES WELL WITH RICE.
...
SECONDS

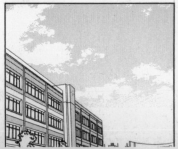

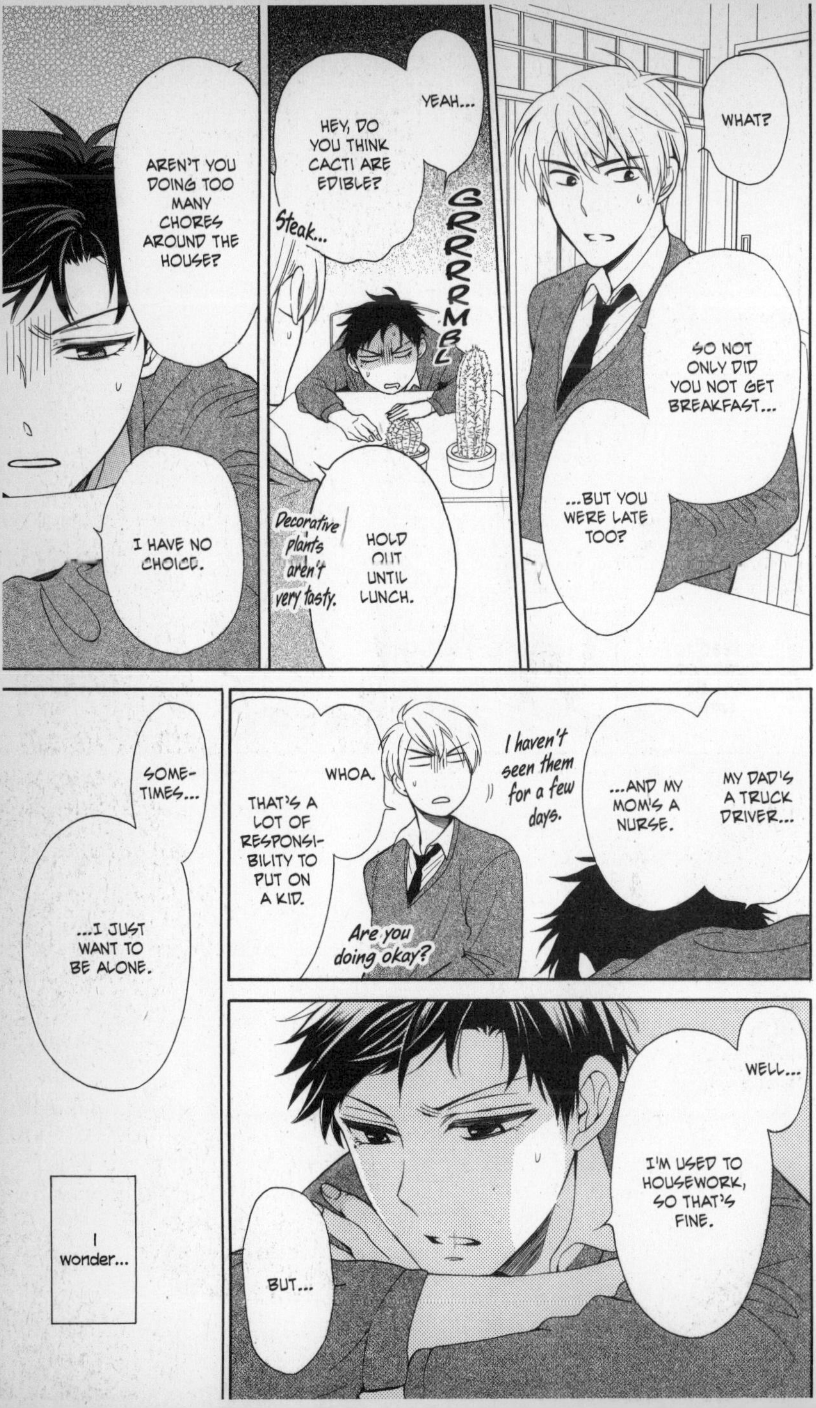
WHAT?
SO NOT ONLY DID YOU NOT GET BREAKFAST...
...BUT YOU WERE LATE TOO?
YEAH...
HEY, DO YOU THINK CACTI ARE EDIBLE?
Steak...
GRRRRRMBL
HOLD OUT UNTIL LUNCH.
Decorative plants aren't very tasty.
AREN'T YOU DOING TOO MANY CHORES AROUND THE HOUSE?
I HAVE NO CHOICE.
MY DAD'S A TRUCK DRIVER...
...AND MY MOM'S A NURSE.
I haven't seen them for a few days.
WHOA.
THAT'S A LOT OF RESPONSIBILITY TO PUT ON A KID.
Are you doing okay?
WELL...
I'M USED TO HOUSEWORK, SO THAT'S FINE.
BUT...
SOME-TIMES...
...I JUST WANT TO BE ALONE.
I wonder...

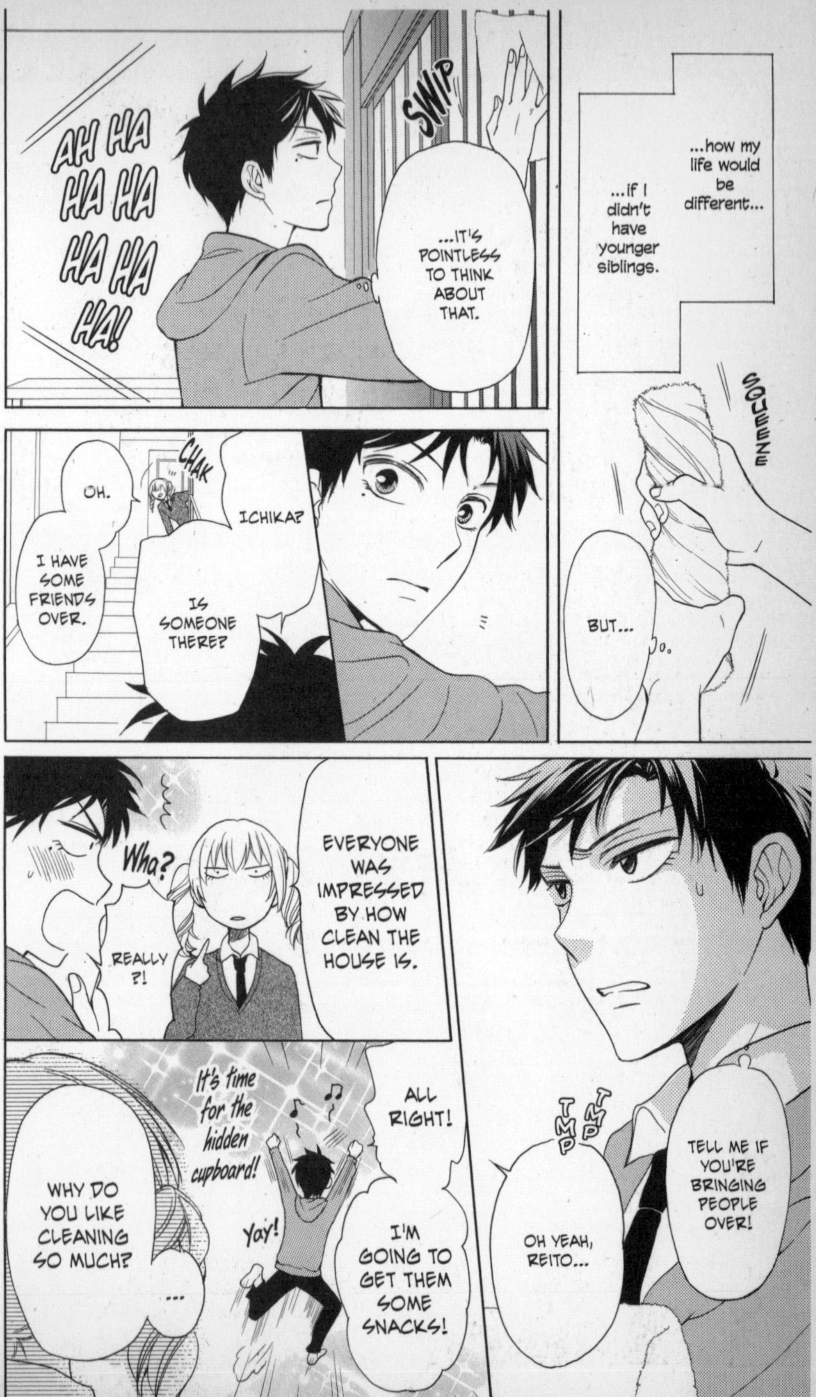
...how my life would be different...
...if I didn't have younger siblings.
SWIP
...IT'S POINTLESS TO THINK ABOUT THAT.
AH HA HA HA HA HA HA HA!
SQUEEZE
BUT...
ICHIKA?
IS SOMEONE THERE?
CHAK
OH.
I HAVE SOME FRIENDS OVER.
TELL ME IF YOU'RE BRINGING PEOPLE OVER!
TMP TMP
OH YEAH, REITO...
EVERYONE WAS IMPRESSED BY HOW CLEAN THE HOUSE IS.
Wha?
REALLY?!
ALL RIGHT!
It's time for the hidden cupboard!
I'M GOING TO GET THEM SOME SNACKS!
Yay!
WHY DO YOU LIKE CLEANING SO MUCH?
...

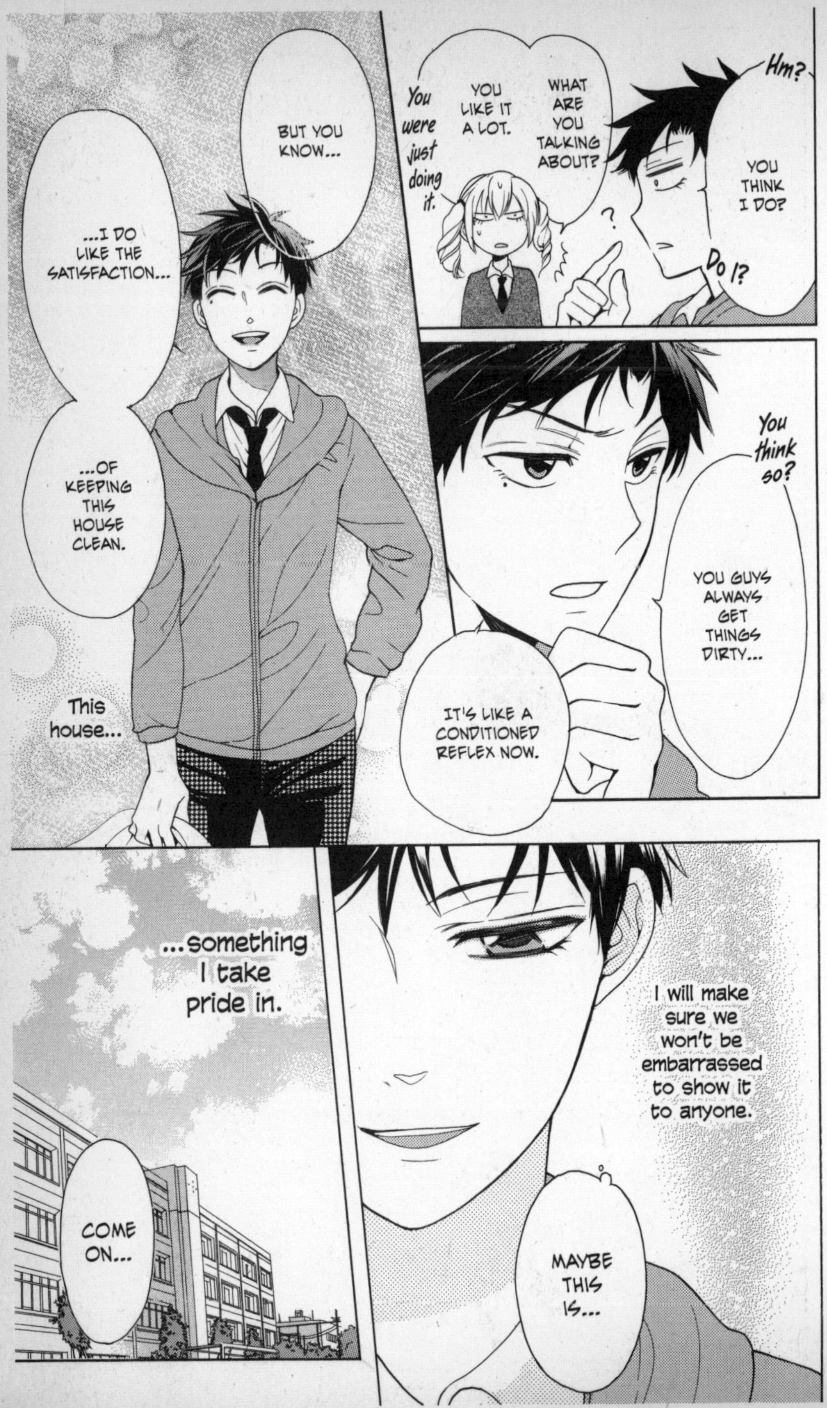
Hm?
YOU THINK I DO?
Do I?
WHAT ARE YOU TALKING ABOUT?
YOU LIKE IT A LOT.
You were just doing it.
You think so?
YOU GUYS ALWAYS GET THINGS DIRTY...
IT'S LIKE A CONDITIONED REFLEX NOW.
BUT YOU KNOW...
...I DO LIKE THE SATISFACTION...
...OF KEEPING THIS HOUSE CLEAN.
This house...
I will make sure we won't be embarrassed to show it to anyone.
MAYBE THIS IS...
...something I take pride in.
COME ON...

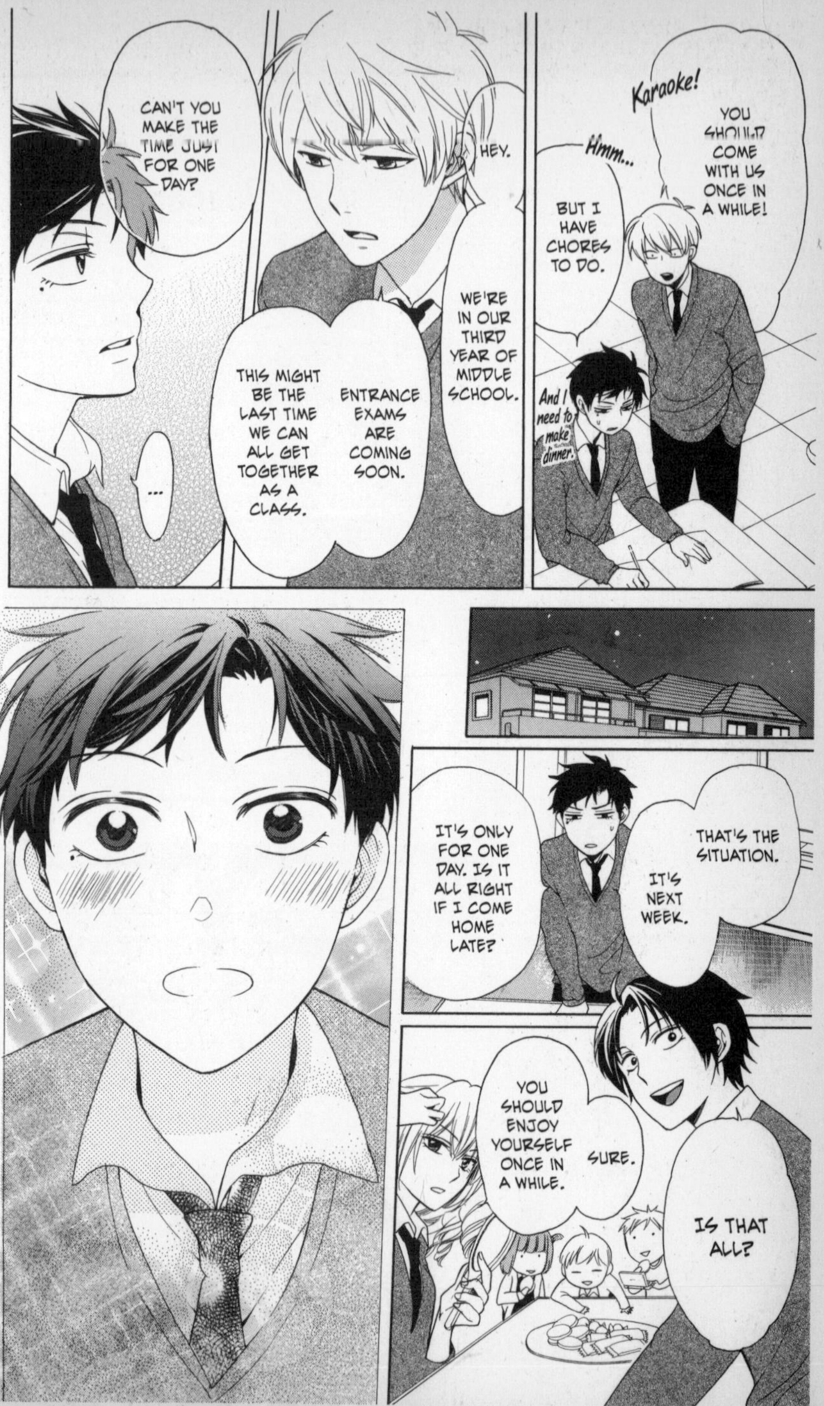
Karaoke!
YOU SHOULD COME WITH US ONCE IN A WHILE!
Hmm...
BUT I HAVE CHORES TO DO.
And I need to make dinner.
HEY.
WE'RE IN OUR THIRD YEAR OF MIDDLE SCHOOL.
ENTRANCE EXAMS ARE COMING SOON.
THIS MIGHT BE THE LAST TIME WE CAN ALL GET TOGETHER AS A CLASS.
CAN'T YOU MAKE THE TIME JUST FOR ONE DAY?
...
THAT'S THE SITUATION.
IT'S NEXT WEEK.
IT'S ONLY FOR ONE DAY. IS IT ALL RIGHT IF I COME HOME LATE?
IS THAT ALL?
SURE.
YOU SHOULD ENJOY YOURSELF ONCE IN A WHILE.

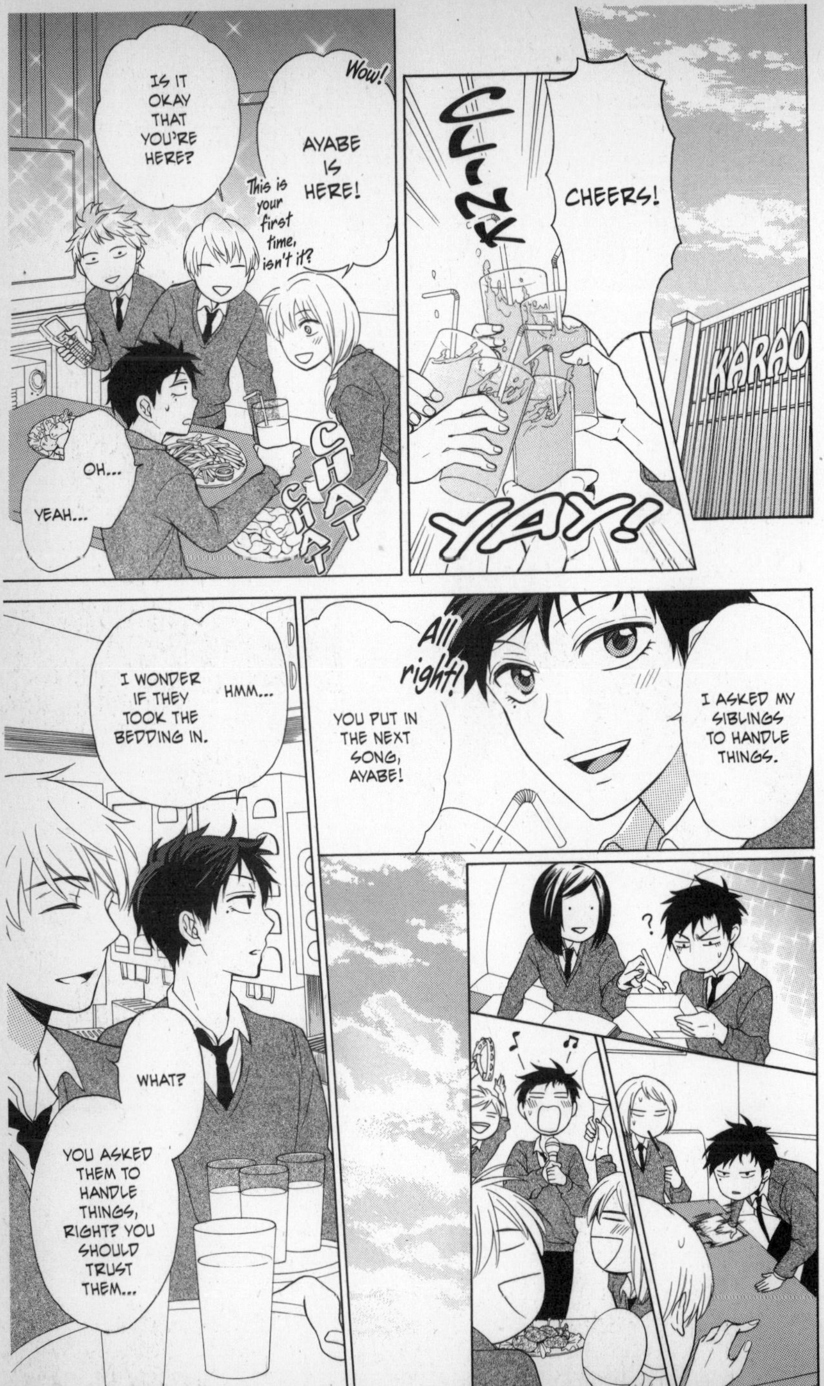
CLI-NK
CHEERS!
KARAO
YAY!
Wow!
AYABE IS HERE!
This is your first time, isn't it?
IS IT OKAY THAT YOU'RE HERE?
CHAT CHAT
OH... YEAH...
I ASKED MY SIBLINGS TO HANDLE THINGS.
All right!
YOU PUT IN THE NEXT SONG, AYABE!
HMM...
I WONDER IF THEY TOOK THE BEDDING IN.
WHAT?
YOU ASKED THEM TO HANDLE THINGS, RIGHT? YOU SHOULD TRUST THEM...

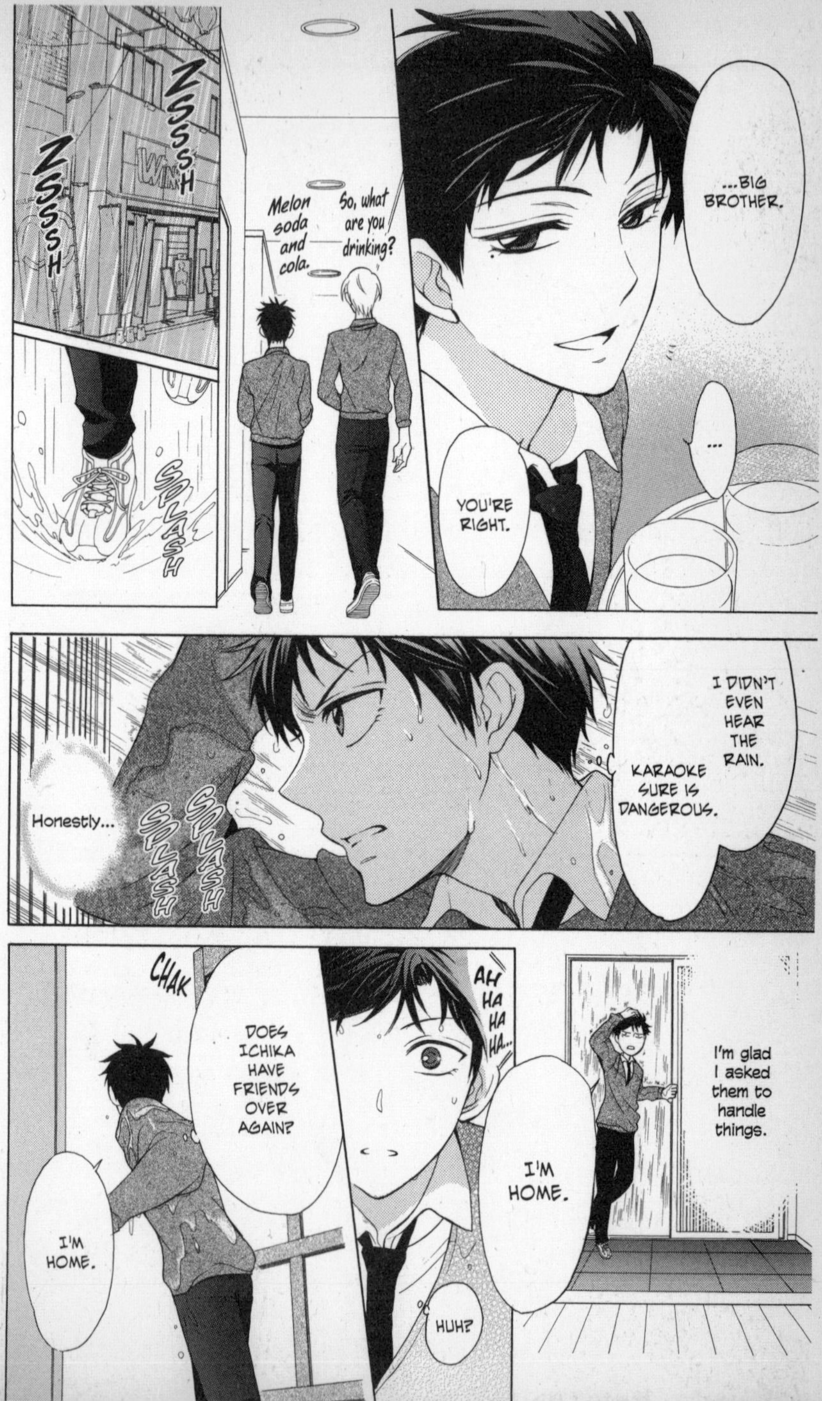
...BIG BROTHER.
...
YOU'RE RIGHT.
So, what are you drinking?
Melon soda and cola.
ZSSSSH
ZSSSH
SPLASH
I DIDN'T EVEN HEAR THE RAIN.
KARAOKE SURE IS DANGEROUS.
SPLASH
SPLASH
Honestly...
I'm glad I asked them to handle things.
AH HA HA HA...
I'M HOME.
HUH?
CHAK
DOES ICHIKA HAVE FRIENDS OVER AGAIN?
I'M HOME.

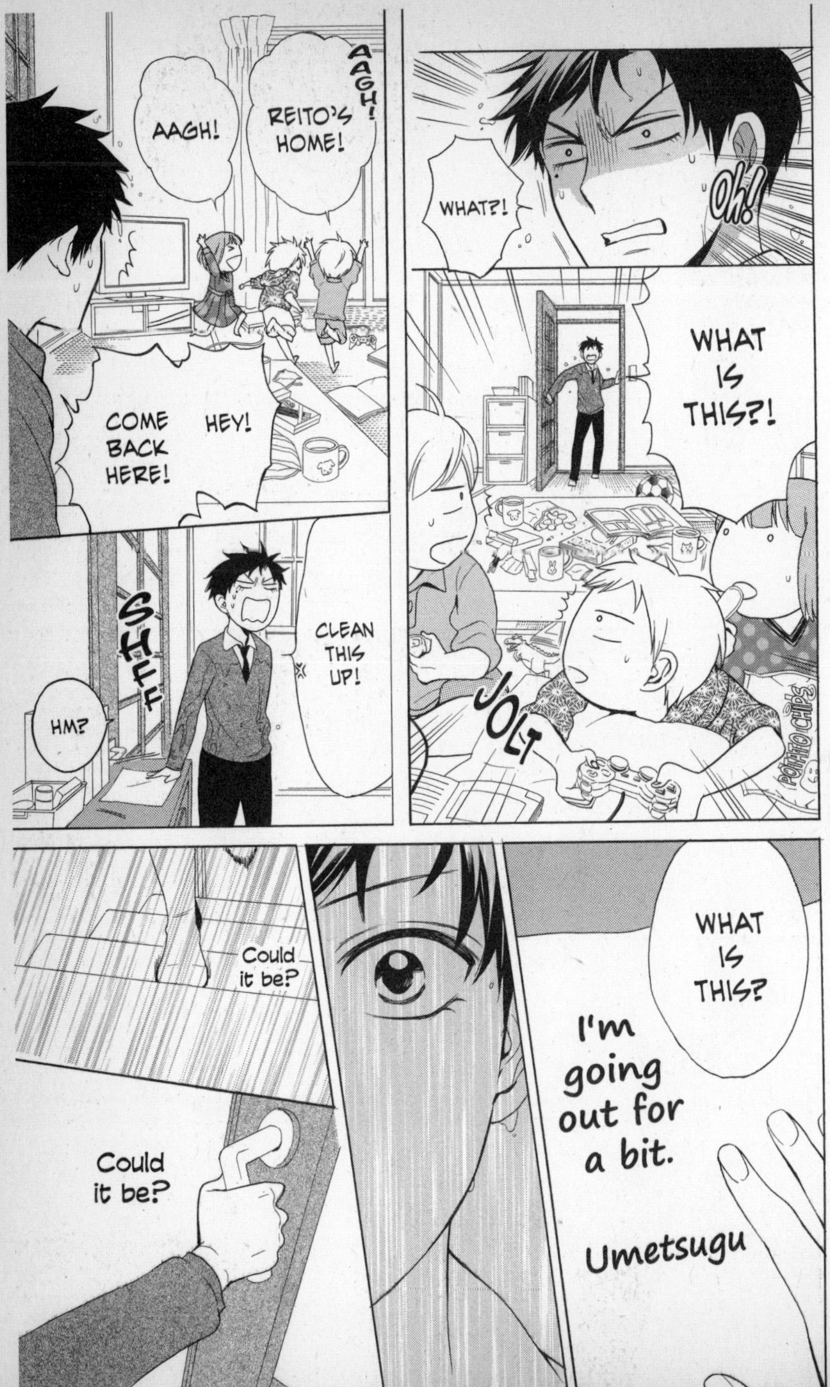
WHAT?!
Oh!
WHAT IS THIS?!
JOLT
POTATO CHIPS
AAGH!
REITO'S HOME!
AAGH!
COME BACK HERE!
HEY!
CLEAN THIS UP!
HM?
SHFF
WHAT IS THIS?
I'm going out for a bit.
Umetsugu
Could it be?
Could it be?

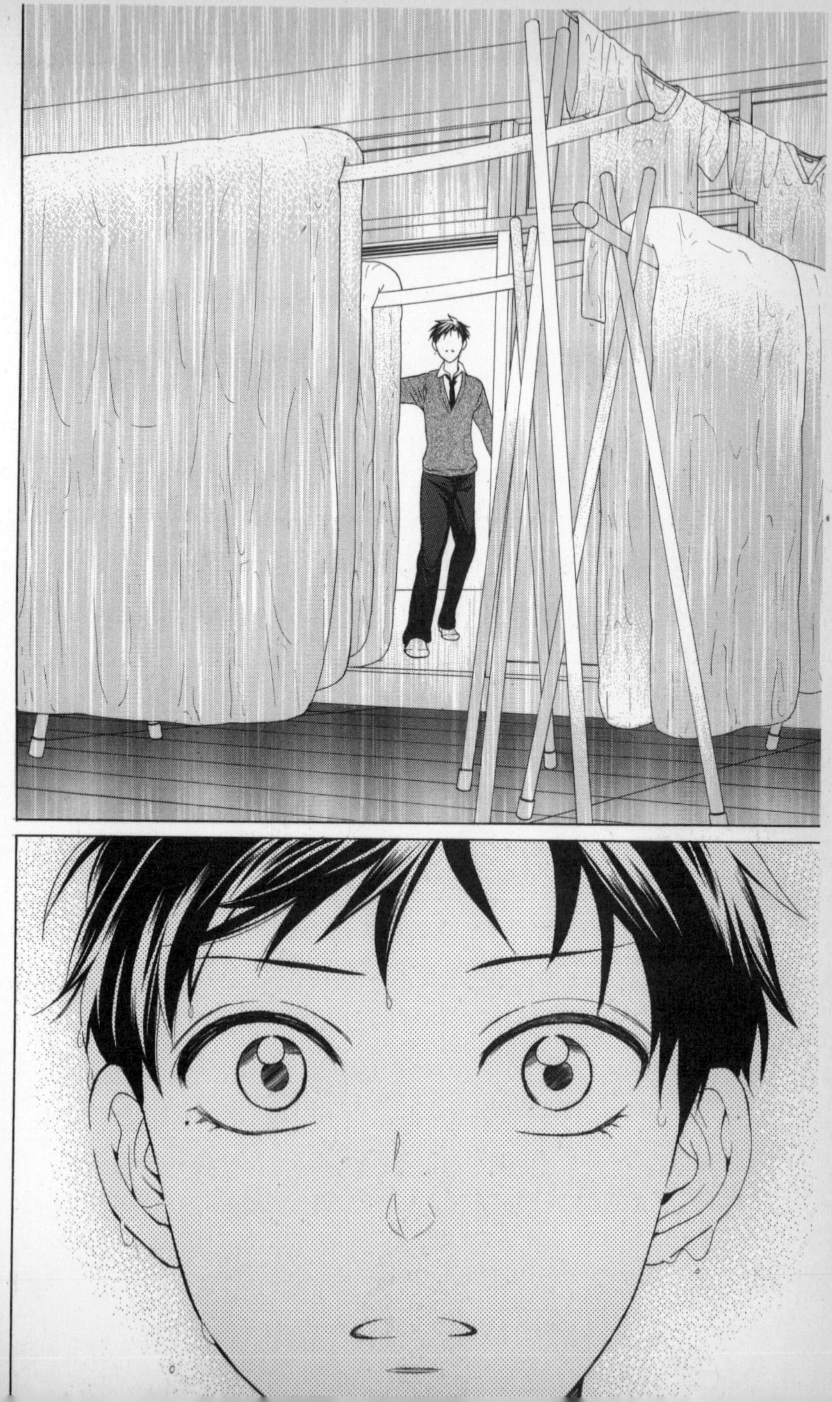

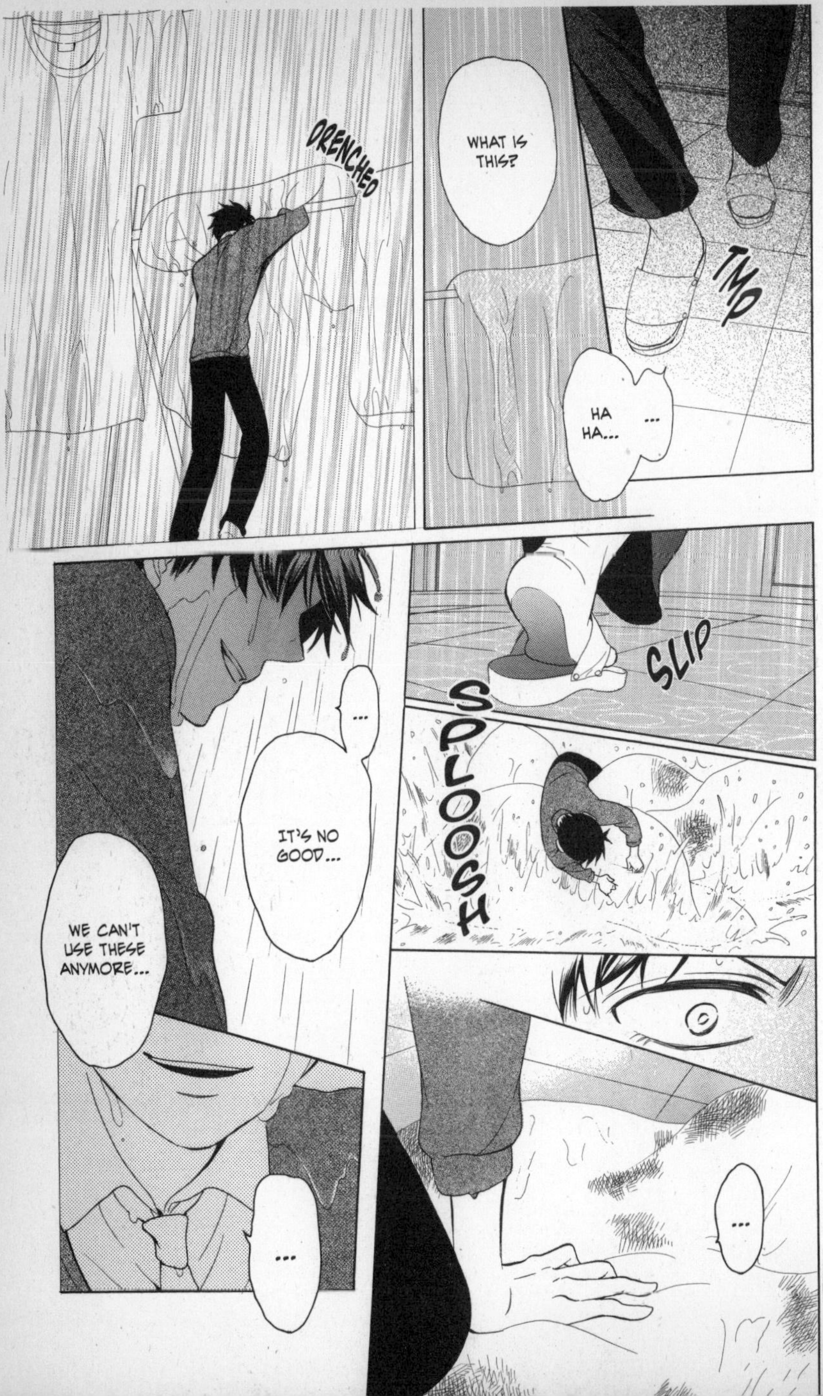
WHAT IS THIS?
TMP
HA HA... ...
DRENCHED
SLIP
SPLOOSH
...
...
IT'S NO GOOD...
WE CAN'T USE THESE ANYMORE...
...

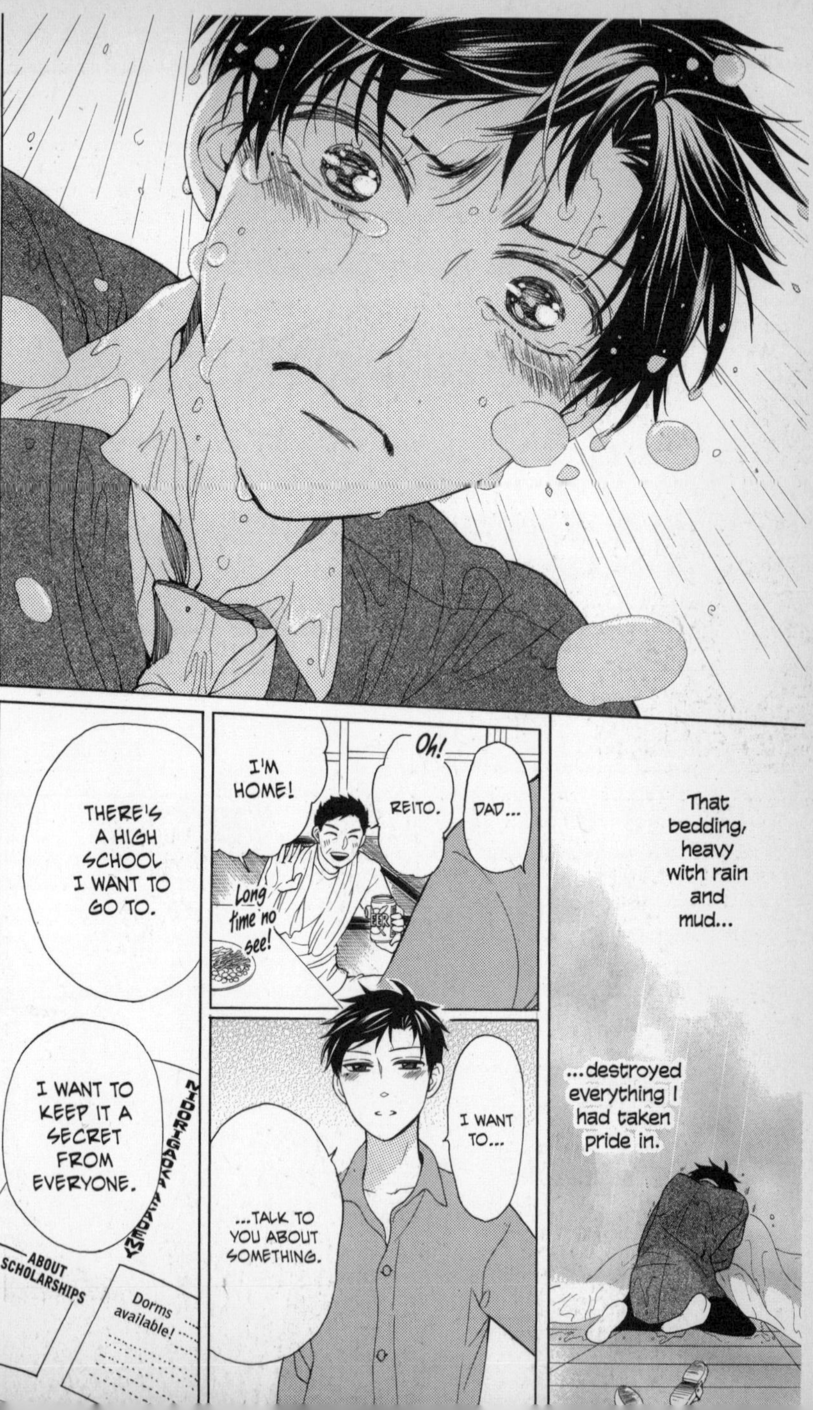
That bedding, heavy with rain and mud...
...destroyed everything I had taken pride in.
DAD...
Oh!
REITO.
I'M HOME!
Long time no see!
I WANT TO...
...TALK TO YOU ABOUT SOMETHING.
THERE'S A HIGH SCHOOL I WANT TO GO TO.
I WANT TO KEEP IT A SECRET FROM EVERYONE.
MIDORIGAOKA ACADEMY
ABOUT SCHOLARSHIPS
Dorms available!

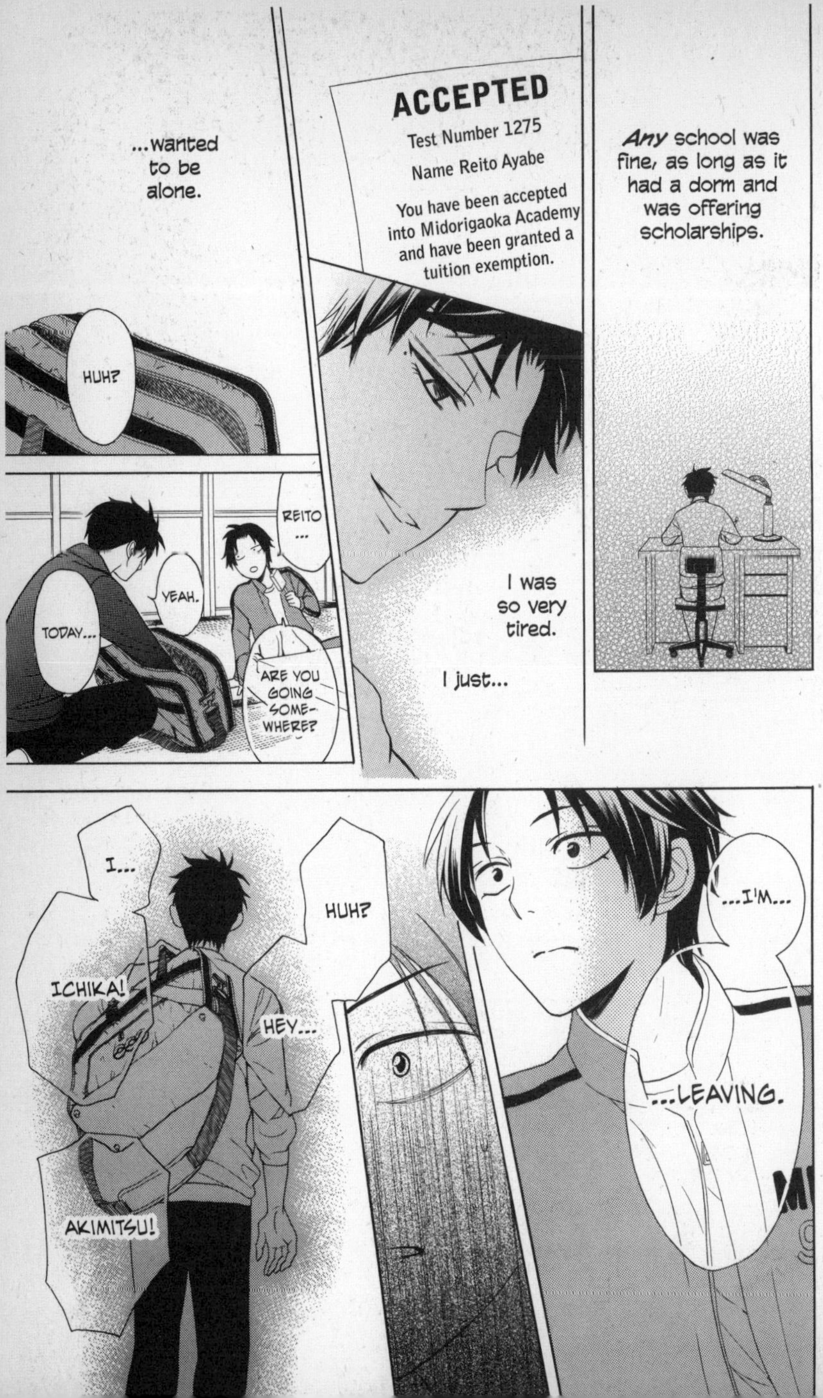

Any school was fine, as long as it had a dorm and was offering scholarships.
ACCEPTED
Test Number 1275
Name Reito Ayabe
You have been accepted into Midorigaoka Academy and have been granted a tuition exemption.
I was so very tired.
I just...
...wanted to be alone.
HUH?
REITO...
YEAH.
TODAY...
ARE YOU GOING SOMEWHERE?
...I'M...
...LEAVING.
HUH?
HEY...
I...
ICHIKA!
AKIMITSU!

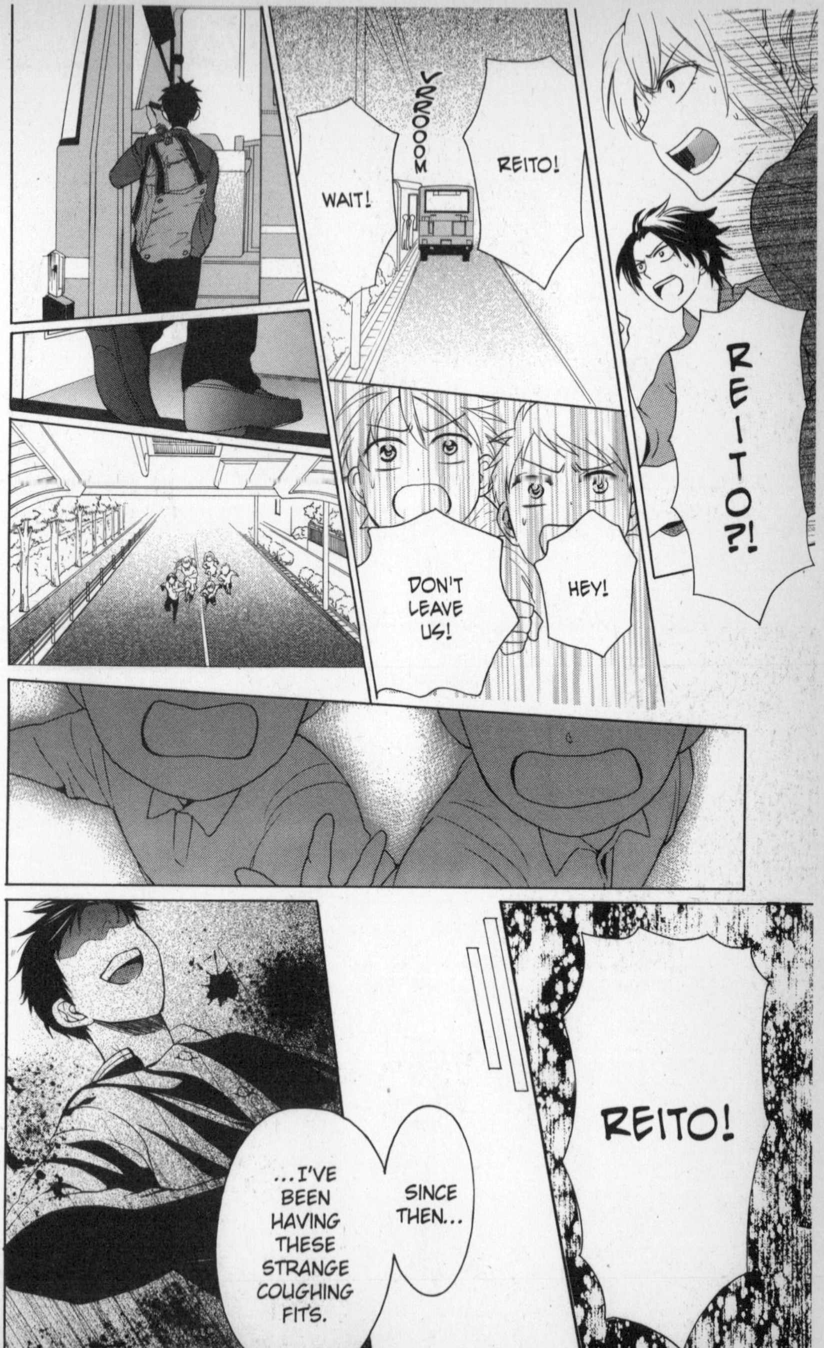
REITO?!
VRROOOM
REITO!
WAIT!
HEY!
DON'T LEAVE US!
REITO!
SINCE THEN...
...I'VE BEEN HAVING THESE STRANGE COUGHING FITS.

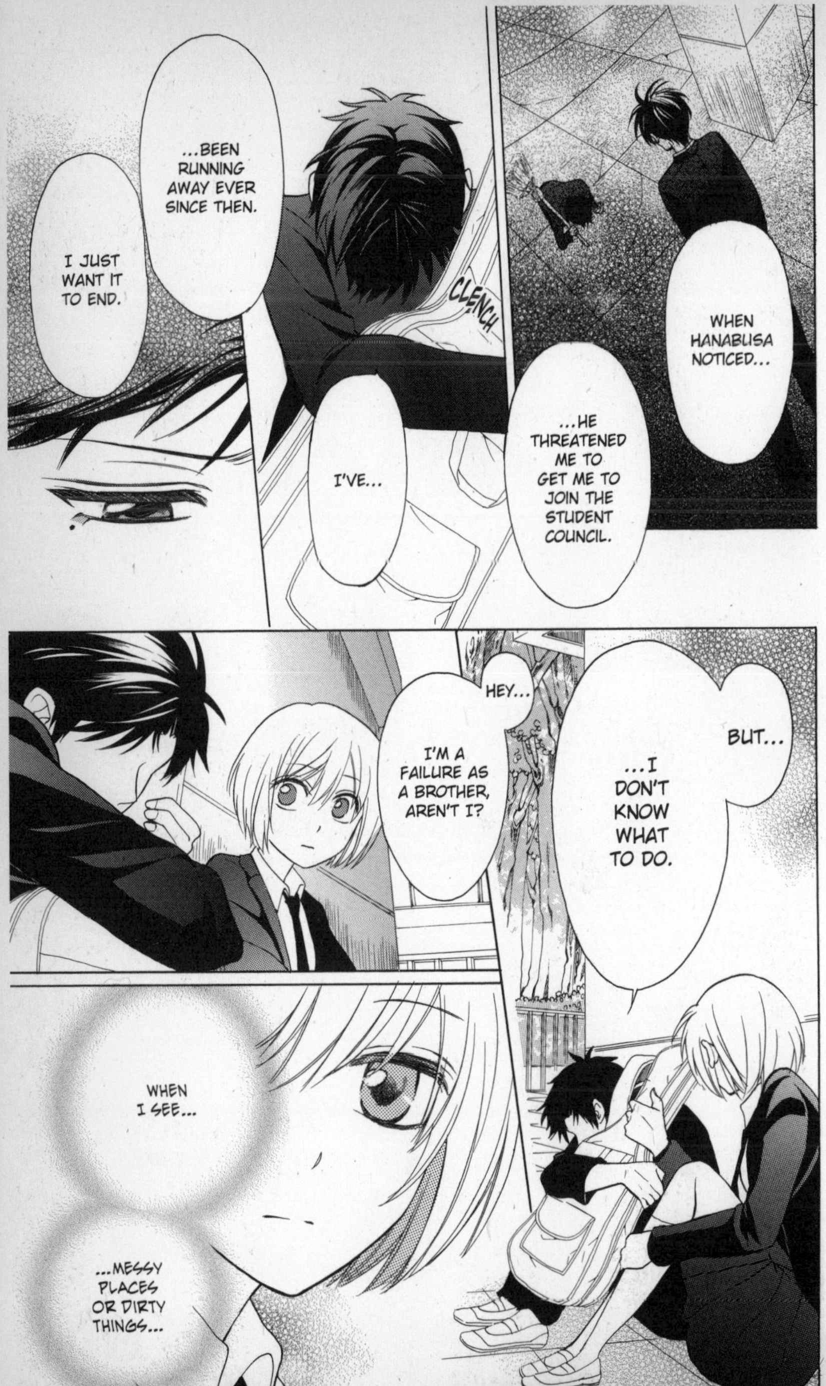
WHEN HANABUSA NOTICED...
...HE THREATENED ME TO GET ME TO JOIN THE STUDENT COUNCIL.
CLENCH
I'VE...
...BEEN RUNNING AWAY EVER SINCE THEN.
I JUST WANT IT TO END.
BUT...
...I DON'T KNOW WHAT TO DO.
HEY...
I'M A FAILURE AS A BROTHER, AREN'T I?
WHEN I SEE...
...MESSY PLACES OR DIRTY THINGS...

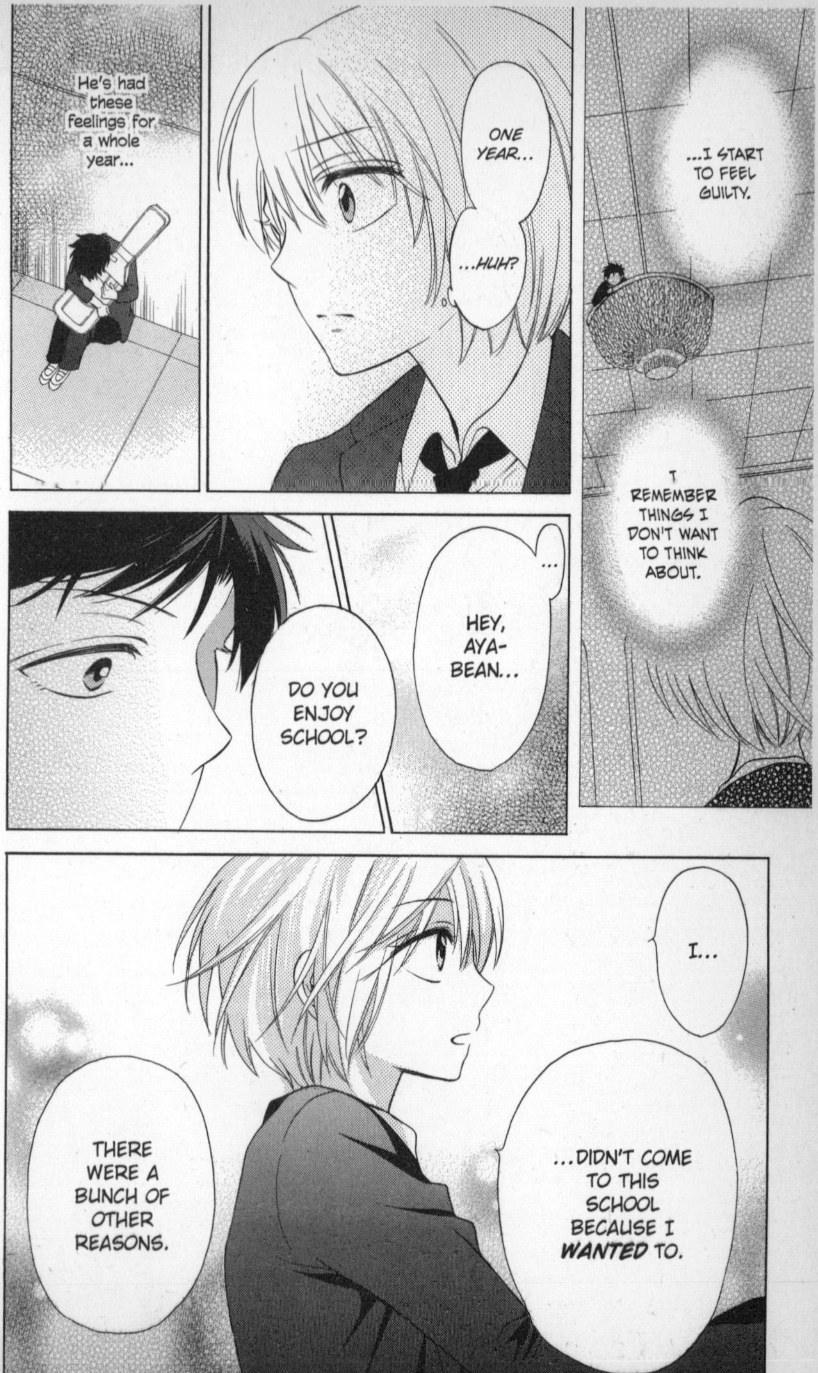
...I START TO FEEL GUILTY.
I REMEMBER THINGS I DON'T WANT TO THINK ABOUT.
ONE YEAR...
...HUH?
He's had these feelings for a whole year...
...
HEY, AYA-BEAN...
DO YOU ENJOY SCHOOL?
I...
...DIDN'T COME TO THIS SCHOOL BECAUSE I **WANTED** TO.
THERE WERE A BUNCH OF OTHER REASONS.

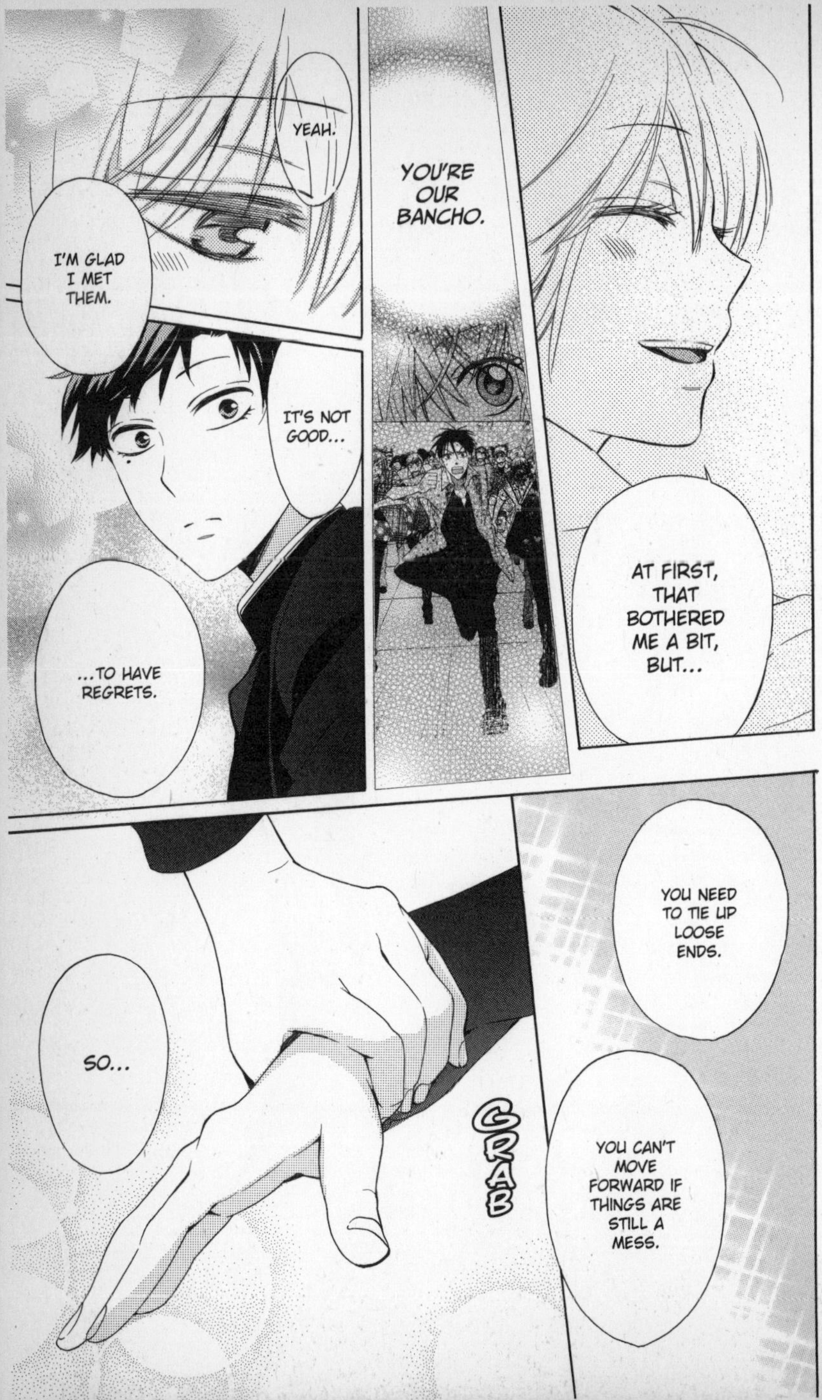
AT FIRST, THAT BOTHERED ME A BIT, BUT...
YOU'RE OUR BANCHO.
YEAH.
I'M GLAD I MET THEM.
IT'S NOT GOOD...
...TO HAVE REGRETS.
YOU NEED TO TIE UP LOOSE ENDS.
YOU CAN'T MOVE FORWARD IF THINGS ARE STILL A MESS.
GRAB
SO...

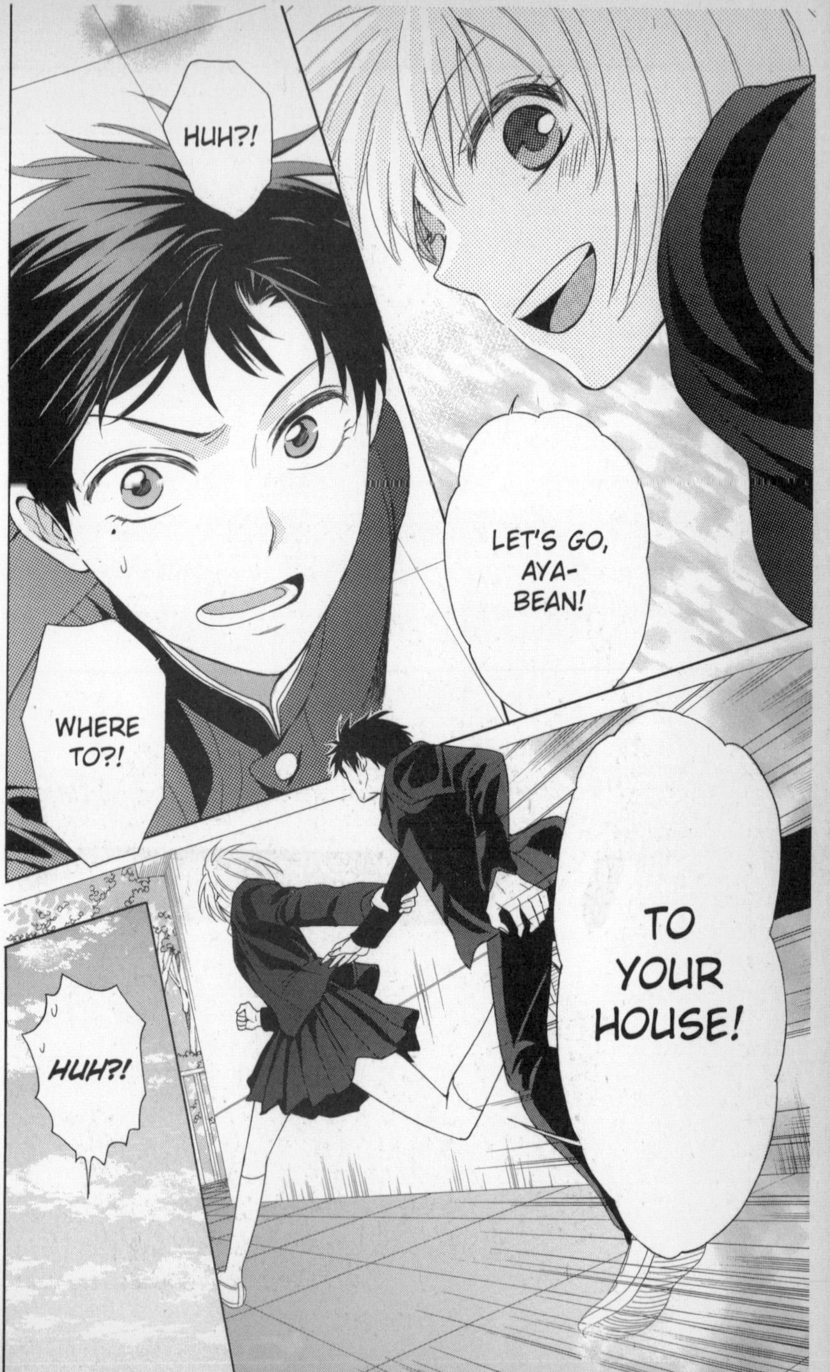
LET'S GO, AYA-BEAN!
HUH?!
WHERE TO?!
TO YOUR HOUSE!
HUH?!

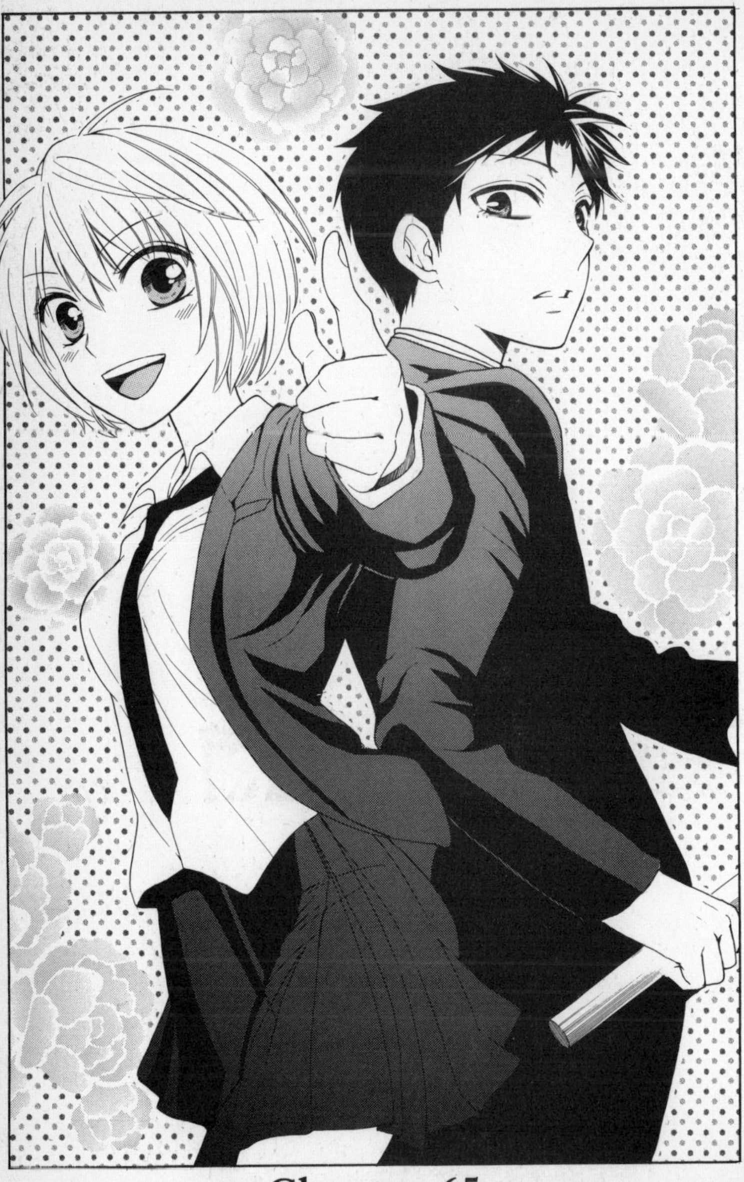

Chapter 65

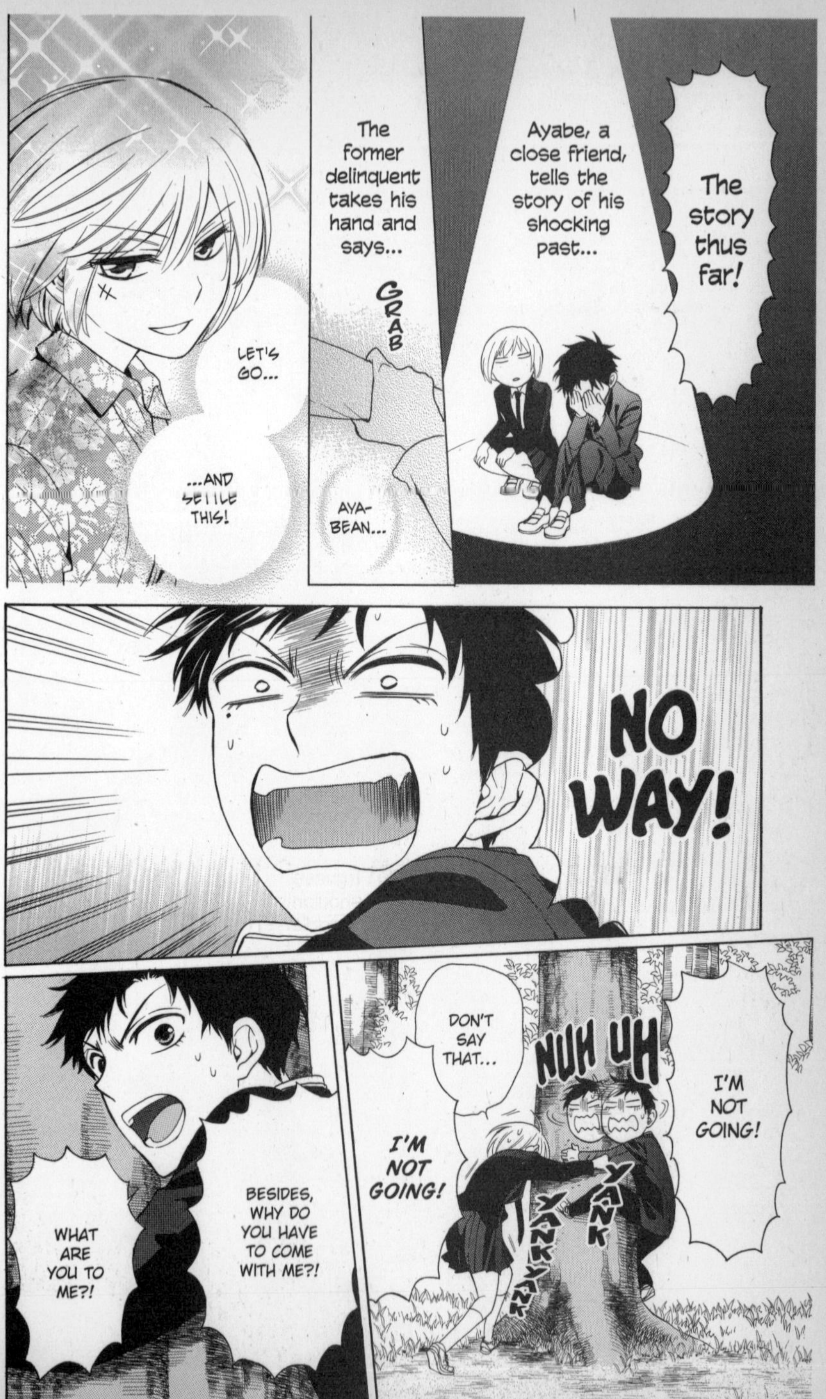
The story thus far!
Ayabe, a close friend, tells the story of his shocking past...
The former delinquent takes his hand and says...
GRAB
AYA-BEAN...
LET'S GO...
...AND SETTLE THIS!
NO WAY!
I'M NOT GOING!
NUH UH
DON'T SAY THAT...
I'M NOT GOING!
YANK
YANK
YANKYANK
BESIDES, WHY DO YOU HAVE TO COME WITH ME?!
WHAT ARE YOU TO ME?!

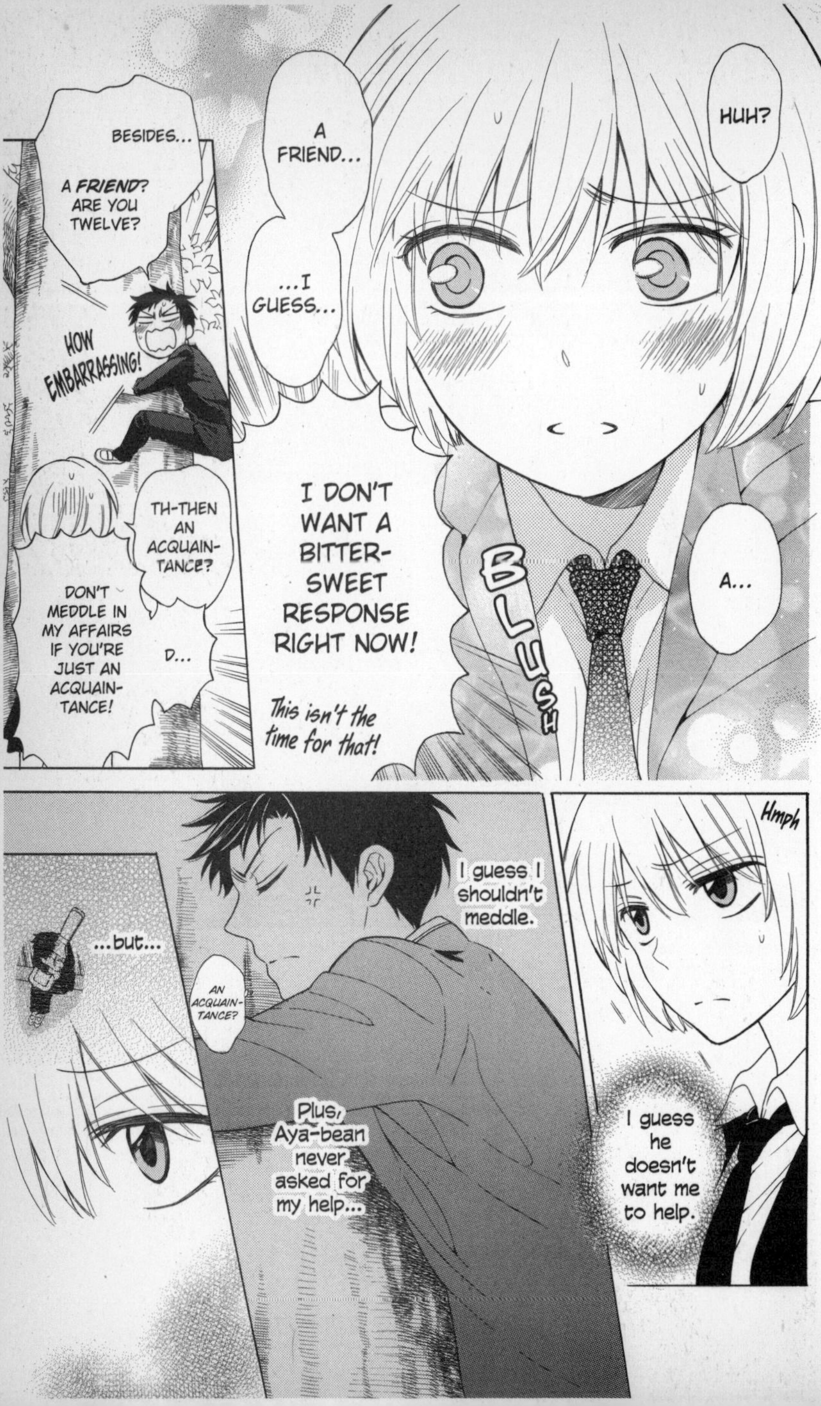
HUH?
A...
A FRIEND...
...I GUESS...
BLUSH
I DON'T WANT A BITTER-SWEET RESPONSE RIGHT NOW!
This isn't the time for that!
BESIDES...
A FRIEND? ARE YOU TWELVE?
HOW EMBARRASSING!
TH-THEN AN ACQUAIN-TANCE?
D...
DON'T MEDDLE IN MY AFFAIRS IF YOU'RE JUST AN ACQUAIN-TANCE!
Hmph
I guess he doesn't want me to help.
I guess I shouldn't meddle.
AN ACQUAIN-TANCE?
Plus, Aya-bean never asked for my help...
...but...

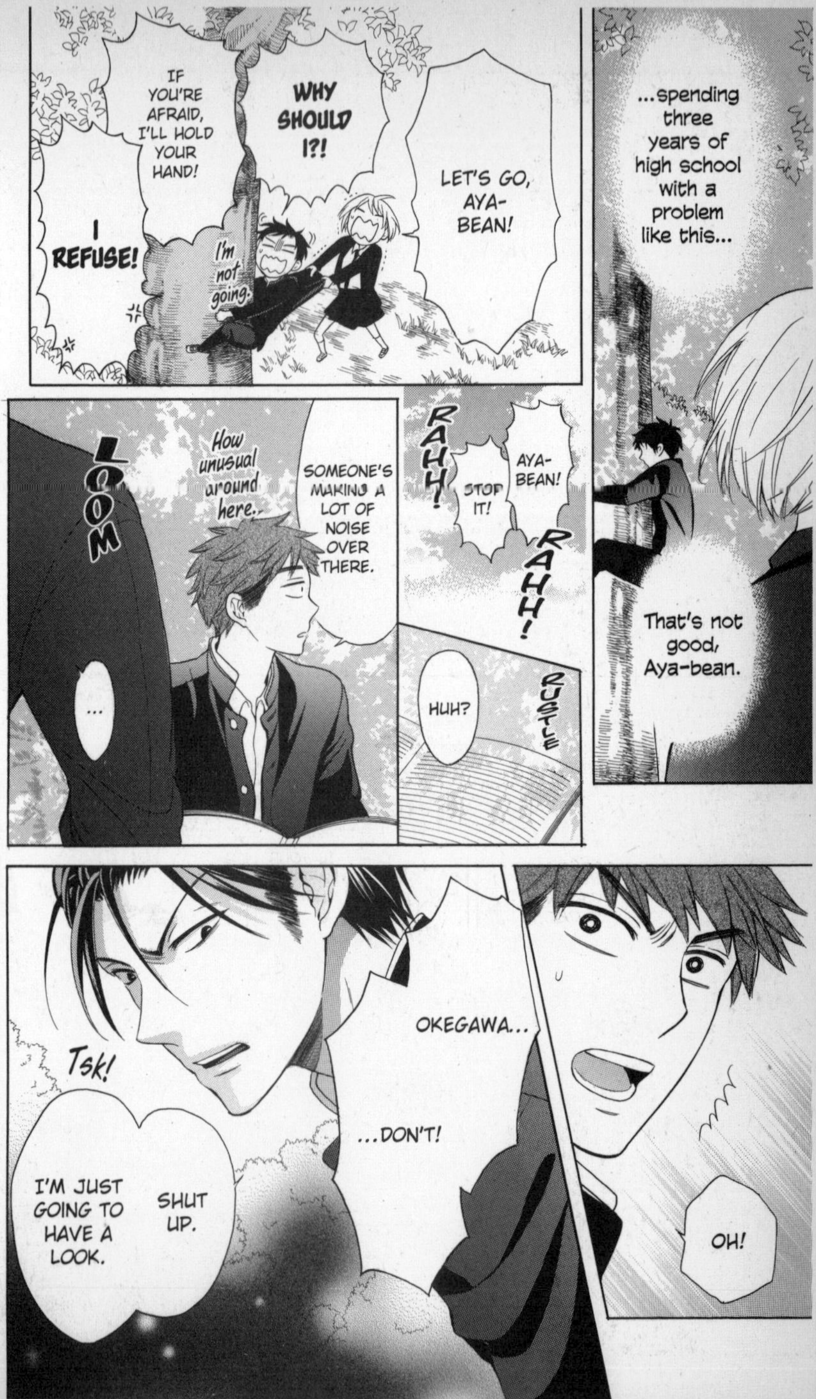
...spending three years of high school with a problem like this...
That's not good, Aya-bean.
LET'S GO, AYA-BEAN!
WHY SHOULD I?!
IF YOU'RE AFRAID, I'LL HOLD YOUR HAND!
I'm not going.
I REFUSE!
RAHH!
AYA-BEAN!
STOP IT!
RAHH!
HUH?
RUSTLE
SOMEONE'S MAKING A LOT OF NOISE OVER THERE.
How unusual around here.
LOOM
...
OH!
OKEGAWA...
...DON'T!
Tsk!
SHUT UP.
I'M JUST GOING TO HAVE A LOOK.

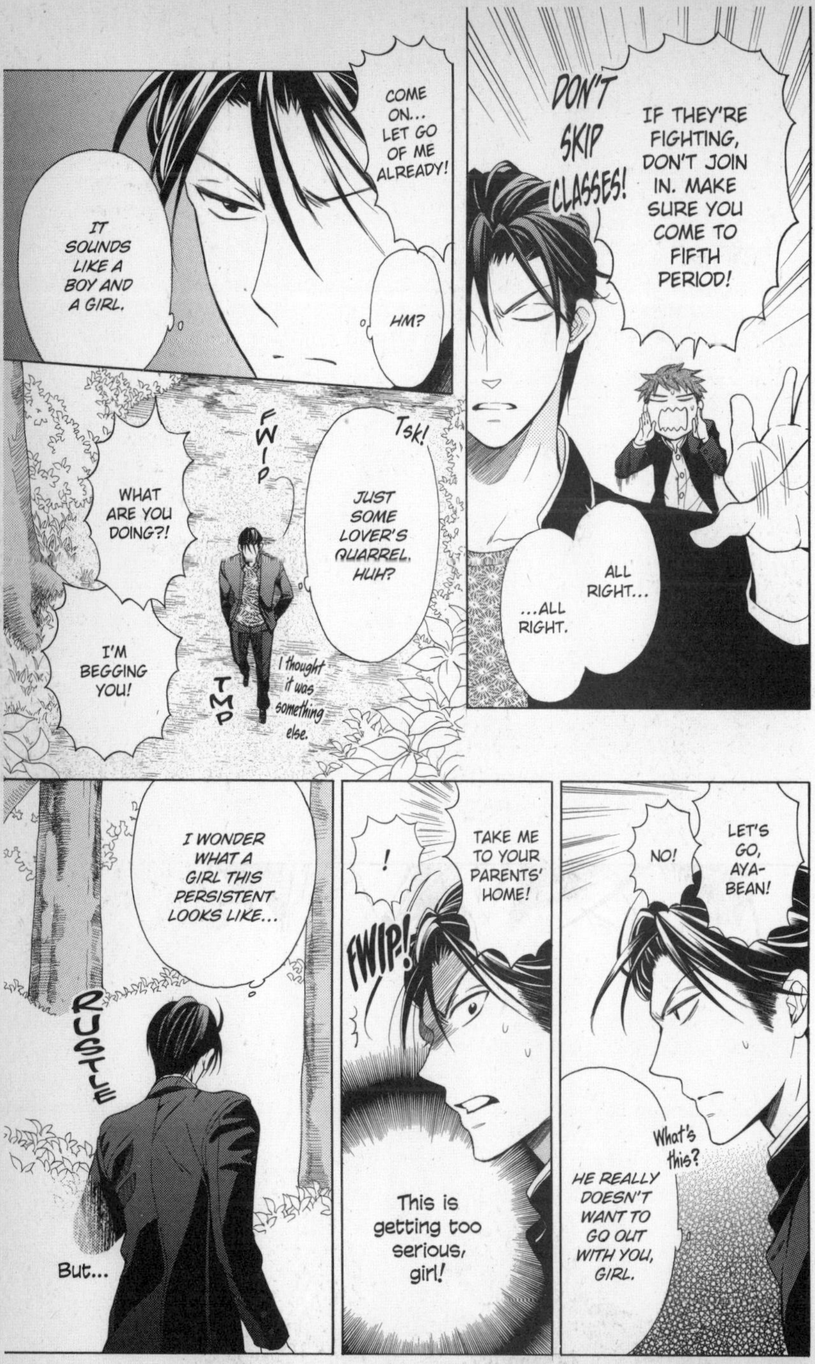
DON'T SKIP CLASSES!
IF THEY'RE FIGHTING, DON'T JOIN IN. MAKE SURE YOU COME TO FIFTH PERIOD!
ALL RIGHT...
...ALL RIGHT.
COME ON... LET GO OF ME ALREADY!
HM?
IT SOUNDS LIKE A BOY AND A GIRL.
Tsk!
JUST SOME LOVER'S QUARREL, HUH?
FWIP
WHAT ARE YOU DOING?!
I'M BEGGING YOU!
TMP
I thought it was something else.
LET'S GO, AYA-BEAN!
NO!
What's this?
HE REALLY DOESN'T WANT TO GO OUT WITH YOU, GIRL.
TAKE ME TO YOUR PARENTS' HOME!
!
FWIP!
This is getting too serious, girl!
I WONDER WHAT A GIRL THIS PERSISTENT LOOKS LIKE...
RUSTLE
But...

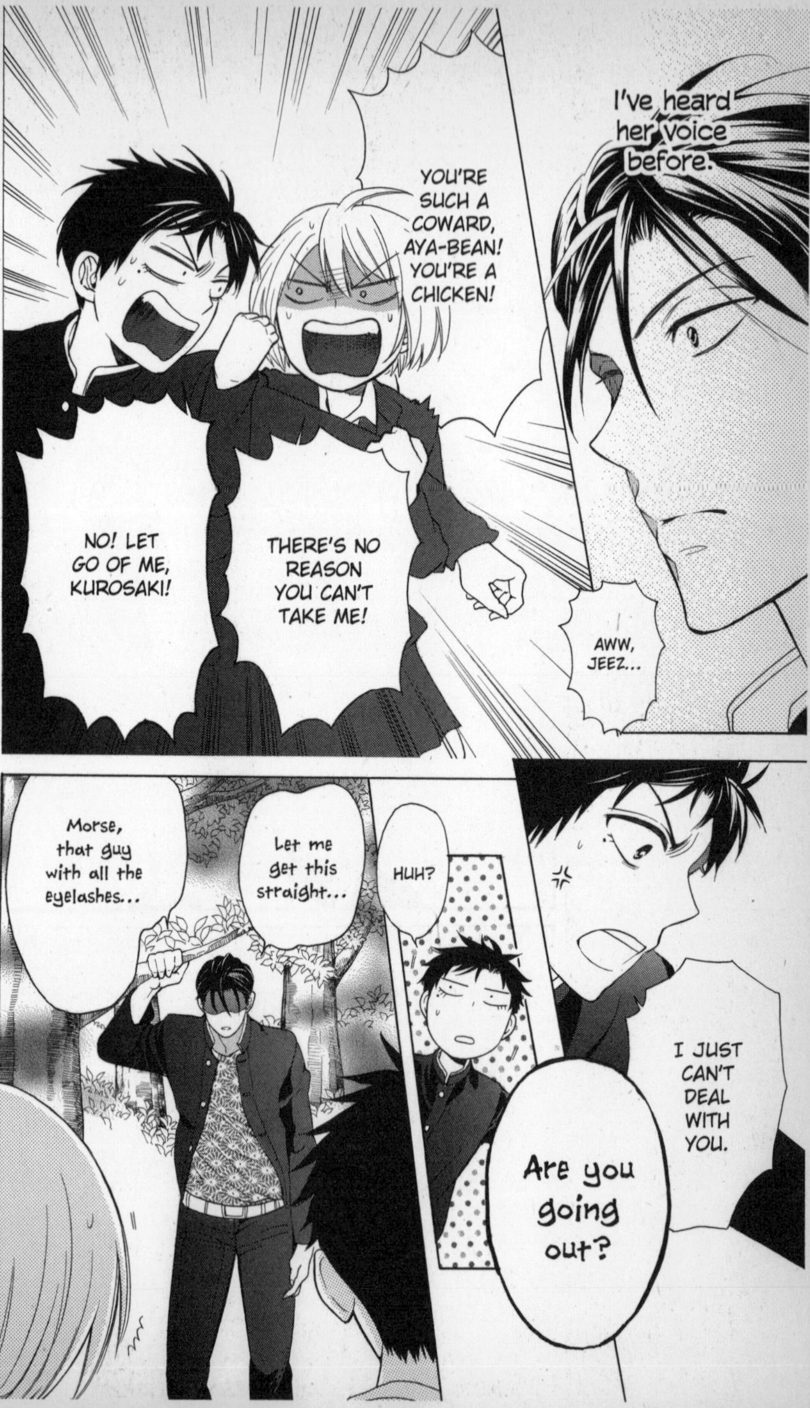
I've heard her voice before.
AWW, JEEZ...
YOU'RE SUCH A COWARD, AYA-BEAN! YOU'RE A CHICKEN!
THERE'S NO REASON YOU CAN'T TAKE ME!
NO! LET GO OF ME, KUROSAKI!
I JUST CAN'T DEAL WITH YOU.
HUH?
Let me get this straight...
Morse, that guy with all the eyelashes...
Are you going out?

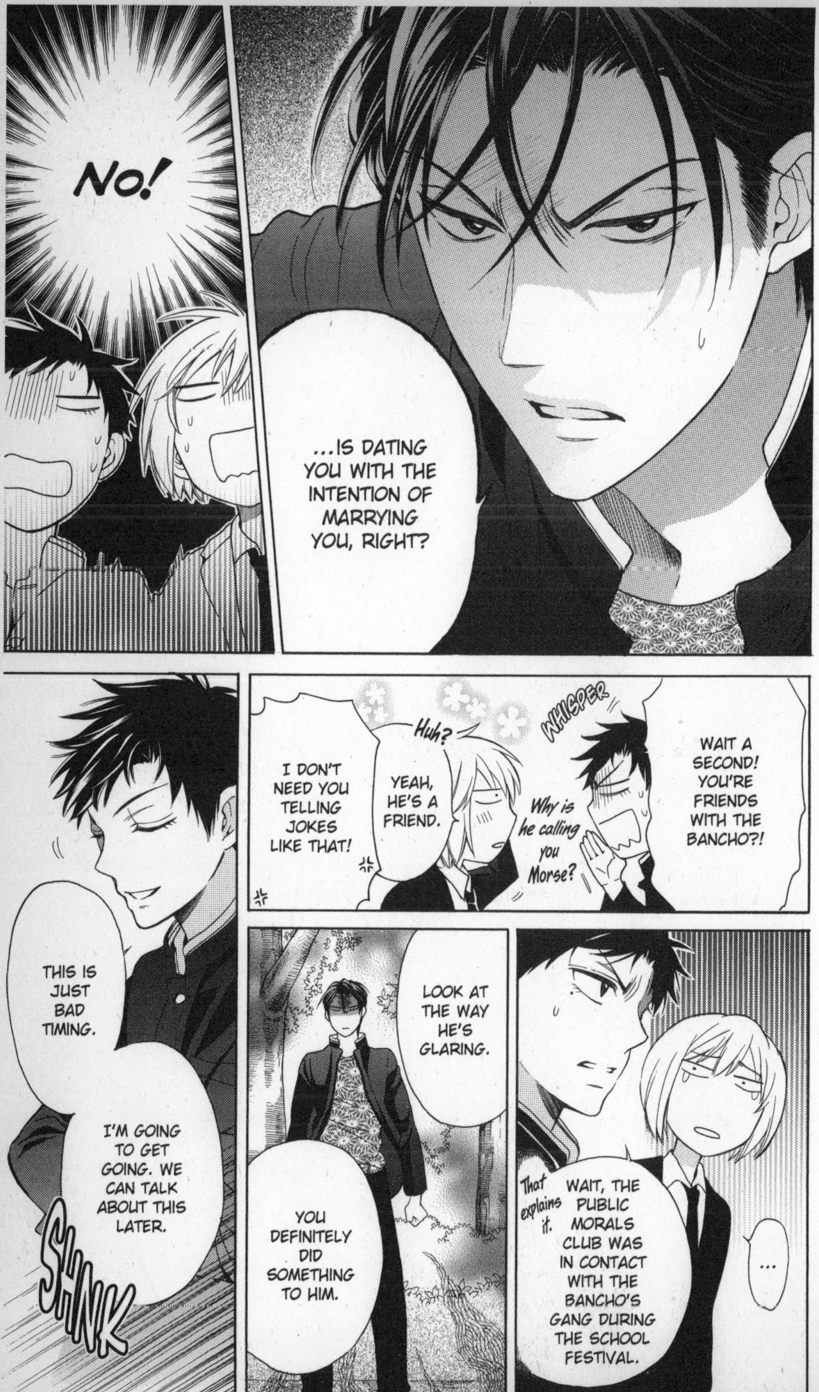
...IS DATING YOU WITH THE INTENTION OF MARRYING YOU, RIGHT?
NO!
WAIT A SECOND! YOU'RE FRIENDS WITH THE BANCHO?!
WHISPER
Why is he calling you Morse?
Huh?
YEAH, HE'S A FRIEND.
I DON'T NEED YOU TELLING JOKES LIKE THAT!
...
WAIT, THE PUBLIC MORALS CLUB WAS IN CONTACT WITH THE BANCHO'S GANG DURING THE SCHOOL FESTIVAL.
That explains it.
LOOK AT THE WAY HE'S GLARING.
YOU DEFINITELY DID SOMETHING TO HIM.
THIS IS JUST BAD TIMING.
I'M GOING TO GET GOING. WE CAN TALK ABOUT THIS LATER.
SHNK

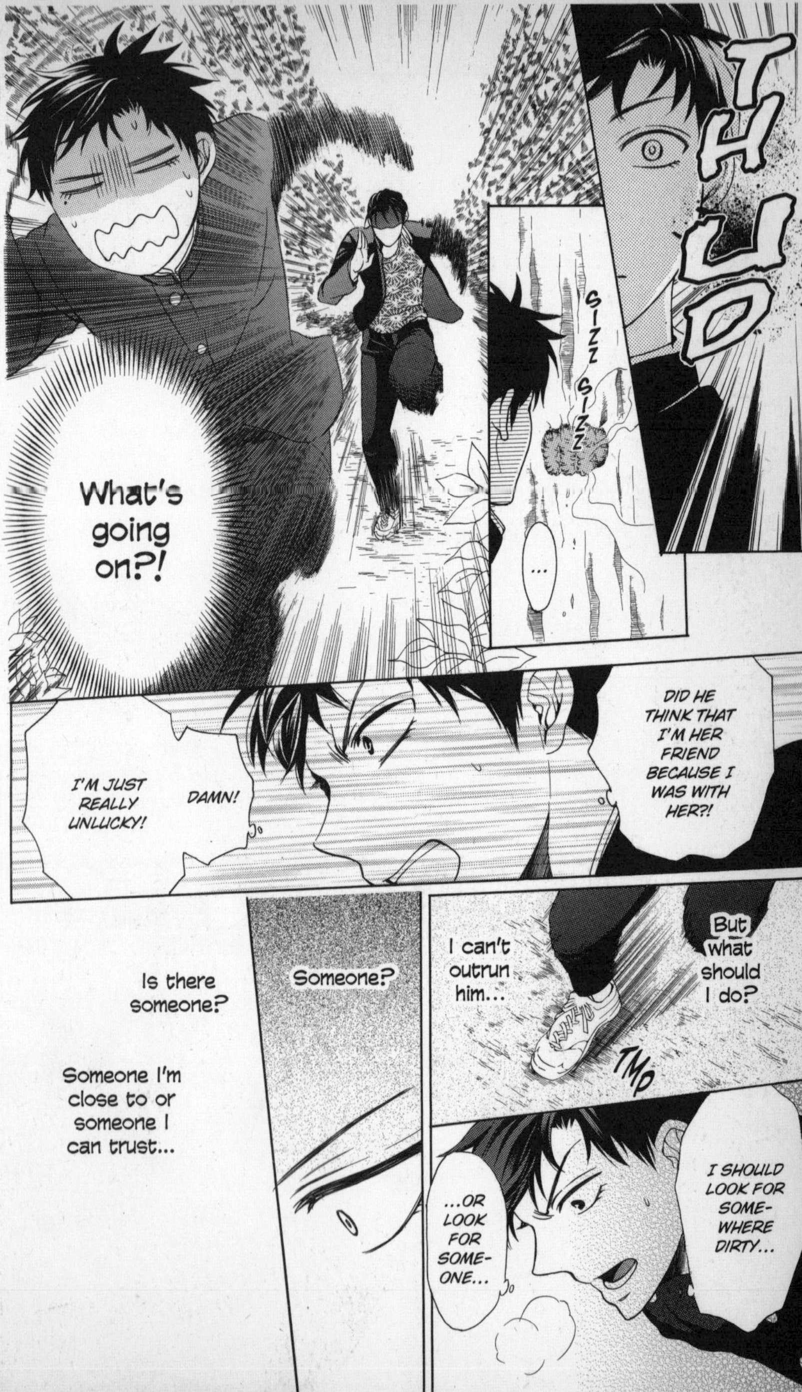
THUD
SIZZ SIZZ
...
What's going on?!
DID HE THINK THAT I'M HER FRIEND BECAUSE I WAS WITH HER?!
DAMN!
I'M JUST REALLY UNLUCKY!
But what should I do?
I can't outrun him...
TMP
I SHOULD LOOK FOR SOME-WHERE DIRTY...
...OR LOOK FOR SOME-ONE...
Someone?
Is there someone?
Someone I'm close to or someone I can trust...

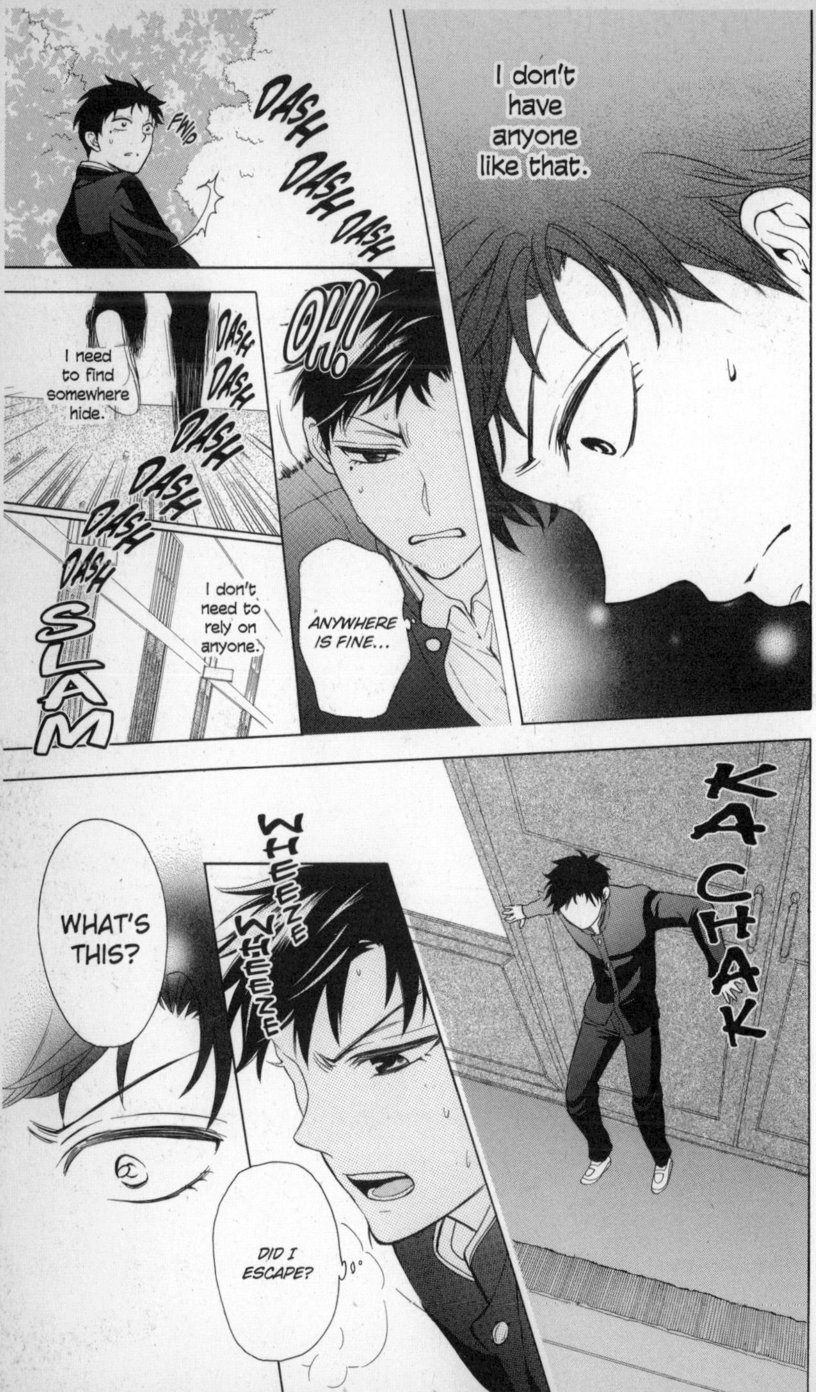
I don't have anyone like that.
FWIP
DASH DASH DASH
OH!!
ANYWHERE IS FINE...
DASH DASH DASH DASH DASH DASH
I need to find somewhere hide.
I don't need to rely on anyone.
SLAM
KA CHAK
WHEEZE WHEEZE
WHAT'S THIS?
DID I ESCAPE?

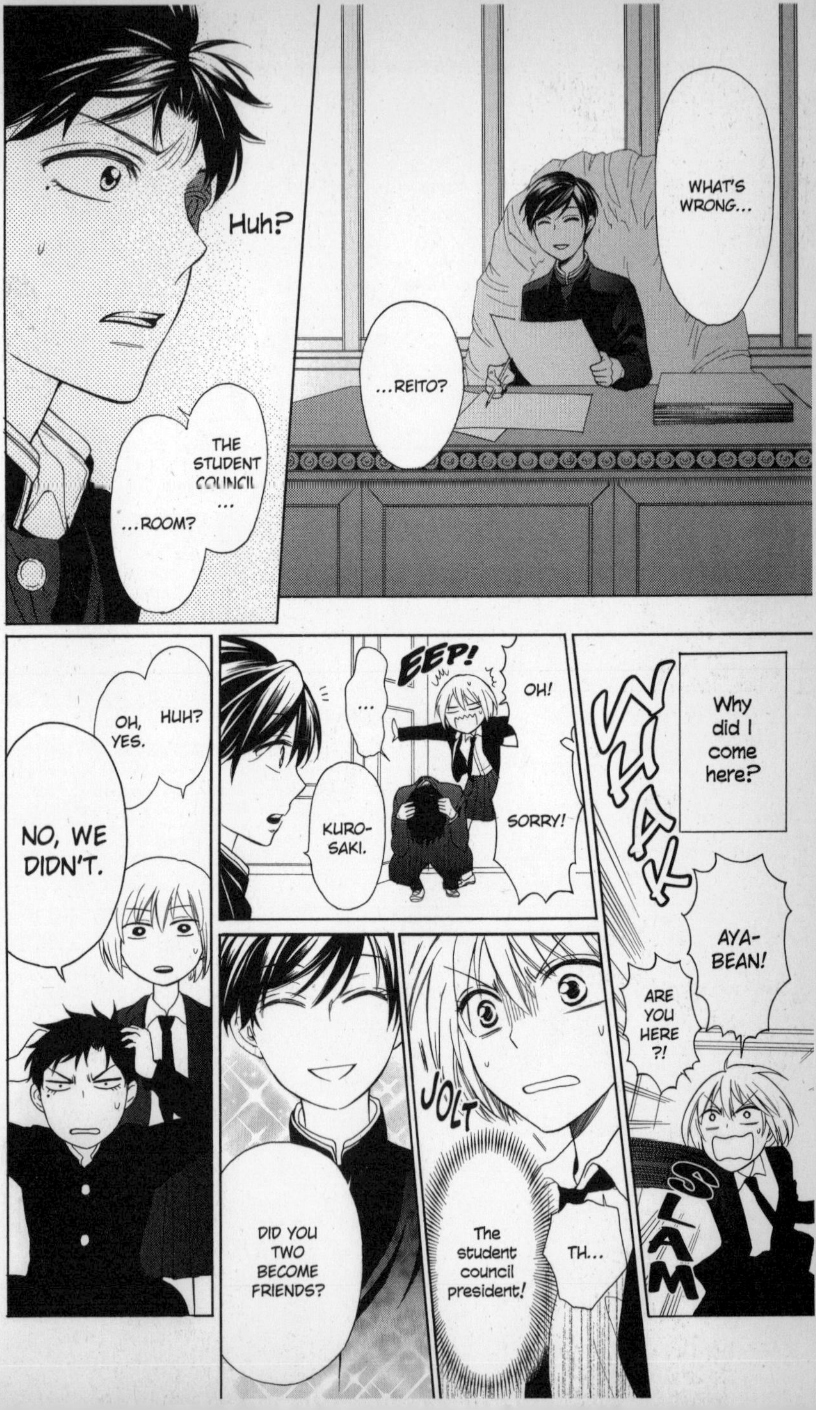
WHAT'S WRONG...
...REITO?
Huh?
THE STUDENT COUNCIL ...
...ROOM?
Why did I come here?
WHAK
AYA-BEAN!
ARE YOU HERE ?!
SLAM
EEP!
OH!
SORRY!
...
KURO-SAKI.
JOLT
TH...
The student council president!
DID YOU TWO BECOME FRIENDS?
HUH?
OH, YES.
NO, WE DIDN'T.

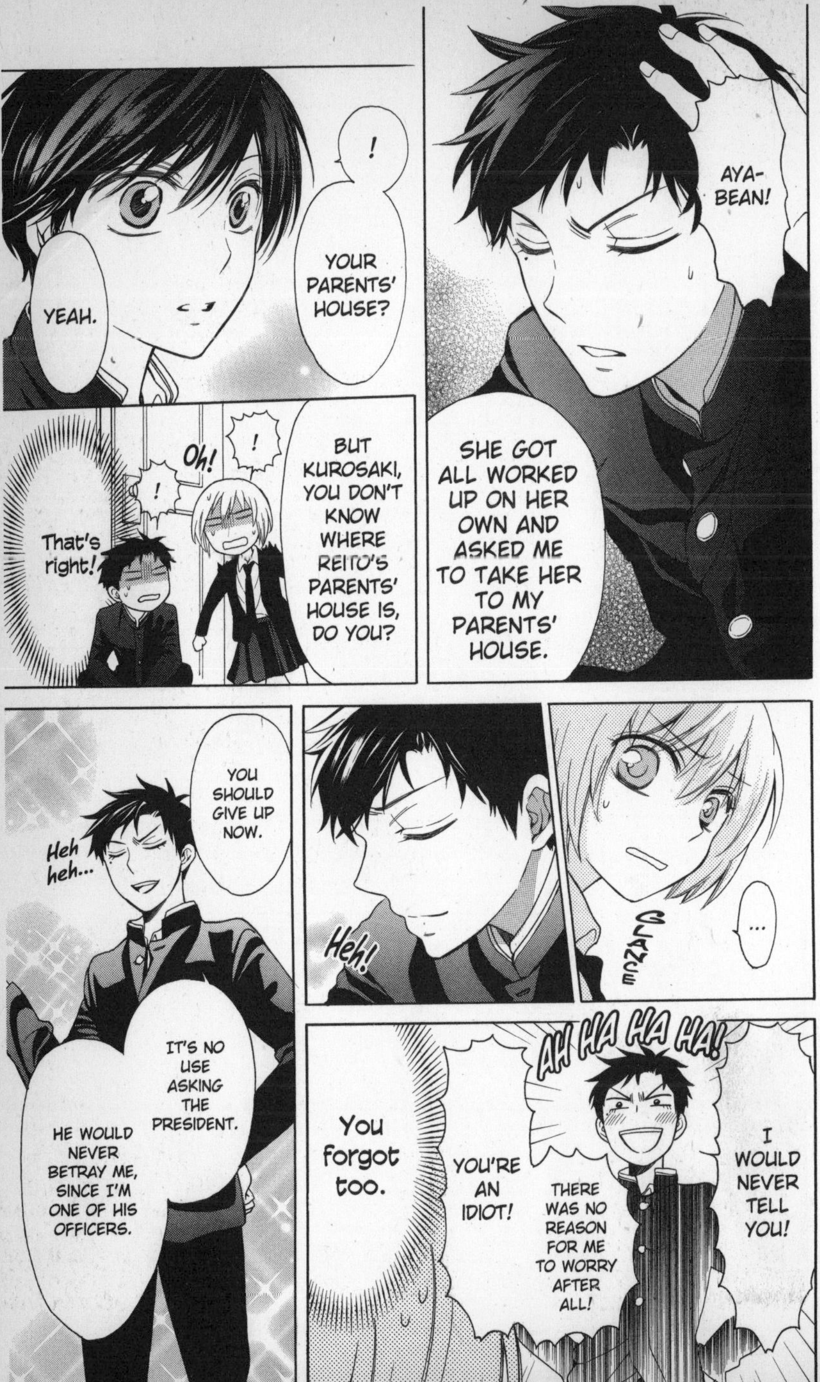
AYA-BEAN!
SHE GOT ALL WORKED UP ON HER OWN AND ASKED ME TO TAKE HER TO MY PARENTS' HOUSE.
!
YOUR PARENTS' HOUSE?
YEAH.
!
BUT KUROSAKI, YOU DON'T KNOW WHERE REITO'S PARENTS' HOUSE IS, DO YOU?
Oh!
!
That's right!
...
GLANCE
Heh!
YOU SHOULD GIVE UP NOW.
Heh heh...
IT'S NO USE ASKING THE PRESIDENT.
HE WOULD NEVER BETRAY ME, SINCE I'M ONE OF HIS OFFICERS.
AH HA HA HA!
I WOULD NEVER TELL YOU!
THERE WAS NO REASON FOR ME TO WORRY AFTER ALL!
YOU'RE AN IDIOT!
You forgot too.

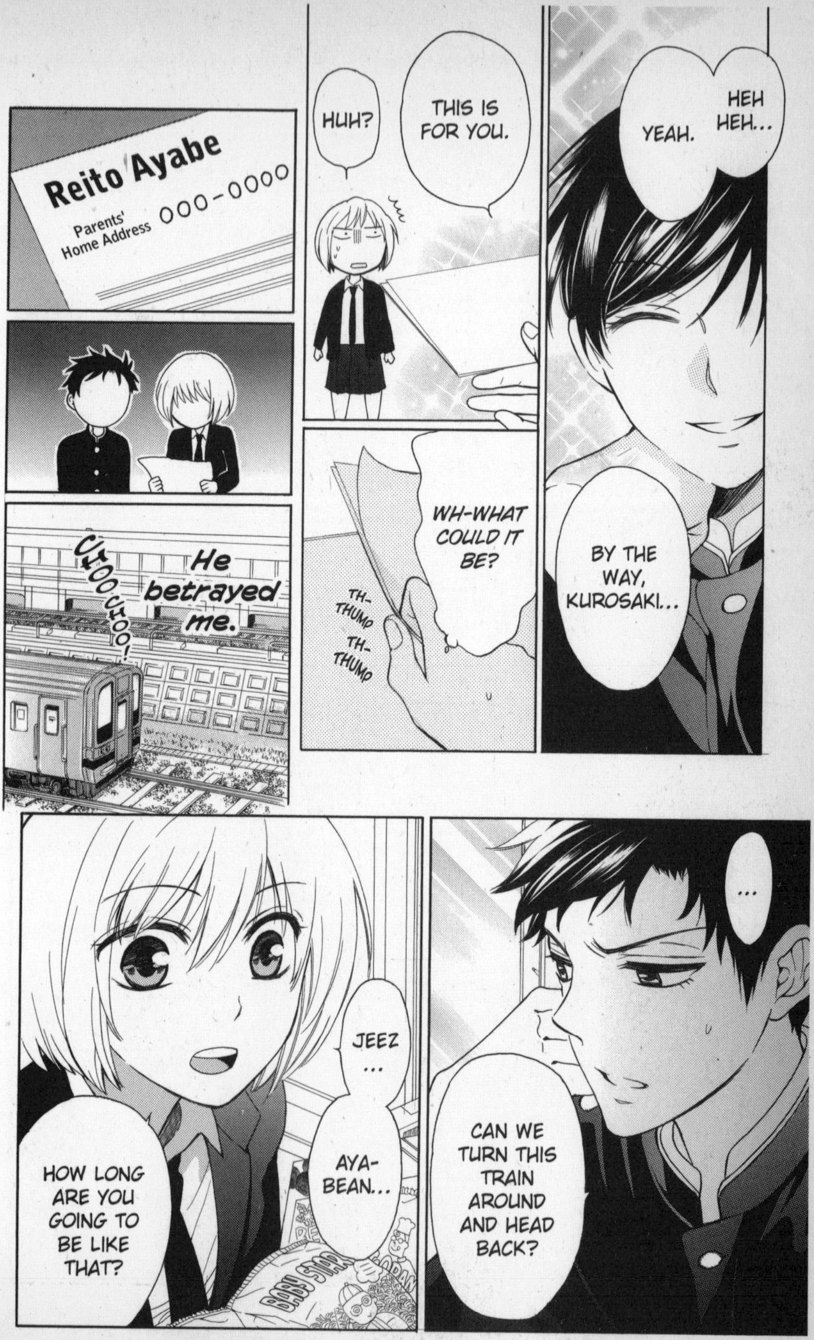
HEH HEH...
YEAH.
BY THE WAY, KUROSAKI...
THIS IS FOR YOU.
HUH?
WH-WHAT COULD IT BE?
TH-THUMP TH-THUMP
Reito Ayabe
Parents' Home Address 000-0000
CHOO CHOO!
He betrayed me.
...
CAN WE TURN THIS TRAIN AROUND AND HEAD BACK?
JEEZ...
AYA-BEAN...
HOW LONG ARE YOU GOING TO BE LIKE THAT?

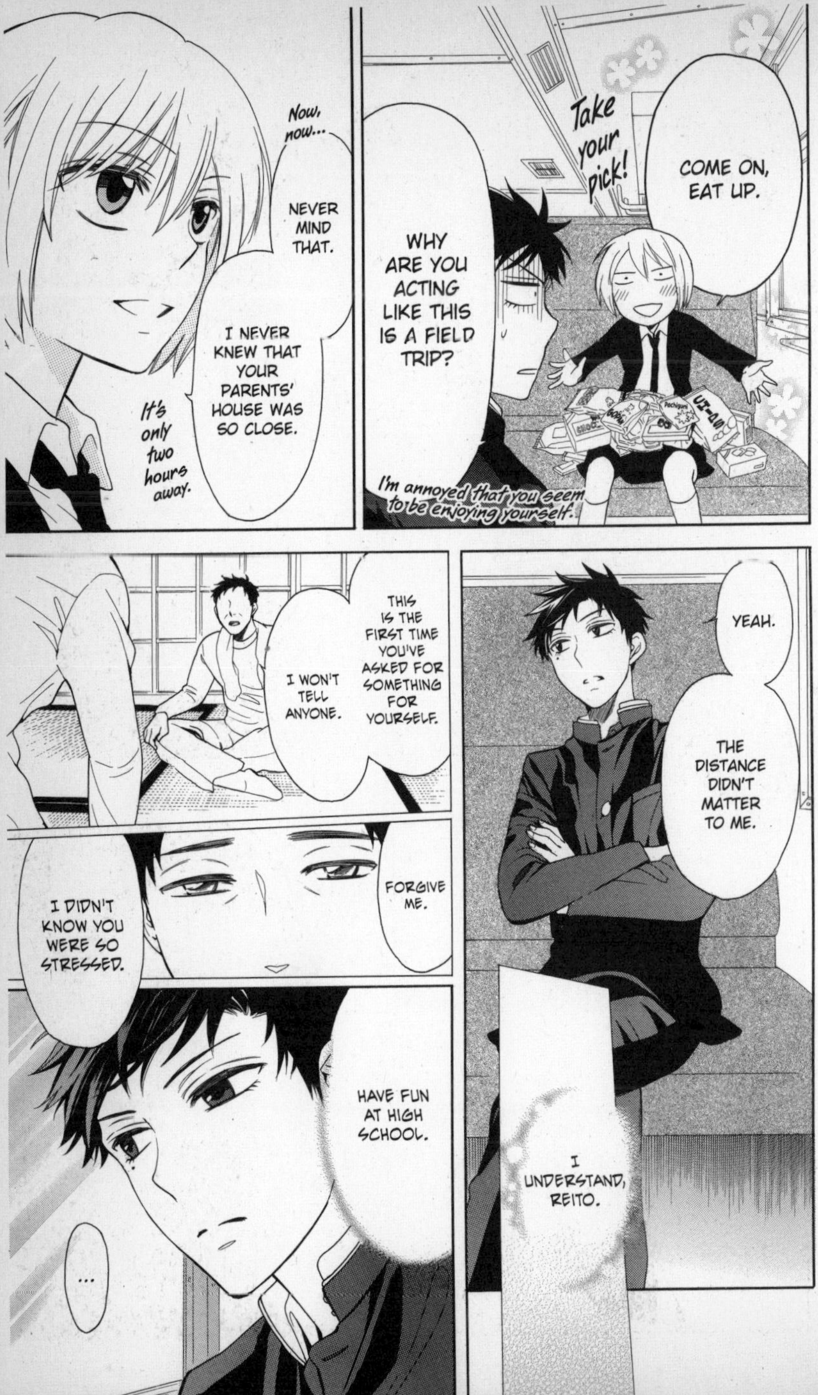
Take your pick!
COME ON, EAT UP.
WHY ARE YOU ACTING LIKE THIS IS A FIELD TRIP?
I'm annoyed that you seem to be enjoying yourself.
Now, now...
NEVER MIND THAT.
I NEVER KNEW THAT YOUR PARENTS' HOUSE WAS SO CLOSE.
It's only two hours away.
YEAH.
THE DISTANCE DIDN'T MATTER TO ME.
I UNDERSTAND, REITO.
THIS IS THE FIRST TIME YOU'VE ASKED FOR SOMETHING FOR YOURSELF.
I WON'T TELL ANYONE.
FORGIVE ME.
I DIDN'T KNOW YOU WERE SO STRESSED.
HAVE FUN AT HIGH SCHOOL.
...

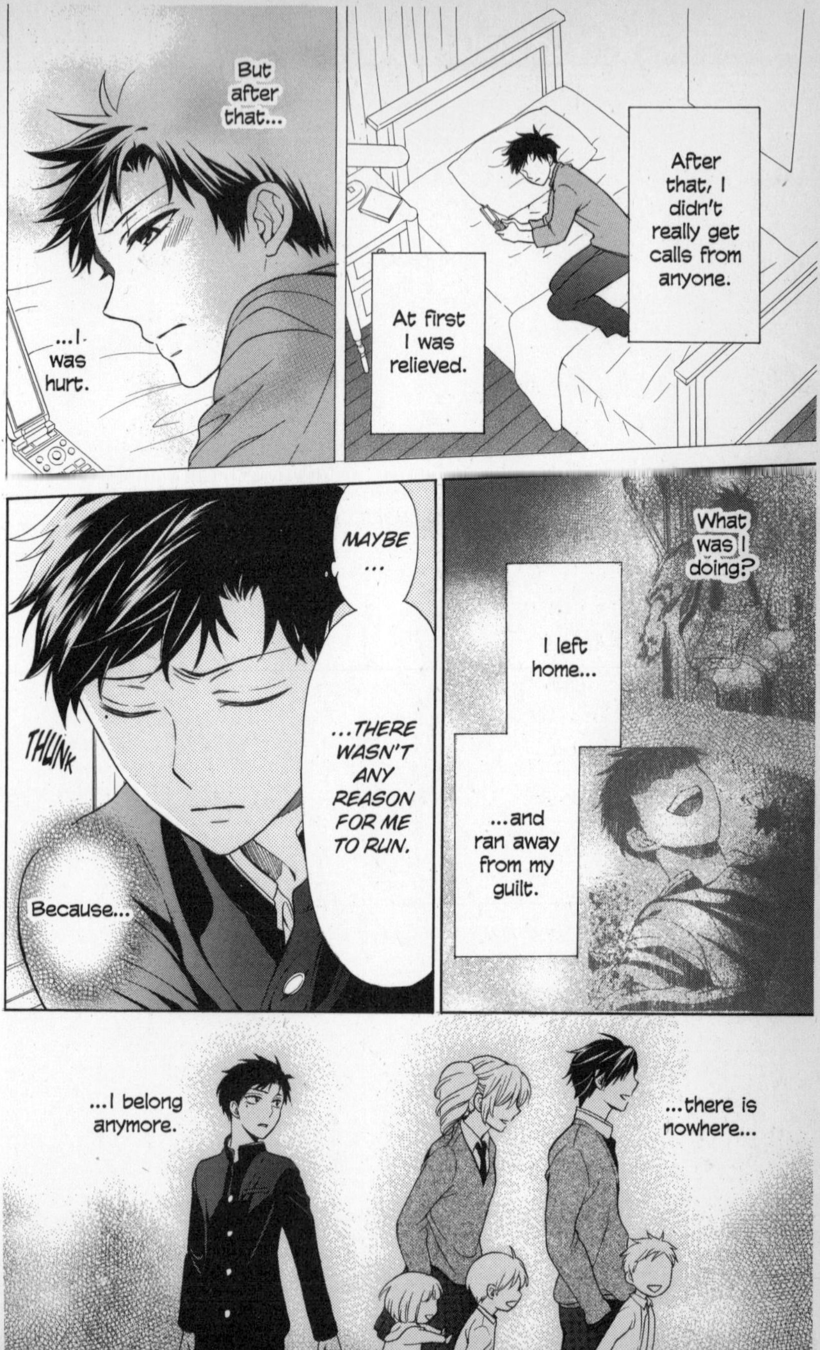
After that, I didn't really get calls from anyone.
At first I was relieved.
But after that...
...I was hurt.
What was I doing?
I left home...
...and ran away from my guilt.
MAYBE ...
...THERE WASN'T ANY REASON FOR ME TO RUN.
THUNK
Because...
...there is nowhere...
...I belong anymore.

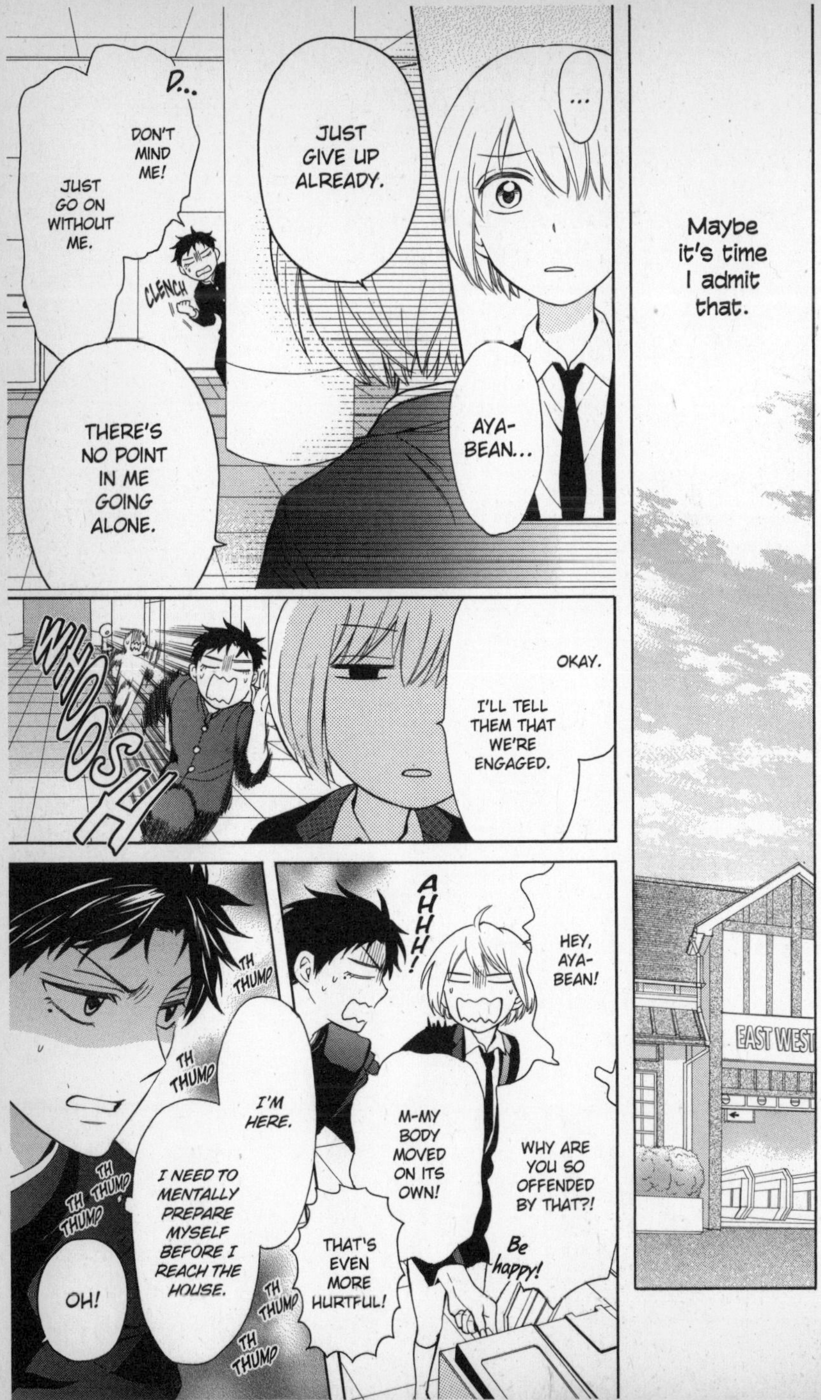
Maybe it's time I admit that.
EAST WEST
...
AYA-BEAN...
JUST GIVE UP ALREADY.
D...
DON'T MIND ME!
JUST GO ON WITHOUT ME.
CLENCH
THERE'S NO POINT IN ME GOING ALONE.
OKAY.
I'LL TELL THEM THAT WE'RE ENGAGED.
WHOOSH
HEY, AYA-BEAN!
AHHH!
WHY ARE YOU SO OFFENDED BY THAT?!
M-MY BODY MOVED ON ITS OWN!
Be happy!
THAT'S EVEN MORE HURTFUL!
TH THUMP
TH THUMP
I'M HERE.
I NEED TO MENTALLY PREPARE MYSELF BEFORE I REACH THE HOUSE.
TH THUMP
TH THUMP
TH THUMP
TH THUMP
OH!

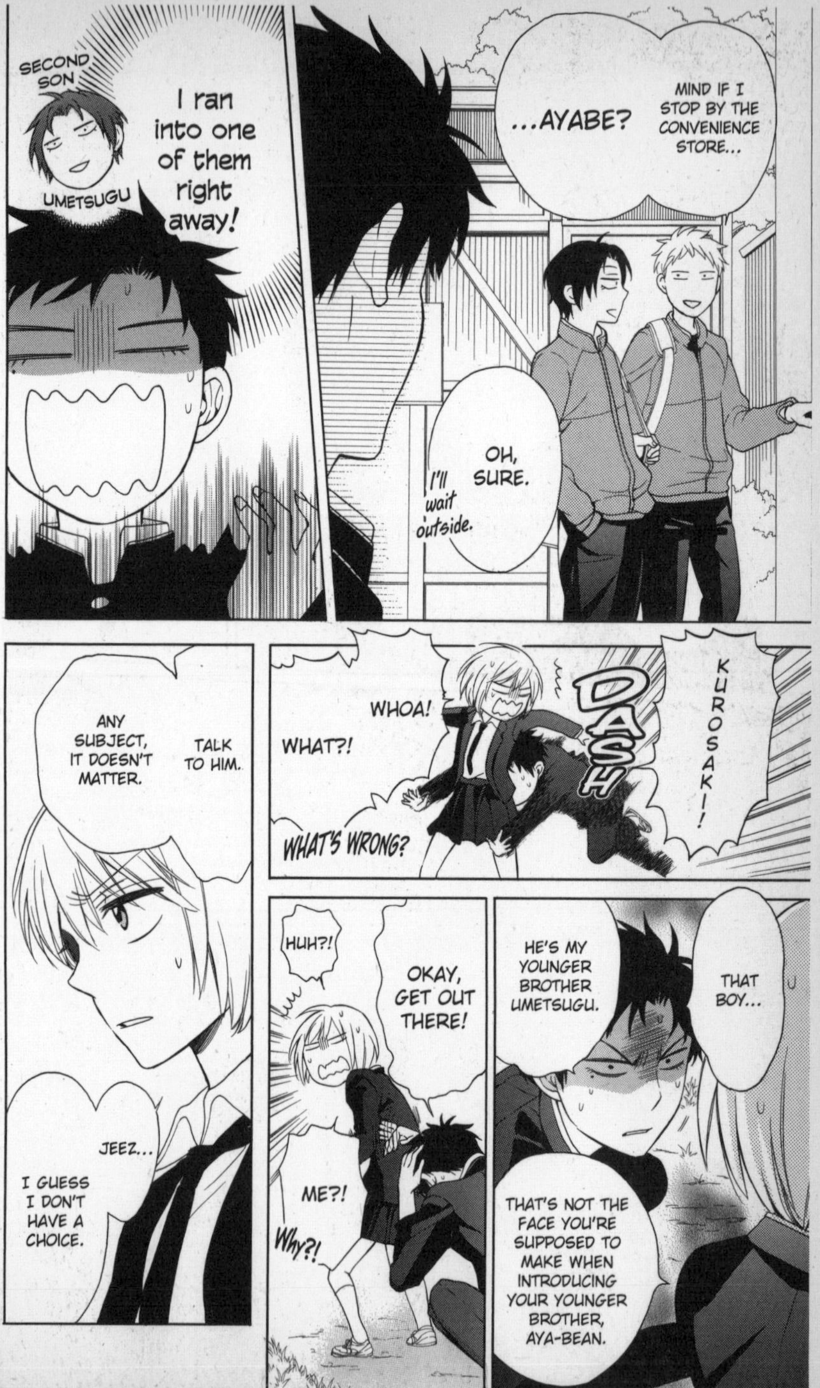
MIND IF I STOP BY THE CONVENIENCE STORE...
...AYABE?
OH, SURE.
I'll wait outside.
I ran into one of them right away!
SECOND SON
UMETSUGU
KUROSAKI!
DASH
WHOA!
WHAT?!
WHAT'S WRONG?
THAT BOY...
HE'S MY YOUNGER BROTHER UMETSUGU.
THAT'S NOT THE FACE YOU'RE SUPPOSED TO MAKE WHEN INTRODUCING YOUR YOUNGER BROTHER, AYA-BEAN.
HUH?!
OKAY, GET OUT THERE!
ME?!
Why?!
TALK TO HIM.
ANY SUBJECT, IT DOESN'T MATTER.
JEEZ...
I GUESS I DON'T HAVE A CHOICE.

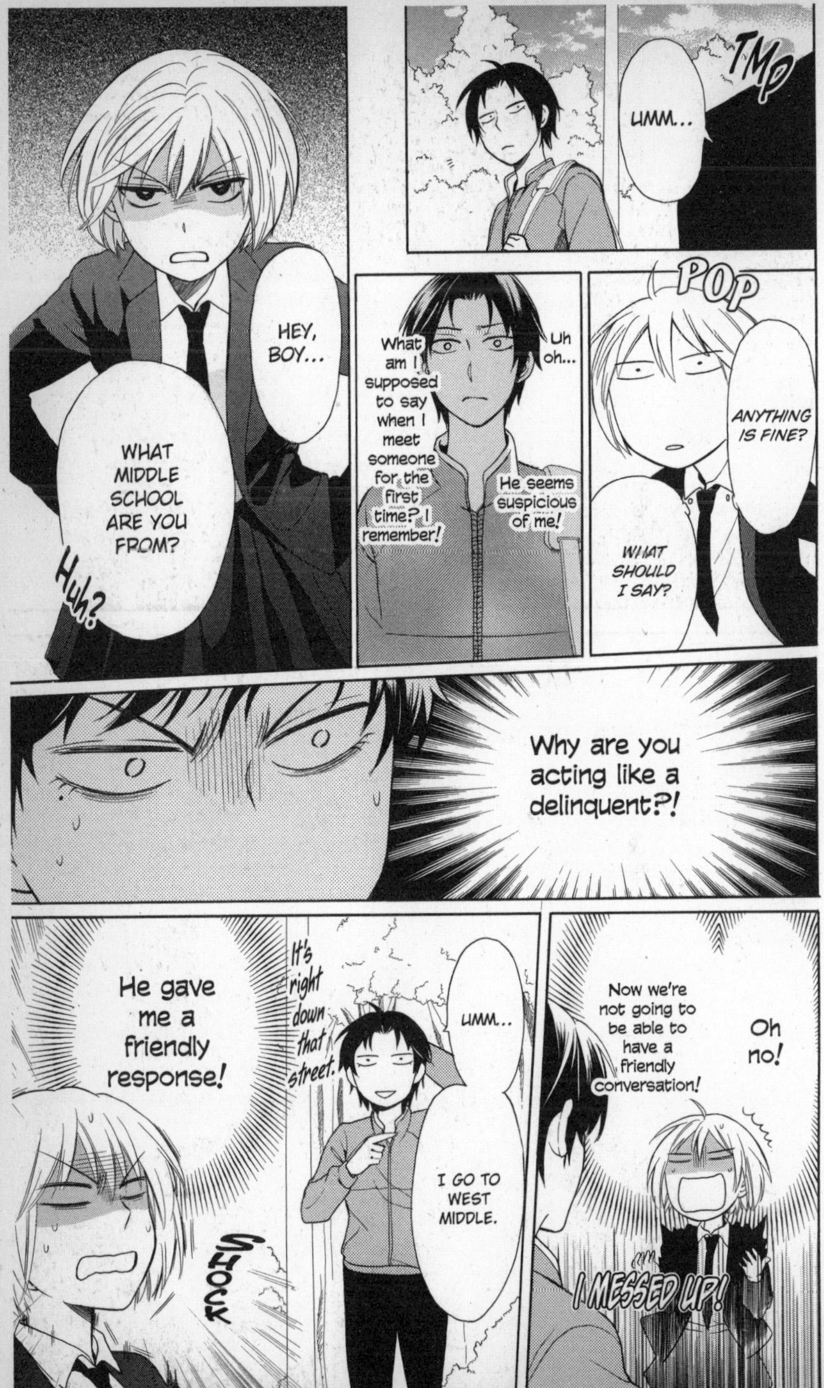
UMM...
TMP
POP
ANYTHING IS FINE?
WHAT SHOULD I SAY?
Uh oh...
He seems suspicious of me!
What am I supposed to say when I meet someone for the first time? I remember!
HEY, BOY...
WHAT MIDDLE SCHOOL ARE YOU FROM?
Huh?
Why are you acting like a delinquent?!
Oh no!
Now we're not going to be able to have a friendly conversation!
I MESSED UP!
UMM...
I GO TO WEST MIDDLE.
It's right down that street.
He gave me a friendly response!
SHOCK

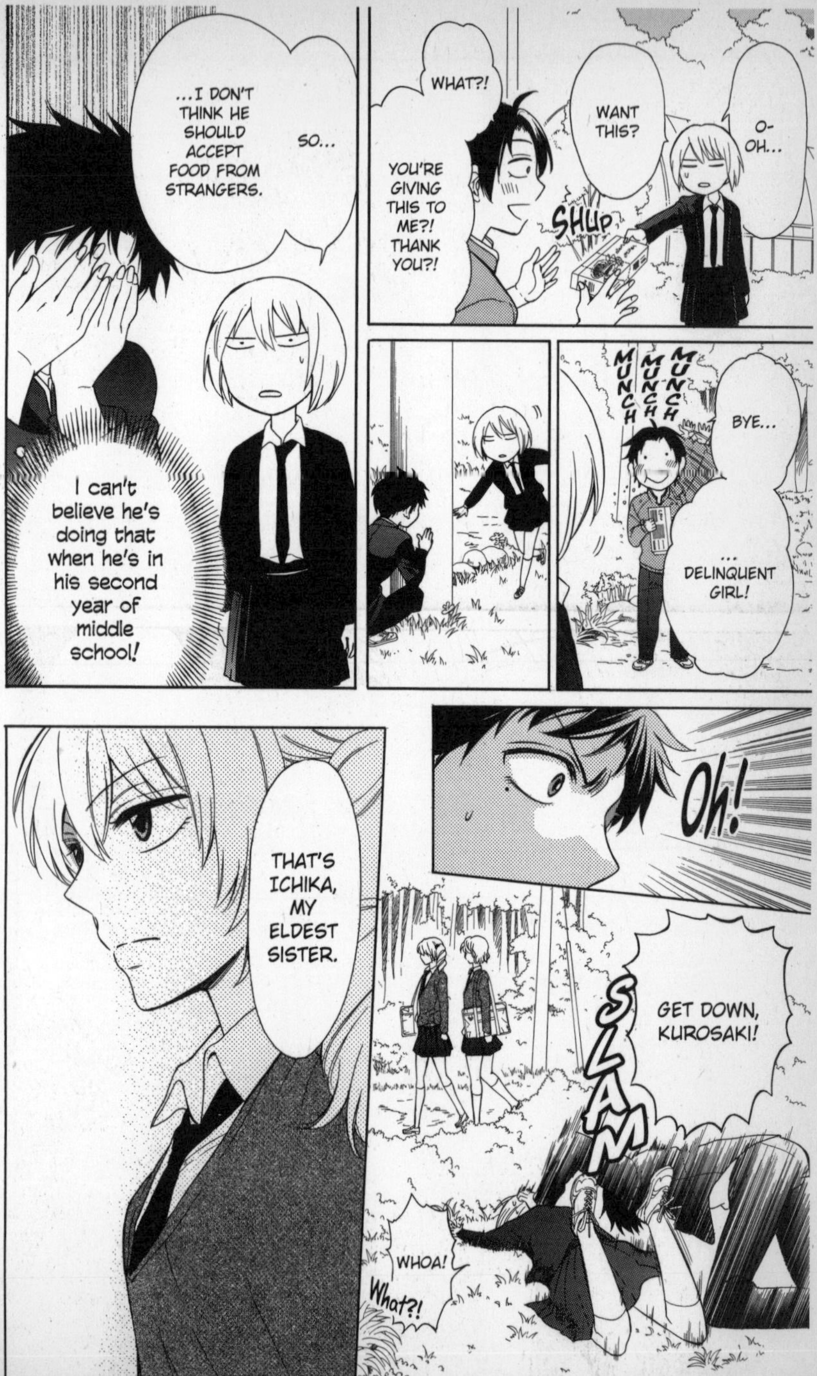
O-OH...
WANT THIS?
SHUP
WHAT?!
YOU'RE GIVING THIS TO ME?! THANK YOU?!
BYE...
... DELINQUENT GIRL!
MUNCH MUNCH MUNCH
SO...
...I DON'T THINK HE SHOULD ACCEPT FOOD FROM STRANGERS.
I can't believe he's doing that when he's in his second year of middle school!
Oh!
GET DOWN, KUROSAKI!
SLAM
WHOA!
What?!
THAT'S ICHIKA, MY ELDEST SISTER.

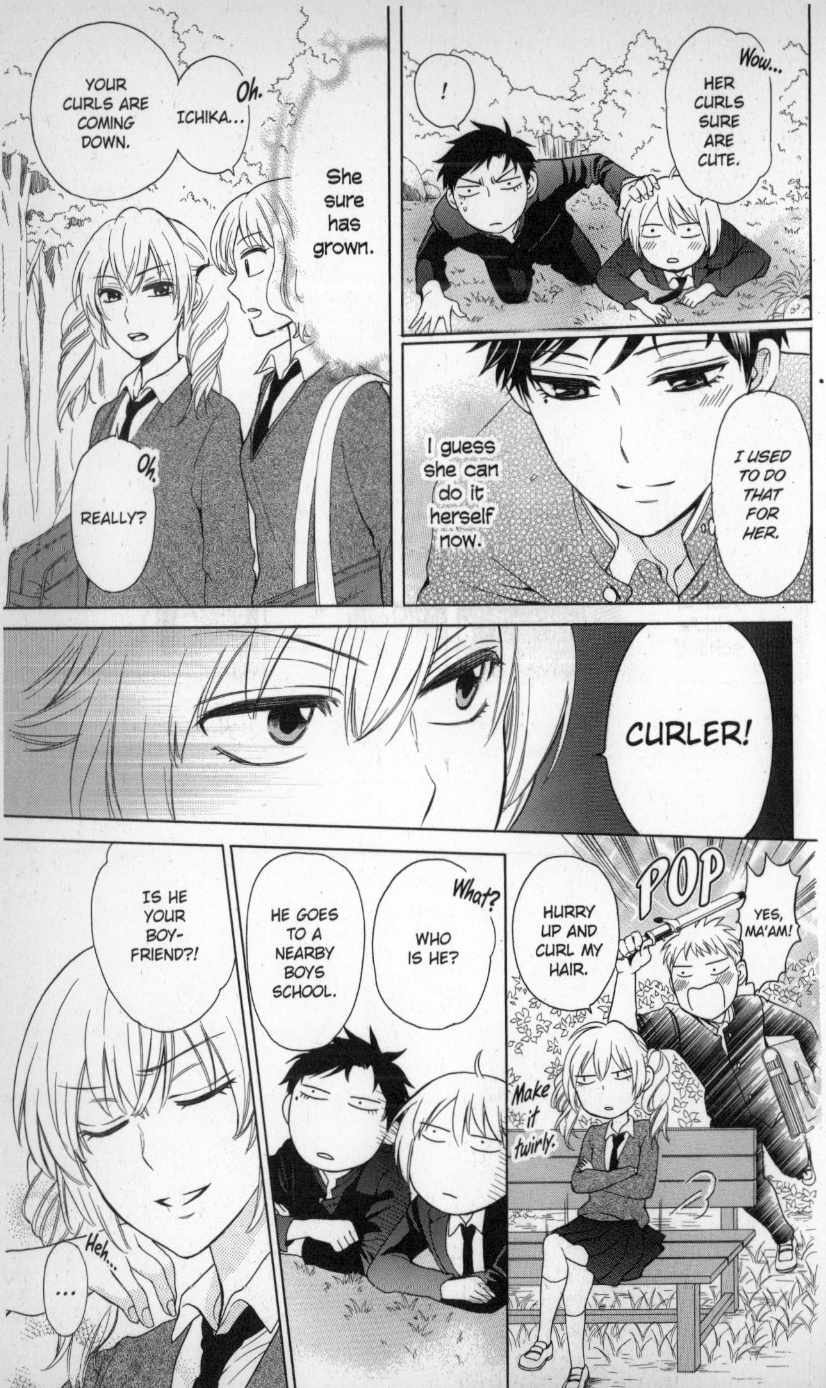
Wow...
HER CURLS SURE ARE CUTE.
!
I USED TO DO THAT FOR HER.
I guess she can do it herself now.
Oh.
ICHIKA...
YOUR CURLS ARE COMING DOWN.
She sure has grown.
Oh.
REALLY?
CURLER!
YES, MA'AM!
POP
HURRY UP AND CURL MY HAIR.
Make it twirly.
What?
WHO IS HE?
HE GOES TO A NEARBY BOYS SCHOOL.
IS HE YOUR BOY-FRIEND?!
Heh...
...

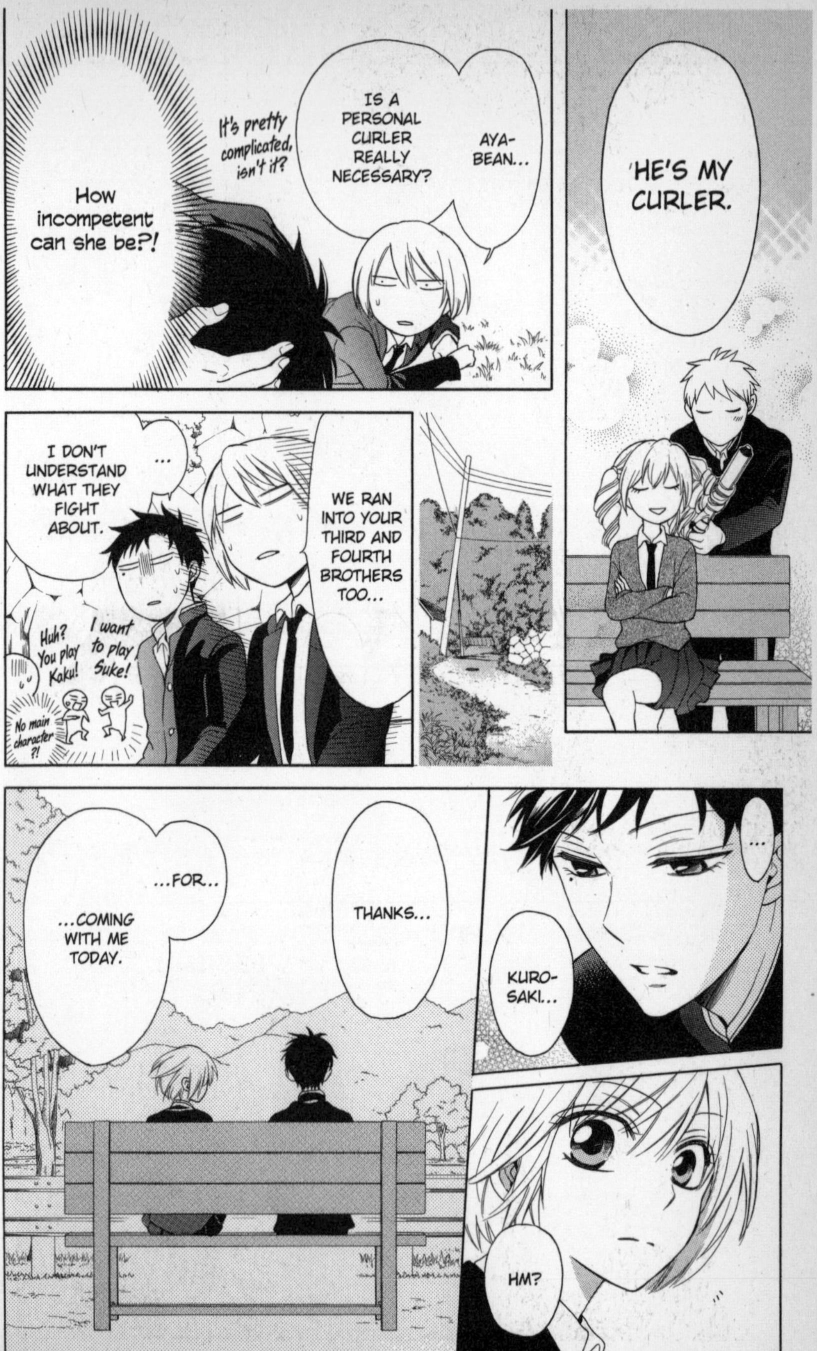
'HE'S MY CURLER.
AYA-BEAN...
IS A PERSONAL CURLER REALLY NECESSARY?
It's pretty complicated, isn't it?
How incompetent can she be?!
WE RAN INTO YOUR THIRD AND FOURTH BROTHERS TOO...
...
I DON'T UNDERSTAND WHAT THEY FIGHT ABOUT.
I want to play Suke!
Huh? You play Kaku!
No main character?!
...
KURO-SAKI...
HM?
THANKS...
...FOR...
...COMING WITH ME TODAY.

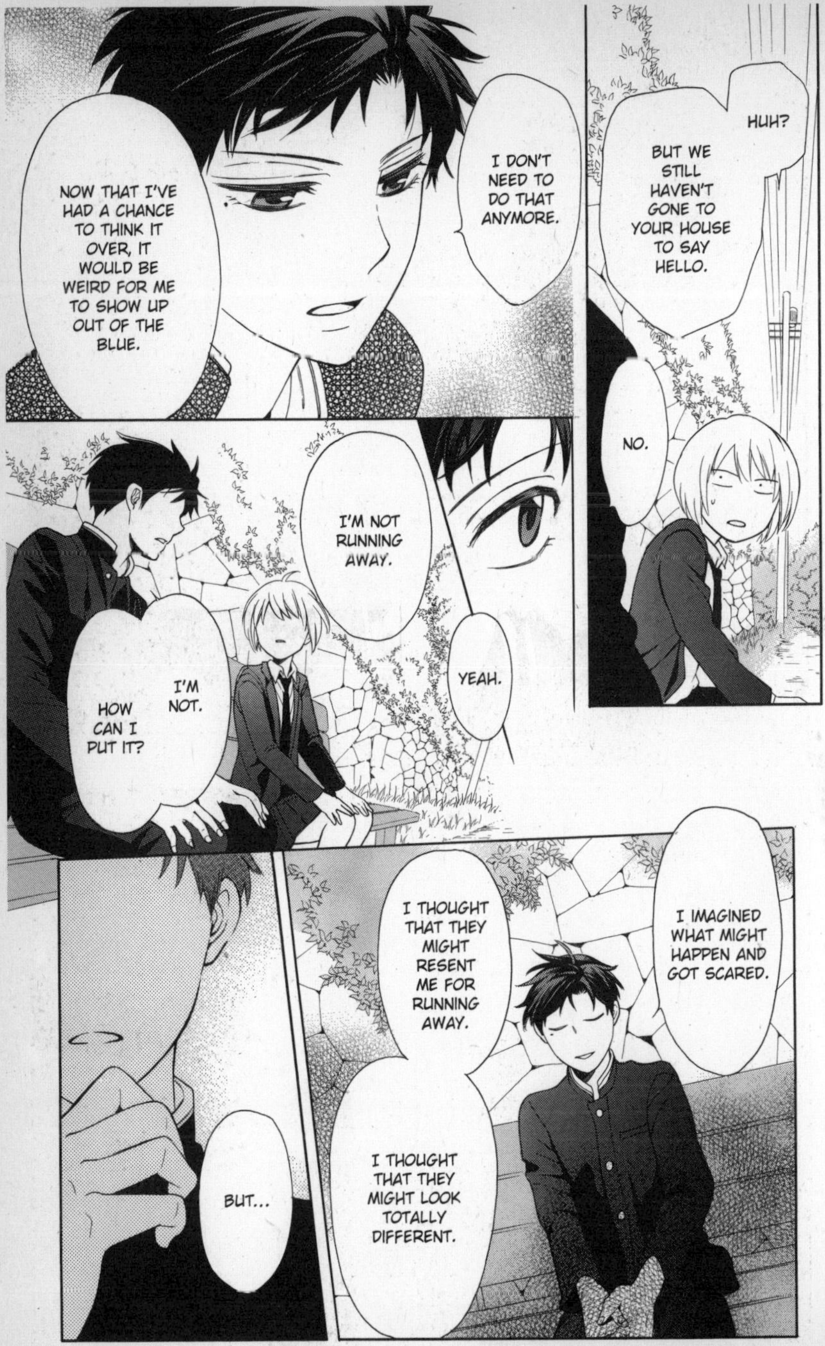
HUH?
BUT WE STILL HAVEN'T GONE TO YOUR HOUSE TO SAY HELLO.
NO.
I DON'T NEED TO DO THAT ANYMORE.
NOW THAT I'VE HAD A CHANCE TO THINK IT OVER, IT WOULD BE WEIRD FOR ME TO SHOW UP OUT OF THE BLUE.
I'M NOT RUNNING AWAY.
YEAH.
I'M NOT.
HOW CAN I PUT IT?
I IMAGINED WHAT MIGHT HAPPEN AND GOT SCARED.
I THOUGHT THAT THEY MIGHT RESENT ME FOR RUNNING AWAY.
I THOUGHT THAT THEY MIGHT LOOK TOTALLY DIFFERENT.
BUT...

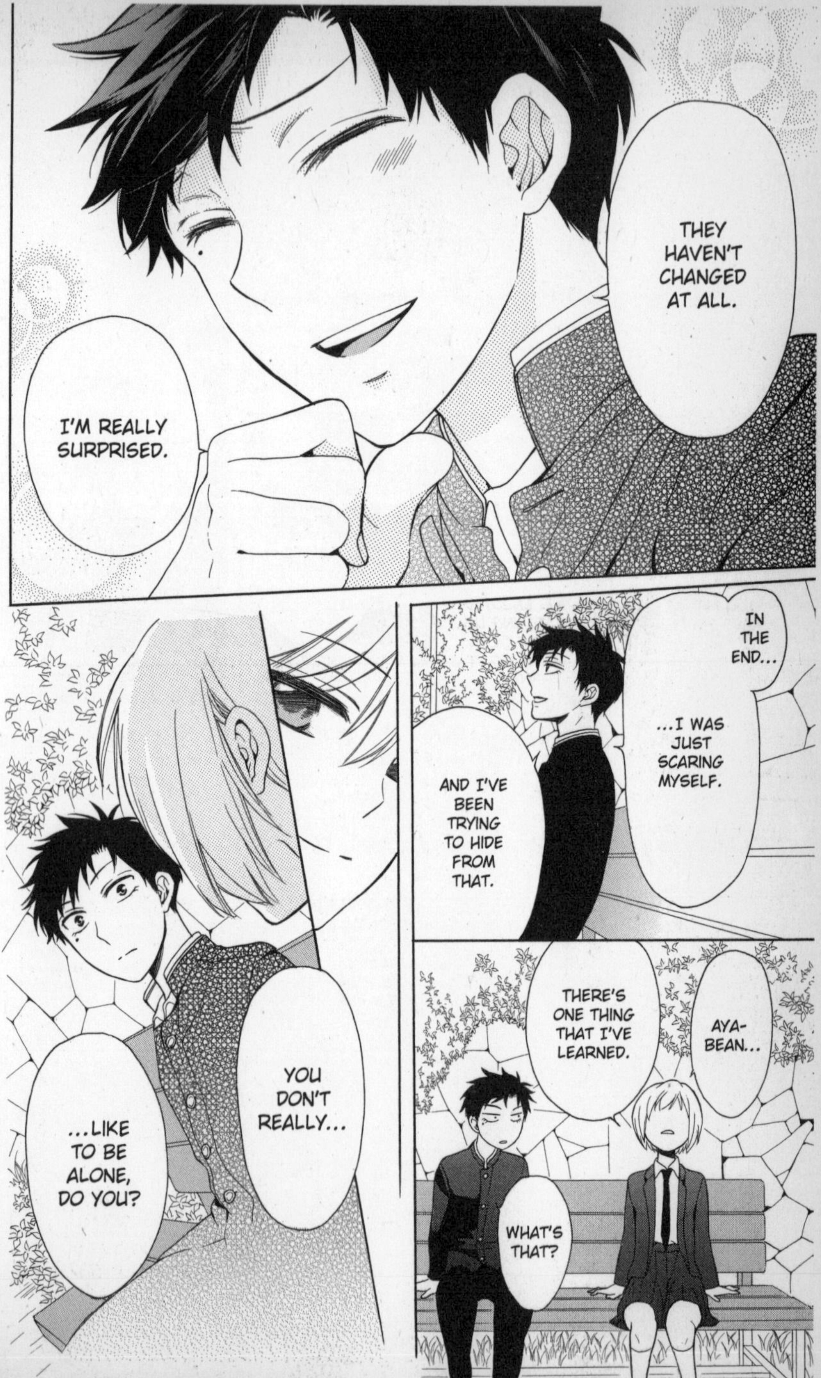
THEY HAVEN'T CHANGED AT ALL.
I'M REALLY SURPRISED.
IN THE END...
...I WAS JUST SCARING MYSELF.
AND I'VE BEEN TRYING TO HIDE FROM THAT.
AYA-BEAN...
THERE'S ONE THING THAT I'VE LEARNED.
WHAT'S THAT?
YOU DON'T REALLY...
...LIKE TO BE ALONE, DO YOU?

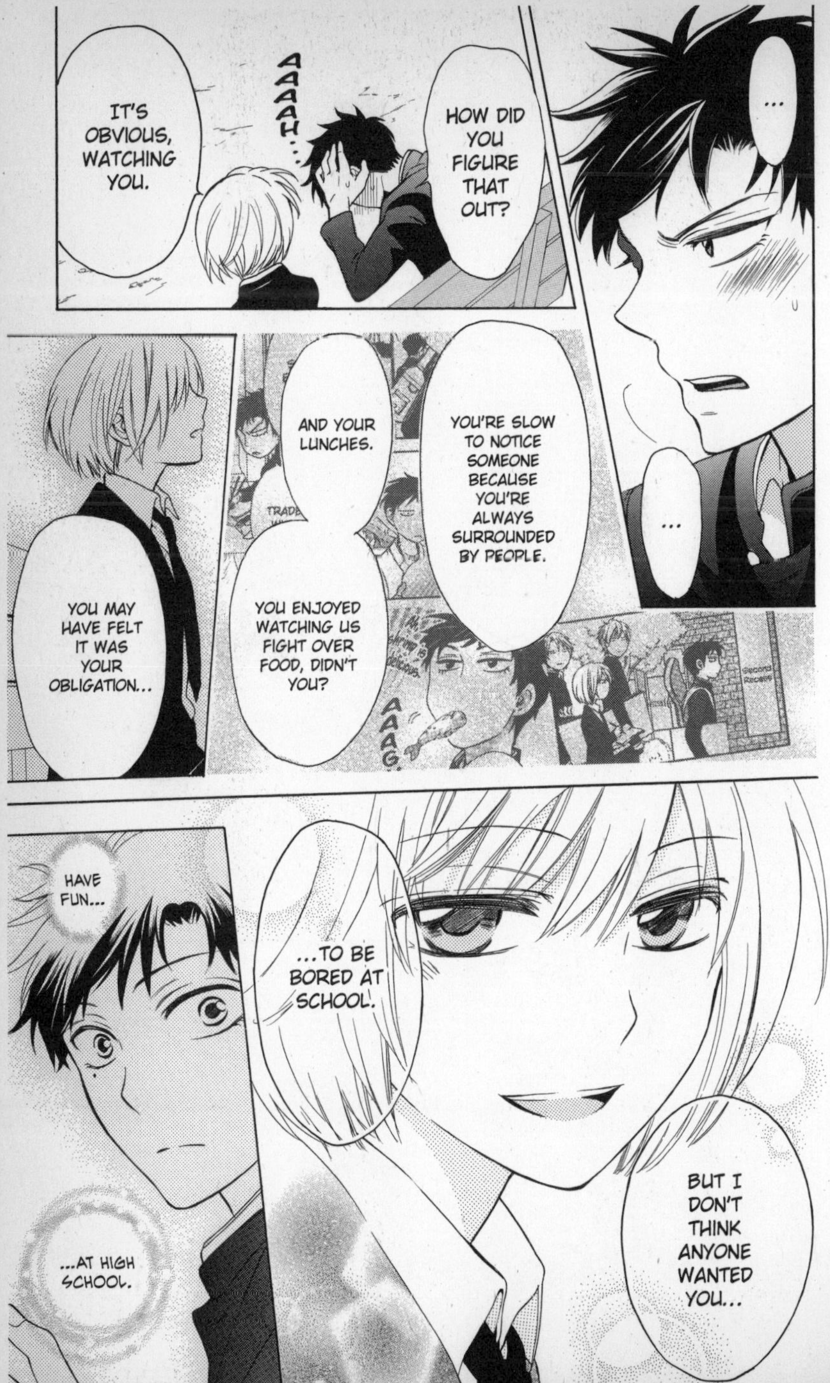
...
...
HOW DID YOU FIGURE THAT OUT?
AAAAAH...
IT'S OBVIOUS, WATCHING YOU.
YOU'RE SLOW TO NOTICE SOMEONE BECAUSE YOU'RE ALWAYS SURROUNDED BY PEOPLE.
AND YOUR LUNCHES.
YOU ENJOYED WATCHING US FIGHT OVER FOOD, DIDN'T YOU?
YOU MAY HAVE FELT IT WAS YOUR OBLIGATION...
BUT I DON'T THINK ANYONE WANTED YOU...
...TO BE BORED AT SCHOOL.
HAVE FUN...
...AT HIGH SCHOOL.

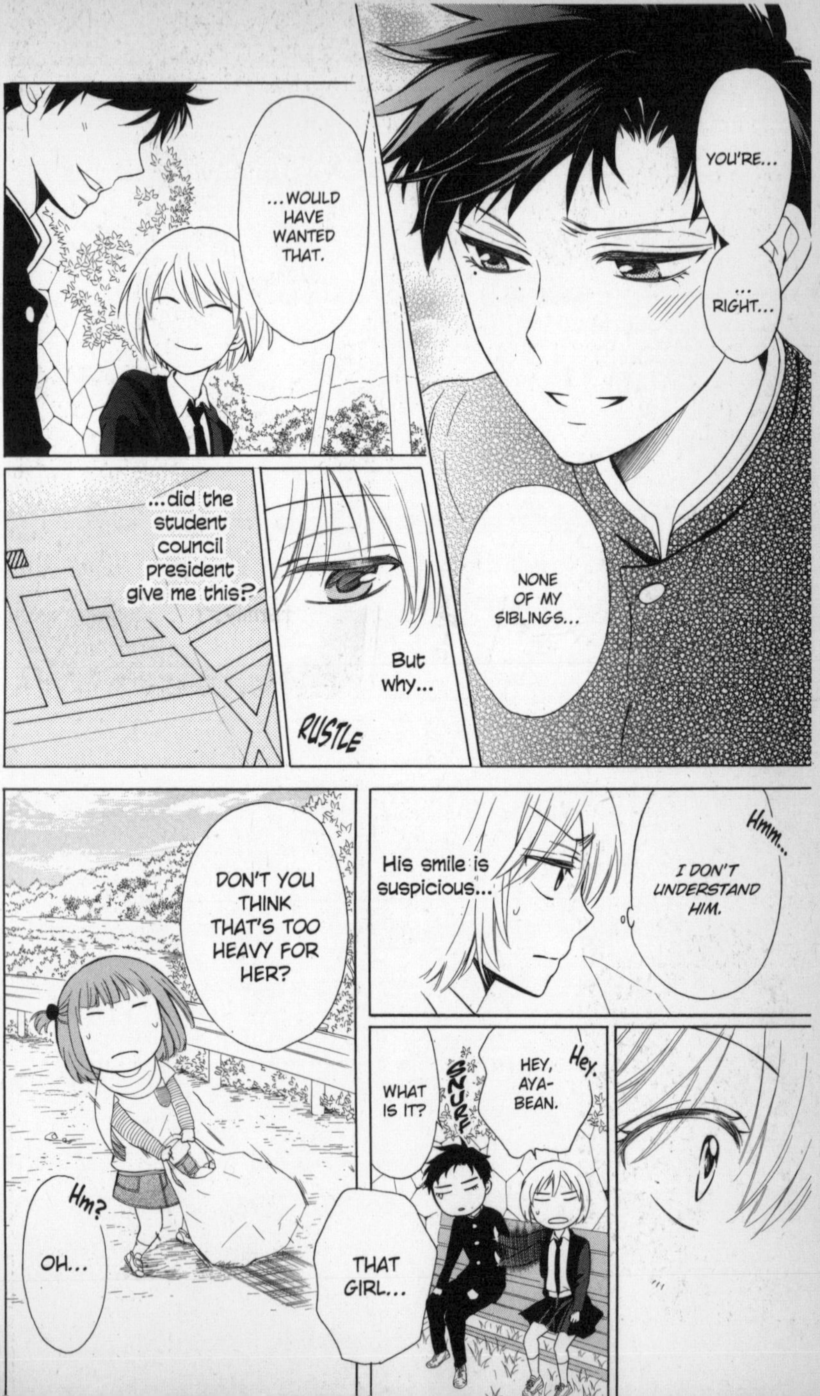
YOU'RE...
...RIGHT...
NONE OF MY SIBLINGS...
...WOULD HAVE WANTED THAT.
But why...
RUSTLE
...did the student council president give me this?
Hmm...
I DON'T UNDERSTAND HIM.
His smile is suspicious...
Hey.
HEY, AYA-BEAN.
SNUFF
WHAT IS IT?
THAT GIRL...
DON'T YOU THINK THAT'S TOO HEAVY FOR HER?
Hm?
OH...

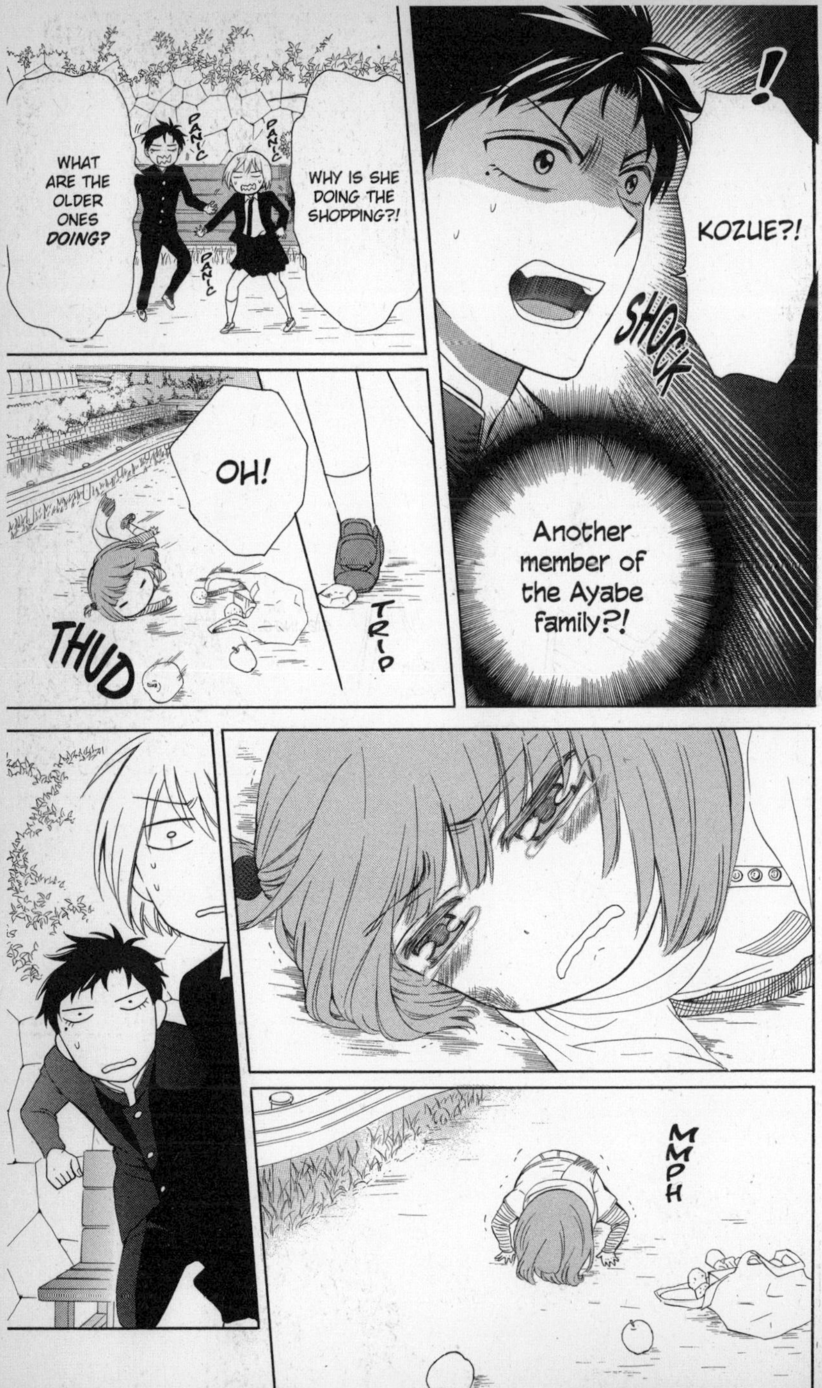
!
KOZUE?!
SHOCK
Another member of the Ayabe family?!
WHY IS SHE DOING THE SHOPPING?!
PANIC
PANIC
PANIC
WHAT ARE THE OLDER ONES *DOING?*
OH!
TRIP
THUD
MMPH

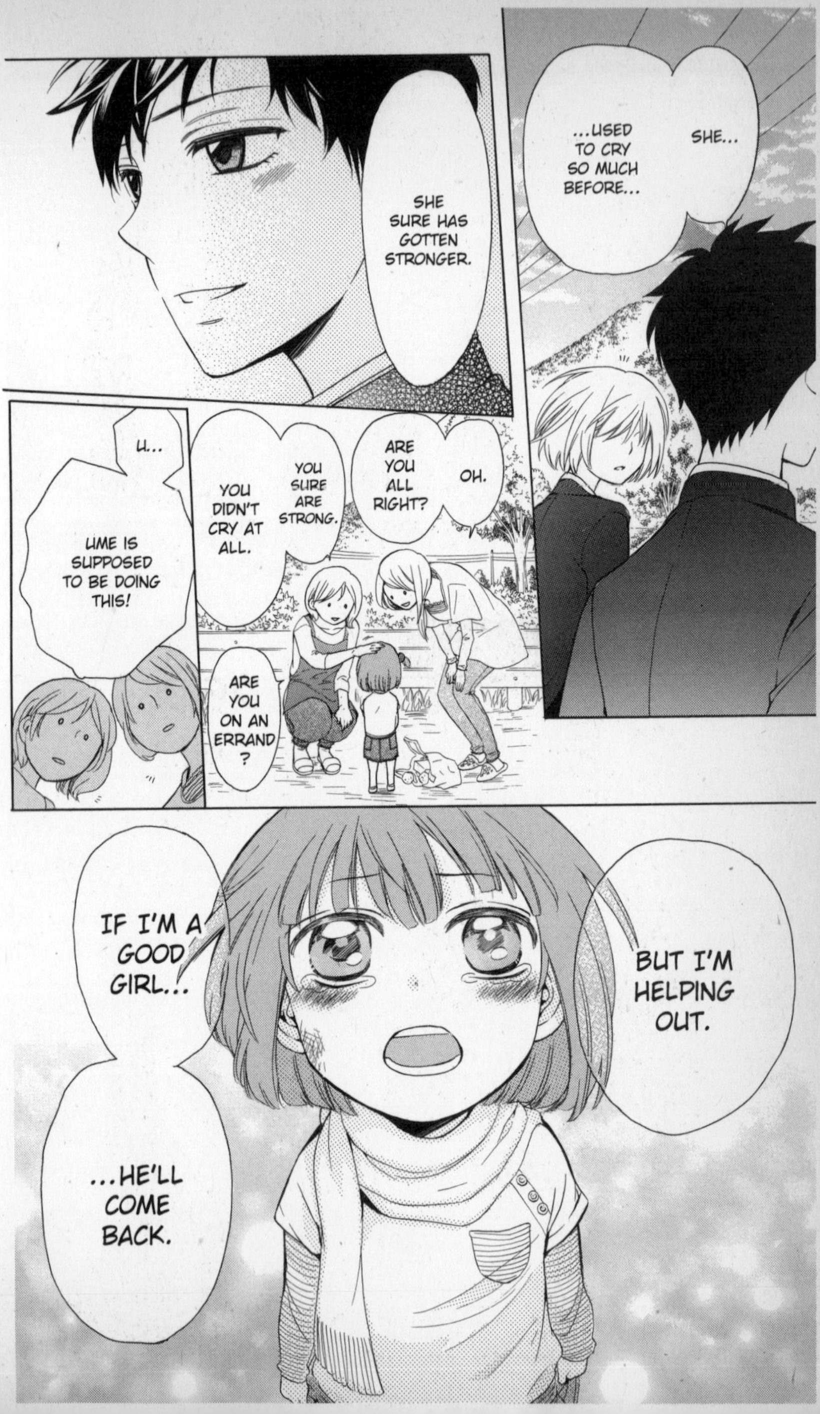
SHE...
...USED TO CRY SO MUCH BEFORE...
SHE SURE HAS GOTTEN STRONGER.
OH.
ARE YOU ALL RIGHT?
YOU SURE ARE STRONG.
YOU DIDN'T CRY AT ALL.
ARE YOU ON AN ERRAND?
U...
UME IS SUPPOSED TO BE DOING THIS!
BUT I'M HELPING OUT.
IF I'M A GOOD GIRL...
...HE'LL COME BACK.

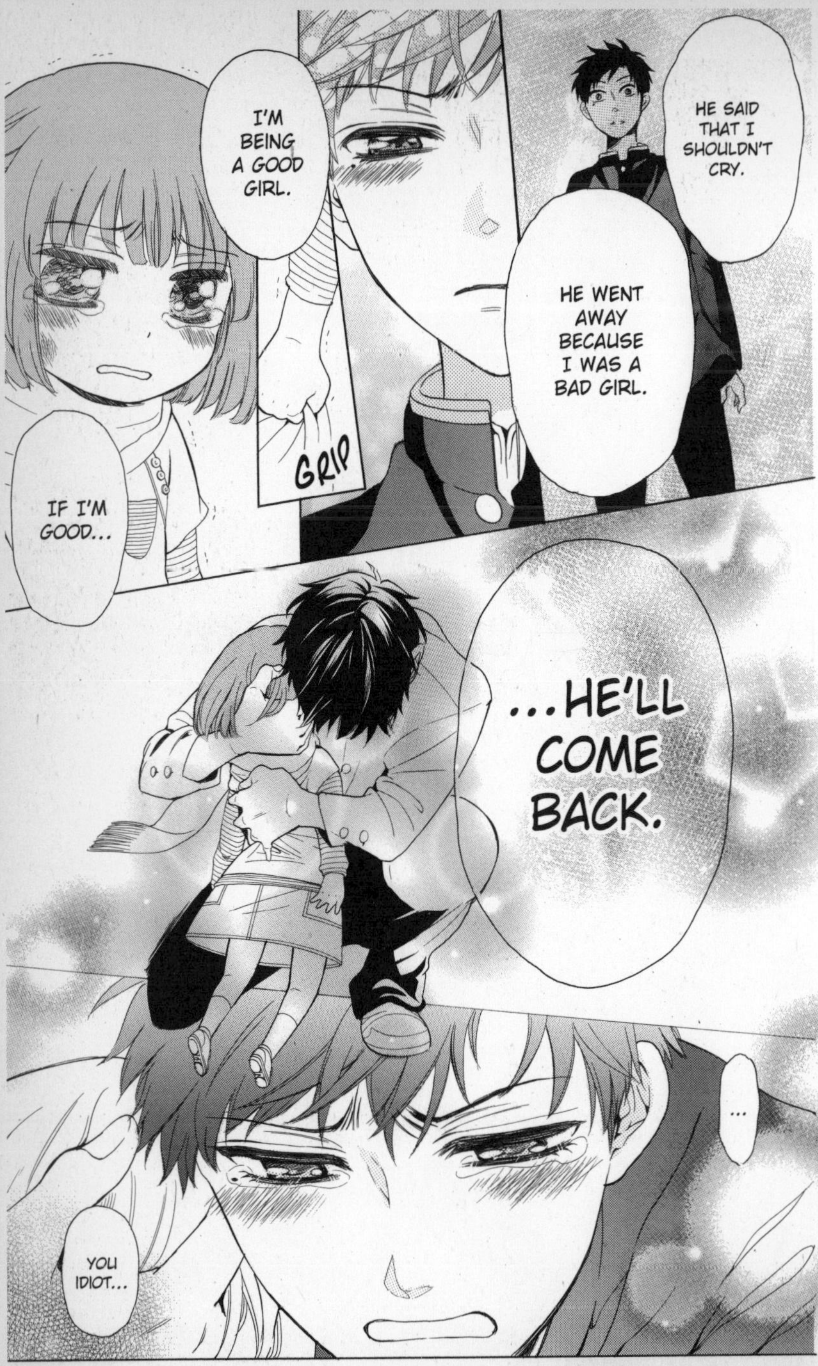
HE SAID THAT I SHOULDN'T CRY.
HE WENT AWAY BECAUSE I WAS A BAD GIRL.
I'M BEING A GOOD GIRL.
GRIP
IF I'M GOOD...
...HE'LL COME BACK.
...
YOU IDIOT...

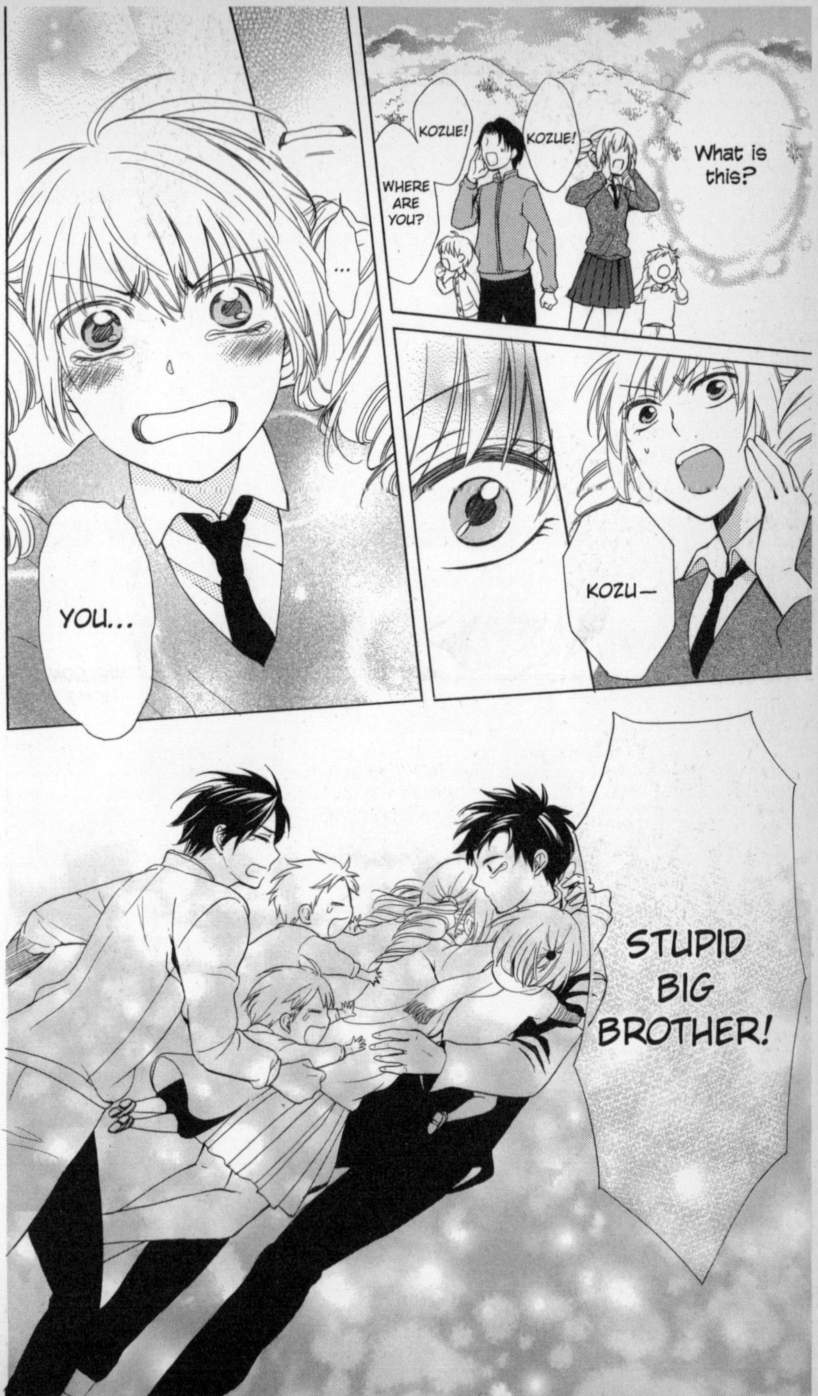
What is this?
KOZUE!
KOZUE!
WHERE ARE YOU?
KOZU—
...
YOU...
STUPID BIG BROTHER!

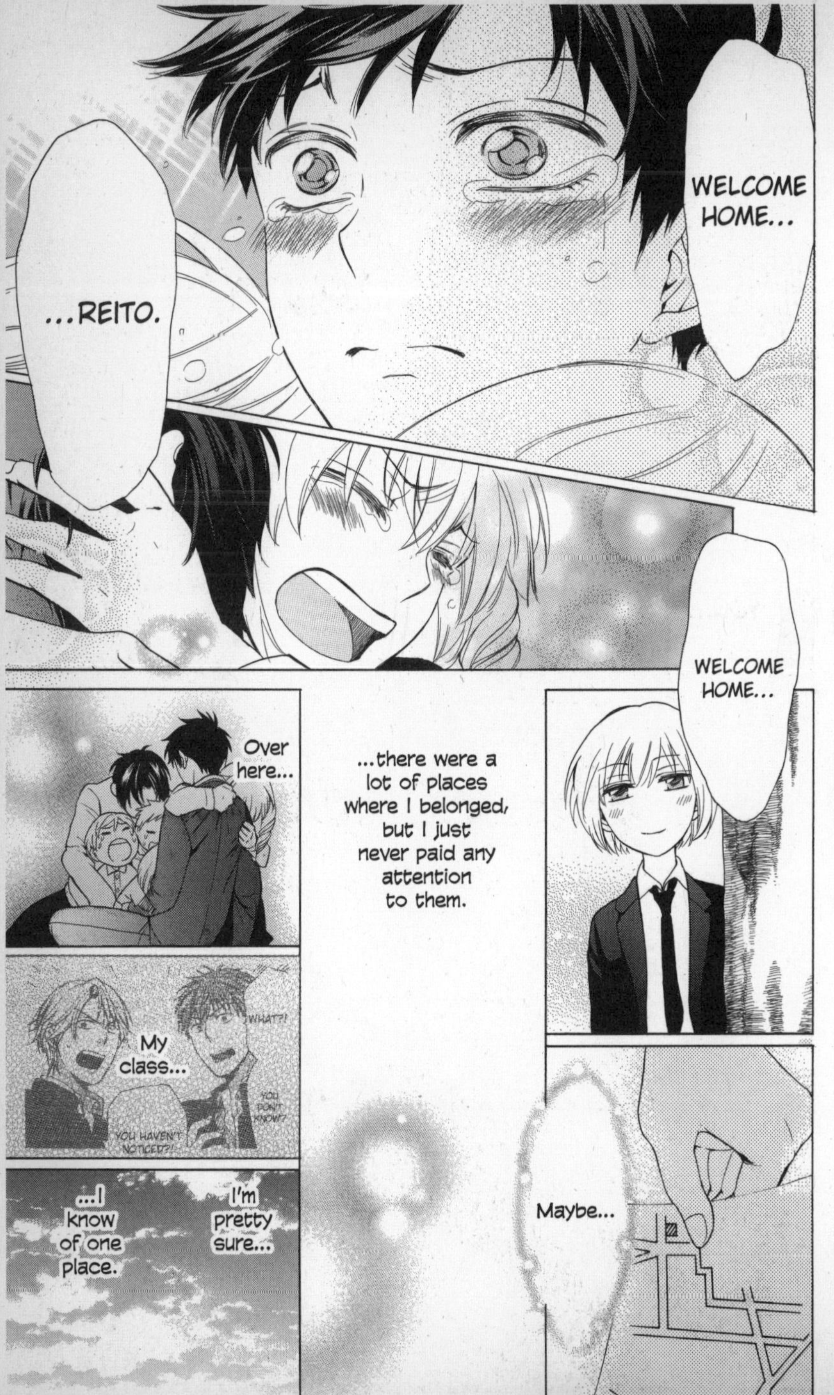
WELCOME HOME...
...REITO.
WELCOME HOME...
...there were a lot of places where I belonged, but I just never paid any attention to them.
Over here...
My class...
WHAT?!
YOU DON'T KNOW?
YOU HAVEN'T NOTICED?!
Maybe...
I'm pretty sure...
...I know of one place.

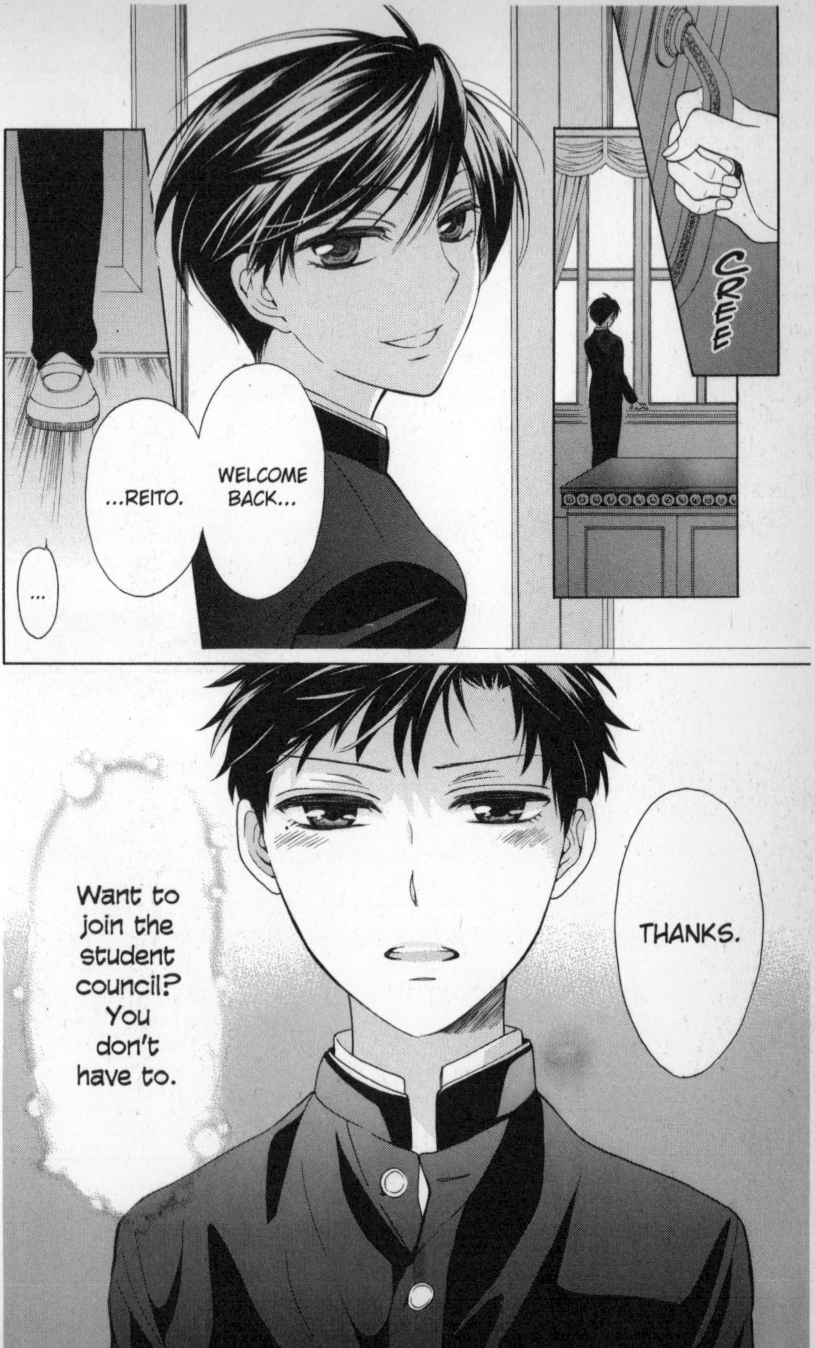
CREE
WELCOME BACK...
...REITO.
...
THANKS.
Want to join the student council? You don't have to.

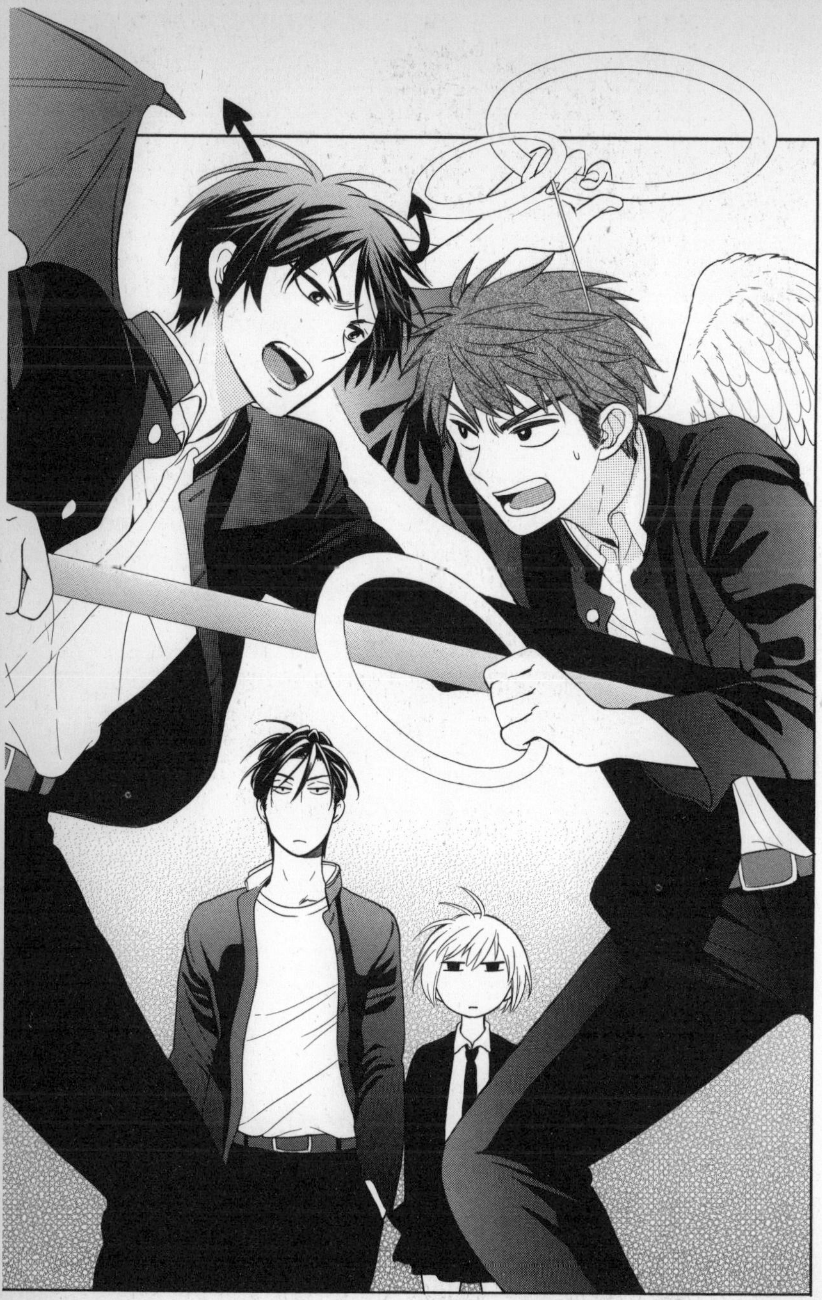

Chapter 66

ONE DAY TO DESTINY

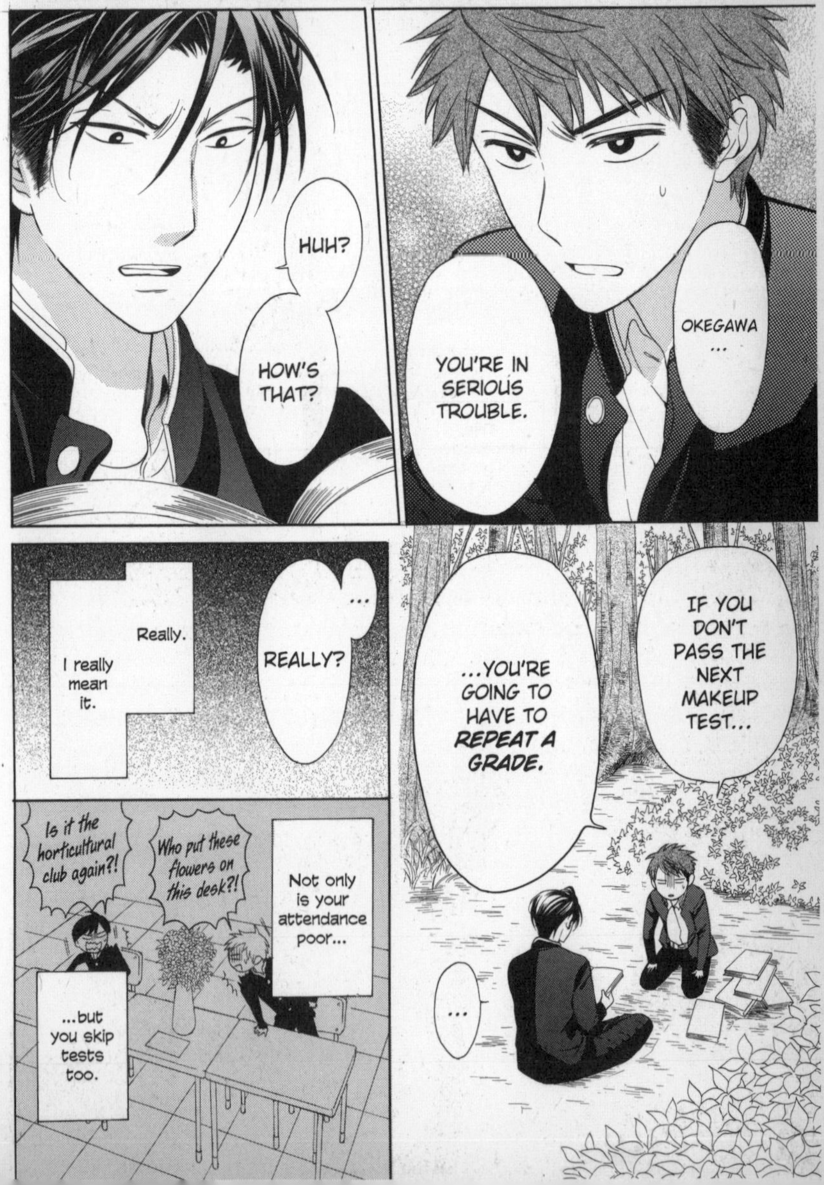
OKEGAWA ...
YOU'RE IN SERIOUS TROUBLE.
HUH?
HOW'S THAT?
IF YOU DON'T PASS THE NEXT MAKEUP TEST...
...YOU'RE GOING TO HAVE TO REPEAT A GRADE.
...
...
REALLY?
Really.
I really mean it.
Not only is your attendance poor...
Who put these flowers on this desk?!
Is it the horticultural club again?!
...but you skip tests too.

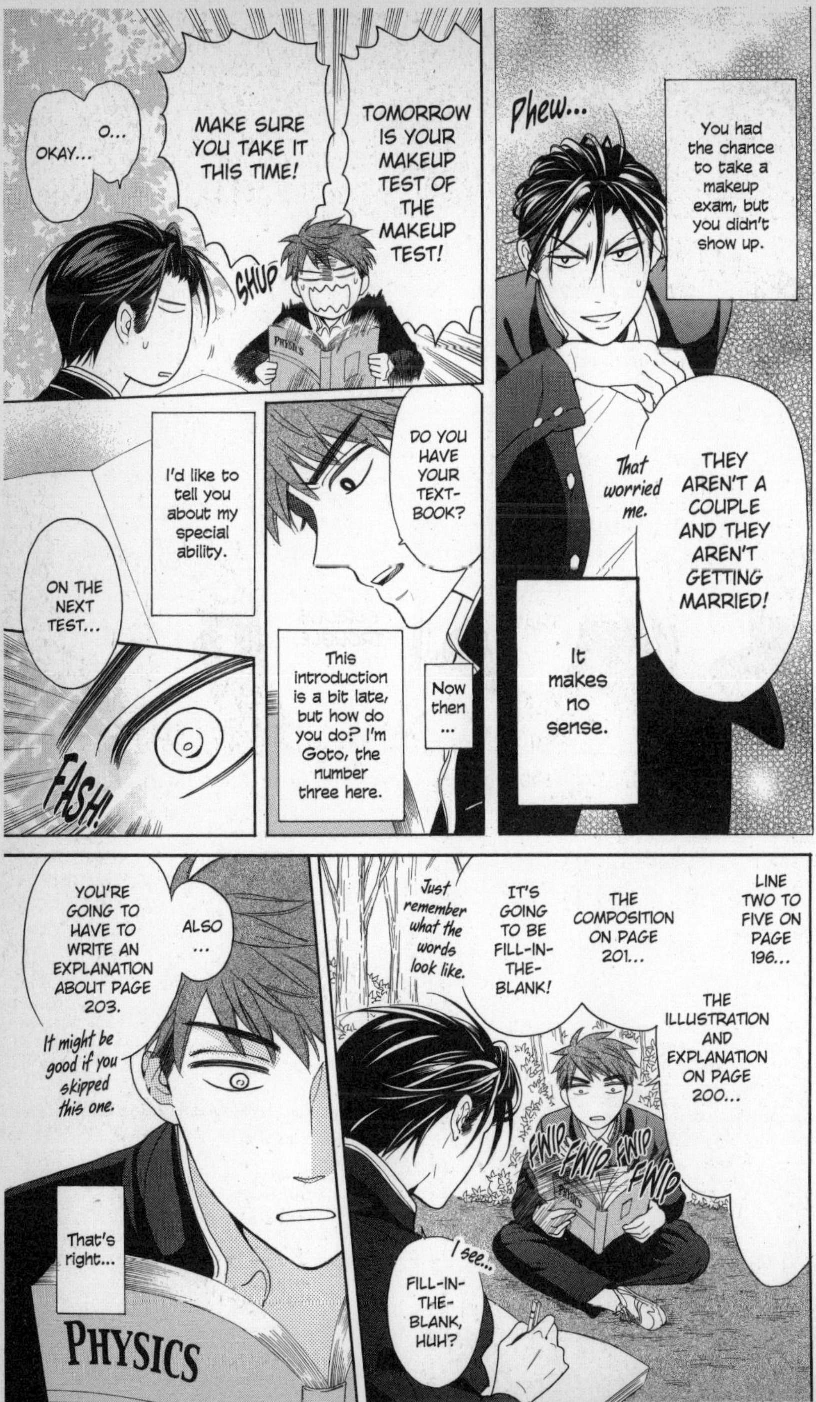
Phew...
You had the chance to take a makeup exam, but you didn't show up.
THEY AREN'T A COUPLE AND THEY AREN'T GETTING MARRIED!
That worried me.
It makes no sense.
TOMORROW IS YOUR MAKEUP TEST OF THE MAKEUP TEST!
MAKE SURE YOU TAKE IT THIS TIME!
O... OKAY...
SHUP
PHYSICS
DO YOU HAVE YOUR TEXT-BOOK?
Now then...
This introduction is a bit late, but how do you do? I'm Goto, the number three here.
I'd like to tell you about my special ability.
ON THE NEXT TEST...
FASH!
LINE TWO TO FIVE ON PAGE 196...
THE COMPOSITION ON PAGE 201...
IT'S GOING TO BE FILL-IN-THE-BLANK!
Just remember what the words look like.
THE ILLUSTRATION AND EXPLANATION ON PAGE 200...
FWIP FWIP FWIP FWIP
PHYSICS
I see...
FILL-IN-THE-BLANK, HUH?
ALSO...
YOU'RE GOING TO HAVE TO WRITE AN EXPLANATION ABOUT PAGE 203.
It might be good if you skipped this one.
That's right...
PHYSICS

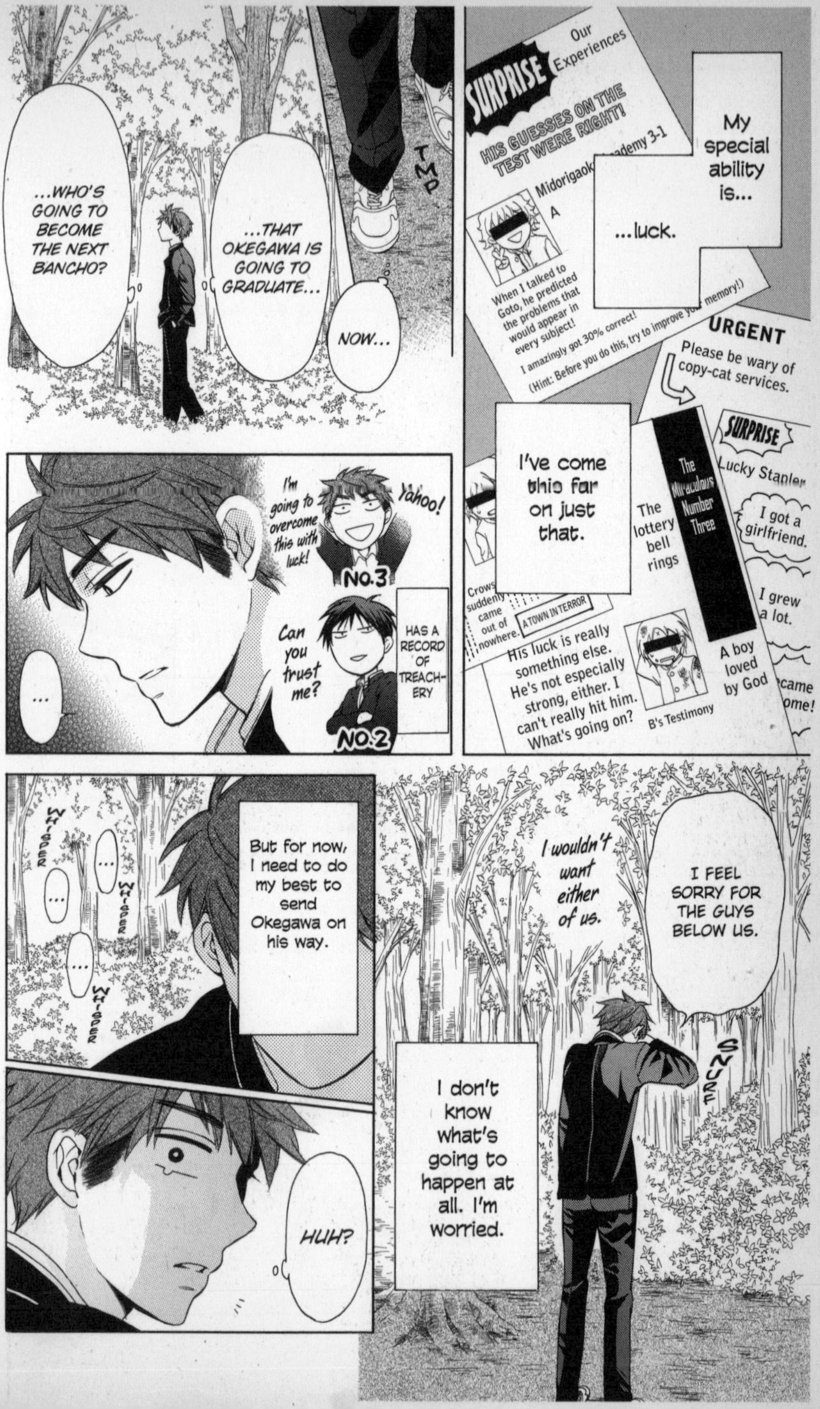

Our Experiences
SURPRISE
HIS GUESSES ON THE TEST WERE RIGHT!
Midorigaok
ademy 3-1
A
When I talked to Goto, he predicted the problems that would appear in every subject!
I amazingly got 30% correct!
(Hint: Before you do this, try to improve your memory!)
My special ability is...
...luck.
URGENT
Please be wary of copy-cat services.
SURPRISE
Lucky Stapler
I got a girlfriend.
I grew a lot.
The Miraculous Number Three
The lottery bell rings
I've come this far on just that.
Crows suddenly came out of nowhere.
A TOWN IN TERROR
His luck is really something else. He's not especially strong, either. I can't really hit him. What's going on?
B's Testimony
A boy loved by God
TMP
NOW...
...THAT OKEGAWA IS GOING TO GRADUATE...
...WHO'S GOING TO BECOME THE NEXT BANCHO?
Yahoo!
I'm going to overcome this with luck!
NO.3
HAS A RECORD OF TREACHERY
Can you trust me?
NO.2
...
I FEEL SORRY FOR THE GUYS BELOW US.
SNURF
I wouldn't want either of us.
I don't know what's going to happen at all. I'm worried.
But for now, I need to do my best to send Okegawa on his way.
WHISPER
...
WHISPER
...
WHISPER
...
HUH?

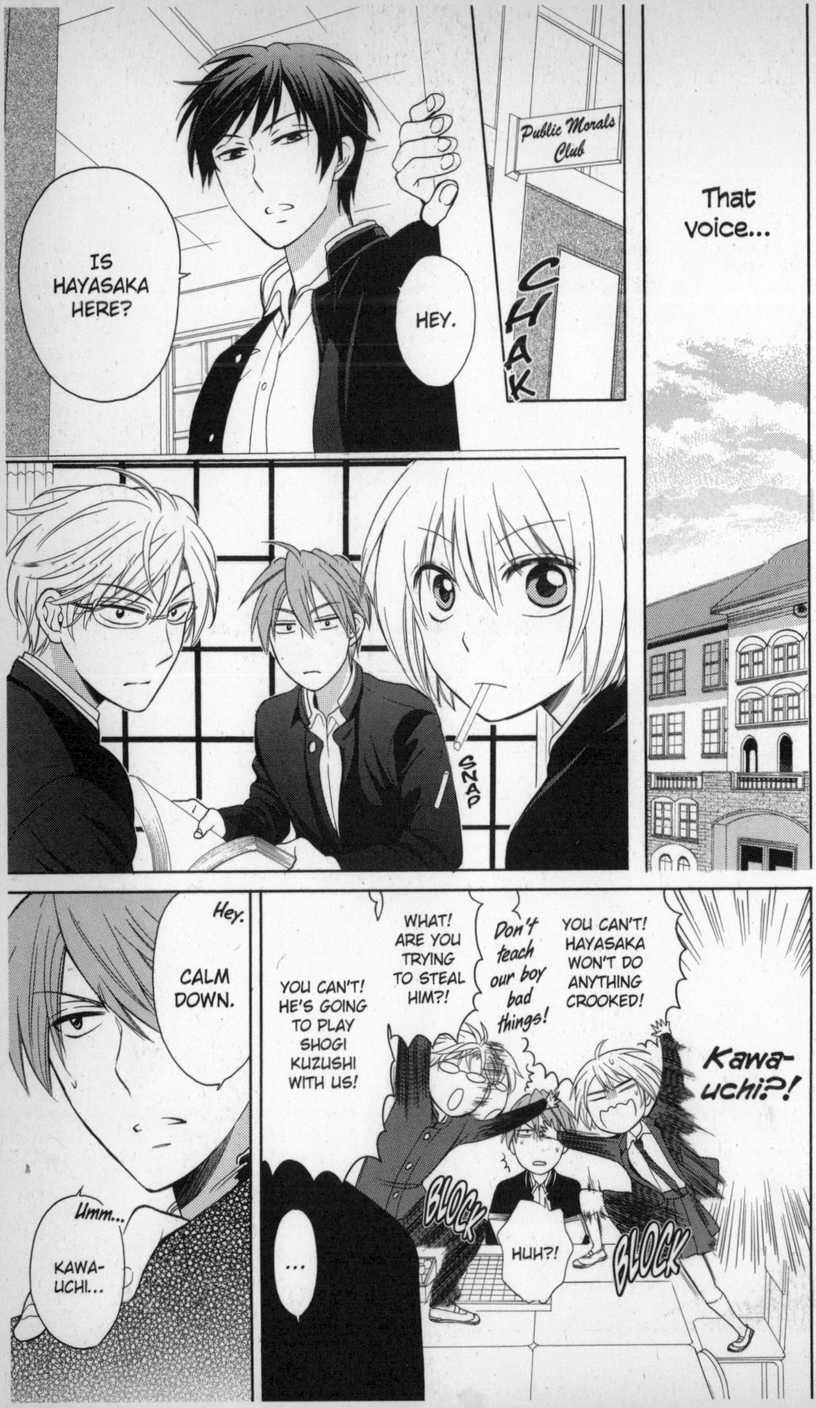
That voice...
Public Morals Club
CHAK
HEY.
IS HAYASAKA HERE?
SNAP
Kawa-uchi?!
YOU CAN'T! HAYASAKA WON'T DO ANYTHING CROOKED!
Don't teach our boy bad things!
WHAT! ARE YOU TRYING TO STEAL HIM?!
YOU CAN'T! HE'S GOING TO PLAY SHOGI KUZUSHI WITH US!
BLOCK
BLOCK
HUH?!
...
Hey. CALM DOWN.
Umm... KAWA-UCHI...

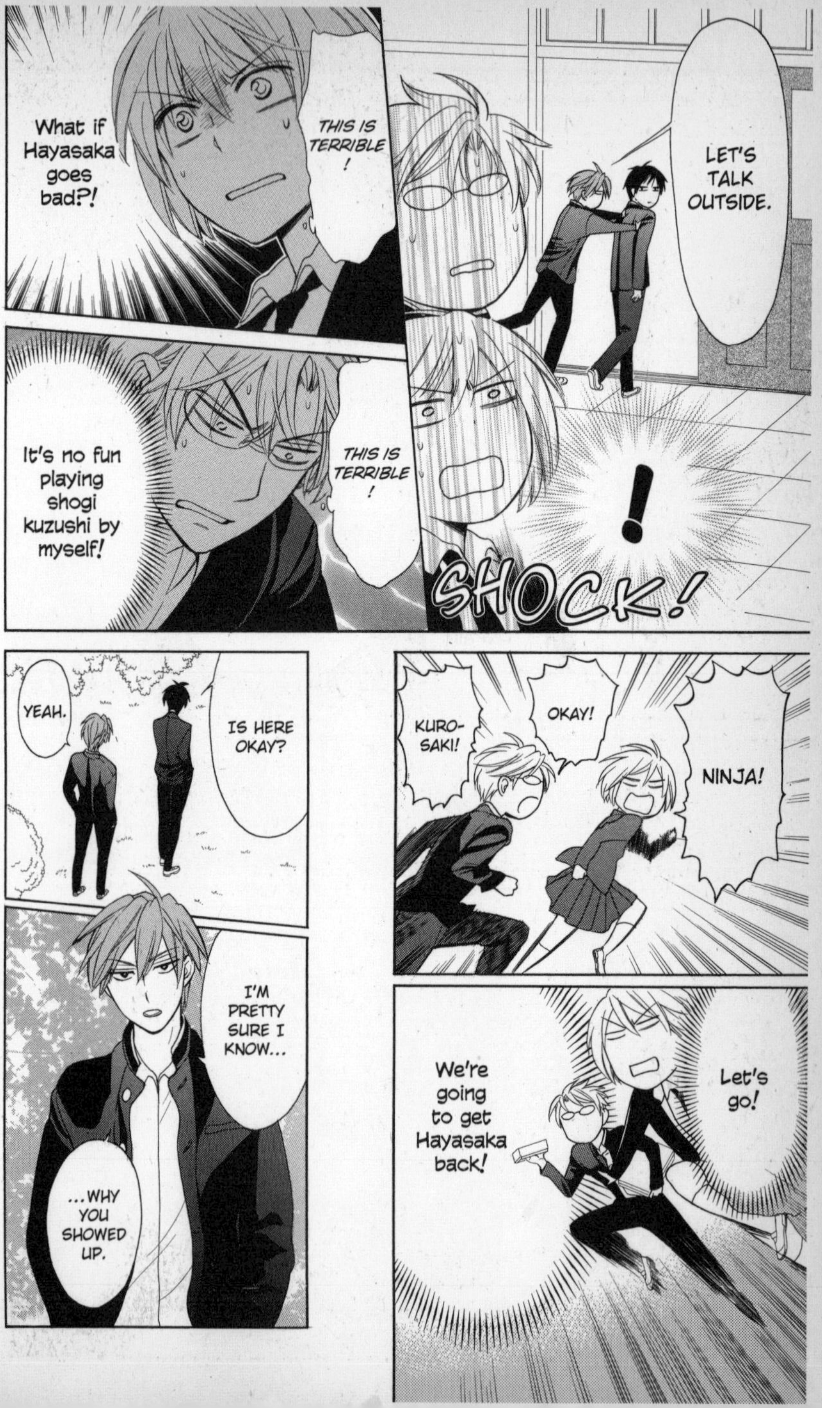
LET'S TALK OUTSIDE.
!
SHOCK!
THIS IS TERRIBLE!
What if Hayasaka goes bad?!
THIS IS TERRIBLE!
It's no fun playing shogi kuzushi by myself!
NINJA!
OKAY!
KURO-SAKI!
Let's go!
We're going to get Hayasaka back!
IS HERE OKAY?
YEAH.
I'M PRETTY SURE I KNOW...
...WHY YOU SHOWED UP.

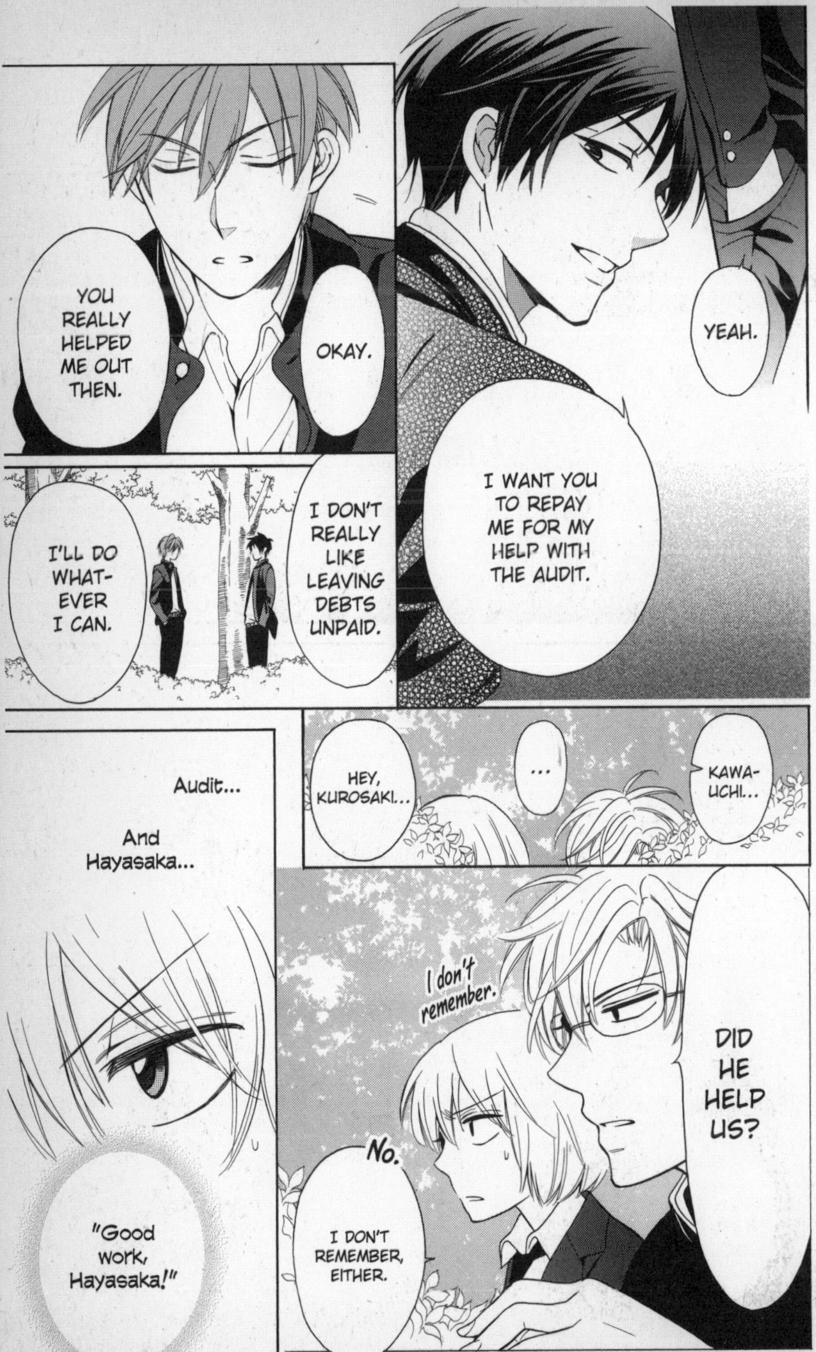
YEAH.
I WANT YOU TO REPAY ME FOR MY HELP WITH THE AUDIT.
OKAY.
YOU REALLY HELPED ME OUT THEN.
I DON'T REALLY LIKE LEAVING DEBTS UNPAID.
I'LL DO WHAT-EVER I CAN.
KAWA-UCHI...
...
HEY, KUROSAKI...
DID HE HELP US?
I don't remember.
No.
I DON'T REMEMBER, EITHER.
Audit...
And Hayasaka...
"Good work, Hayasaka!"

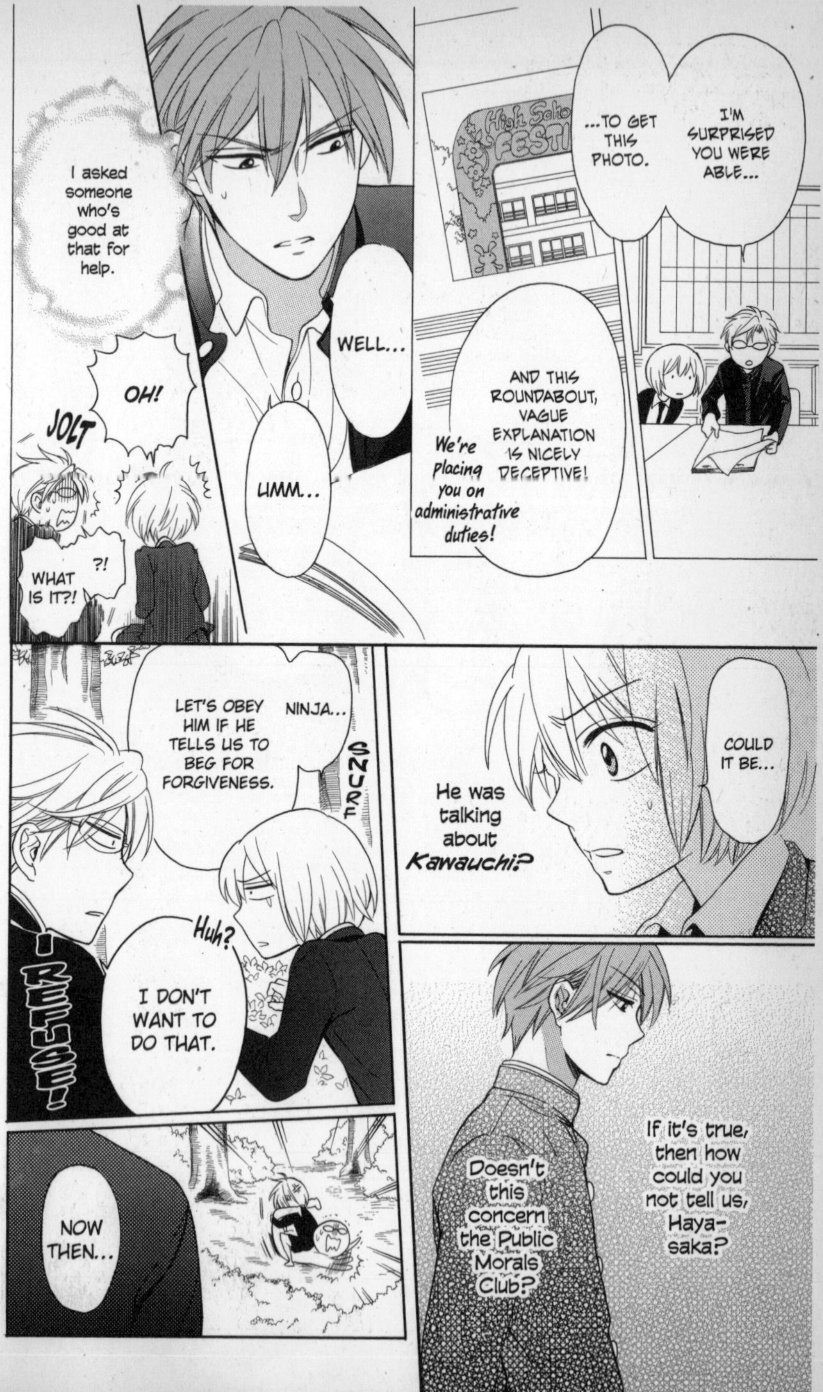
I'M SURPRISED YOU WERE ABLE...
...TO GET THIS PHOTO.
AND THIS ROUNDABOUT, VAGUE EXPLANATION IS NICELY DECEPTIVE!
We're placing you on administrative duties!
WELL...
UMM...
I asked someone who's good at that for help.
OH!
JOLT
?!
WHAT IS IT?!
COULD IT BE...
He was talking about Kawauchi?
If it's true, then how could you not tell us, Haya-saka?
Doesn't this concern the Public Morals Club?
NINJA...
LET'S OBEY HIM IF HE TELLS US TO BEG FOR FORGIVENESS.
SNURF
Huh?
I DON'T WANT TO DO THAT.
REFUSE!
NOW THEN...

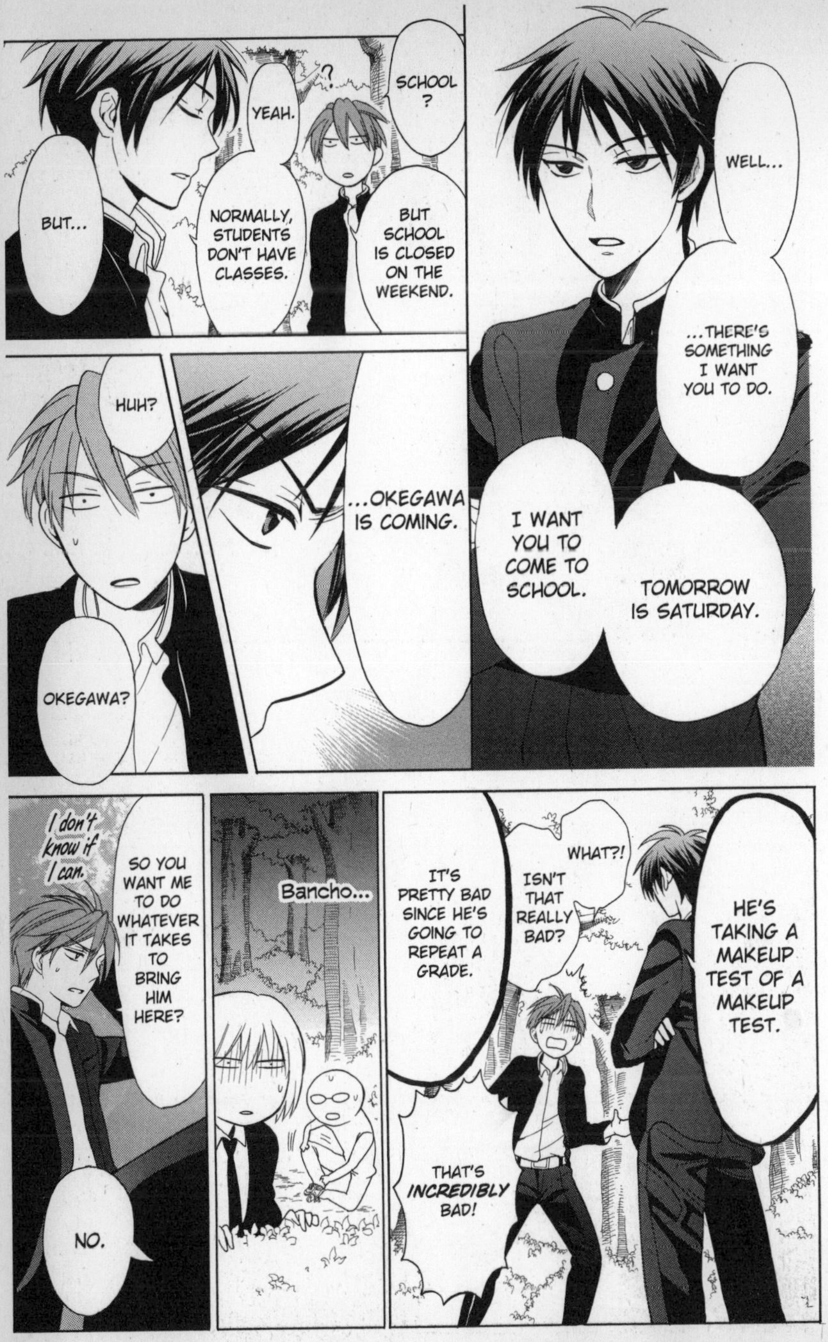
WELL...
...THERE'S SOMETHING I WANT YOU TO DO.
TOMORROW IS SATURDAY.
I WANT YOU TO COME TO SCHOOL.
SCHOOL?
BUT SCHOOL IS CLOSED ON THE WEEKEND.
YEAH.
NORMALLY, STUDENTS DON'T HAVE CLASSES.
BUT...
...OKEGAWA IS COMING.
HUH?
OKEGAWA?
HE'S TAKING A MAKEUP TEST OF A MAKEUP TEST.
WHAT?! ISN'T THAT REALLY BAD?
IT'S PRETTY BAD SINCE HE'S GOING TO REPEAT A GRADE.
THAT'S *INCREDIBLY* BAD!
Bancho...
SO YOU WANT ME TO DO WHATEVER IT TAKES TO BRING HIM HERE?
I don't know if I can.
NO.

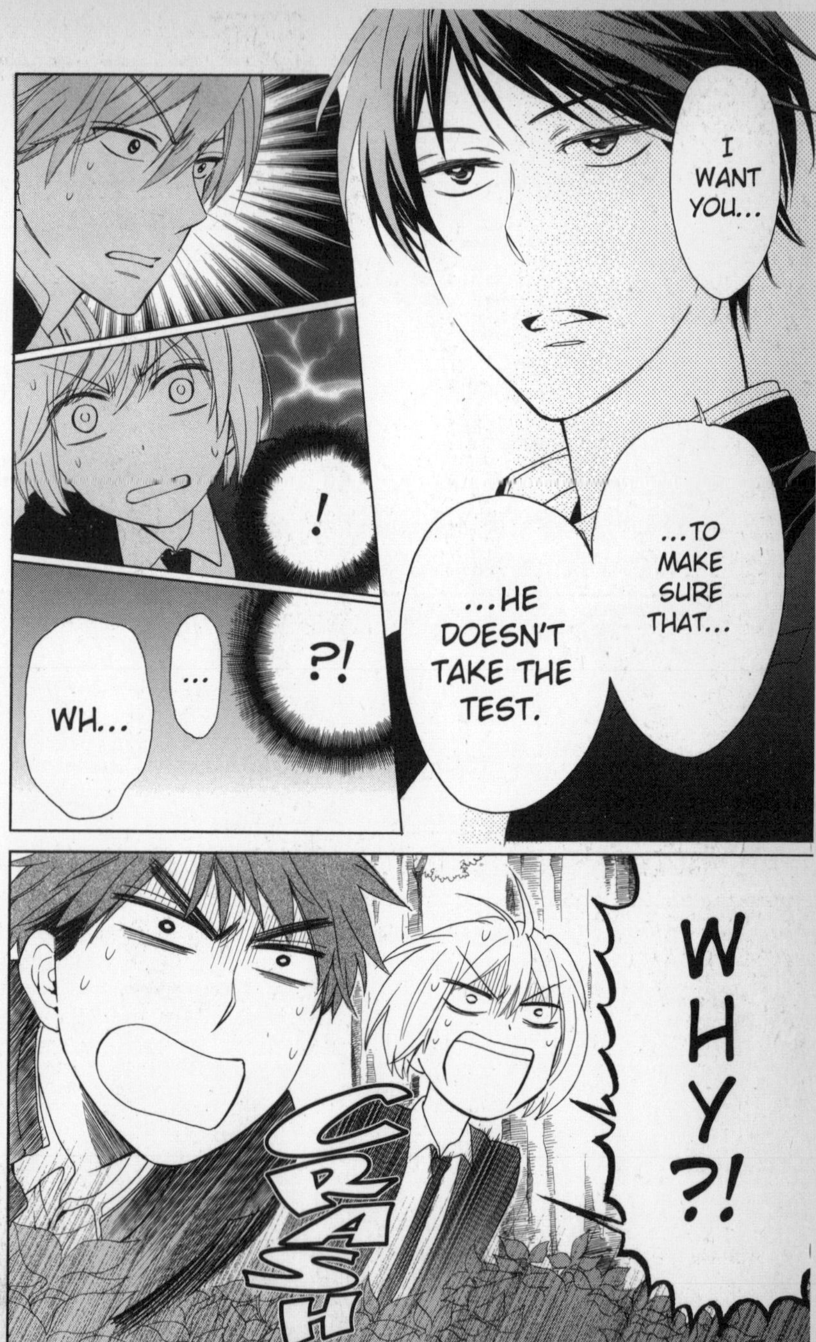
I WANT YOU...
...TO MAKE SURE THAT...
...HE DOESN'T TAKE THE TEST.
!
?!
...
WH...
WHY?!
CRASH

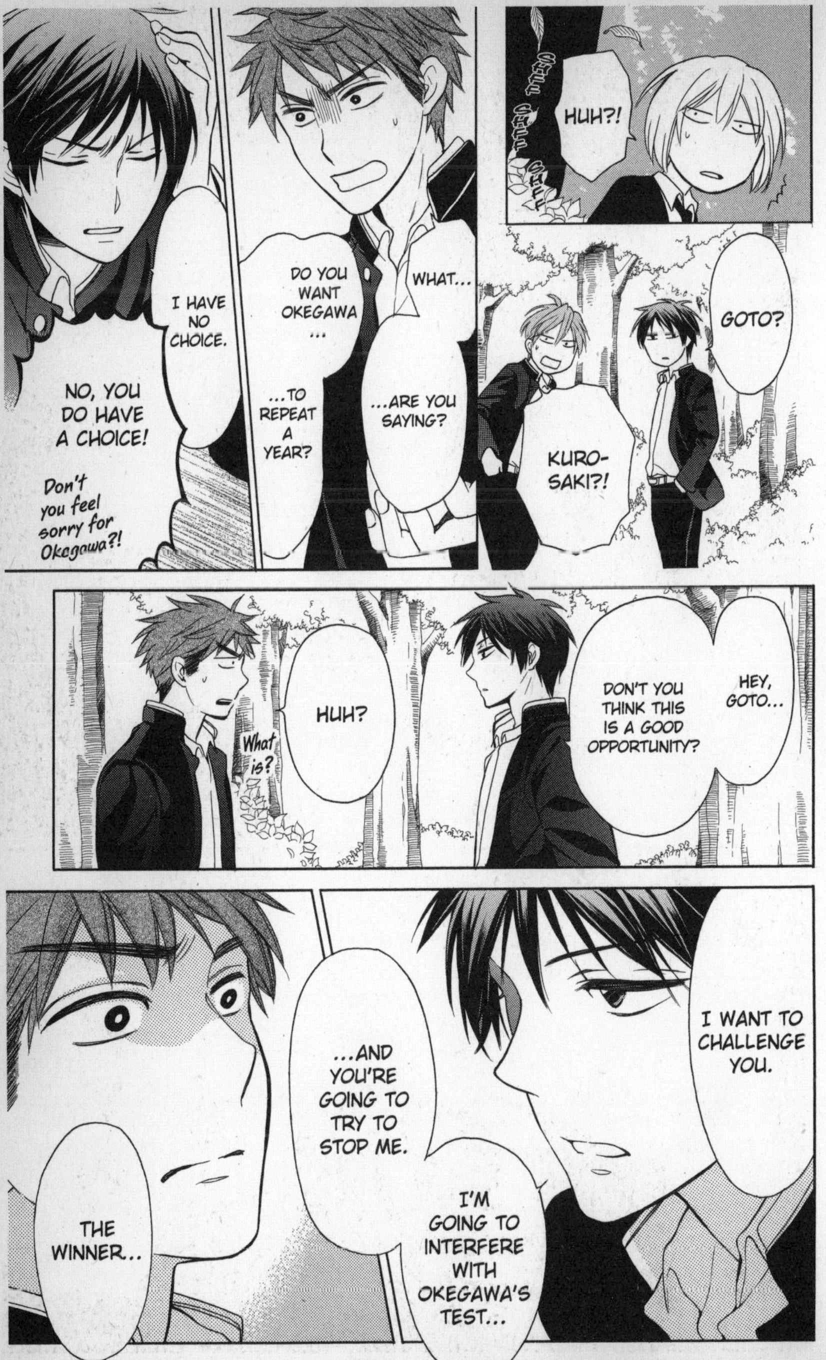
SHFF SHFF SHFF
HUH?!
GOTO?
KURO-SAKI?!
WHAT...
DO YOU WANT OKEGAWA ...
...ARE YOU SAYING?
...TO REPEAT A YEAR?
I HAVE NO CHOICE.
NO, YOU DO HAVE A CHOICE!
Don't you feel sorry for Okegawa?!
HEY, GOTO...
DON'T YOU THINK THIS IS A GOOD OPPORTUNITY?
HUH?
What is?
I WANT TO CHALLENGE YOU.
I'M GOING TO INTERFERE WITH OKEGAWA'S TEST...
...AND YOU'RE GOING TO TRY TO STOP ME.
THE WINNER...

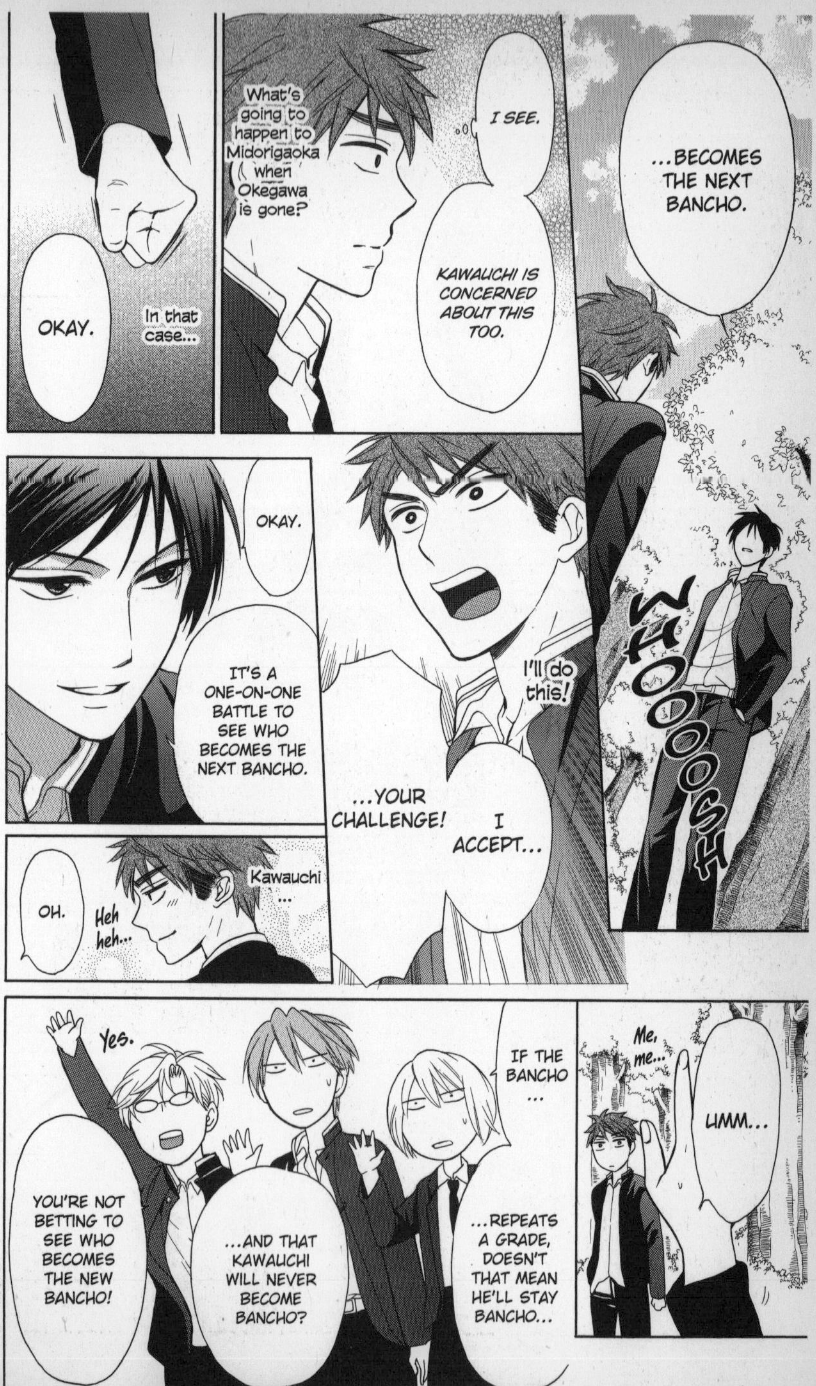
...BECOMES THE NEXT BANCHO.
WHOOOOOSH
I SEE.
KAWAUCHI IS CONCERNED ABOUT THIS TOO.
What's going to happen to Midorigaoka when Okegawa is gone?
In that case...
OKAY.
I'll do this!
I ACCEPT...
...YOUR CHALLENGE!
OKAY.
IT'S A ONE-ON-ONE BATTLE TO SEE WHO BECOMES THE NEXT BANCHO.
Kawauchi...
Heh heh...
OH.
Me, me...
UMM...
IF THE BANCHO...
...REPEATS A GRADE, DOESN'T THAT MEAN HE'LL STAY BANCHO...
Yes.
...AND THAT KAWAUCHI WILL NEVER BECOME BANCHO?
YOU'RE NOT BETTING TO SEE WHO BECOMES THE NEW BANCHO!

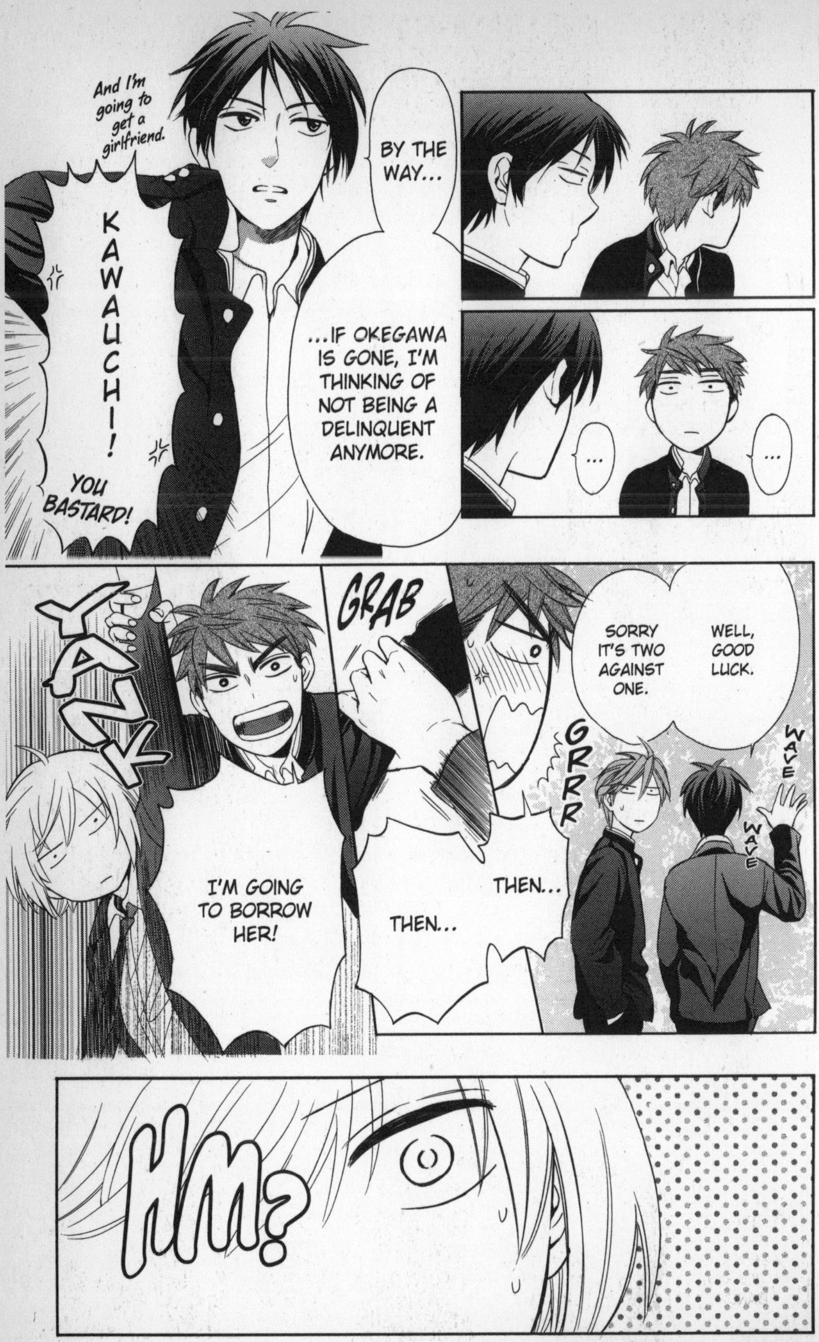
...
...
BY THE WAY...
...IF OKEGAWA IS GONE, I'M THINKING OF NOT BEING A DELINQUENT ANYMORE.
And I'm going to get a girlfriend.
KAWAUCHI!
YOU BASTARD!
WELL, GOOD LUCK.
SORRY IT'S TWO AGAINST ONE.
WAVE
WAVE
GRRR
THEN...
THEN...
GRAB
YANK
I'M GOING TO BORROW HER!
HM?

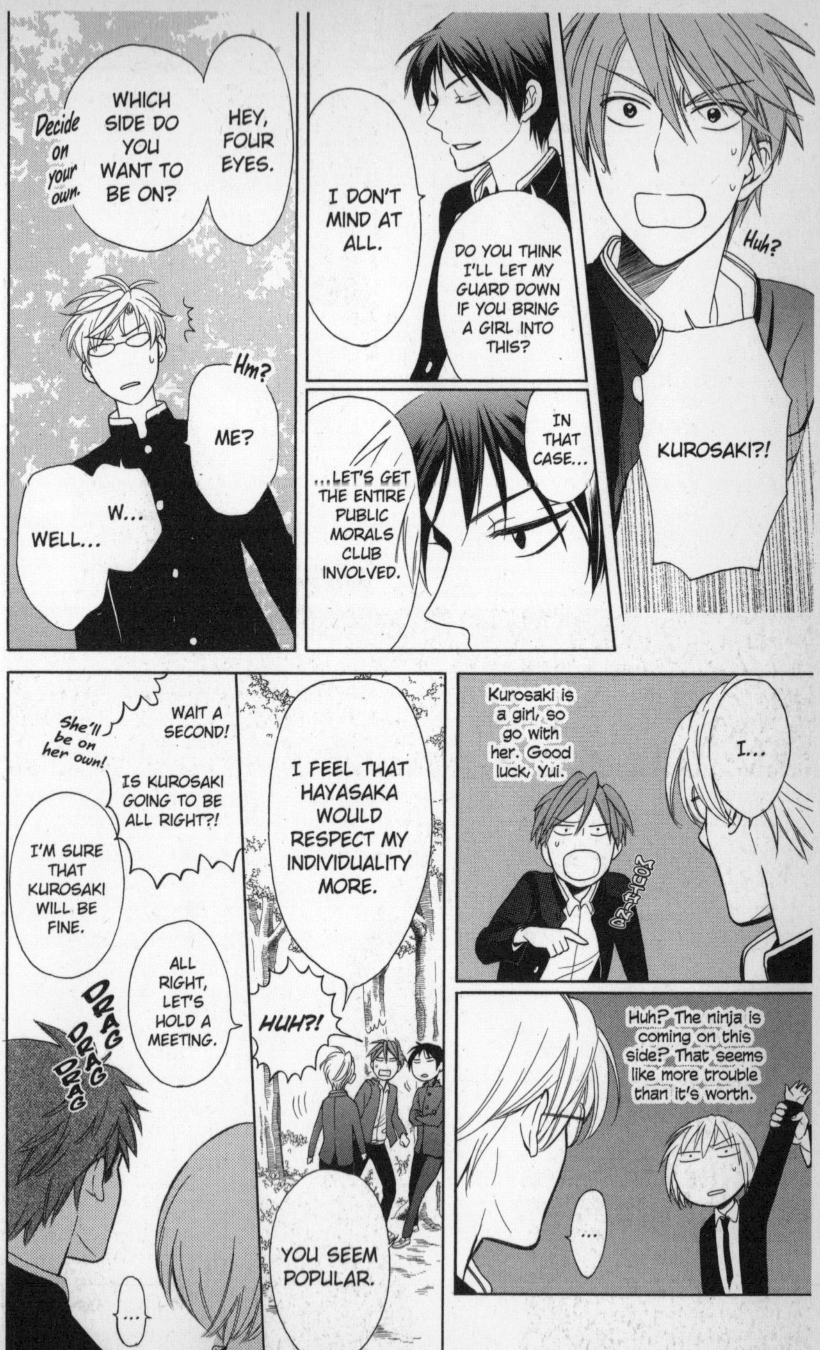
Huh?
KUROSAKI?!
DO YOU THINK I'LL LET MY GUARD DOWN IF YOU BRING A GIRL INTO THIS?
I DON'T MIND AT ALL.
IN THAT CASE...
...LET'S GET THE ENTIRE PUBLIC MORALS CLUB INVOLVED.
HEY, FOUR EYES.
WHICH SIDE DO YOU WANT TO BE ON?
Decide on your own.
Hm?
ME?
W...
WELL...
I...
Kurosaki is a girl, so go with her. Good luck, Yui.
Huh? The ninja is coming on this side? That seems like more trouble than it's worth.
...
I FEEL THAT HAYASAKA WOULD RESPECT MY INDIVIDUALITY MORE.
HUH?!
YOU SEEM POPULAR.
WAIT A SECOND!
She'll be on her own!
IS KUROSAKI GOING TO BE ALL RIGHT?!
I'M SURE THAT KUROSAKI WILL BE FINE.
ALL RIGHT, LET'S HOLD A MEETING.
DRAG DRAG DRAG
...

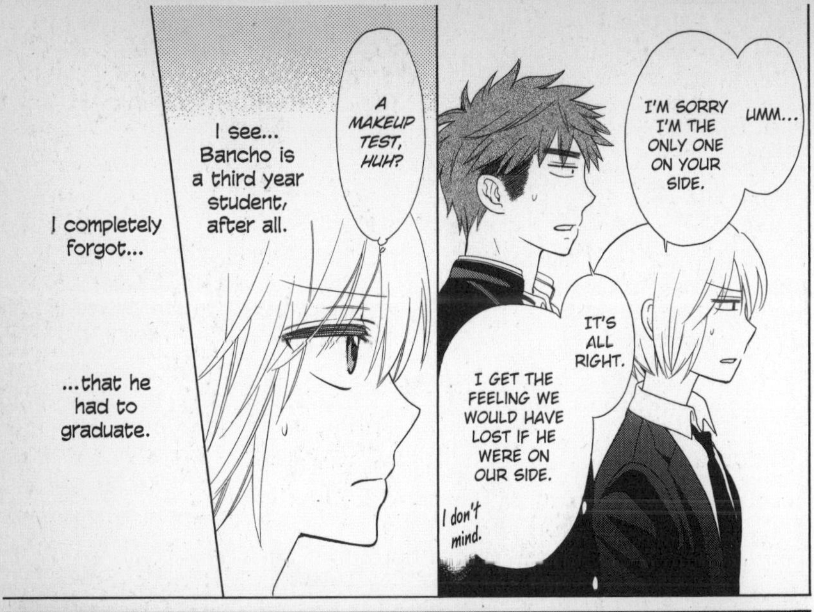
UMM...
I'M SORRY I'M THE ONLY ONE ON YOUR SIDE.
IT'S ALL RIGHT.
I GET THE FEELING WE WOULD HAVE LOST IF HE WERE ON OUR SIDE.
I don't mind.
A MAKEUP TEST, HUH?
I see... Bancho is a third year student, after all.
I completely forgot...
...that he had to graduate.

THE DAY OF DESTINY

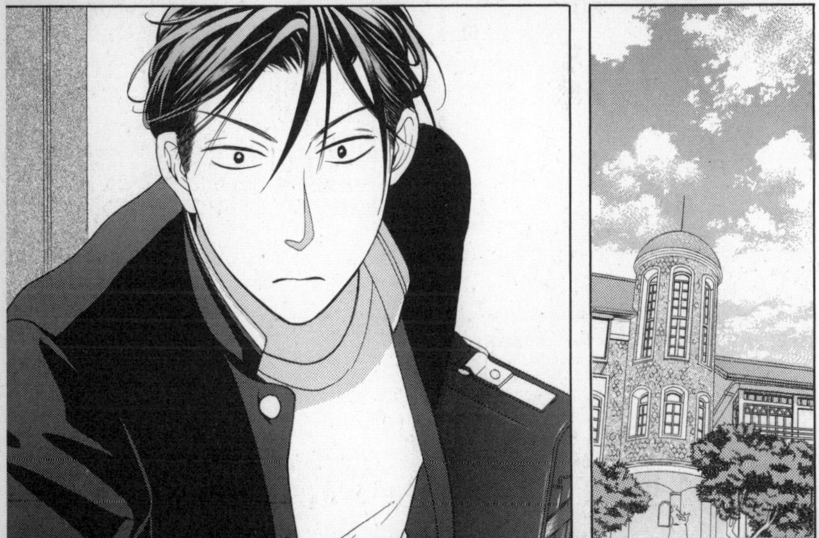

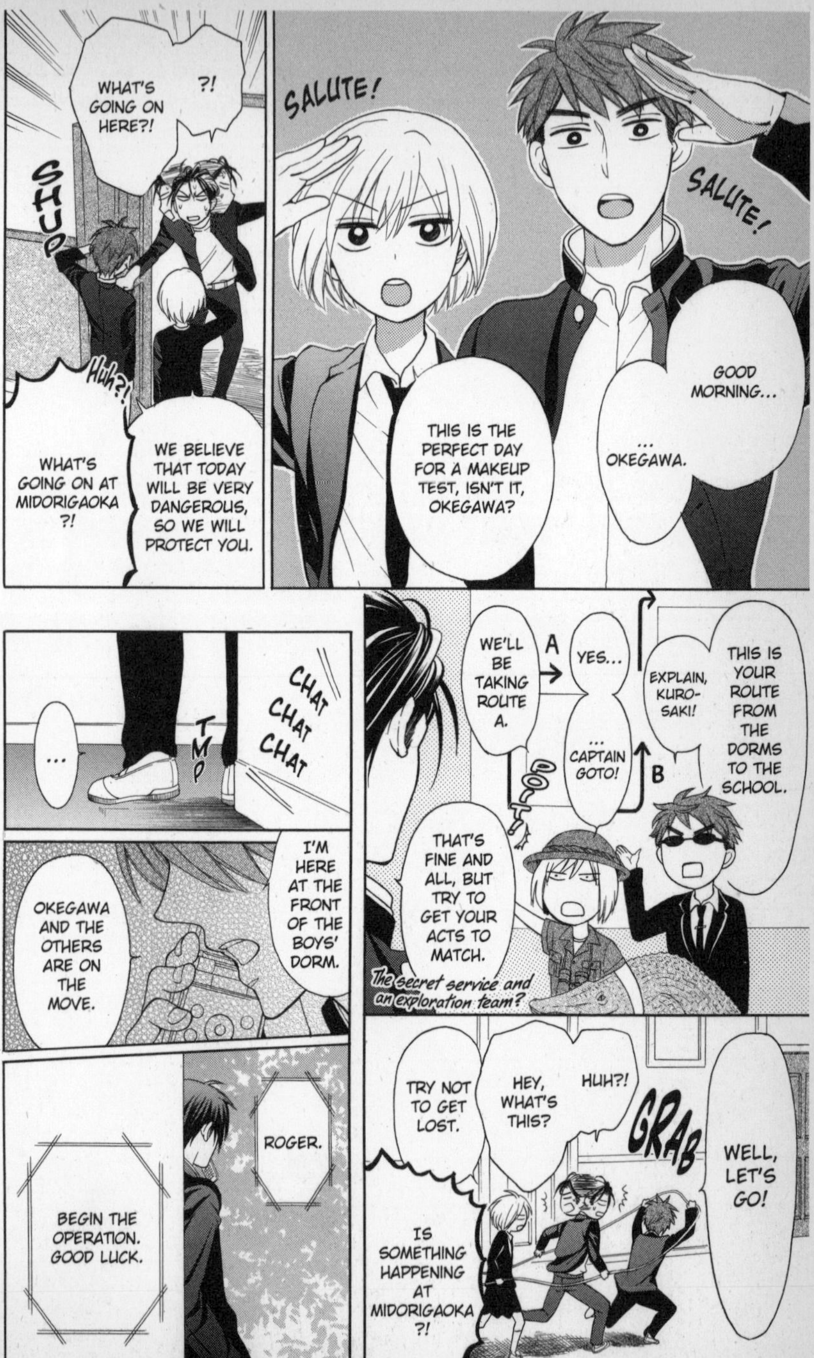
SALUTE!
SALUTE!
GOOD MORNING...
...OKEGAWA.
THIS IS THE PERFECT DAY FOR A MAKEUP TEST, ISN'T IT, OKEGAWA?
?!
WHAT'S GOING ON HERE?!
SHUP
Huh?!
WE BELIEVE THAT TODAY WILL BE VERY DANGEROUS, SO WE WILL PROTECT YOU.
WHAT'S GOING ON AT MIDORIGAOKA?!
THIS IS YOUR ROUTE FROM THE DORMS TO THE SCHOOL.
EXPLAIN, KURO-SAKI!
YES...
...CAPTAIN GOTO!
WE'LL BE TAKING ROUTE A.
A
B
POIT
THAT'S FINE AND ALL, BUT TRY TO GET YOUR ACTS TO MATCH.
The secret service and an exploration team?
CHAT CHAT CHAT
TMP
...
I'M HERE AT THE FRONT OF THE BOYS' DORM.
OKEGAWA AND THE OTHERS ARE ON THE MOVE.
WELL, LET'S GO!
GRAB
HUH?!
HEY, WHAT'S THIS?
TRY NOT TO GET LOST.
IS SOMETHING HAPPENING AT MIDORIGAOKA?!
ROGER.
BEGIN THE OPERATION. GOOD LUCK.

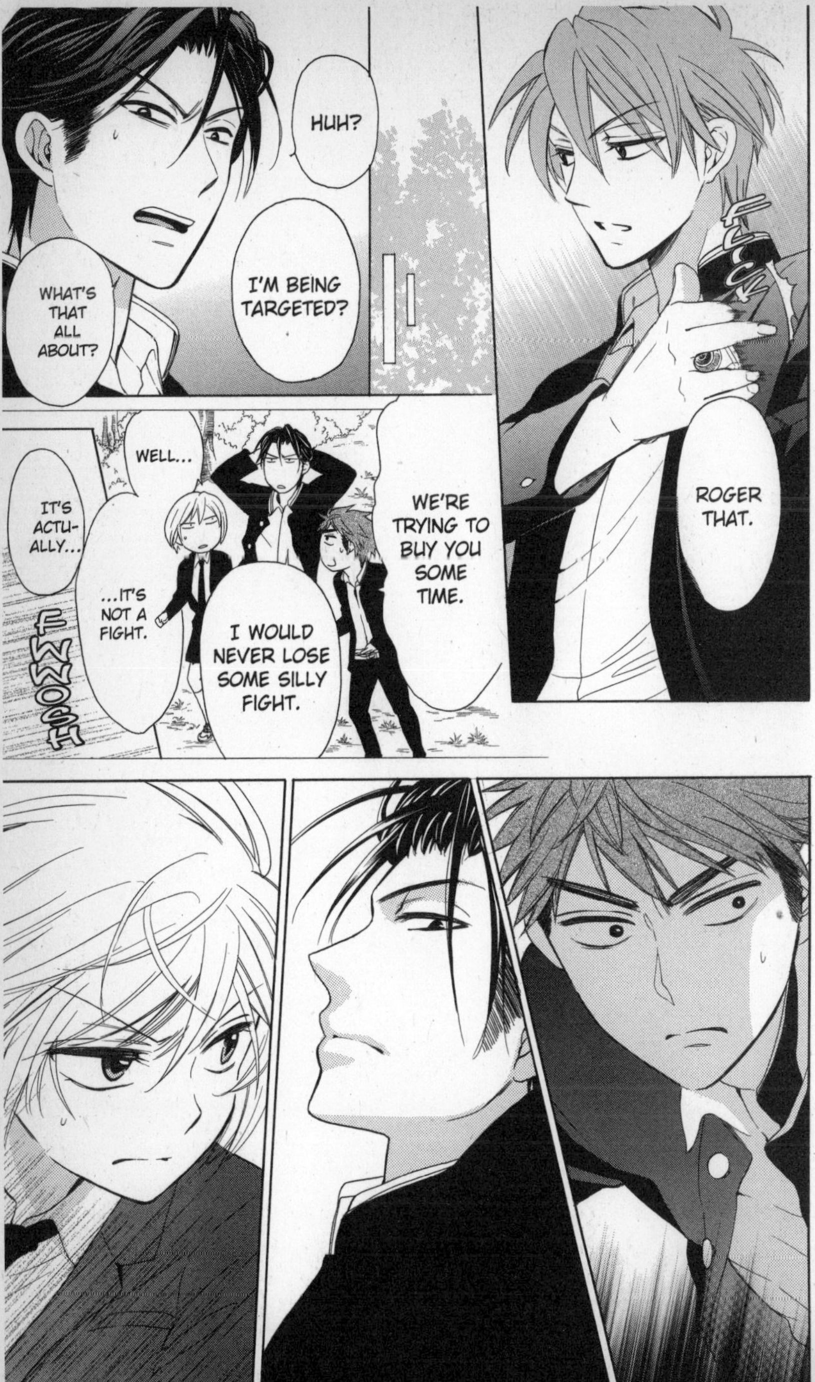
FLICK
ROGER THAT.
HUH?
I'M BEING TARGETED?
WHAT'S THAT ALL ABOUT?
WE'RE TRYING TO BUY YOU SOME TIME.
I WOULD NEVER LOSE SOME SILLY FIGHT.
WELL...
IT'S ACTU-ALLY...
...IT'S NOT A FIGHT.
FWWOSH

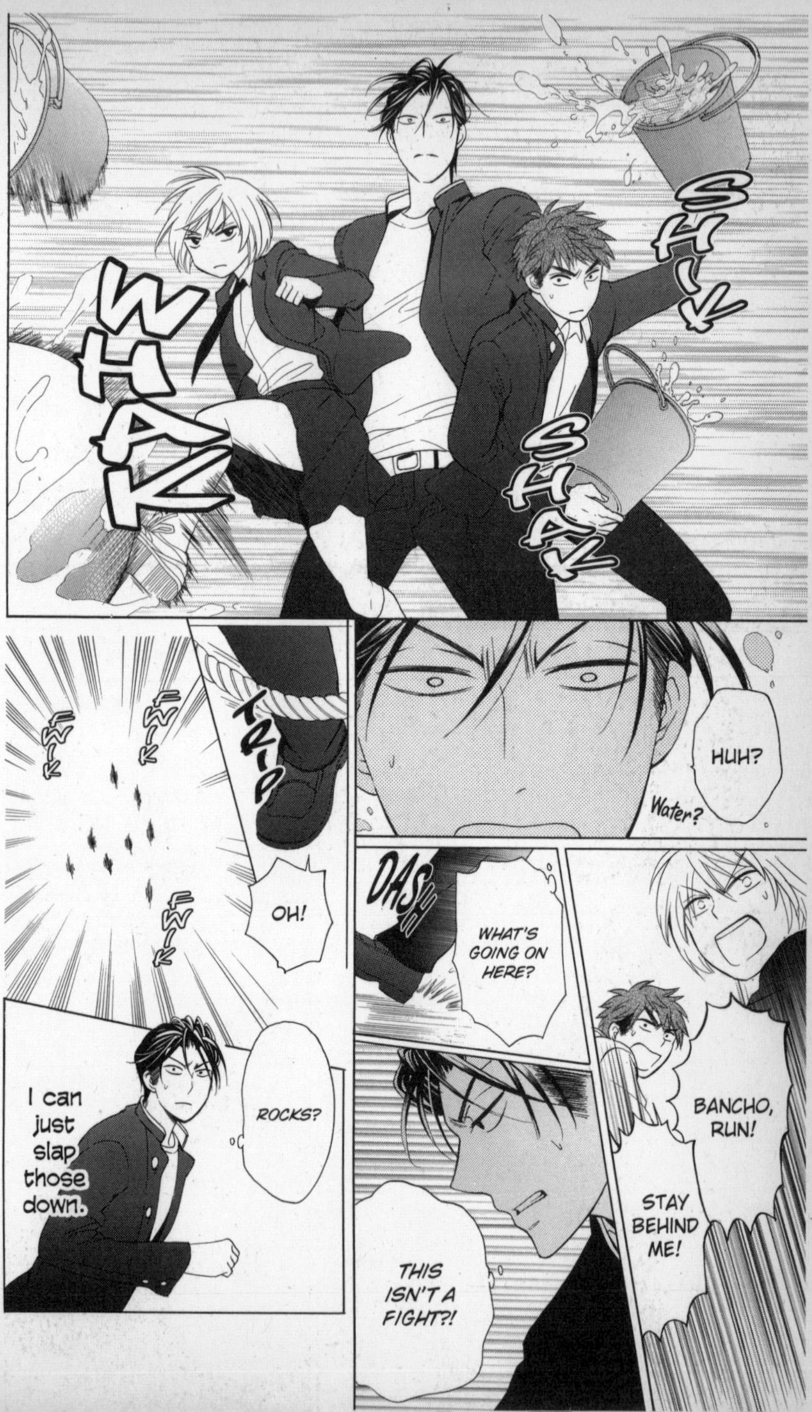
SHIK
SHAK
WHAK
HUH?
Water?
TRIP
OH!
FWIK
FWIK
FWIK
BANCHO, RUN!
STAY BEHIND ME!
DASH
WHAT'S GOING ON HERE?
THIS ISN'T A FIGHT?!
ROCKS?
I can just slap those down.

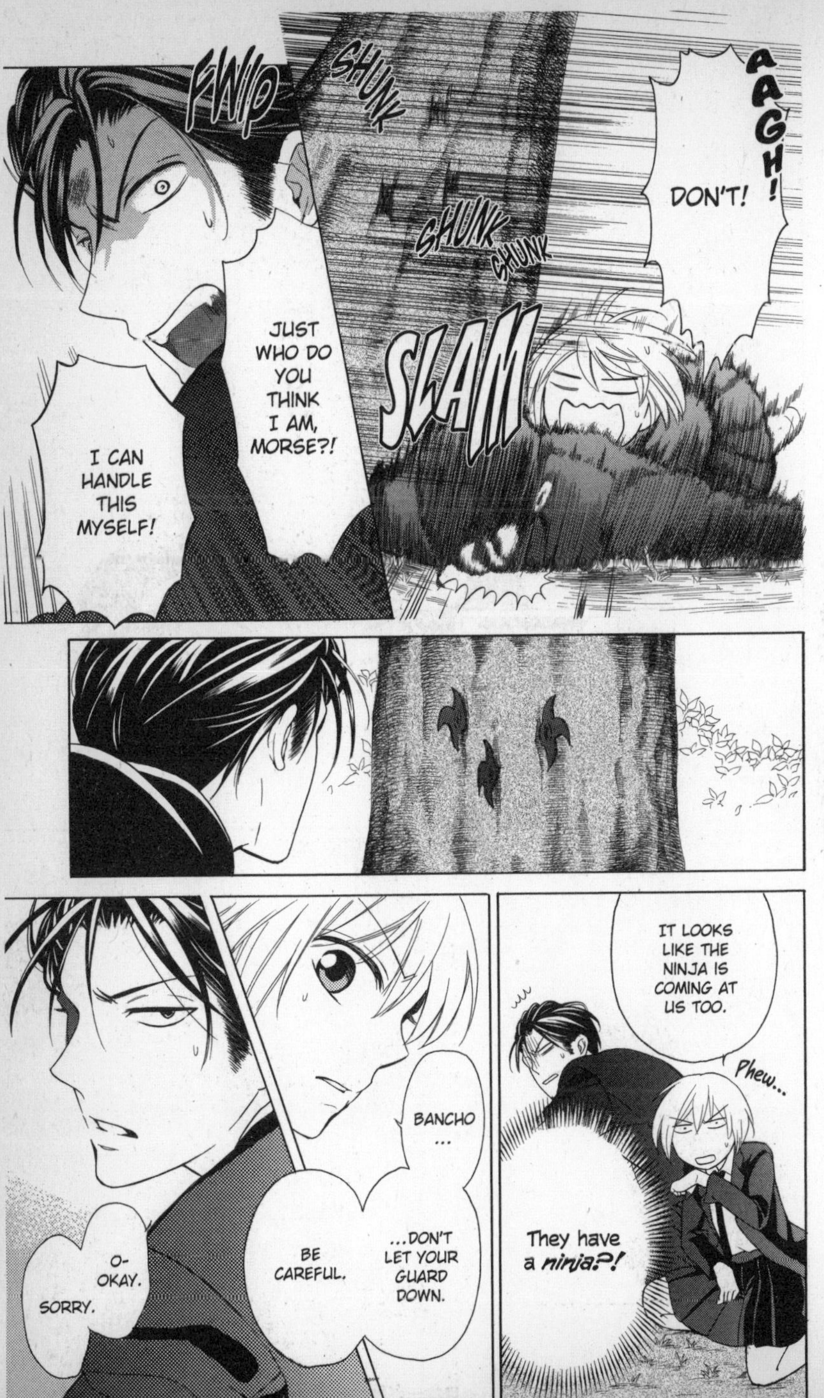
SHUNK
AAGH!
DON'T!
SHUNK
CHUNK
SLAM
FWIP
JUST WHO DO YOU THINK I AM, MORSE?!
I CAN HANDLE THIS MYSELF!
IT LOOKS LIKE THE NINJA IS COMING AT US TOO.
Phew...
They have a *ninja*?!
BANCHO...
...DON'T LET YOUR GUARD DOWN.
BE CAREFUL.
O-OKAY.
SORRY.

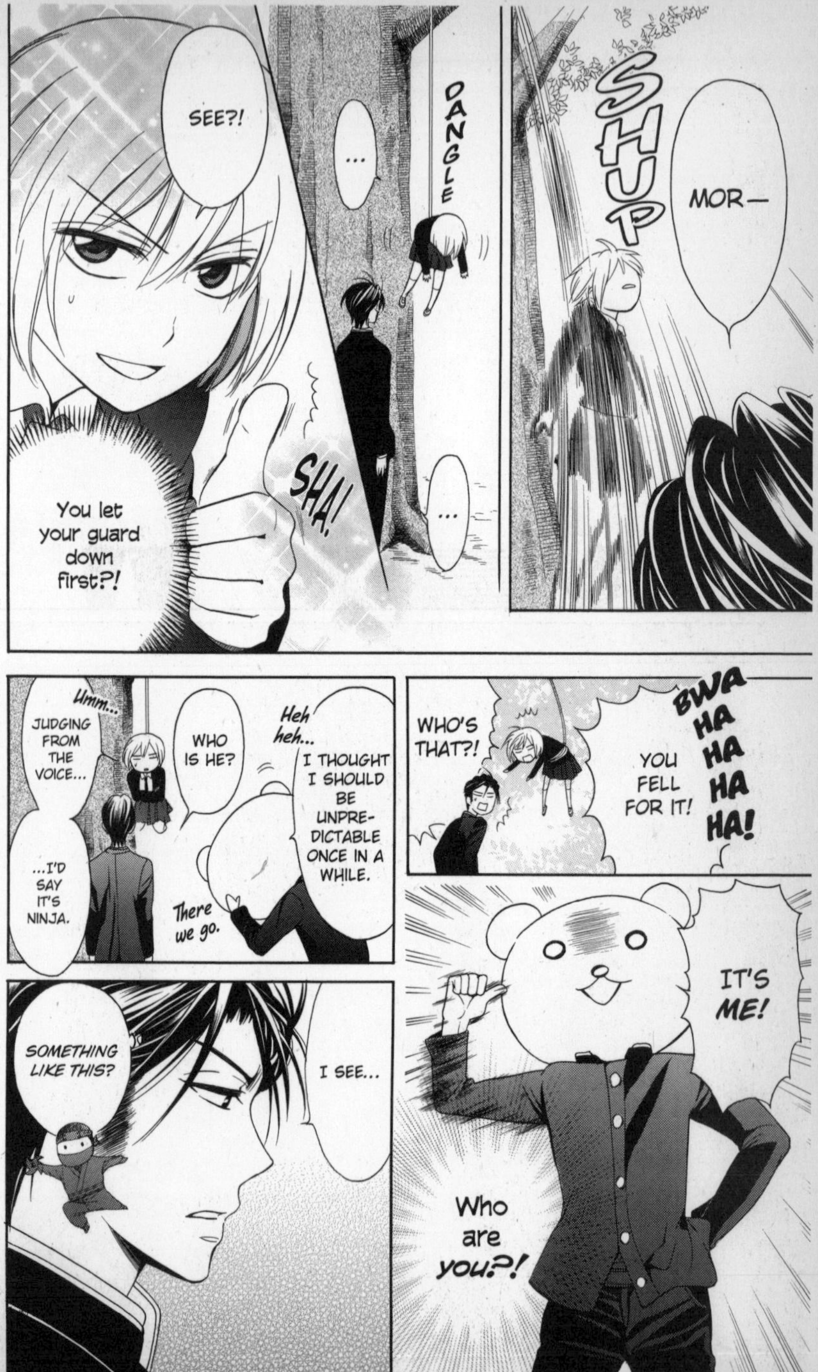
SHUP
MOR—
DANGLE
...
...
SEE?!
SHA!
You let your guard down first?!
WHO'S THAT?!
BWA HA HA HA HA!
YOU FELL FOR IT!
IT'S ME!
Who are you?!
Heh heh... I THOUGHT I SHOULD BE UNPREDICTABLE ONCE IN A WHILE.
WHO IS HE?
Umm... JUDGING FROM THE VOICE...
There we go.
...I'D SAY IT'S NINJA.
I SEE...
SOMETHING LIKE THIS?

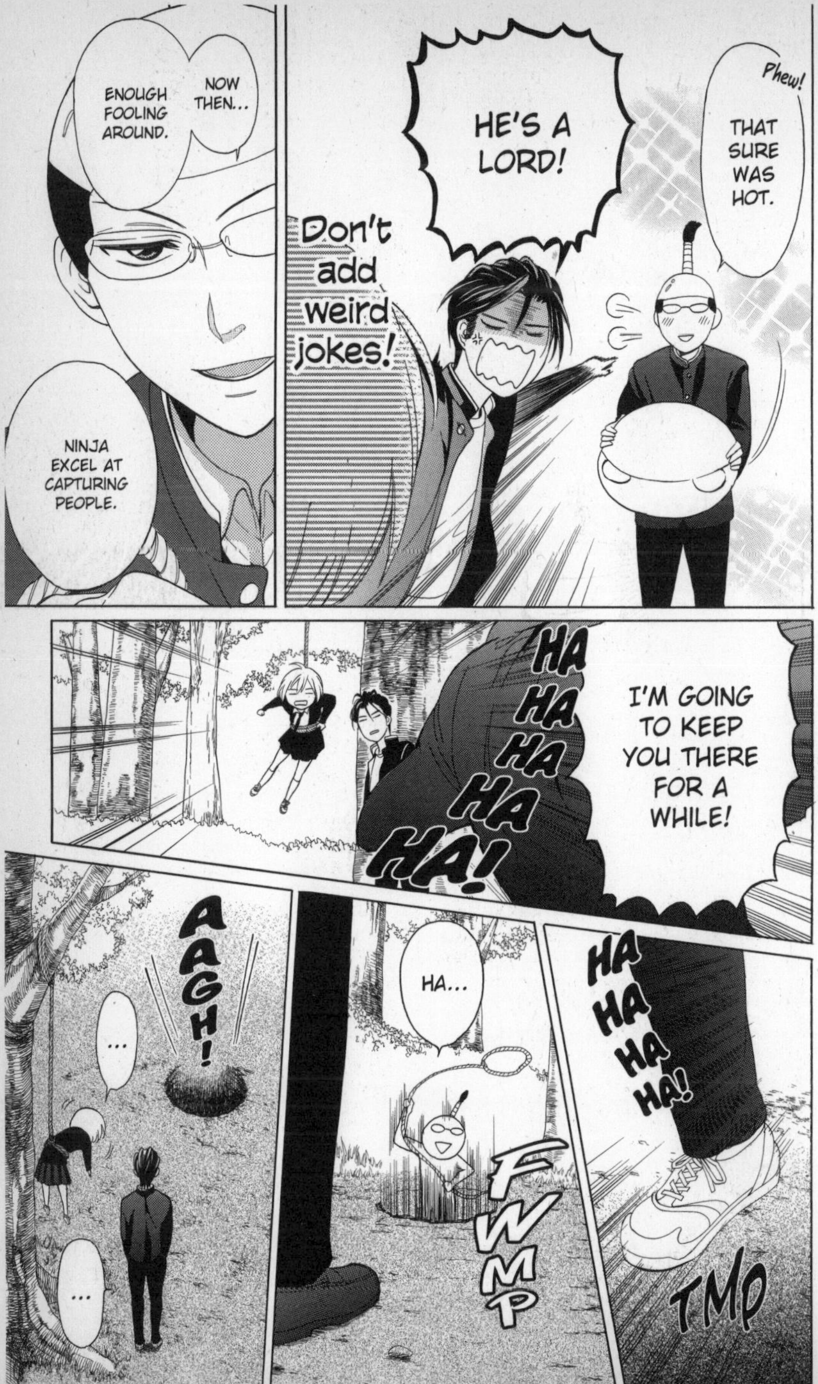
Phew!
THAT SURE WAS HOT.
HE'S A LORD!
Don't add weird jokes!
NOW THEN...
ENOUGH FOOLING AROUND.
NINJA EXCEL AT CAPTURING PEOPLE.
I'M GOING TO KEEP YOU THERE FOR A WHILE!
HA HA HA HA HA!
HA HA HA HA!
TMP
HA...
FWMP
AAGH!
...
...

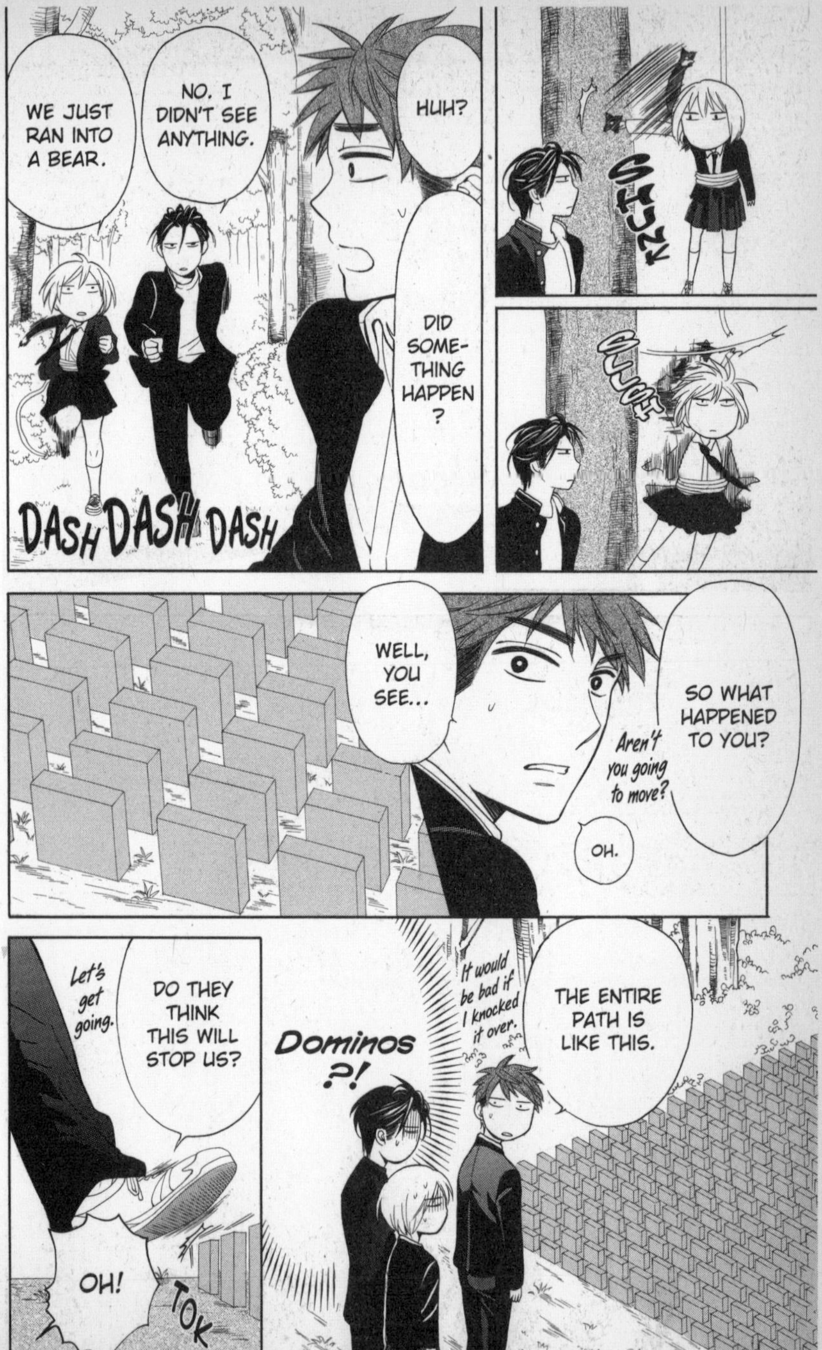
SHUNK
SLUNK
HUH?
DID SOMETHING HAPPEN?
NO. I DIDN'T SEE ANYTHING.
WE JUST RAN INTO A BEAR.
DASH DASH DASH
SO WHAT HAPPENED TO YOU?
Aren't you going to move?
OH.
WELL, YOU SEE...
THE ENTIRE PATH IS LIKE THIS.
It would be bad if I knocked it over.
Dominos ?!
DO THEY THINK THIS WILL STOP US?
Let's get going.
OH!
TOK

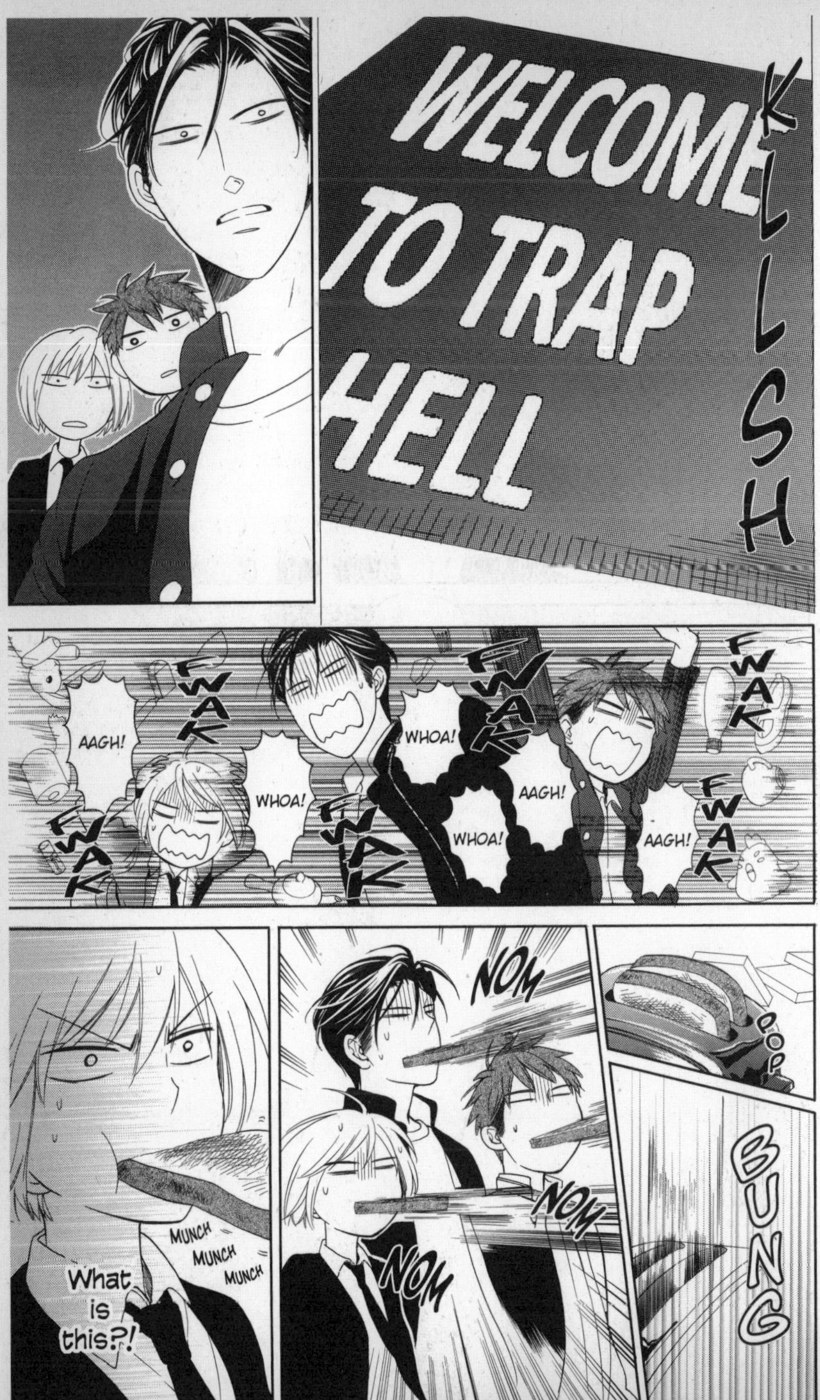
KLLSH
WELCOME TO TRAP HELL
FWAK
FWAK
AAGH!
FWAK
AAGH!
WHOA!
FWAK
WHOA!
WHOA!
FWAK
FWAK
AAGH!
POP
BUNG
NOM
NOM
NOM
MUNCH
MUNCH
MUNCH
What is this?!

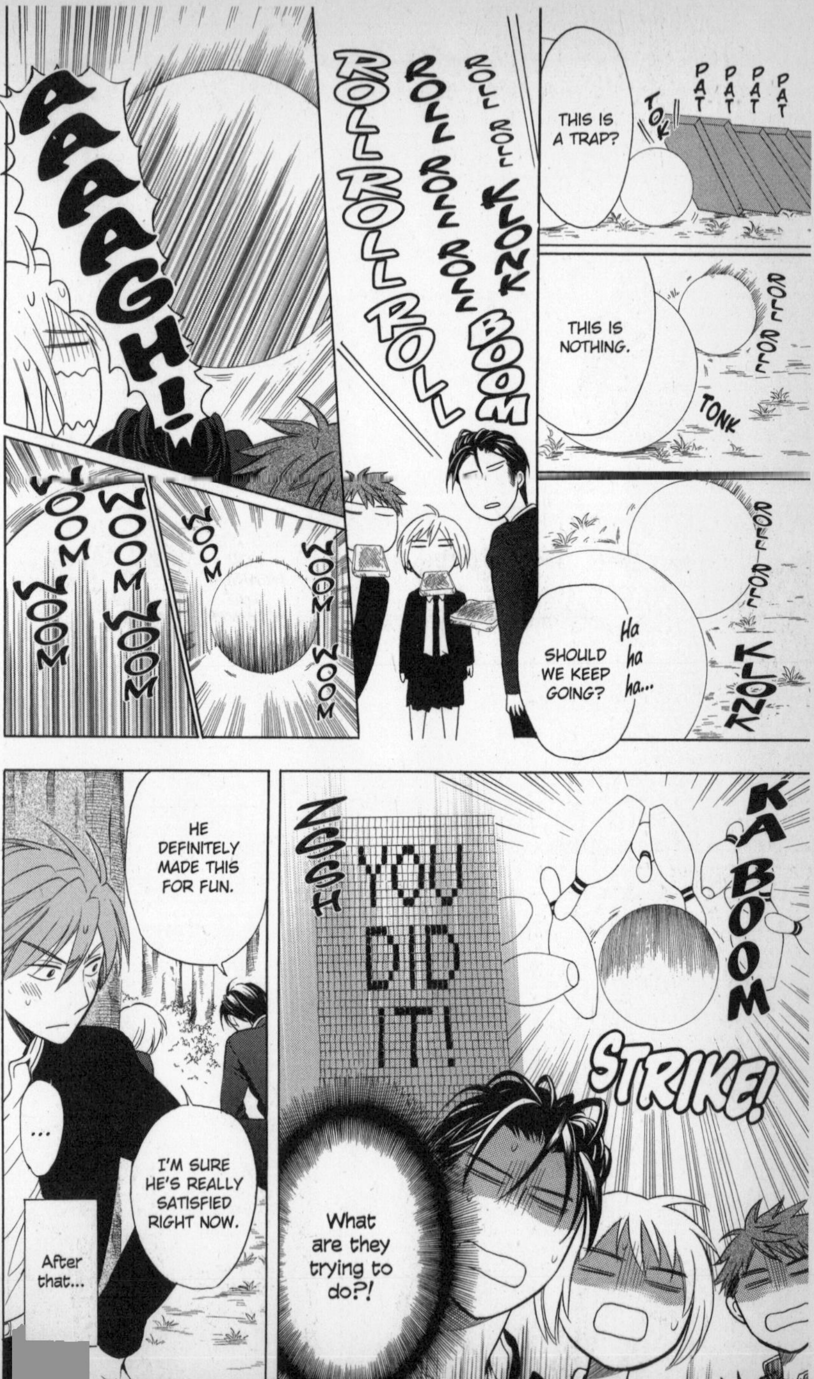
TOK
PAT PAT PAT PAT
THIS IS A TRAP?
ROLL ROLL
TONK
THIS IS NOTHING.
ROLL ROLL
KLONK
SHOULD WE KEEP GOING?
Ha ha ha...
ROLL ROLL KLONK
ROLL ROLL ROLL BOOM
ROLL ROLL ROLL
AAAAGH!
WOOM WOOM
WOOM
WOOM WOOM
WOOM WOOM
KA BOOM
YOU DID IT!
ZSSH
STRIKE!
What are they trying to do?!
HE DEFINITELY MADE THIS FOR FUN.
...
I'M SURE HE'S REALLY SATISFIED RIGHT NOW.
After that...

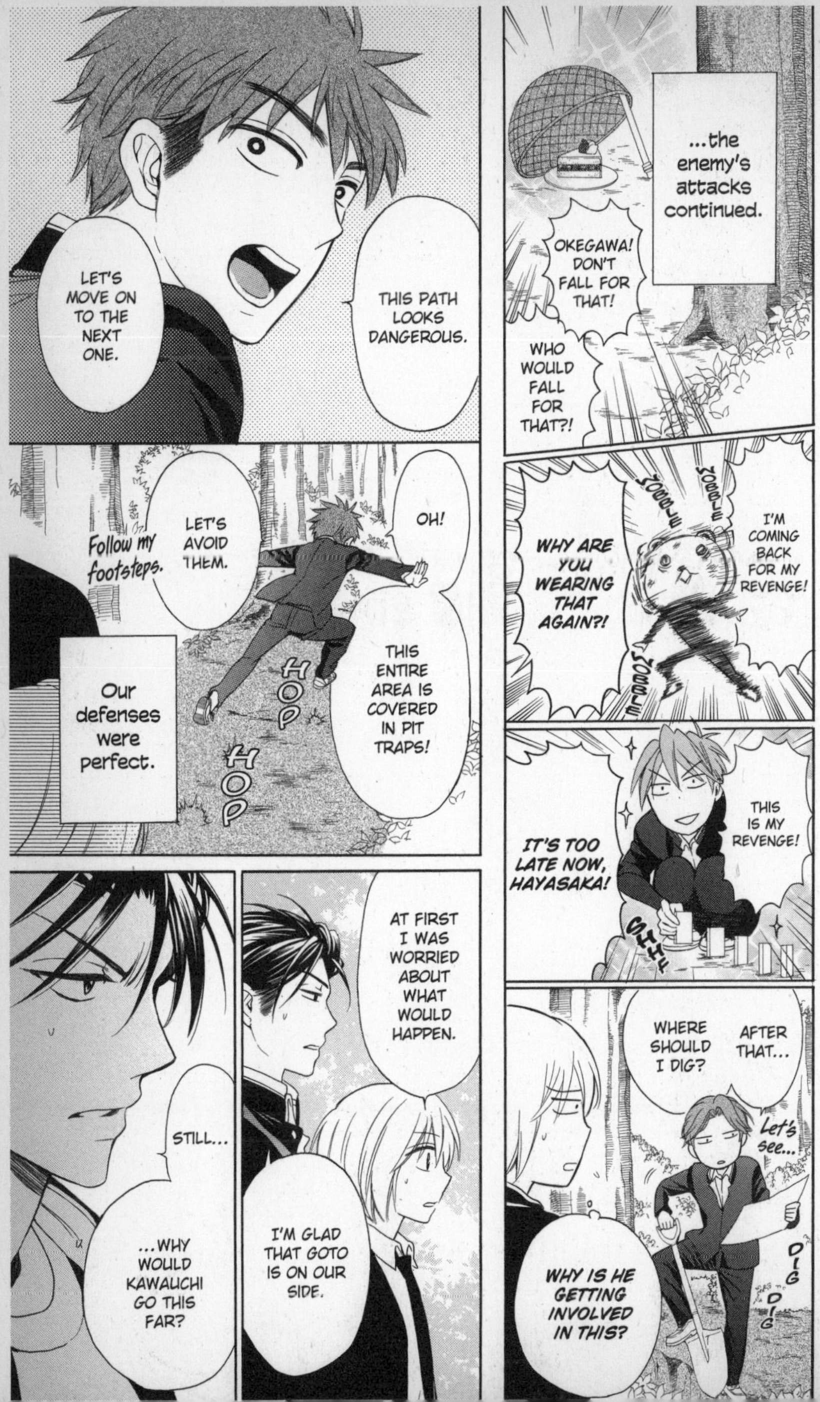
...the enemy's attacks continued.
OKEGAWA! DON'T FALL FOR THAT!
WHO WOULD FALL FOR THAT?!
WOBBLE WOBBLE
I'M COMING BACK FOR MY REVENGE!
WHY ARE YOU WEARING THAT AGAIN?!
WOBBLE
THIS IS MY REVENGE!
IT'S TOO LATE NOW, HAYASAKA!
SHH
AFTER THAT...
WHERE SHOULD I DIG?
Let's see...
DIG DIG
WHY IS HE GETTING INVOLVED IN THIS?
THIS PATH LOOKS DANGEROUS.
LET'S MOVE ON TO THE NEXT ONE.
OH!
LET'S AVOID THEM.
Follow my footsteps.
THIS ENTIRE AREA IS COVERED IN PIT TRAPS!
HOP HOP
Our defenses were perfect.
AT FIRST I WAS WORRIED ABOUT WHAT WOULD HAPPEN.
I'M GLAD THAT GOTO IS ON OUR SIDE.
STILL...
...WHY WOULD KAWAUCHI GO THIS FAR?

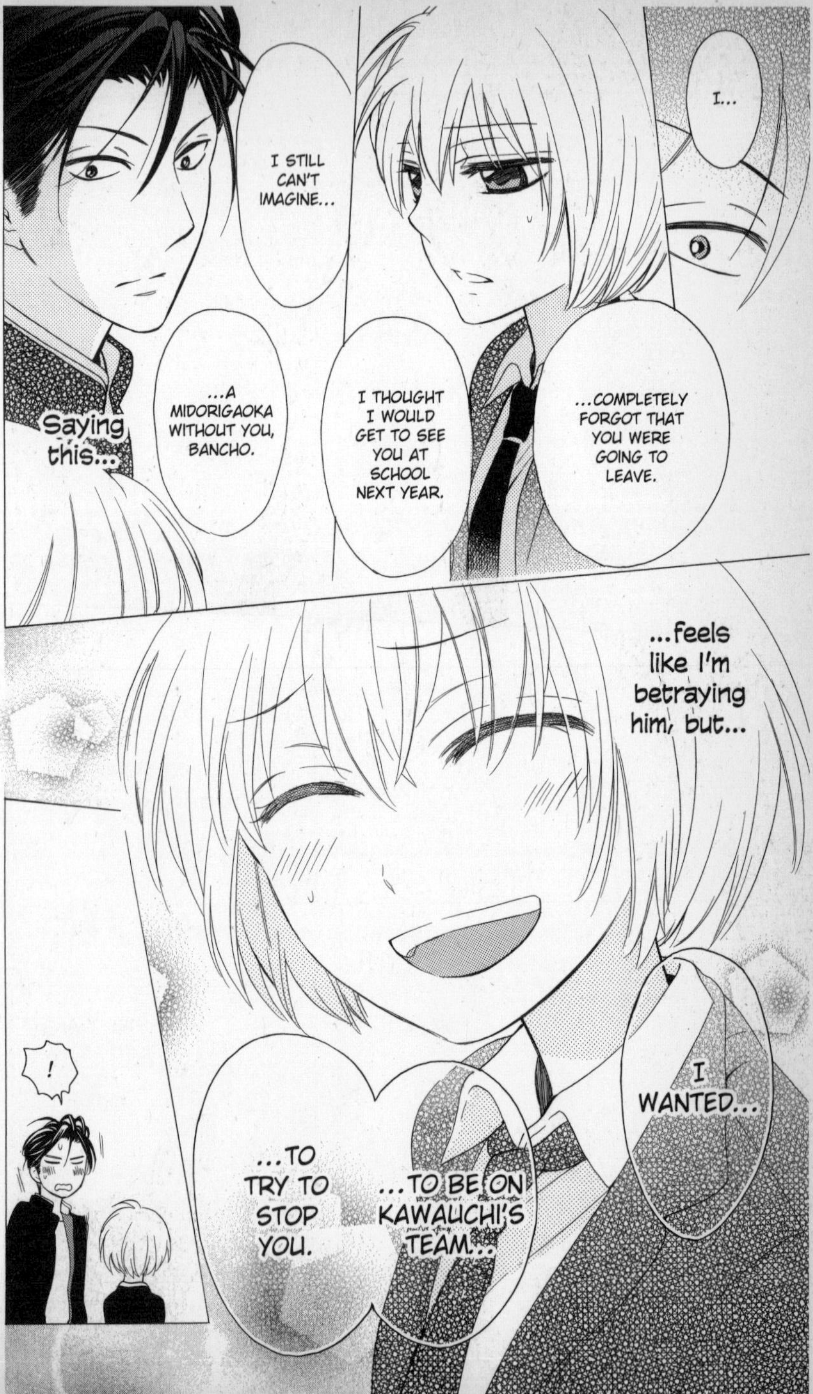
I...
...COMPLETELY FORGOT THAT YOU WERE GOING TO LEAVE.
I THOUGHT I WOULD GET TO SEE YOU AT SCHOOL NEXT YEAR.
I STILL CAN'T IMAGINE...
...A MIDORIGAOKA WITHOUT YOU, BANCHO.
Saying this...
...feels like I'm betraying him, but...
I WANTED...
...TO BE ON KAWAUCHI'S TEAM...
...TO TRY TO STOP YOU.
!

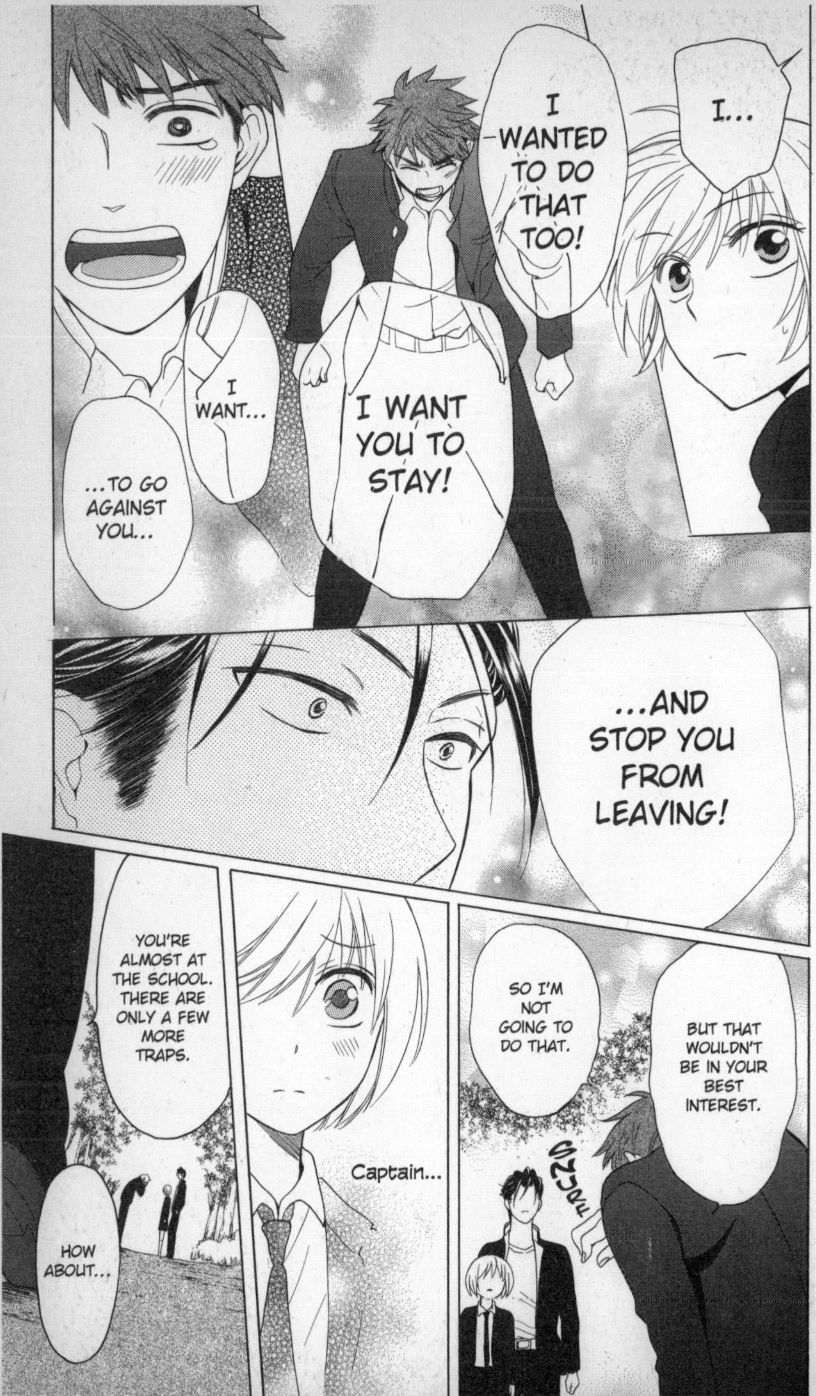
I...
I WANTED TO DO THAT TOO!
I WANT YOU TO STAY!
I WANT...
...TO GO AGAINST YOU...
...AND STOP YOU FROM LEAVING!
BUT THAT WOULDN'T BE IN YOUR BEST INTEREST.
SO I'M NOT GOING TO DO THAT.
SNURF
Captain...
YOU'RE ALMOST AT THE SCHOOL. THERE ARE ONLY A FEW MORE TRAPS.
HOW ABOUT...

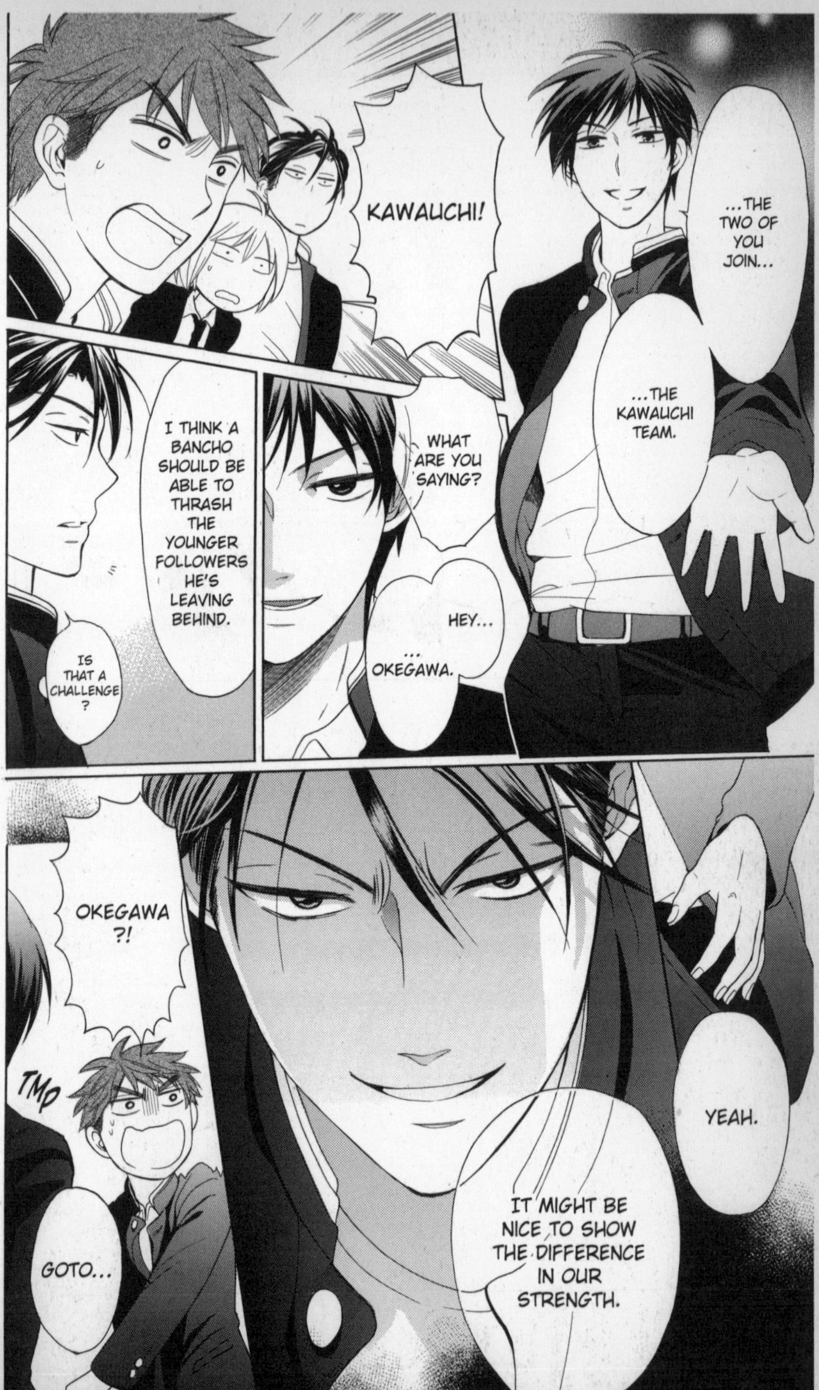

...THE TWO OF YOU JOIN...
...THE KAWAUCHI TEAM.
KAWAUCHI!
WHAT ARE YOU SAYING?
HEY... ...OKEGAWA.
I THINK A BANCHO SHOULD BE ABLE TO THRASH THE YOUNGER FOLLOWERS HE'S LEAVING BEHIND.
IS THAT A CHALLENGE?
IT MIGHT BE NICE TO SHOW THE DIFFERENCE IN OUR STRENGTH.
YEAH.
OKEGAWA?!
TMP
GOTO...

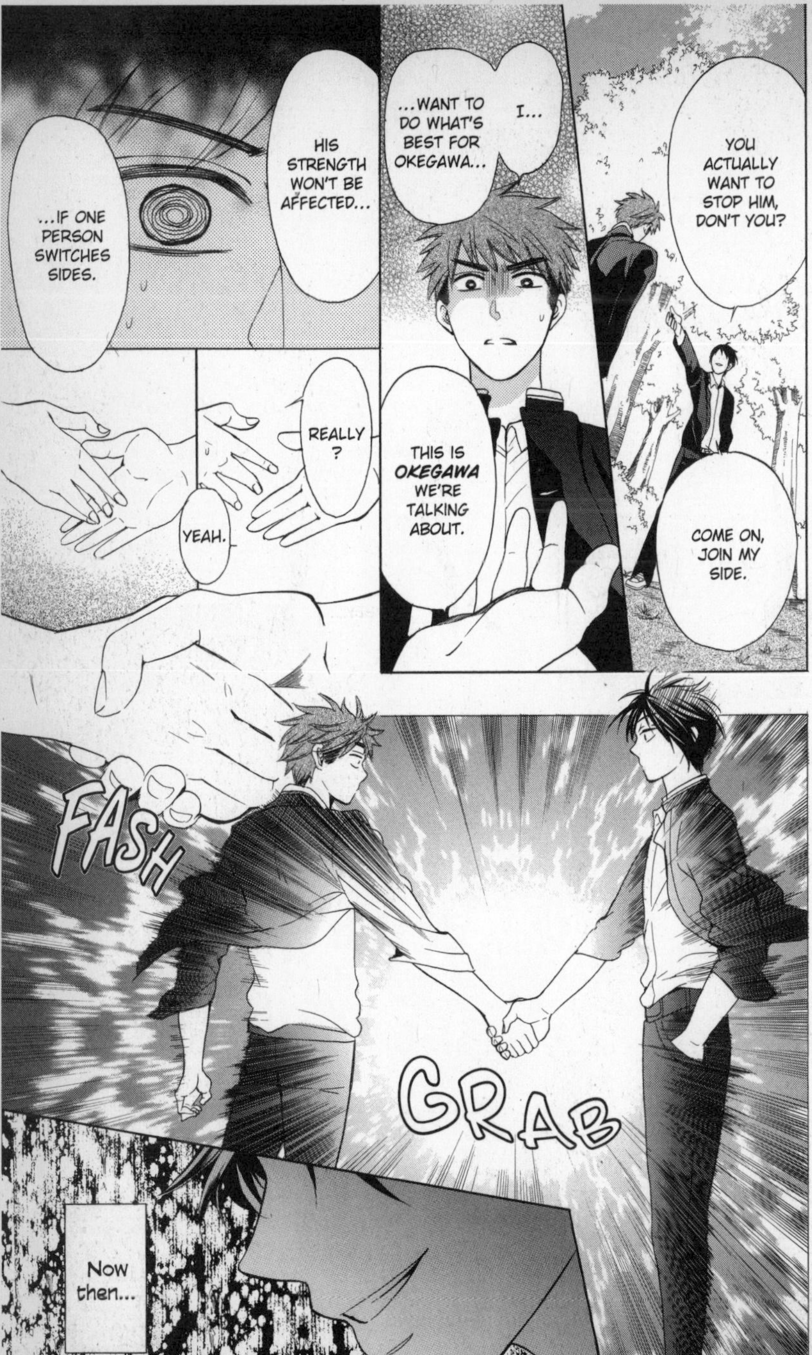
YOU ACTUALLY WANT TO STOP HIM, DON'T YOU?
COME ON, JOIN MY SIDE.
I...
...WANT TO DO WHAT'S BEST FOR OKEGAWA...
THIS IS OKEGAWA WE'RE TALKING ABOUT.
HIS STRENGTH WON'T BE AFFECTED...
...IF ONE PERSON SWITCHES SIDES.
REALLY?
YEAH.
FASH
GRAB
Now then...

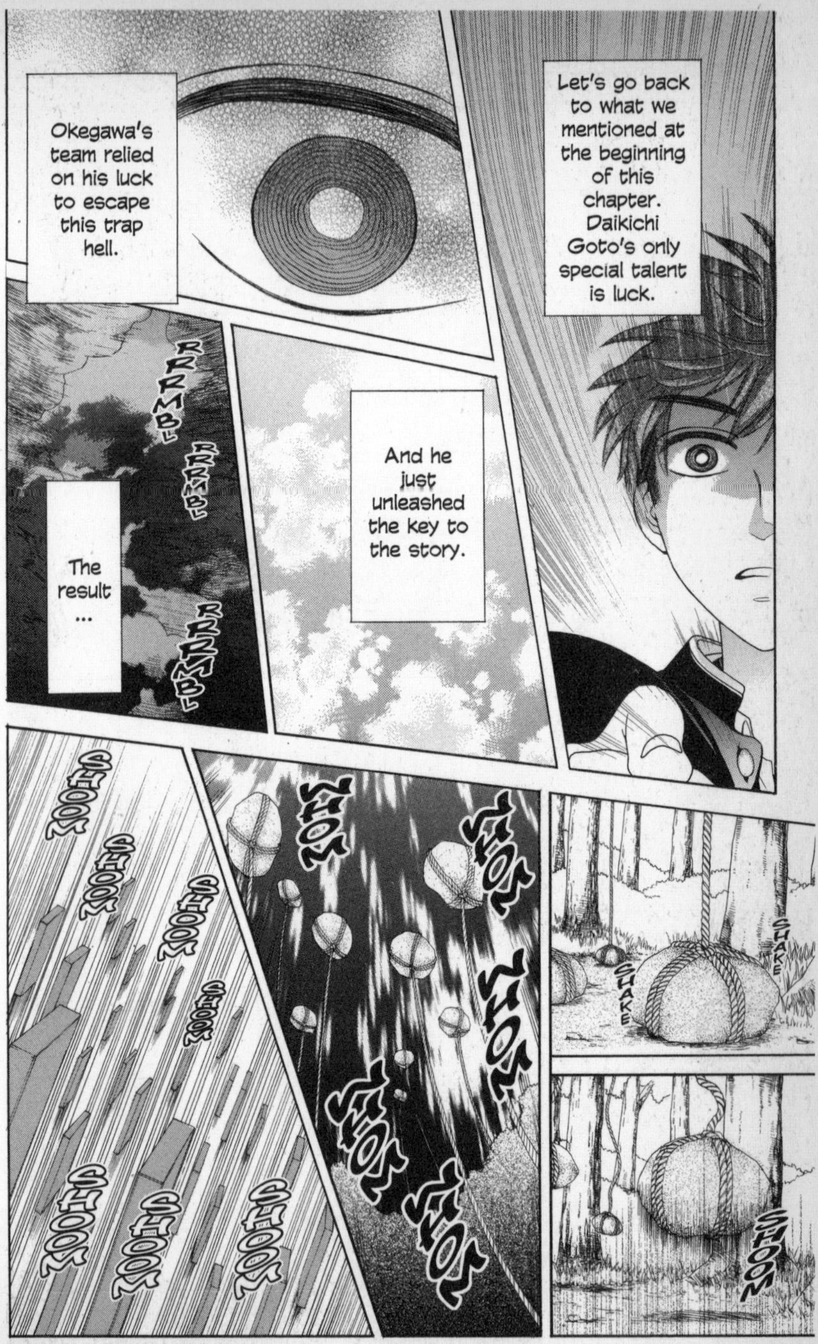
Let's go back to what we mentioned at the beginning of this chapter. Daikichi Goto's only special talent is luck.
Okegawa's team relied on his luck to escape this trap hell.
And he just unleashed the key to the story.
RRRMBL
RRRMBL
RRRMBL
The result ...
SHAKE
SHAKE
SHOOM
ZOOM
ZOOM
ZOOM
ZOOM
ZOOM
SHOOM
SHOOM
SHOOM
SHOOM
SHOOM
SHOOM
SHOOM

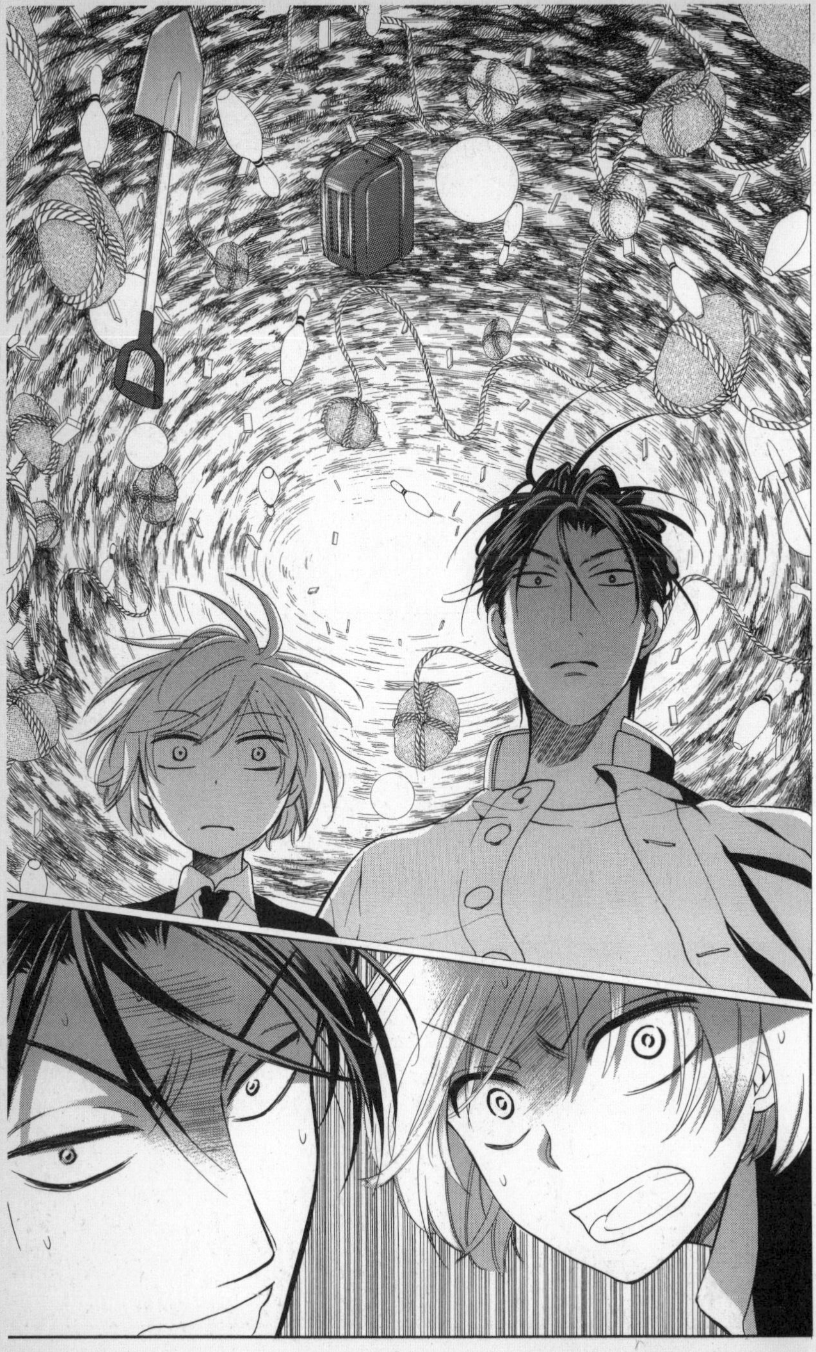

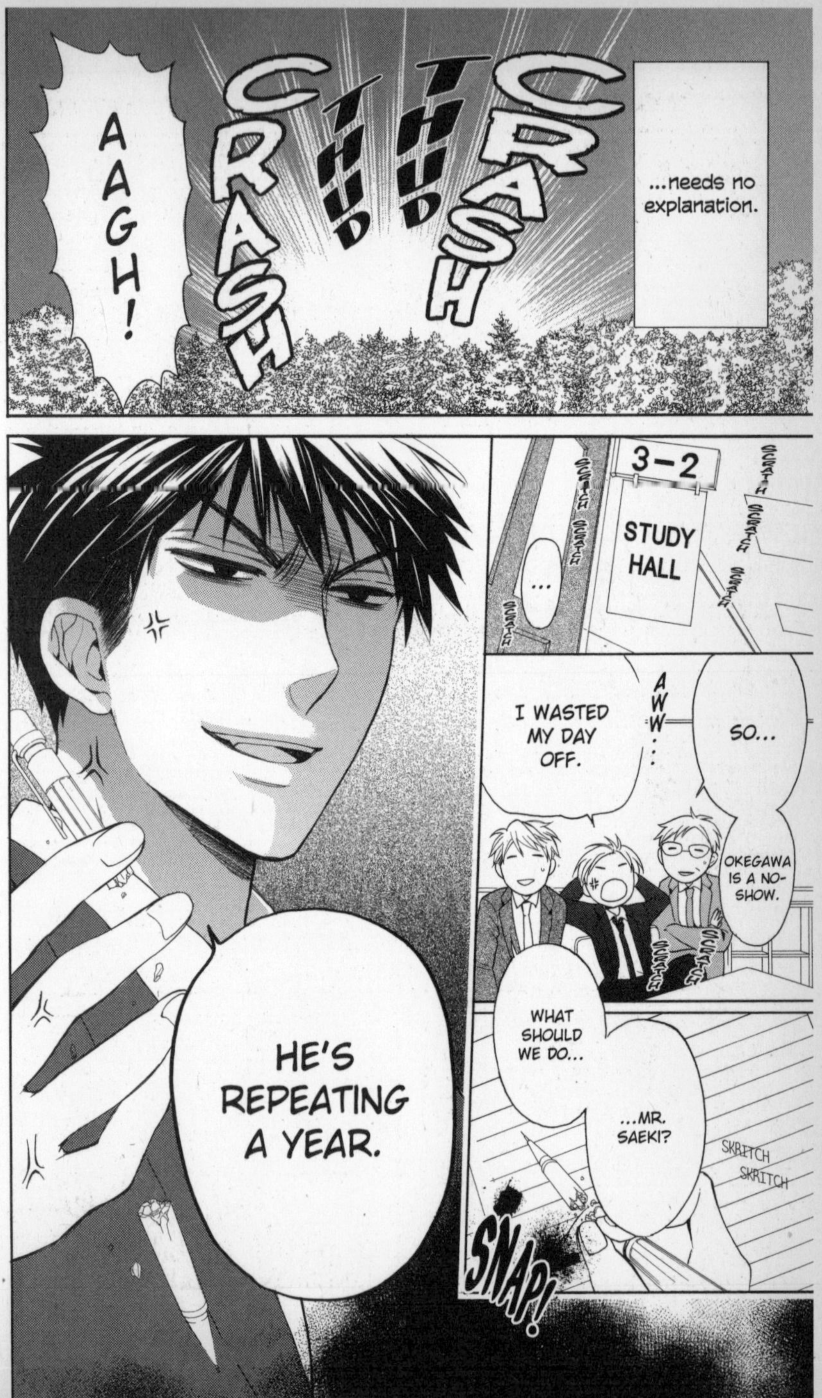
...needs no explanation.
CRASH
THUD
THUD
CRASH
AAGH!
3-2
STUDY HALL
SCRATCH SCRATCH SCRATCH
SCRATCH SCRATCH SCRATCH
...
SO...
OKEGAWA IS A NO-SHOW.
AWW...
I WASTED MY DAY OFF.
SCRATCH SCRATCH
WHAT SHOULD WE DO...
...MR. SAEKI?
SKRITCH SKRITCH
SNAP!
HE'S REPEATING A YEAR.

KOSAKA'S MELANCHOLY

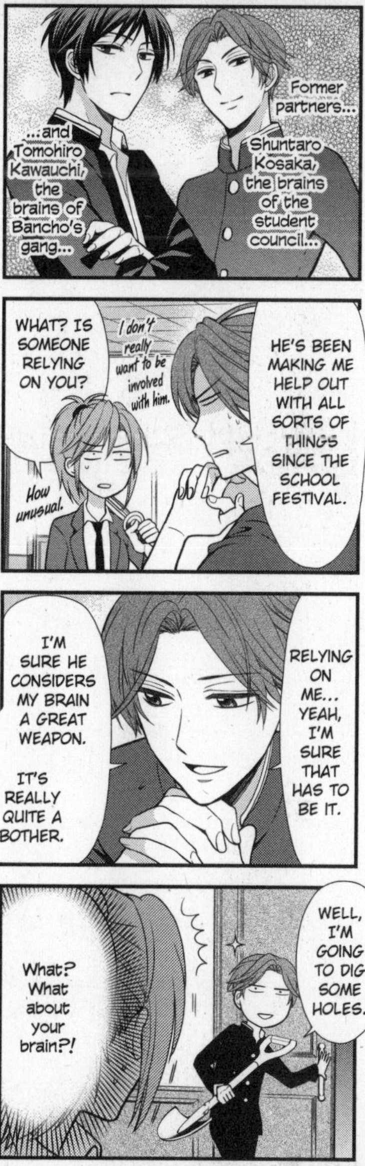
Former partners...
Shuntaro Kosaka, the brains of the student council...
...and Tomohiro Kawauchi, the brains of Bancho's gang...
HE'S BEEN MAKING ME HELP OUT WITH ALL SORTS OF THINGS SINCE THE SCHOOL FESTIVAL.
I don't really want to be involved with him.
WHAT? IS SOMEONE RELYING ON YOU?
How unusual.
RELYING ON ME... YEAH, I'M SURE THAT HAS TO BE IT.
I'M SURE HE CONSIDERS MY BRAIN A GREAT WEAPON.
IT'S REALLY QUITE A BOTHER.
WELL, I'M GOING TO DIG SOME HOLES.
What? What about your brain?!

KAWAUCHI'S AGONY

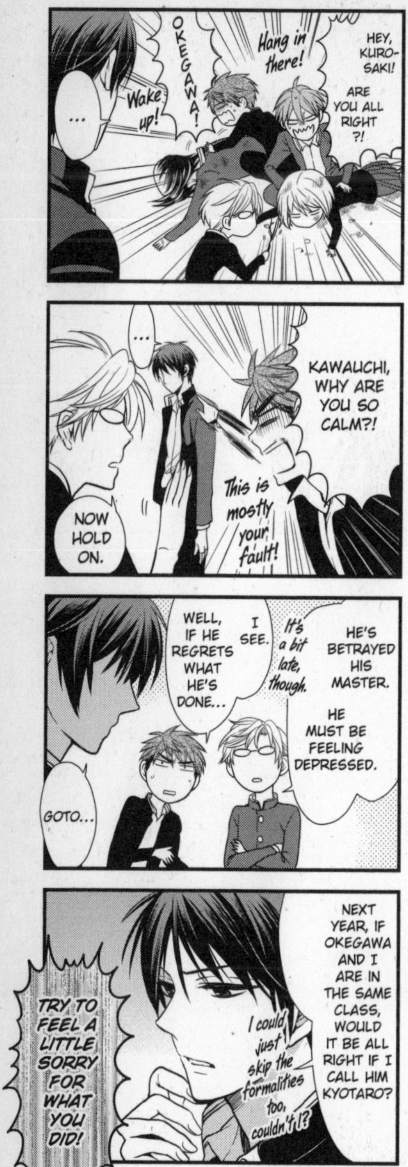
HEY, KURO-SAKI!
ARE YOU ALL RIGHT?!
Hang in there!
OKEGAWA!
Wake up!
...
KAWAUCHI, WHY ARE YOU SO CALM?!
This is mostly your fault!
...
NOW HOLD ON.
HE'S BETRAYED HIS MASTER.
HE MUST BE FEELING DEPRESSED.
It's a bit late, though.
I SEE.
WELL, IF HE REGRETS WHAT HE'S DONE...
GOTO...
NEXT YEAR, IF OKEGAWA AND I ARE IN THE SAME CLASS, WOULD IT BE ALL RIGHT IF I CALL HIM KYOTARO?
I could just skip the formalities too, couldn't I?
TRY TO FEEL A LITTLE SORRY FOR WHAT YOU DID!

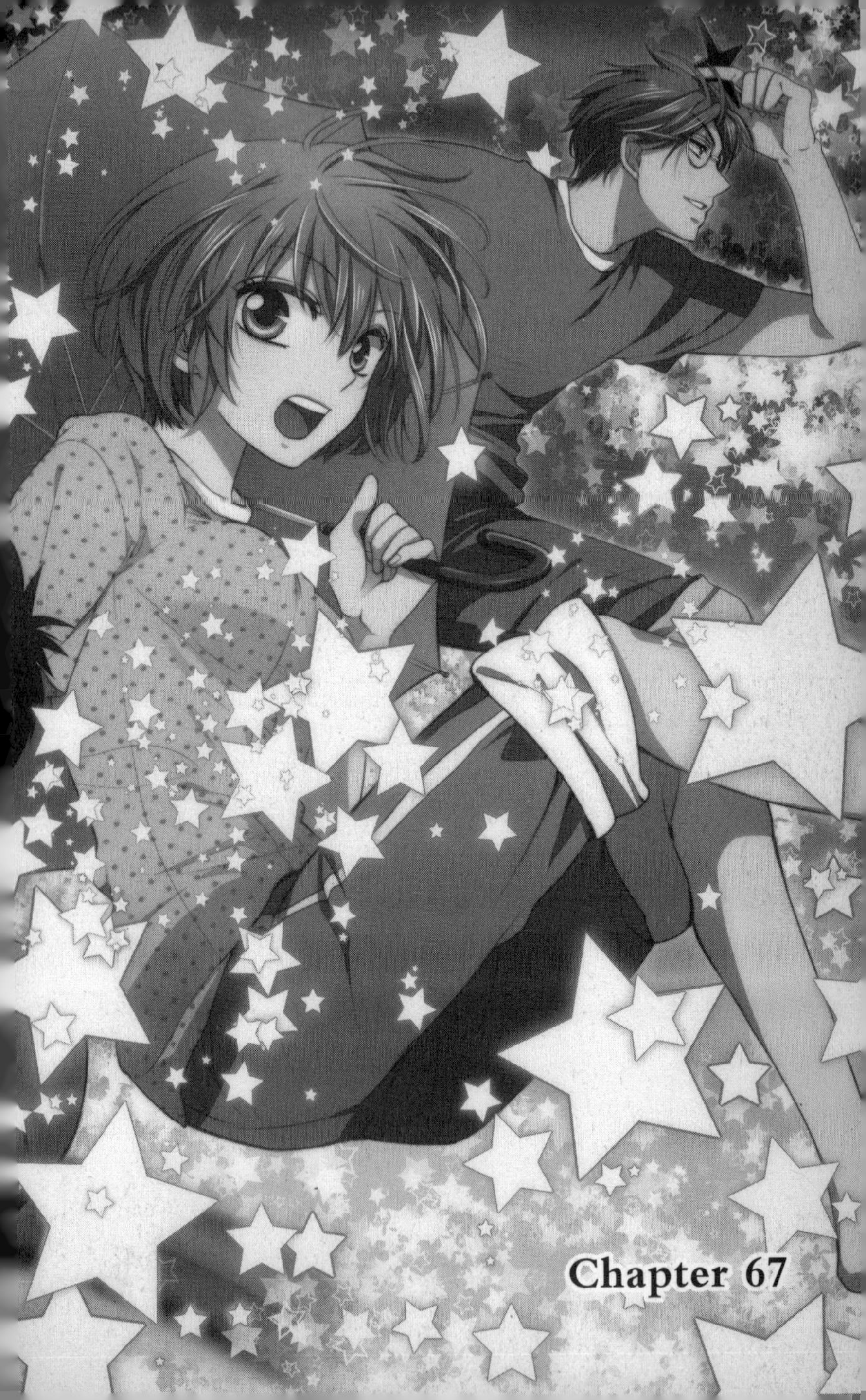
Chapter 67

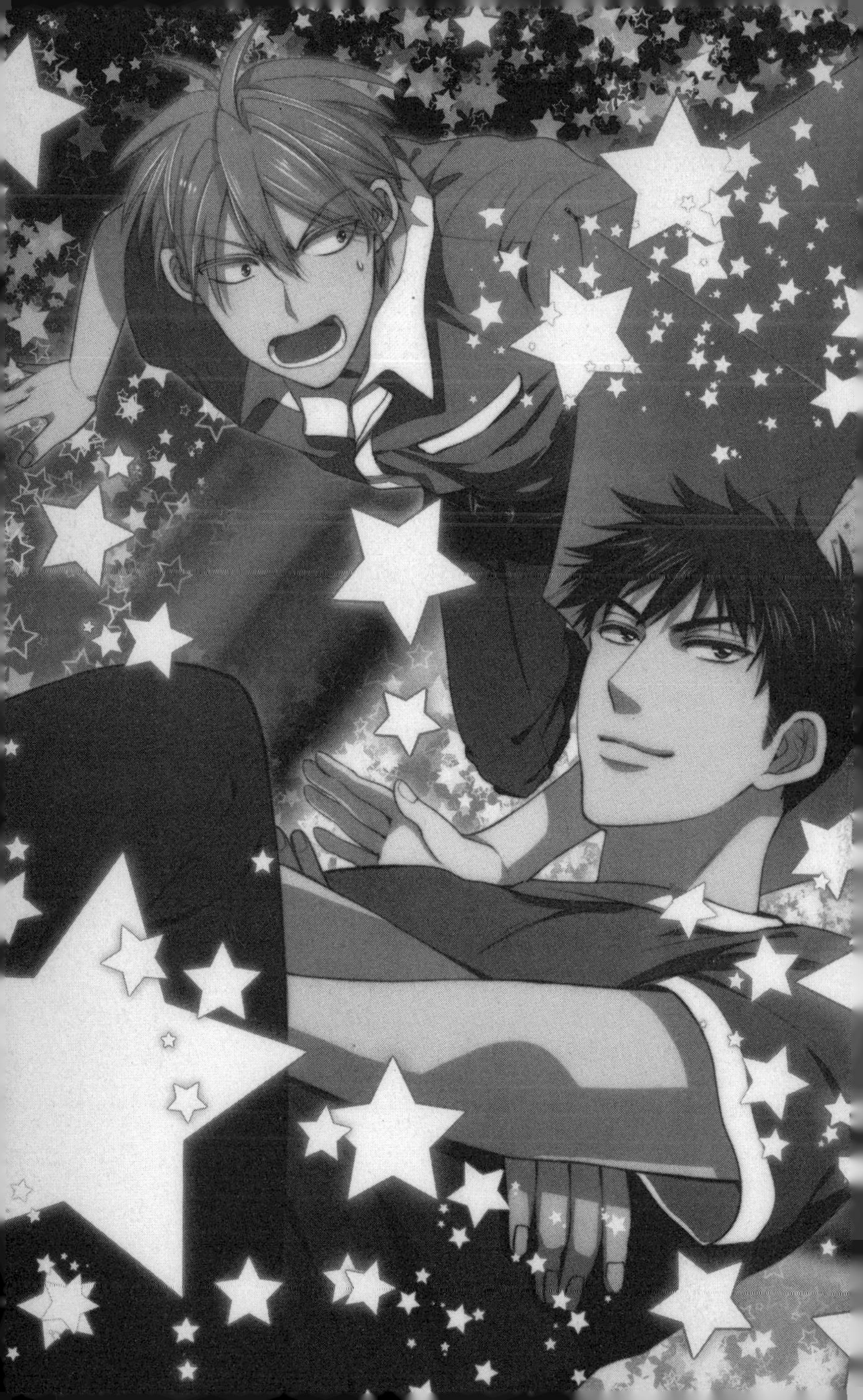

NO DISTINCTION

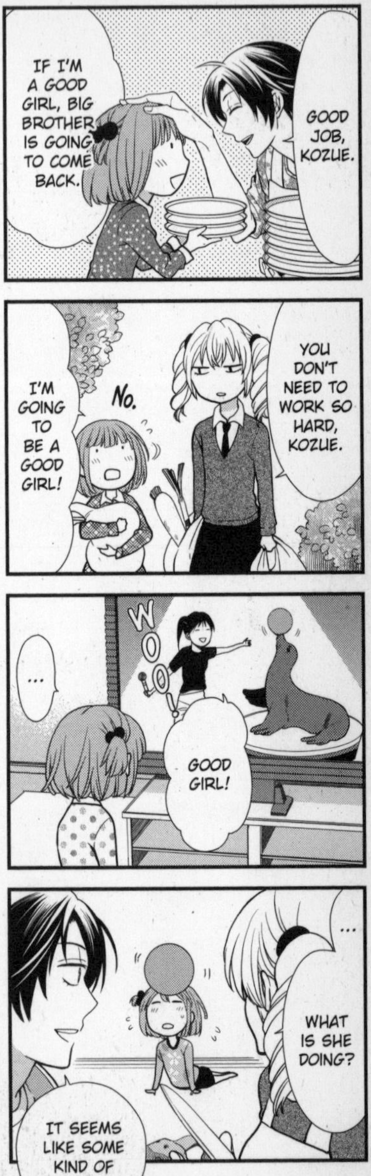
GOOD JOB, KOZUE.
IF I'M A GOOD GIRL, BIG BROTHER IS GOING TO COME BACK.
YOU DON'T NEED TO WORK SO HARD, KOZUE.
No.
I'M GOING TO BE A GOOD GIRL!
WOO!
...
GOOD GIRL!
...
WHAT IS SHE DOING?
IT SEEMS LIKE SOME KIND OF FAD.

AYABE FAMILY + 1

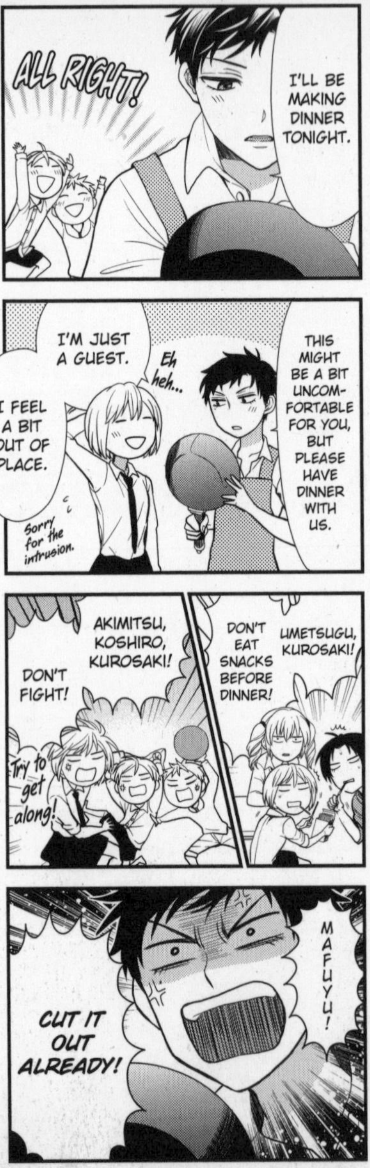
I'LL BE MAKING DINNER TONIGHT.
ALL RIGHT!
THIS MIGHT BE A BIT UNCOMFORTABLE FOR YOU, BUT PLEASE HAVE DINNER WITH US.
Eh heh...
I'M JUST A GUEST.
I FEEL A BIT OUT OF PLACE.
Sorry for the intrusion.
UMETSUGU, KUROSAKI!
DON'T EAT SNACKS BEFORE DINNER!
AKIMITSU, KOSHIRO, KUROSAKI!
DON'T FIGHT!
Try to get along!
MAFUYU!
CUT IT OUT ALREADY!

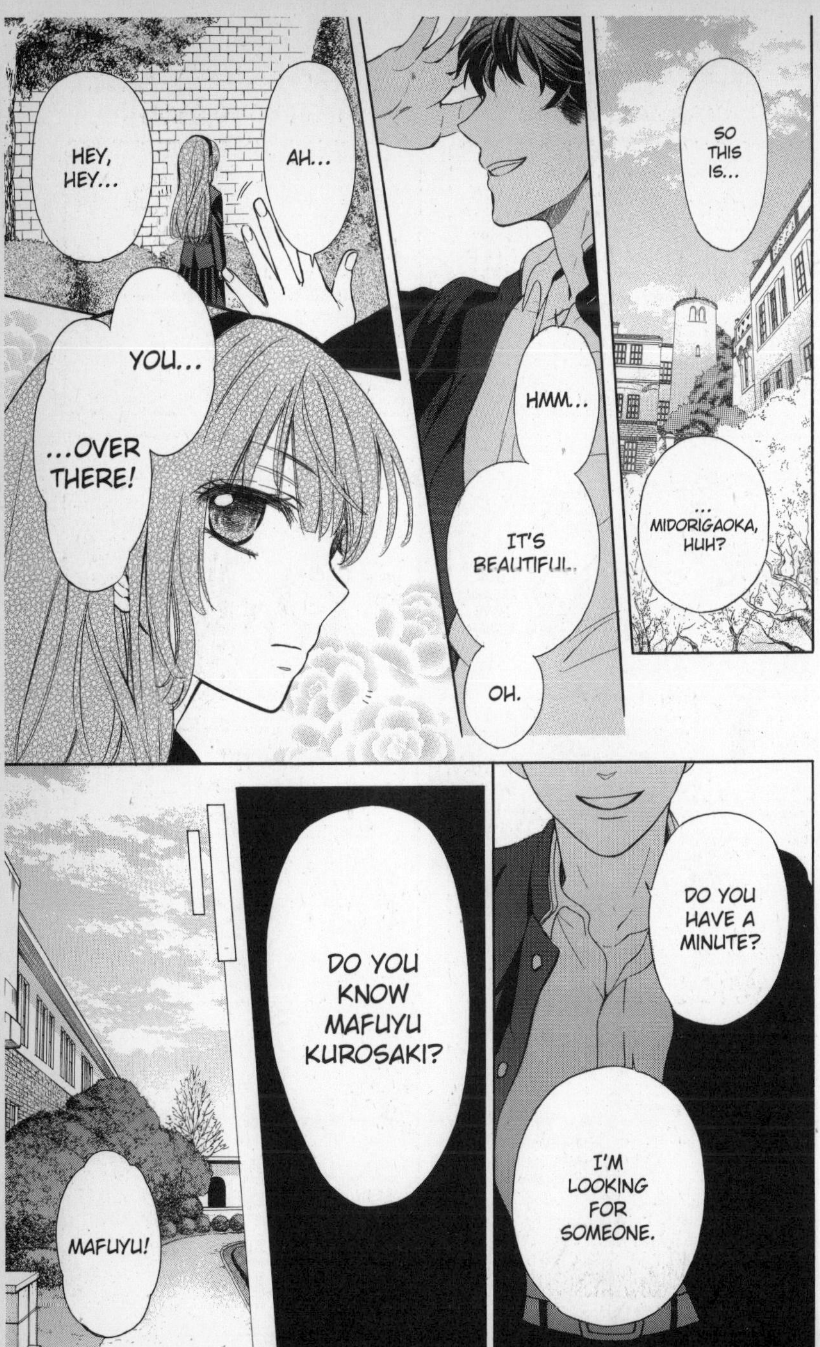
SO THIS IS...
...MIDORIGAOKA, HUH?
HMM...
IT'S BEAUTIFUL.
OH.
AH...
HEY, HEY...
YOU...
...OVER THERE!
DO YOU HAVE A MINUTE?
I'M LOOKING FOR SOMEONE.
DO YOU KNOW MAFUYU KUROSAKI?
MAFUYU!

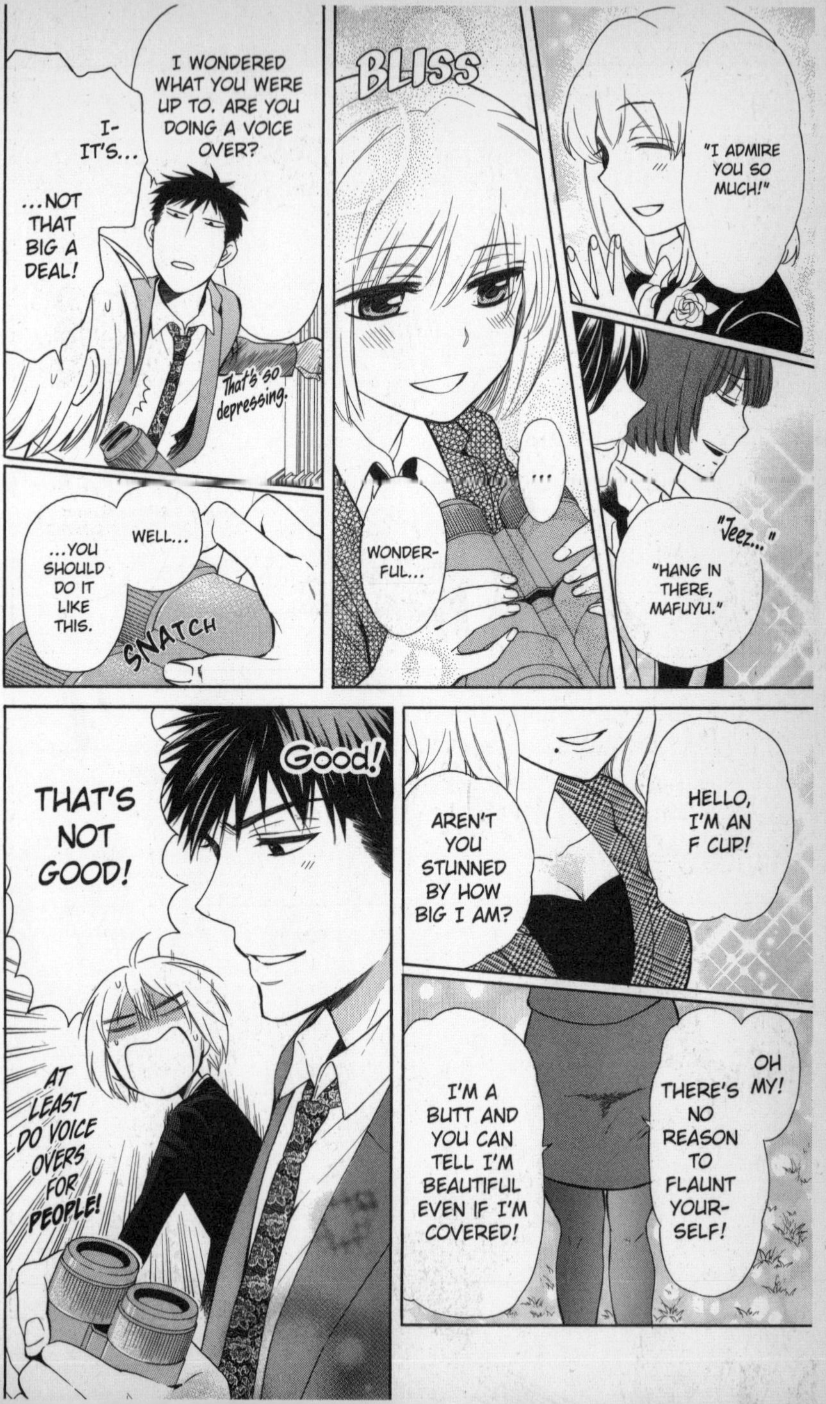
"I ADMIRE YOU SO MUCH!"
"Jeez..."
"HANG IN THERE, MAFUYU."
BLISS
...
WONDERFUL...
I WONDERED WHAT YOU WERE UP TO. ARE YOU DOING A VOICE OVER?
I- IT'S...
...NOT THAT BIG A DEAL!
That's so depressing.
WELL...
...YOU SHOULD DO IT LIKE THIS.
SNATCH
HELLO, I'M AN F CUP!
AREN'T YOU STUNNED BY HOW BIG I AM?
OH MY!
THERE'S NO REASON TO FLAUNT YOURSELF!
I'M A BUTT AND YOU CAN TELL I'M BEAUTIFUL EVEN IF I'M COVERED!
Good!
THAT'S NOT GOOD!
AT LEAST DO VOICE OVERS FOR PEOPLE!

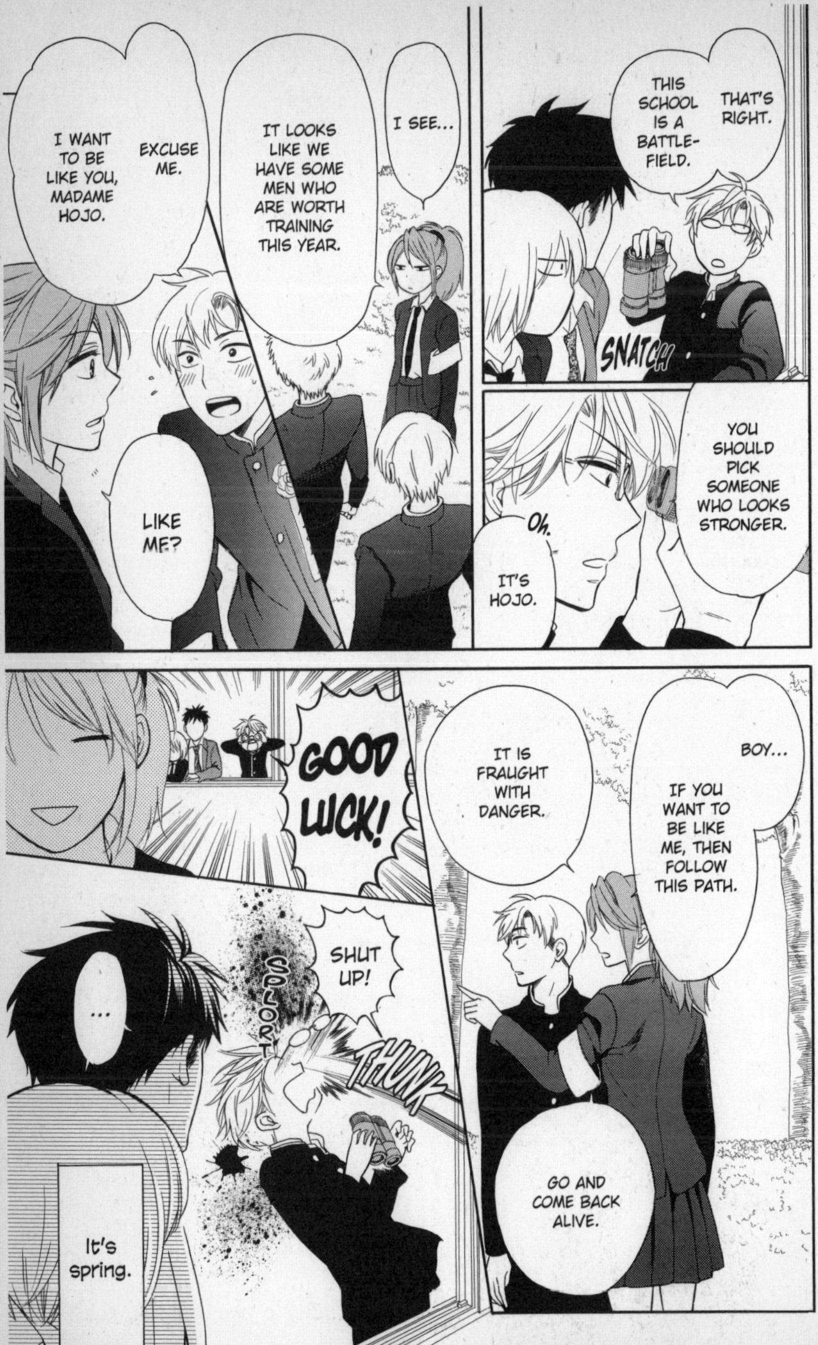
THAT'S RIGHT.
THIS SCHOOL IS A BATTLE-FIELD.
SNATCH
YOU SHOULD PICK SOMEONE WHO LOOKS STRONGER.
Oh.
IT'S HOJO.
I SEE...
IT LOOKS LIKE WE HAVE SOME MEN WHO ARE WORTH TRAINING THIS YEAR.
EXCUSE ME.
I WANT TO BE LIKE YOU, MADAME HOJO.
LIKE ME?
BOY...
IF YOU WANT TO BE LIKE ME, THEN FOLLOW THIS PATH.
IT IS FRAUGHT WITH DANGER.
GO AND COME BACK ALIVE.
GOOD LUCK!
SHUT UP!
SPLORT
THUNK
...
It's spring.

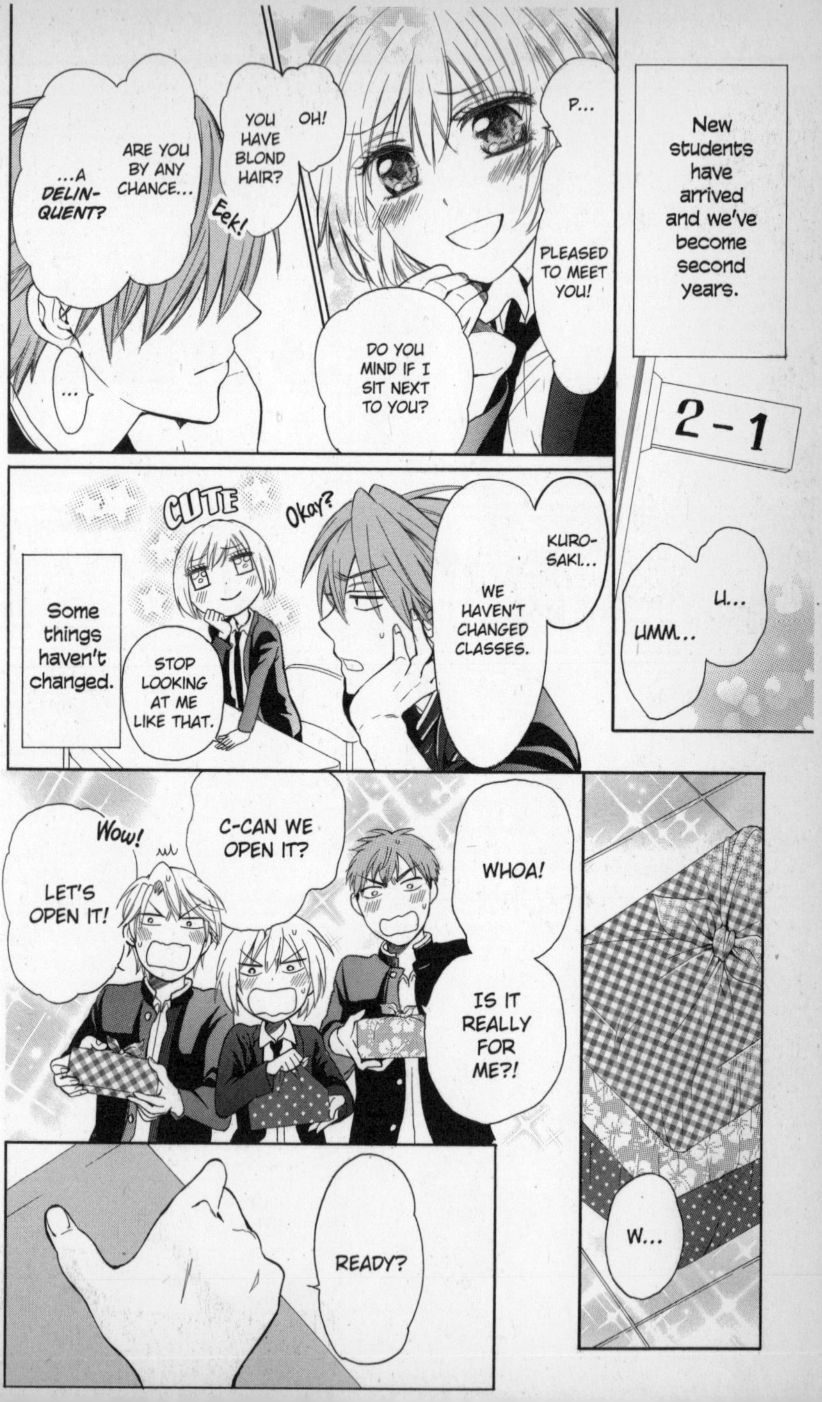
New students have arrived and we've become second years.
2-1
U...
UMM...
P...
PLEASED TO MEET YOU!
DO YOU MIND IF I SIT NEXT TO YOU?
OH!
YOU HAVE BLOND HAIR?
Eek!
ARE YOU BY ANY CHANCE...
...A DELINQUENT?
...
KURO-SAKI...
WE HAVEN'T CHANGED CLASSES.
Okay?
CUTE
STOP LOOKING AT ME LIKE THAT.
Some things haven't changed.
W...
WHOA!
IS IT REALLY FOR ME?!
C-CAN WE OPEN IT?
Wow!
LET'S OPEN IT!
READY?

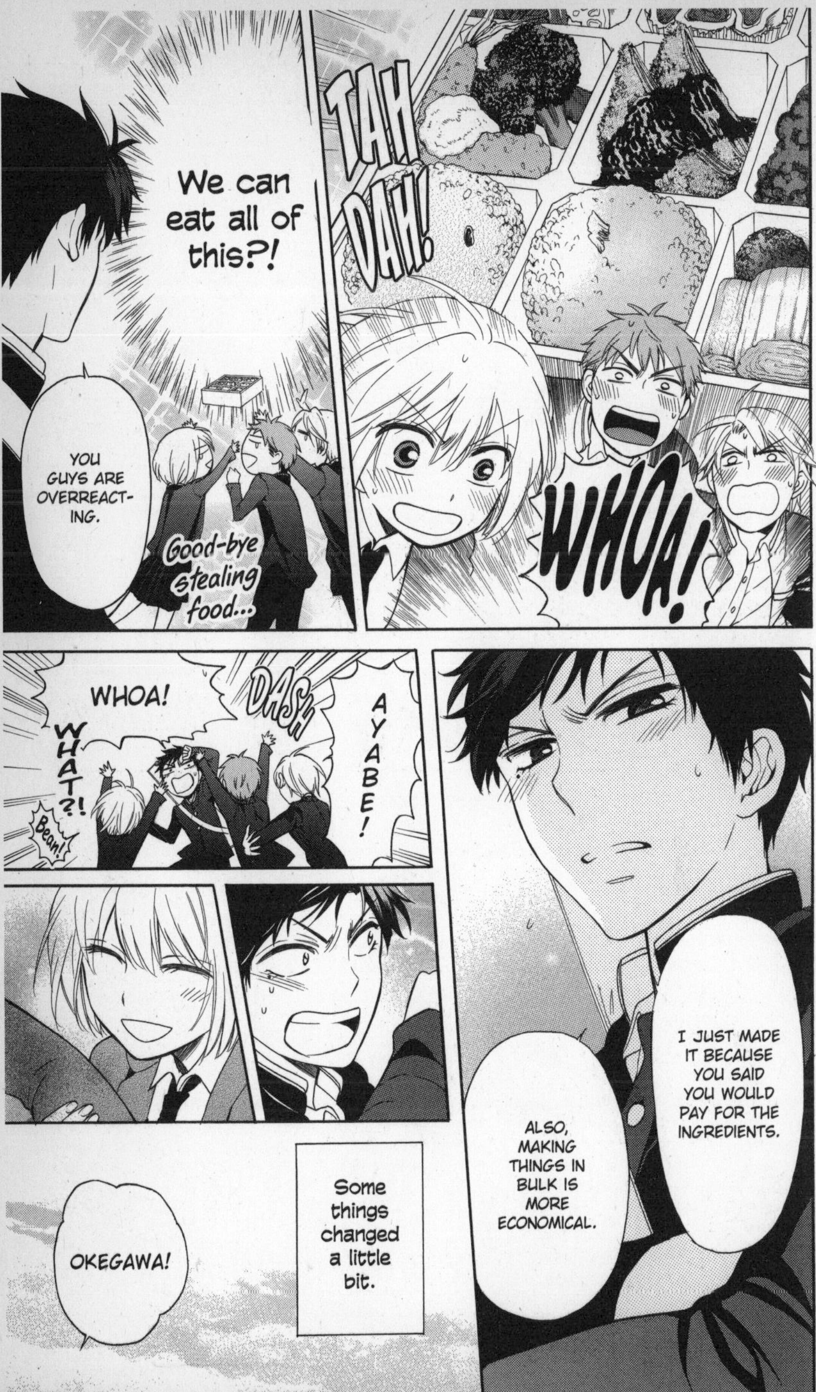
TAH DAH!
WHOA!
We can eat all of this?!
YOU GUYS ARE OVERREACTING.
Good-bye stealing food...
I JUST MADE IT BECAUSE YOU SAID YOU WOULD PAY FOR THE INGREDIENTS.
ALSO, MAKING THINGS IN BULK IS MORE ECONOMICAL.
AYABE!
DASH
WHOA!
WHAT?!
Bean!
Some things changed a little bit.
OKEGAWA!

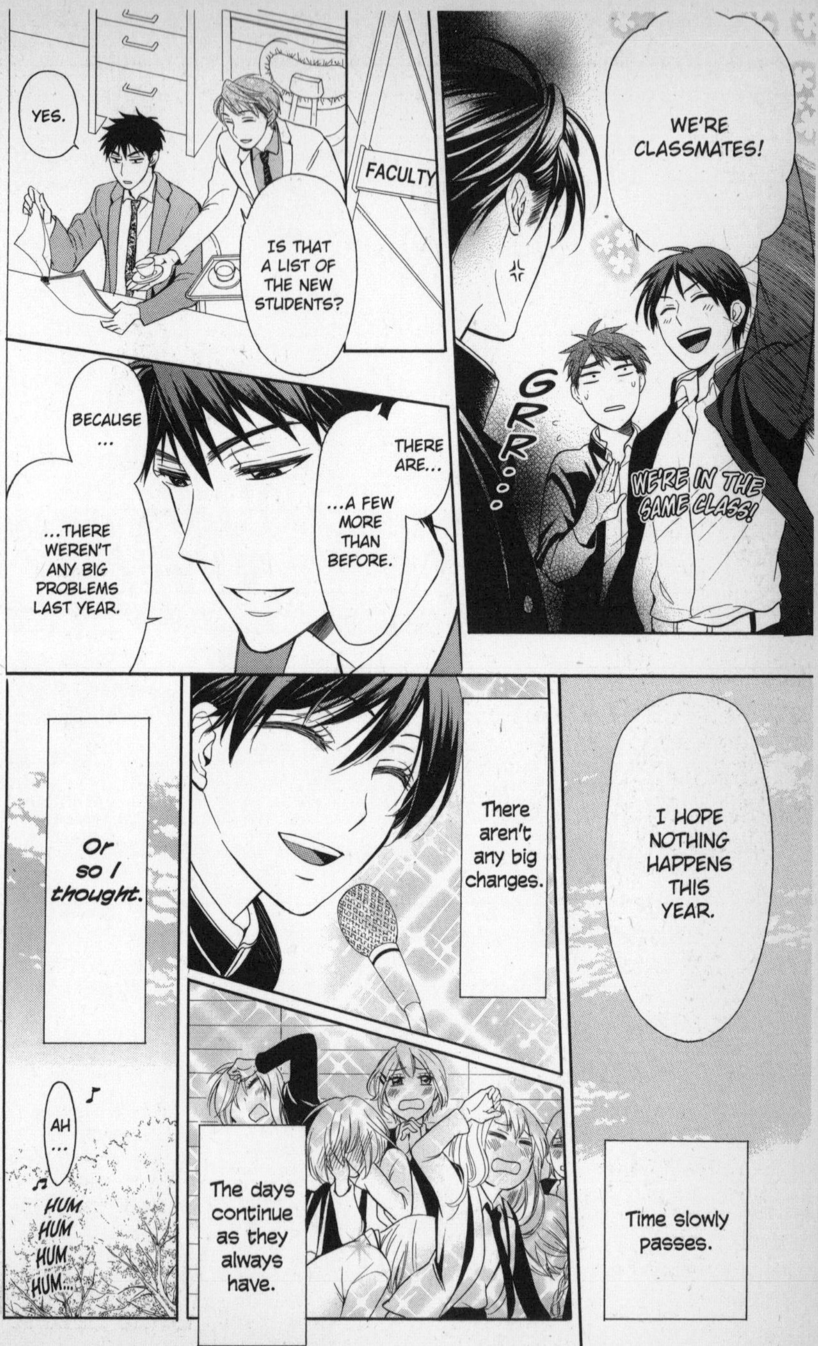
WE'RE CLASSMATES!
GRR...
WE'RE IN THE SAME CLASS!
FACULTY
IS THAT A LIST OF THE NEW STUDENTS?
YES.
THERE ARE...
...A FEW MORE THAN BEFORE.
BECAUSE...
...THERE WEREN'T ANY BIG PROBLEMS LAST YEAR.
I HOPE NOTHING HAPPENS THIS YEAR.
Time slowly passes.
There aren't any big changes.
The days continue as they always have.
Or so I thought.
AH...
HUM HUM HUM HUM...

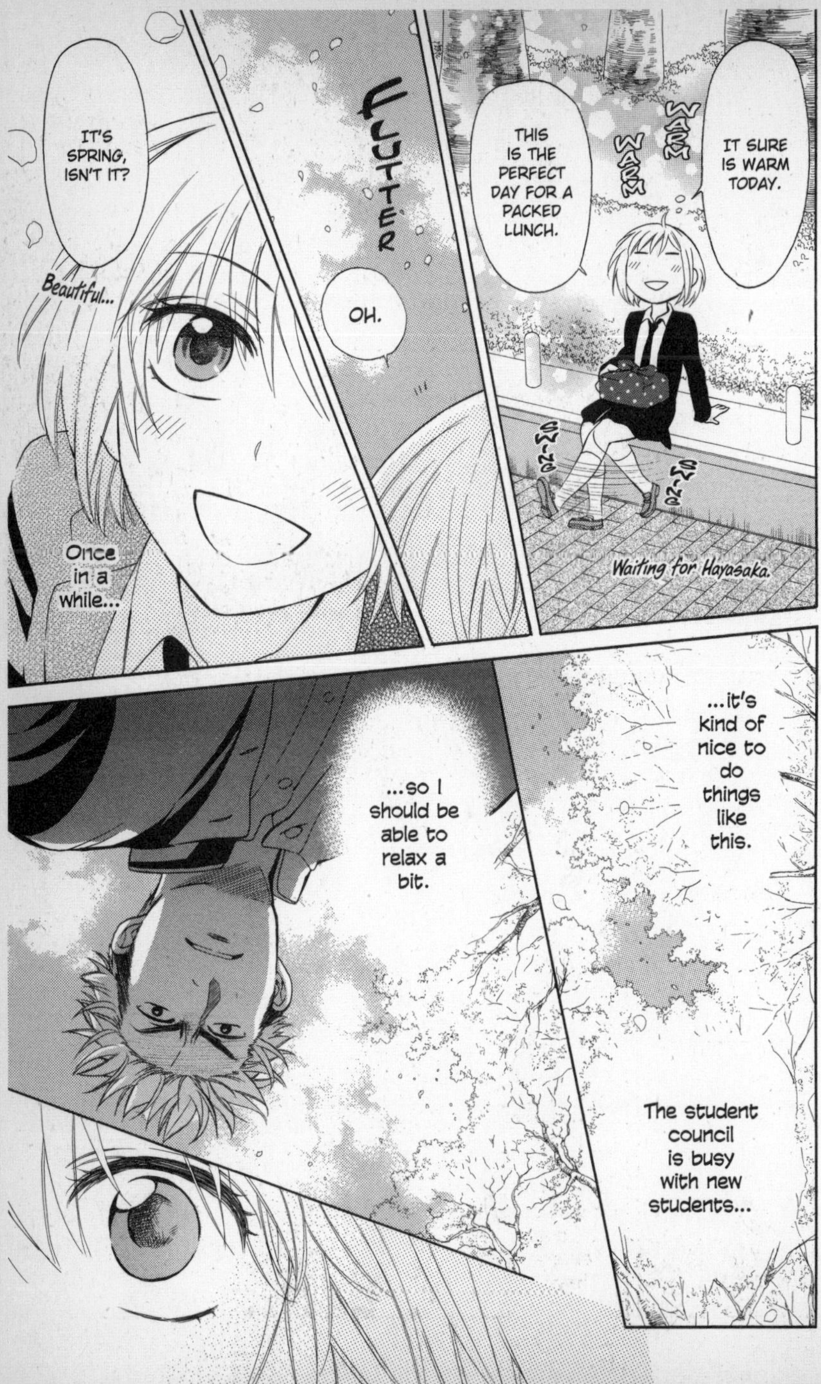
IT SURE IS WARM TODAY.
WARM WARM
THIS IS THE PERFECT DAY FOR A PACKED LUNCH.
SWING SWING
Waiting for Hayasaka.
FLUTTER
OH.
IT'S SPRING, ISN'T IT?
Beautiful...
Once in a while...
...it's kind of nice to do things like this.
The student council is busy with new students...
...so I should be able to relax a bit.

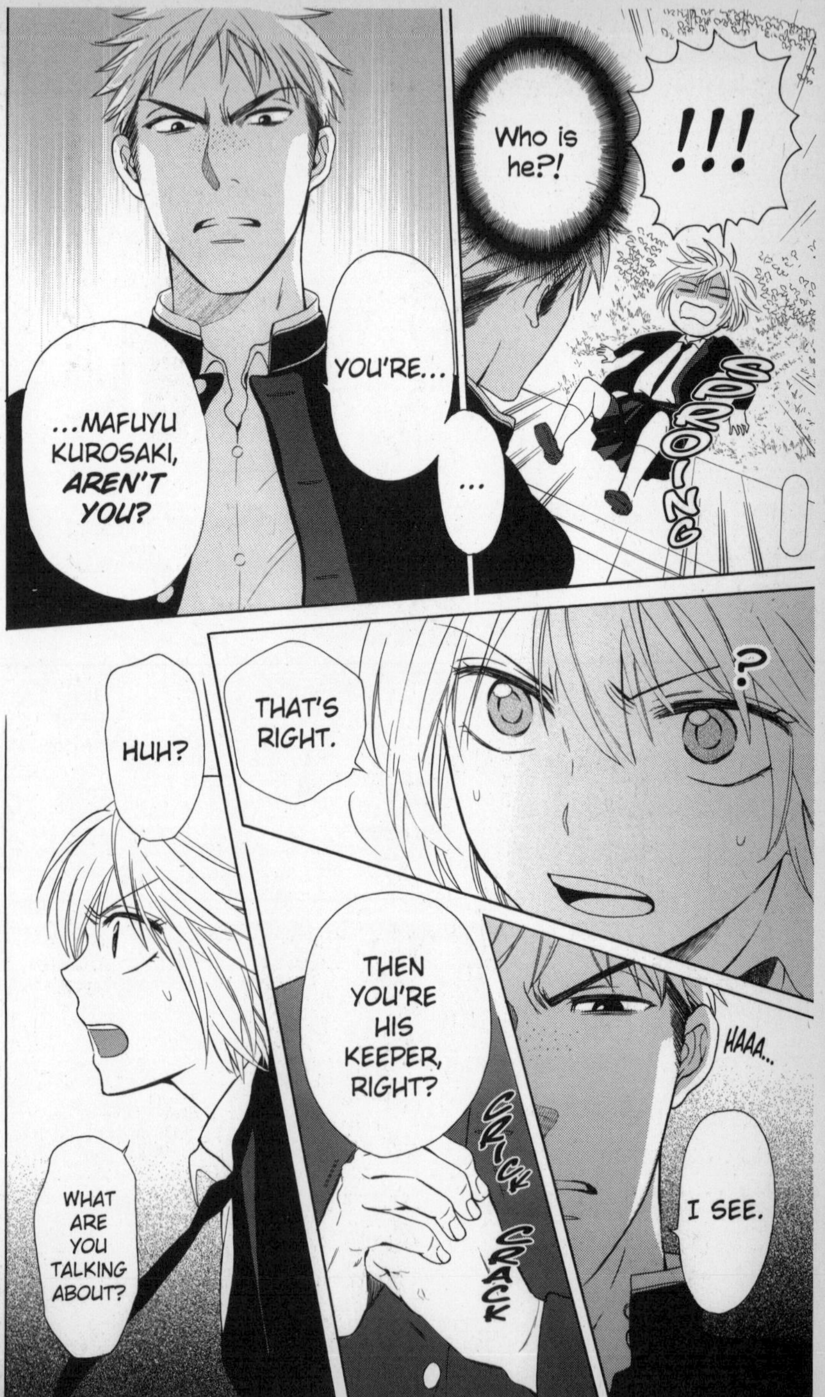
!!!
Who is he?!
SPROING
YOU'RE...
...
...MAFUYU KUROSAKI, AREN'T YOU?
?
THAT'S RIGHT.
HAAA...
I SEE.
THEN YOU'RE HIS KEEPER, RIGHT?
CRICK
CRACK
HUH?
WHAT ARE YOU TALKING ABOUT?

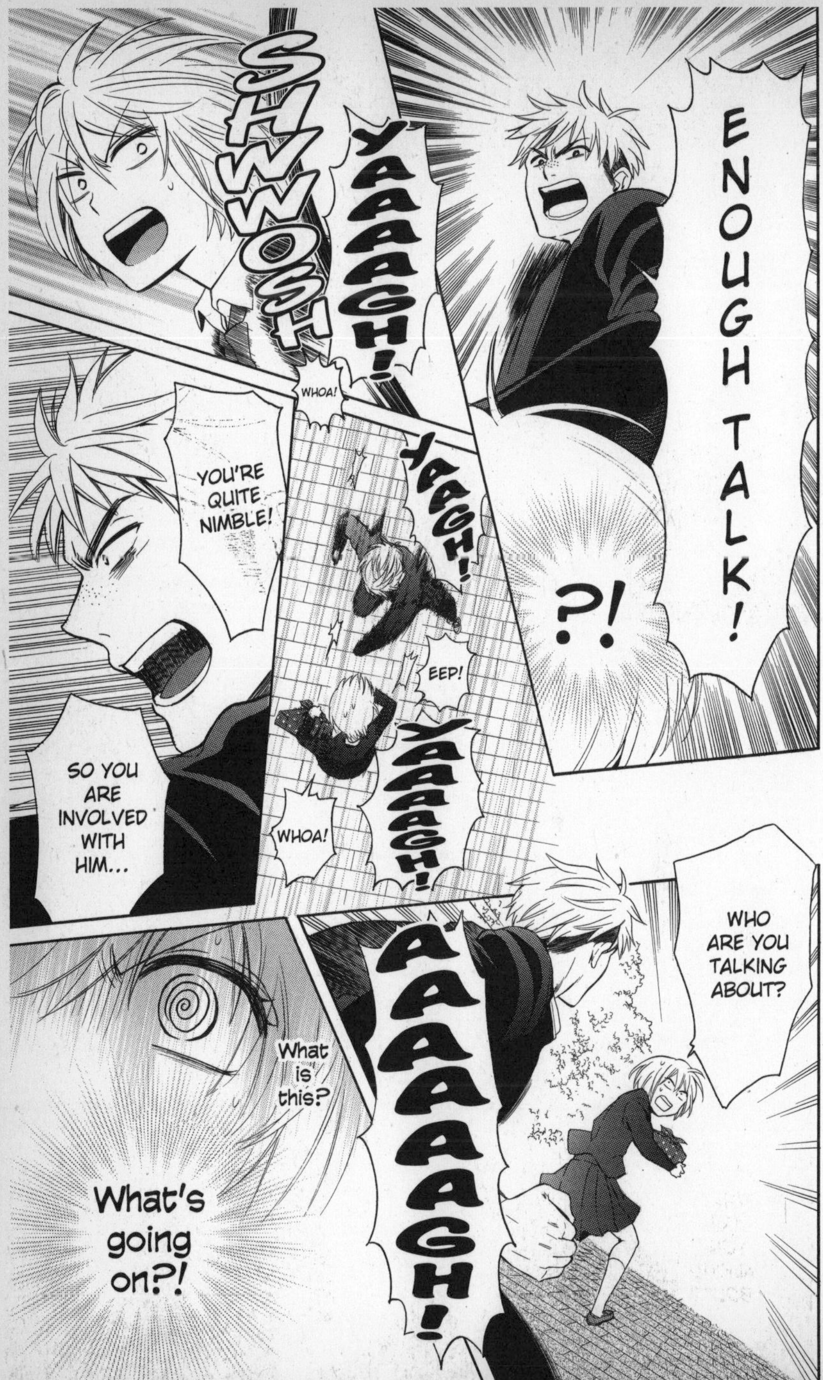
ENOUGH TALK!
?!
YAAAAAGH!
SHWWOSH
WHOA!
YAAGH!
EEP!
YAAAAAAGH!
WHOA!
YOU'RE QUITE NIMBLE!
SO YOU ARE INVOLVED WITH HIM...
WHO ARE YOU TALKING ABOUT?
AAAAAAAGH!
What is this?
What's going on?!

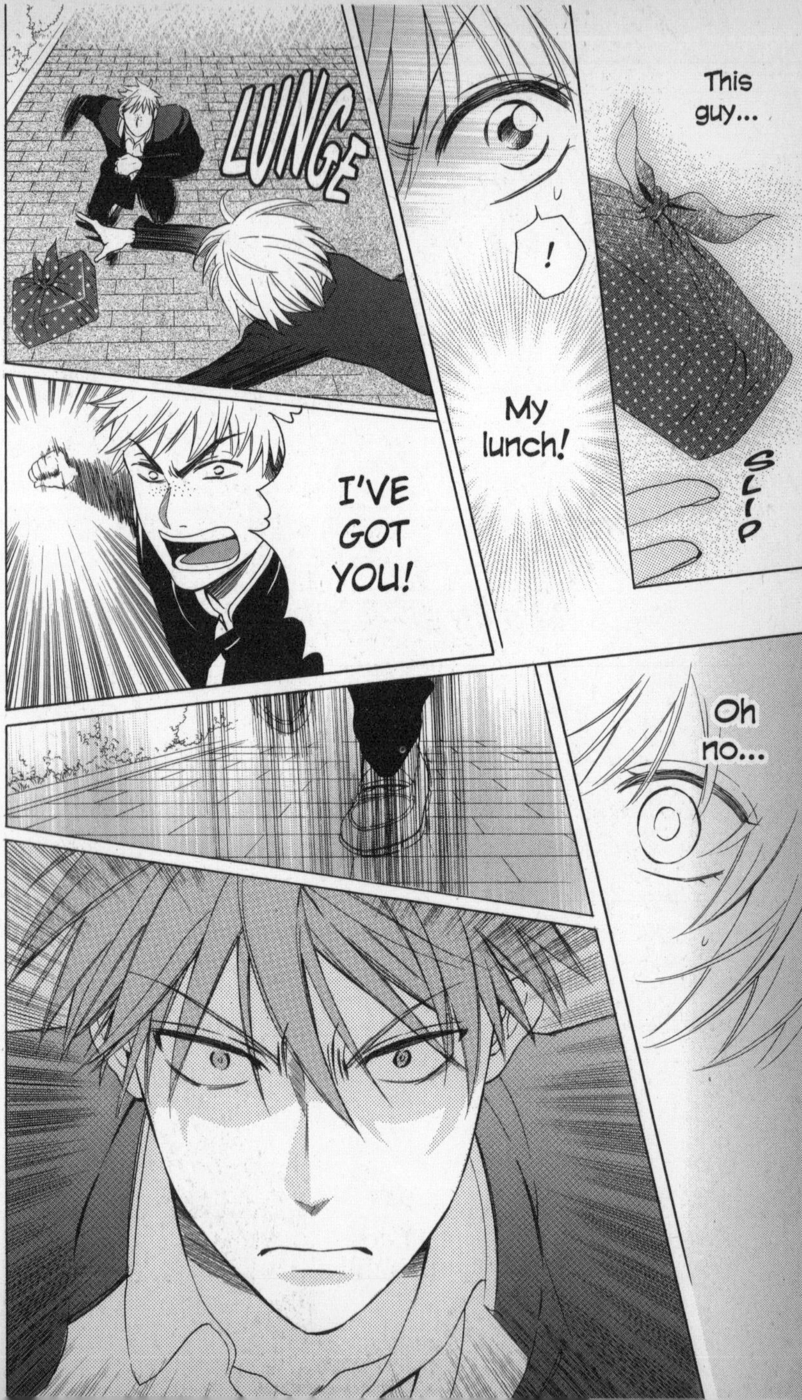
This guy...
!
My lunch!
SLIP
LUNGE
I'VE GOT YOU!
Oh no...

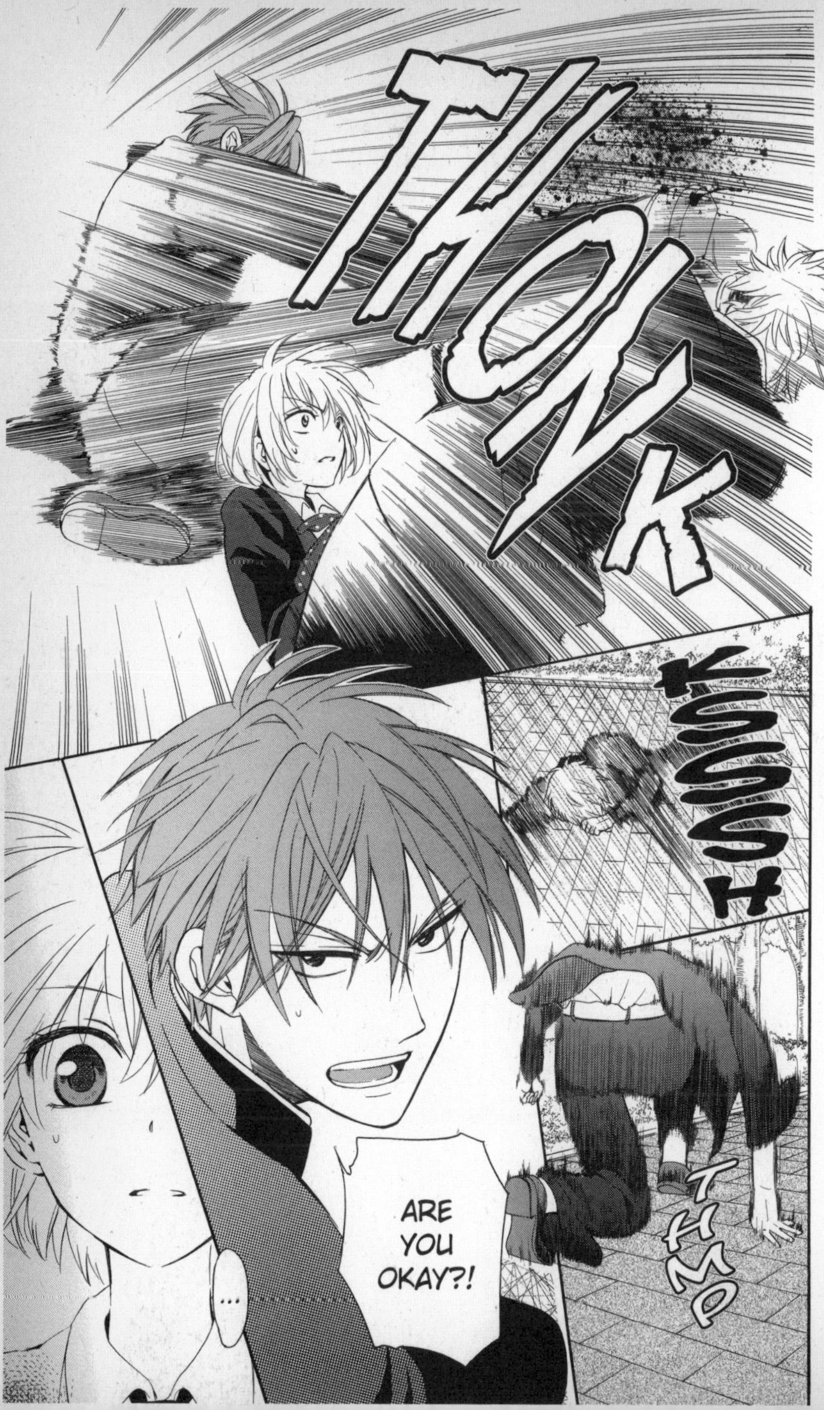
THONK
KSSSH
THMP
ARE YOU OKAY?!
...

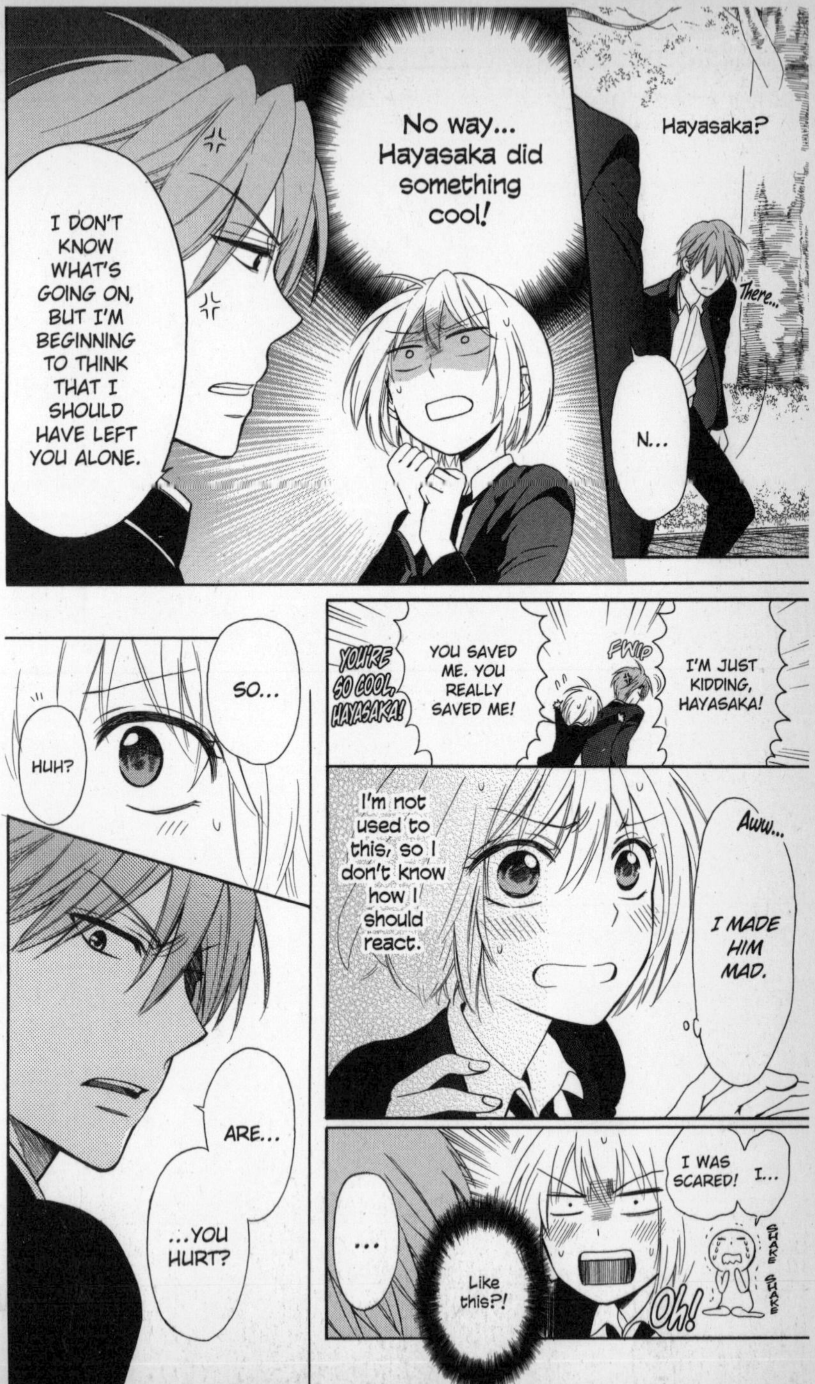
Hayasaka?
There...
N...
No way... Hayasaka did something cool!
I DON'T KNOW WHAT'S GOING ON, BUT I'M BEGINNING TO THINK THAT I SHOULD HAVE LEFT YOU ALONE.
I'M JUST KIDDING, HAYASAKA!
FWIP
YOU SAVED ME. YOU REALLY SAVED ME!
YOU'RE SO COOL, HAYASAKA!
Aww...
I MADE HIM MAD.
I'm not used to this, so I don't know how I should react.
I WAS SCARED! I...
SHAKE SHAKE
Oh!
Like this?!
...
SO...
HUH?
ARE...
...YOU HURT?

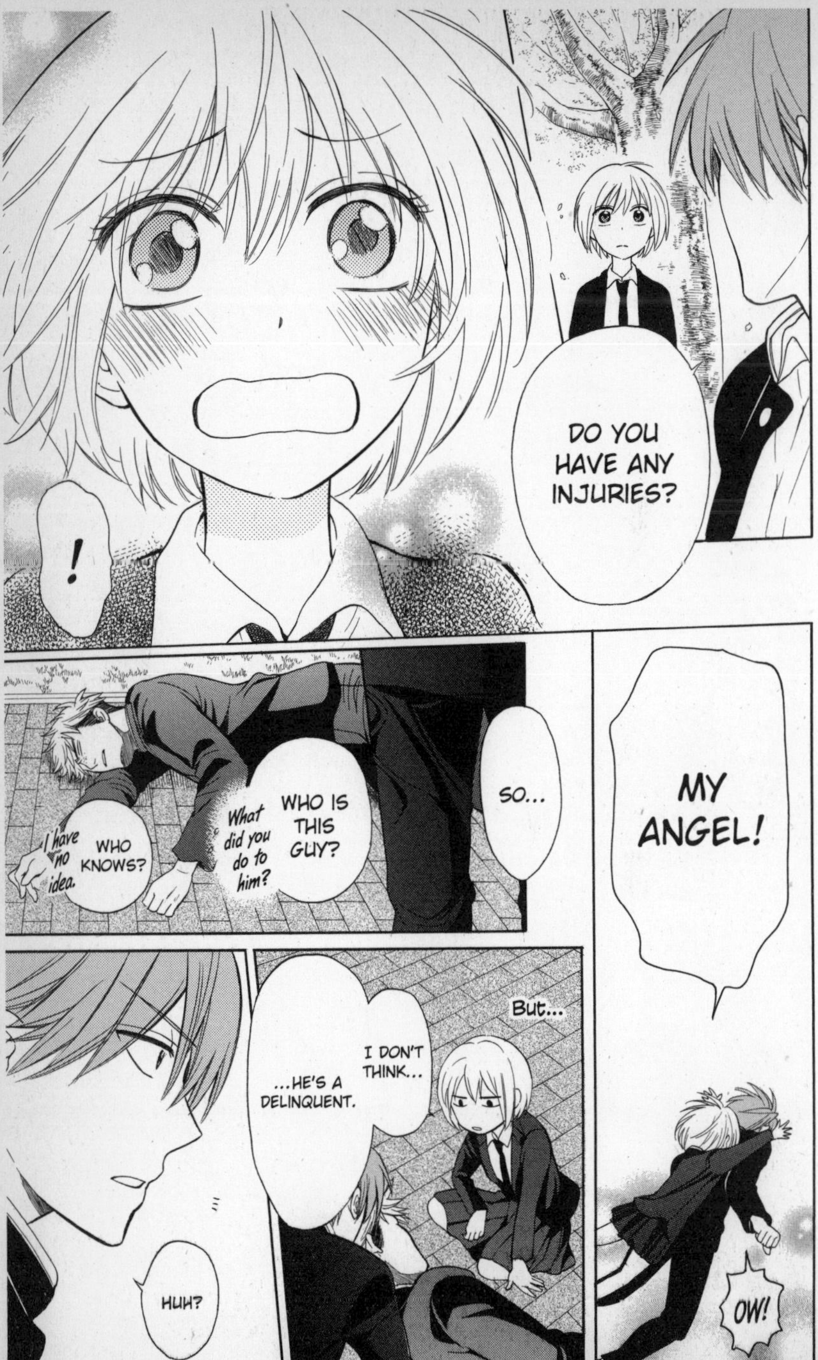
DO YOU HAVE ANY INJURIES?
!
MY ANGEL!
OW!
SO...
WHO IS THIS GUY?
What did you do to him?
WHO KNOWS?
I have no idea.
But...
I DON'T THINK...
...HE'S A DELINQUENT.
HUH?

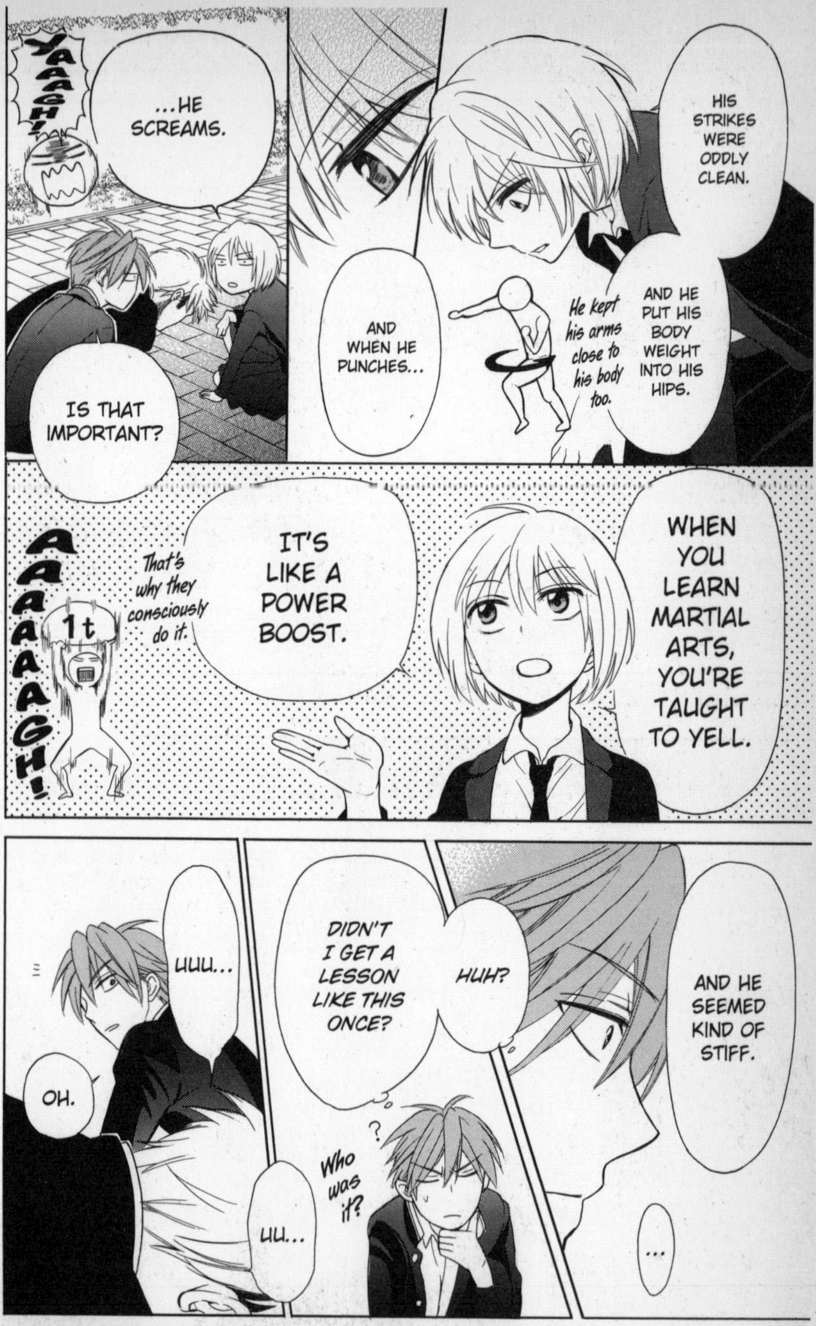
HIS STRIKES WERE ODDLY CLEAN.
AND HE PUT HIS BODY WEIGHT INTO HIS HIPS.
He kept his arms close to his body too.
AND WHEN HE PUNCHES...
...HE SCREAMS.
YAAAGH!
IS THAT IMPORTANT?
WHEN YOU LEARN MARTIAL ARTS, YOU'RE TAUGHT TO YELL.
IT'S LIKE A POWER BOOST.
That's why they consciously do it.
1t
AAAAAAAAGH!
AND HE SEEMED KIND OF STIFF.
...
HUH?
DIDN'T I GET A LESSON LIKE THIS ONCE?
Who was it?
UUU...
OH.
UU...

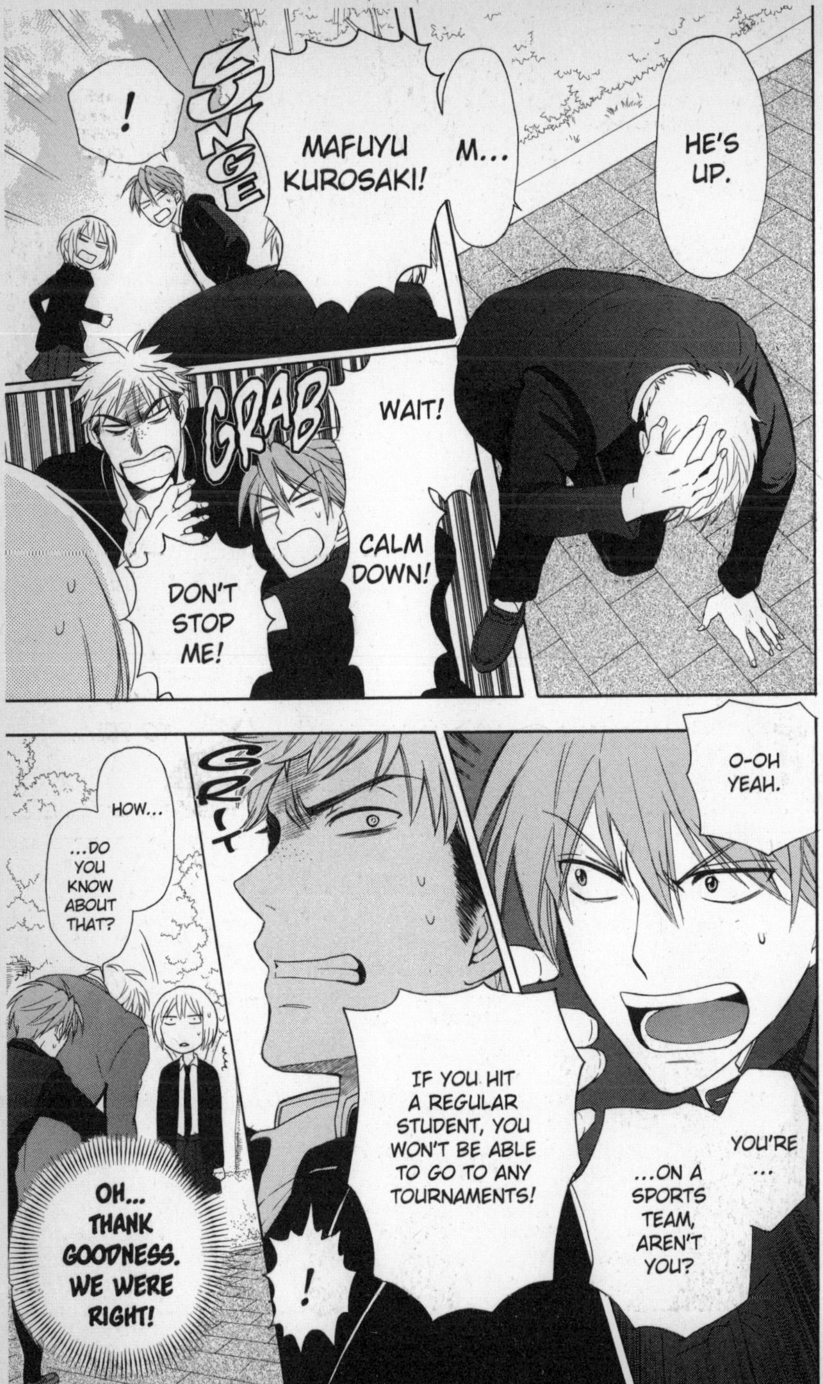
HE'S UP.
M...
MAFUYU KUROSAKI!
LUNGE
!
WAIT!
CALM DOWN!
GRAB
DON'T STOP ME!
O-OH YEAH.
YOU'RE ...
...ON A SPORTS TEAM, AREN'T YOU?
GRIT
IF YOU HIT A REGULAR STUDENT, YOU WON'T BE ABLE TO GO TO ANY TOURNAMENTS!
!
HOW...
...DO YOU KNOW ABOUT THAT?
OH... THANK GOODNESS. WE WERE RIGHT!

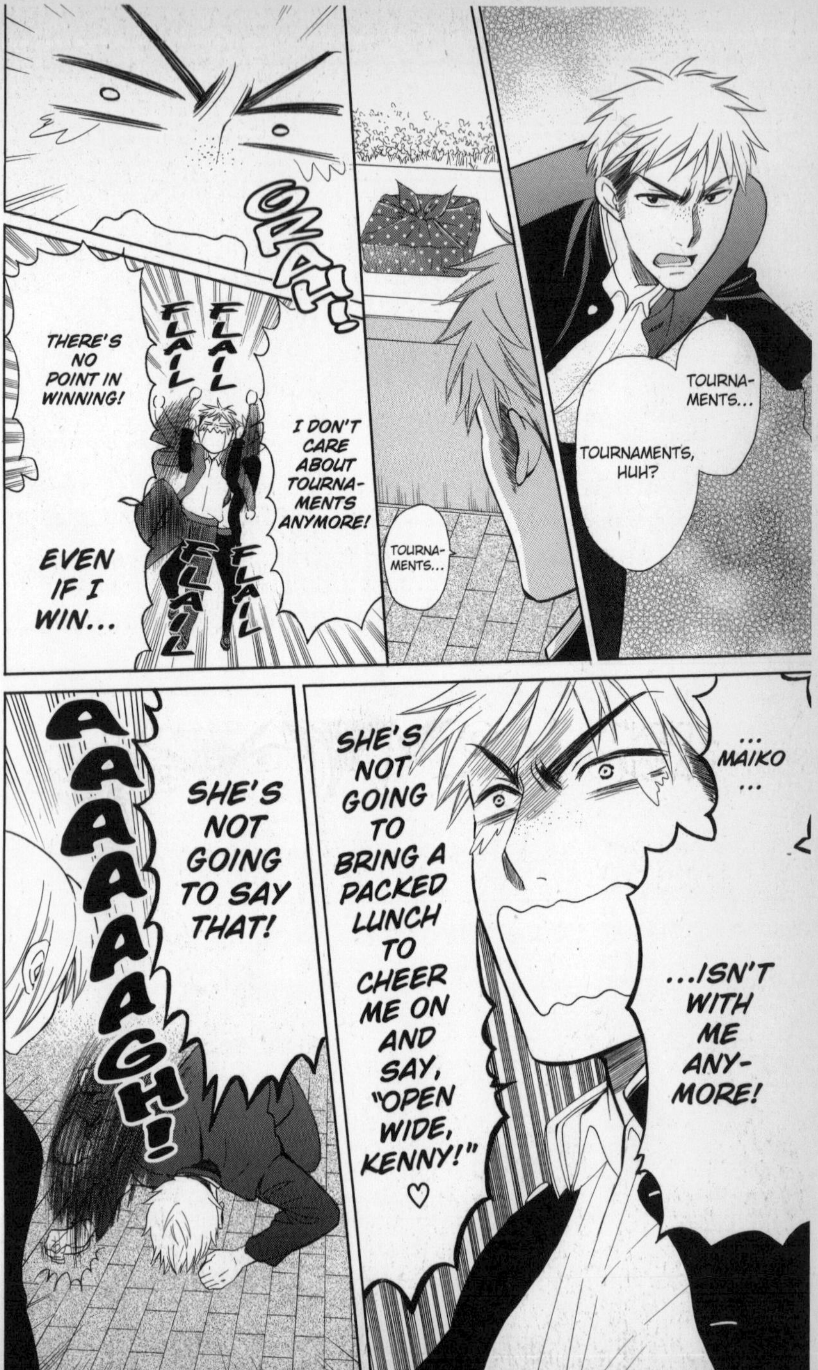
TOURNAMENTS...
TOURNAMENTS, HUH?
TOURNAMENTS...
I DON'T CARE ABOUT TOURNAMENTS ANYMORE!
FLAIL FLAIL
THERE'S NO POINT IN WINNING!
FLAIL FLAIL
EVEN IF I WIN...
...MAIKO...
...ISN'T WITH ME ANYMORE!
SHE'S NOT GOING TO BRING A PACKED LUNCH TO CHEER ME ON AND SAY, "OPEN WIDE, KENNY!" ♡
SHE'S NOT GOING TO SAY THAT!
AAAAAAAGH!

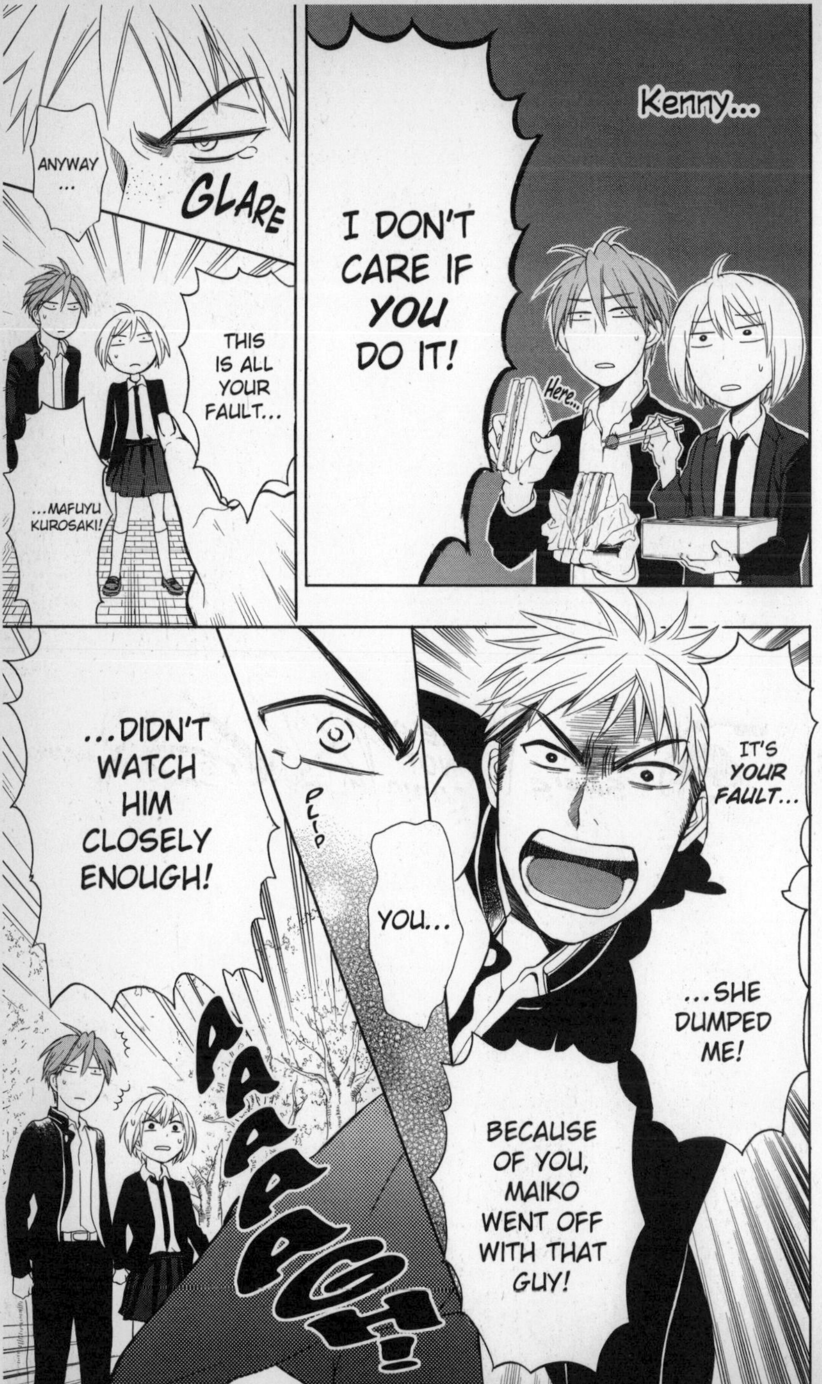
Kenny...
I DON'T CARE IF YOU DO IT!
Here...
ANYWAY...
GLARE
THIS IS ALL YOUR FAULT...
...MAFUYU KUROSAKI!
IT'S YOUR FAULT...
YOU...
...DIDN'T WATCH HIM CLOSELY ENOUGH!
PLIP
...SHE DUMPED ME!
BECAUSE OF YOU, MAIKO WENT OFF WITH THAT GUY!
PAAAACH!

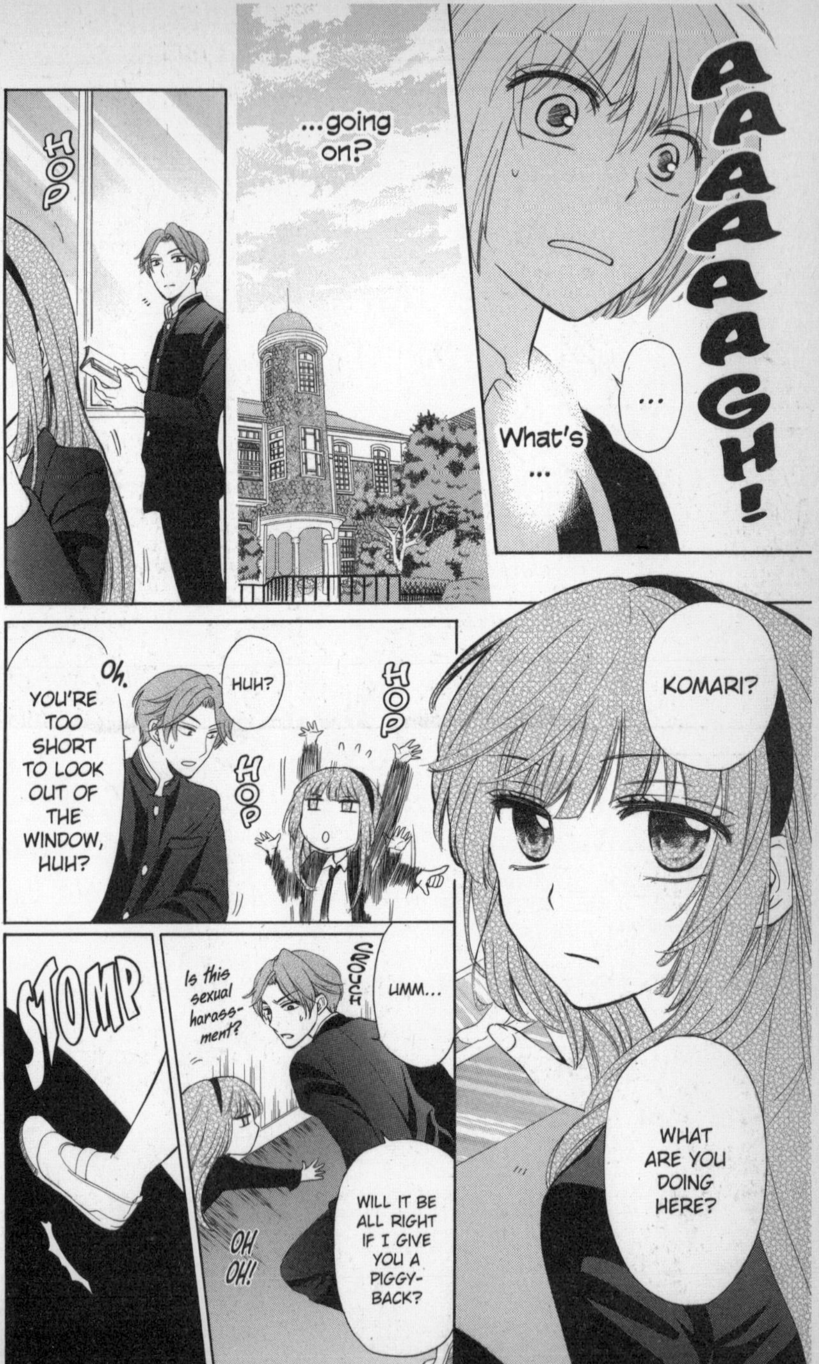
AAAAAAGH!
...
What's ...
...going on?
HOP
KOMARI?
WHAT ARE YOU DOING HERE?
HOP HOP
HUH?
Oh.
YOU'RE TOO SHORT TO LOOK OUT OF THE WINDOW, HUH?
UMM...
CROUCH
Is this sexual harass-ment?
WILL IT BE ALL RIGHT IF I GIVE YOU A PIGGY-BACK?
OH OH!
STOMP

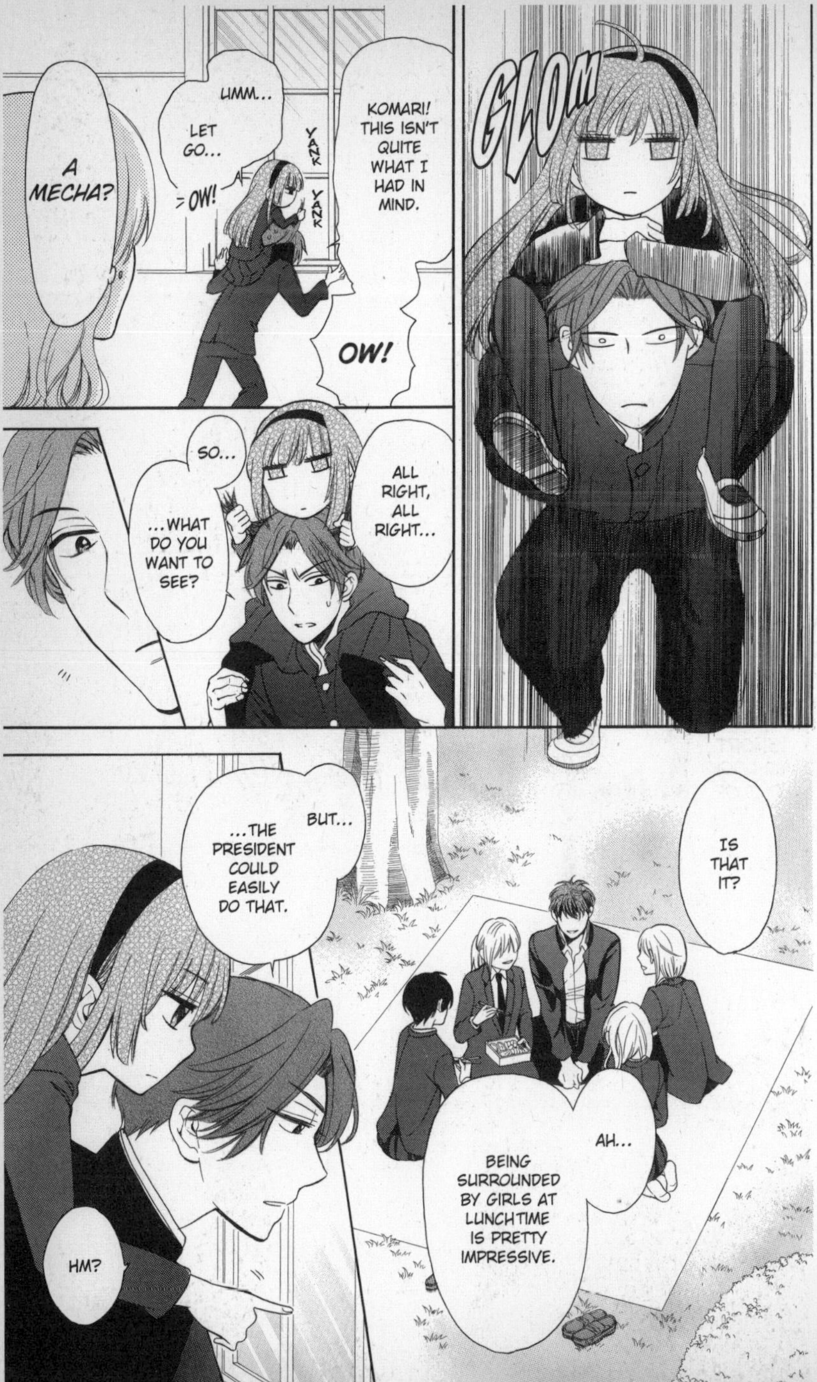
GLOM
KOMARI! THIS ISN'T QUITE WHAT I HAD IN MIND.
YANK
YANK
UMM...
LET GO...
OW!
OW!
A MECHA?
ALL RIGHT, ALL RIGHT...
SO...
...WHAT DO YOU WANT TO SEE?
IS THAT IT?
BUT...
...THE PRESIDENT COULD EASILY DO THAT.
AH...
BEING SURROUNDED BY GIRLS AT LUNCHTIME IS PRETTY IMPRESSIVE.
HM?

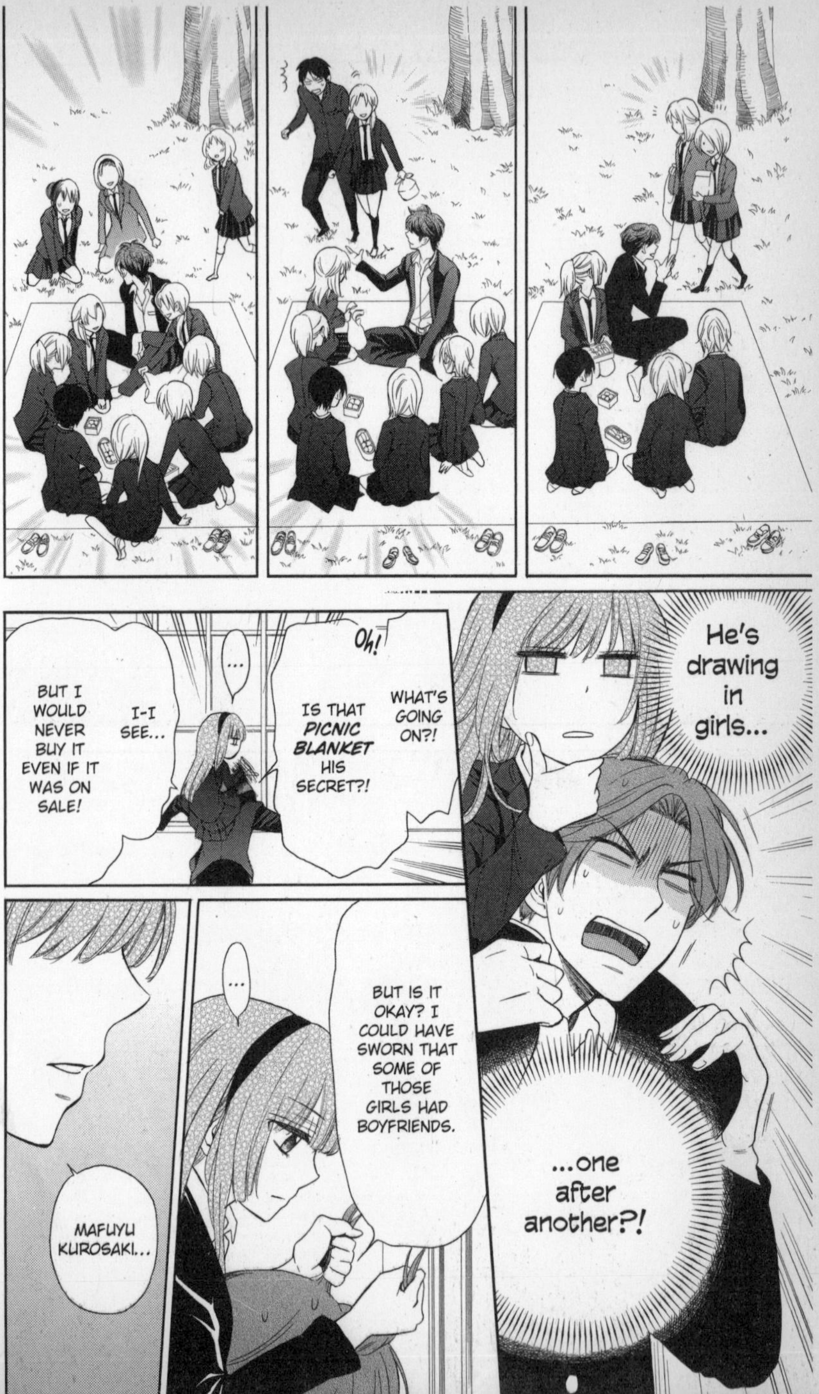
He's drawing in girls...
...one after another?!
WHAT'S GOING ON?!
Oh!
IS THAT PICNIC BLANKET HIS SECRET?!
...
I-I SEE...
BUT I WOULD NEVER BUY IT EVEN IF IT WAS ON SALE!
...
BUT IS IT OKAY? I COULD HAVE SWORN THAT SOME OF THOSE GIRLS HAD BOYFRIENDS.
MAFUYU KUROSAKI...

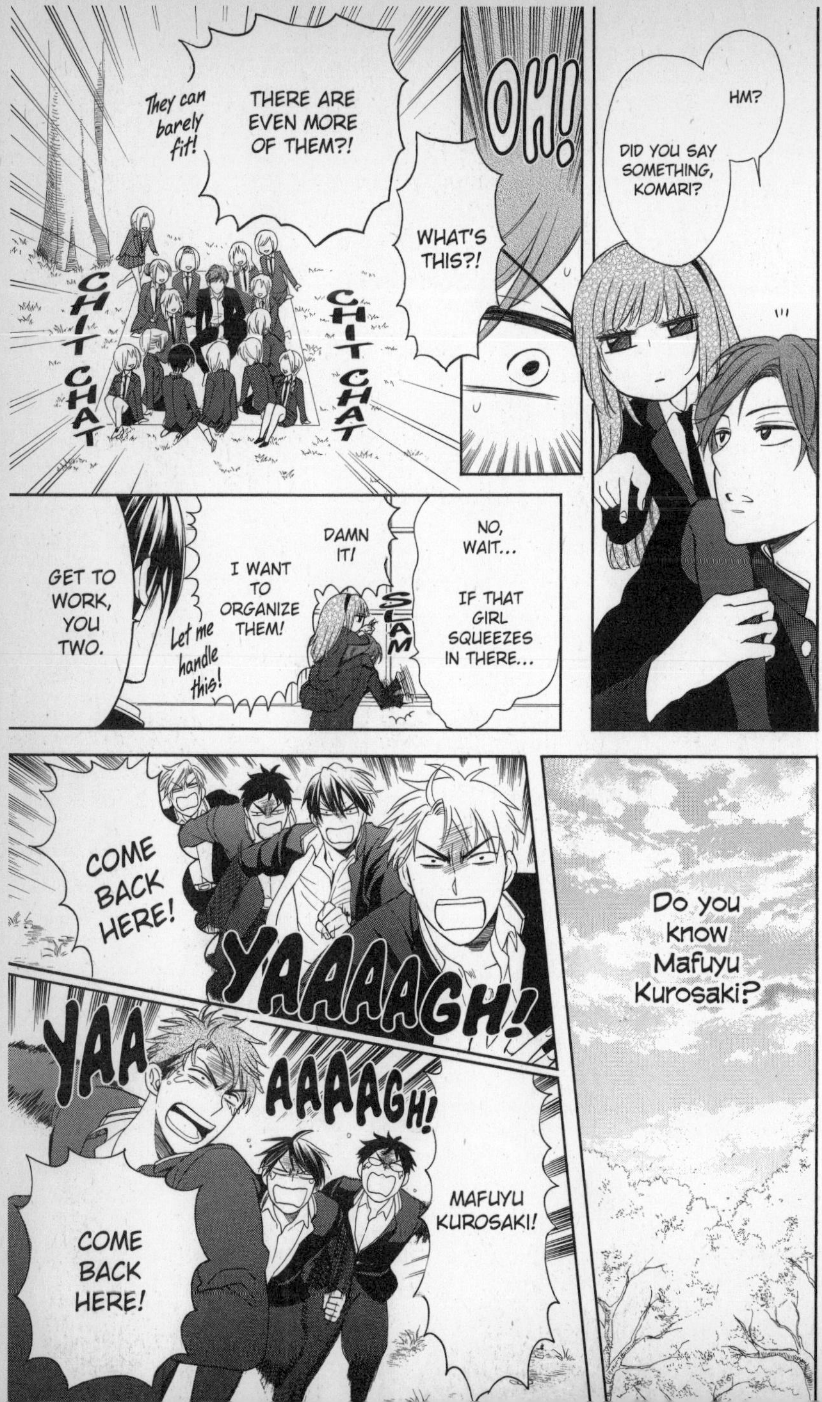
HM?
DID YOU SAY SOMETHING, KOMARI?
OH!
WHAT'S THIS?!
THERE ARE EVEN MORE OF THEM?!
They can barely fit!
CHIT CHAT
CHIT CHAT
NO, WAIT...
IF THAT GIRL SQUEEZES IN THERE...
SLAM
DAMN IT!
I WANT TO ORGANIZE THEM!
Let me handle this!
GET TO WORK, YOU TWO.
Do you know Mafuyu Kurosaki?
COME BACK HERE!
YAAAAAGH!
YAAAAAAGH!
MAFUYU KUROSAKI!
COME BACK HERE!

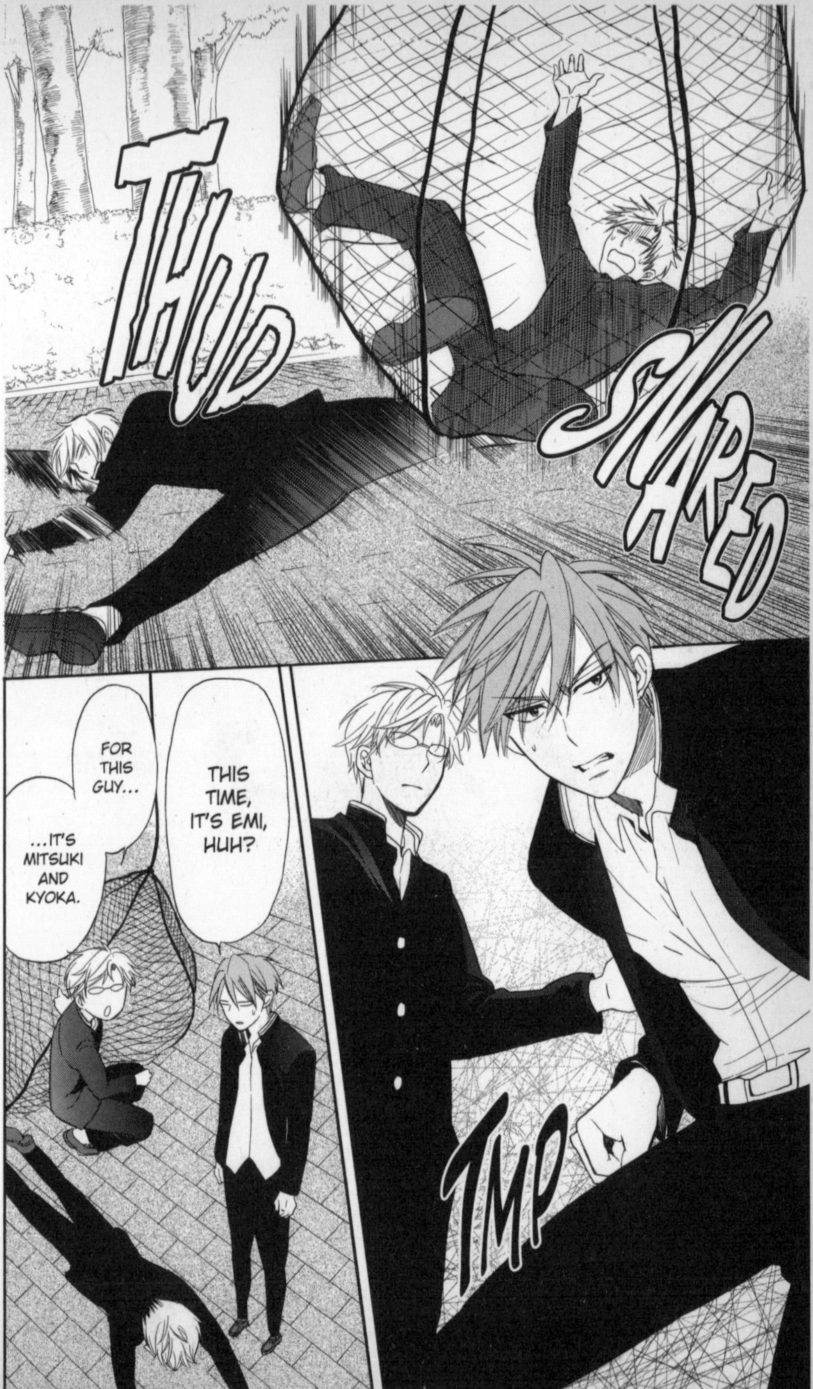
SNARED
THUD
TMP
THIS TIME, IT'S EMI, HUH?
FOR THIS GUY...
...IT'S MITSUKI AND KYOKA.

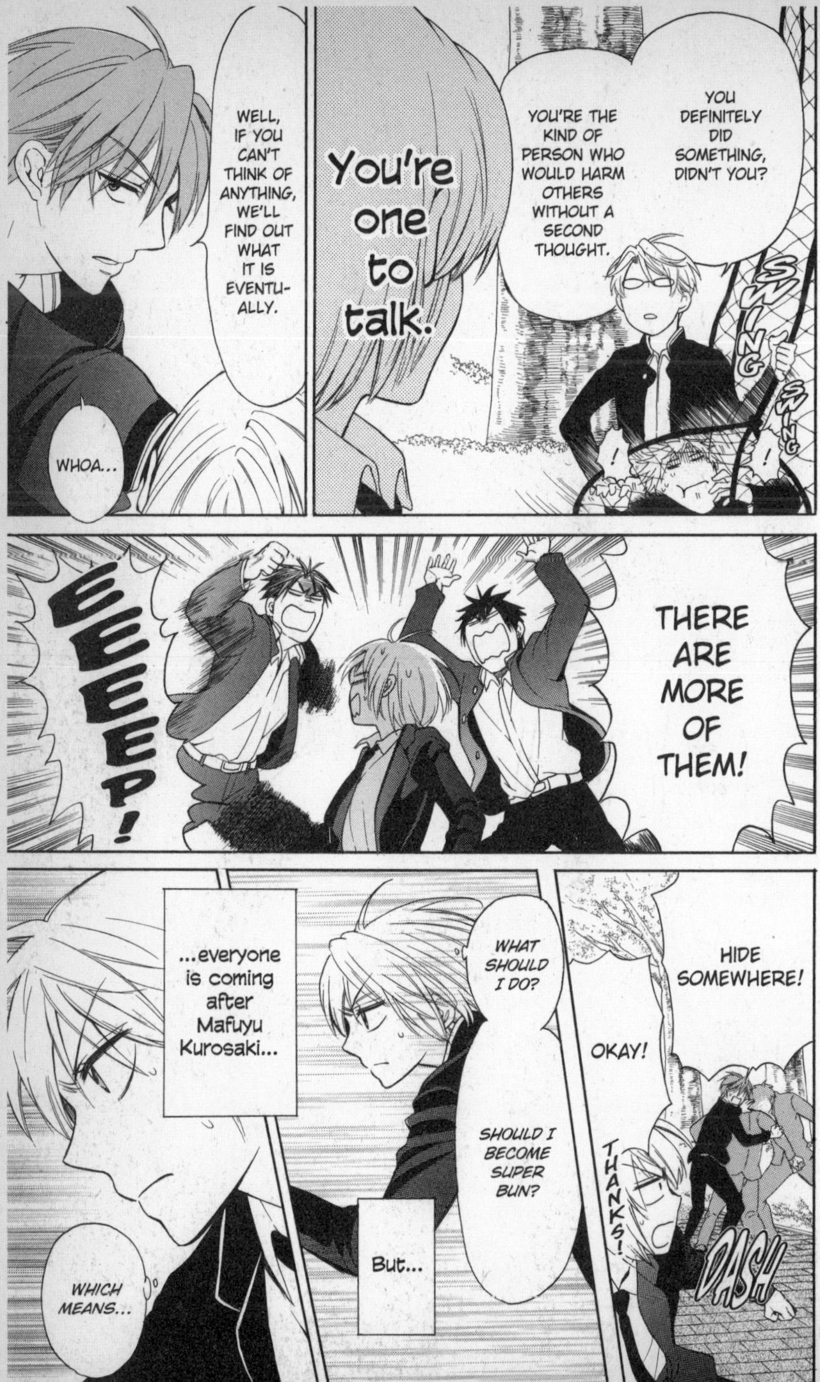
YOU DEFINITELY DID SOMETHING, DIDN'T YOU?
YOU'RE THE KIND OF PERSON WHO WOULD HARM OTHERS WITHOUT A SECOND THOUGHT.
SWING
SWING
!
!
You're one to talk.
WELL, IF YOU CAN'T THINK OF ANYTHING, WE'LL FIND OUT WHAT IT IS EVENTUALLY.
WHOA...
THERE ARE MORE OF THEM!
EEEEEP!
HIDE SOMEWHERE!
OKAY!
THANKS!
DASH
WHAT SHOULD I DO?
...everyone is coming after Mafuyu Kurosaki...
SHOULD I BECOME SUPER BUN?
But...
WHICH MEANS...

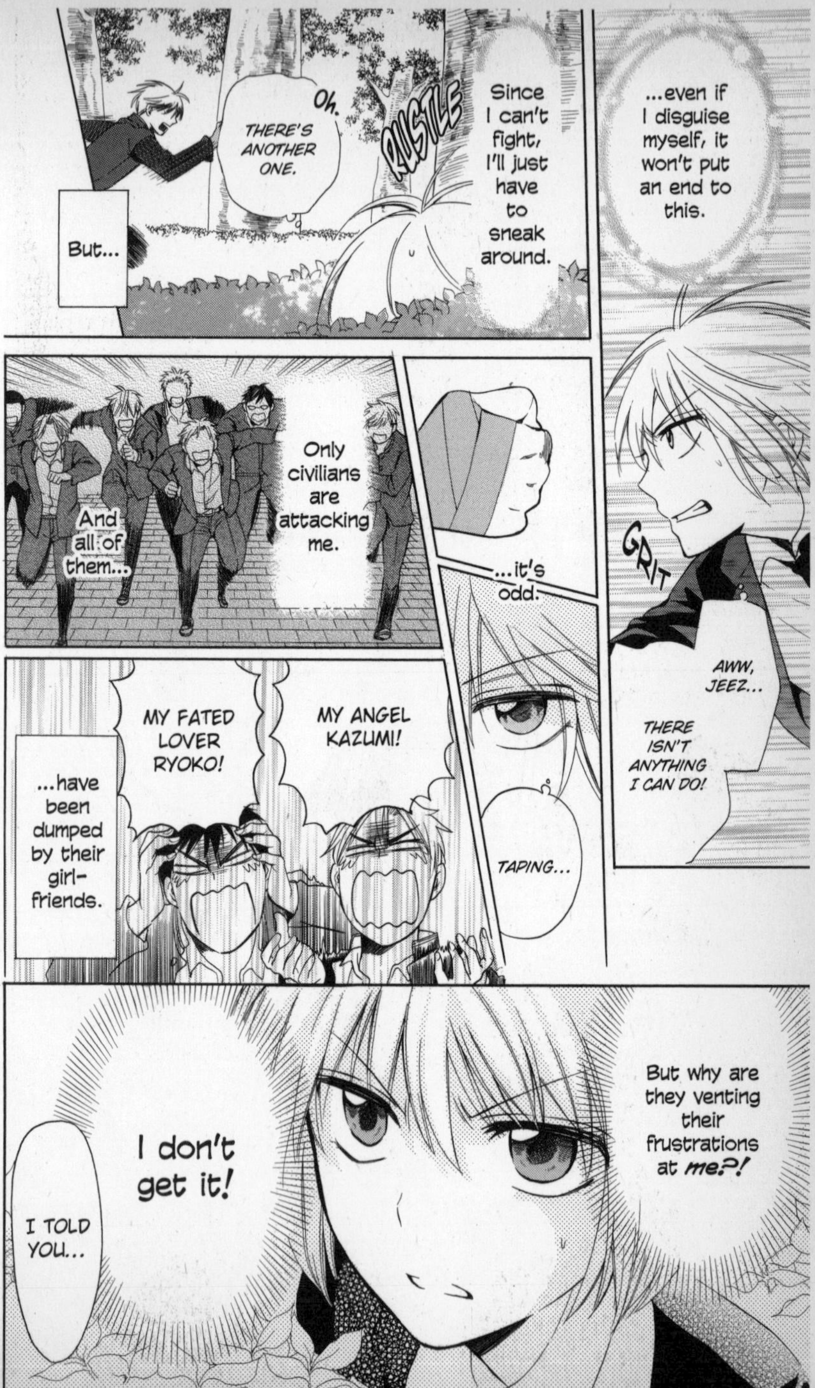
Since I can't fight, I'll just have to sneak around.
RUSTLE
Oh.
THERE'S ANOTHER ONE.
But...
...even if I disguise myself, it won't put an end to this.
GRIT
AWW, JEEZ...
THERE ISN'T ANYTHING I CAN DO!
...it's odd.
Only civilians are attacking me.
And all of them...
TAPING...
MY ANGEL KAZUMI!
MY FATED LOVER RYOKO!
...have been dumped by their girl-friends.
But why are they venting their frustrations at *me*?!
I don't get it!
I TOLD YOU...

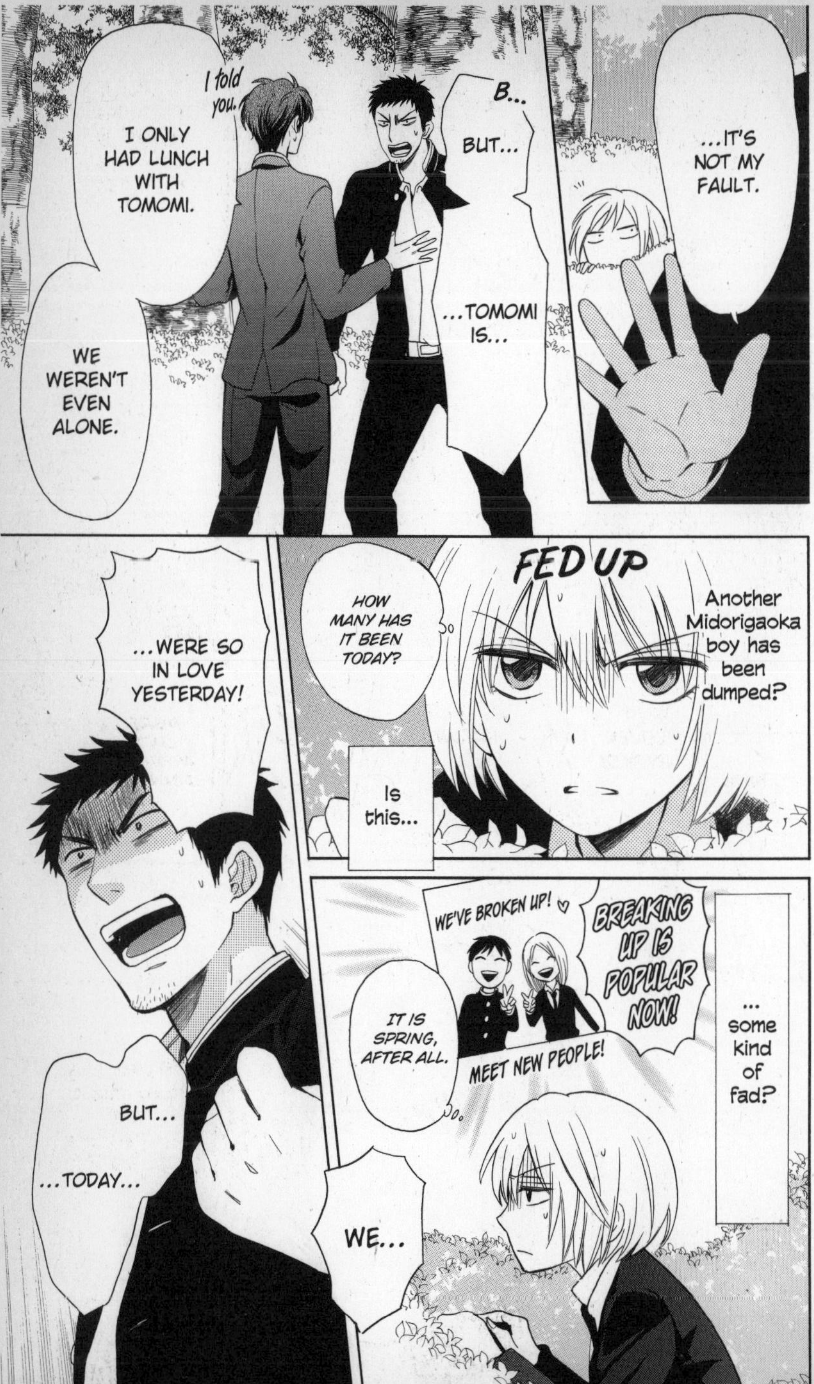
...IT'S NOT MY FAULT.
B...
BUT...
...TOMOMI IS...
I told you.
I ONLY HAD LUNCH WITH TOMOMI.
WE WEREN'T EVEN ALONE.
FED UP
Another Midorigaoka boy has been dumped?
HOW MANY HAS IT BEEN TODAY?
Is this...
... some kind of fad?
BREAKING UP IS POPULAR NOW!
WE'VE BROKEN UP!
IT IS SPRING, AFTER ALL.
MEET NEW PEOPLE!
WE...
...WERE SO IN LOVE YESTERDAY!
BUT...
...TODAY...

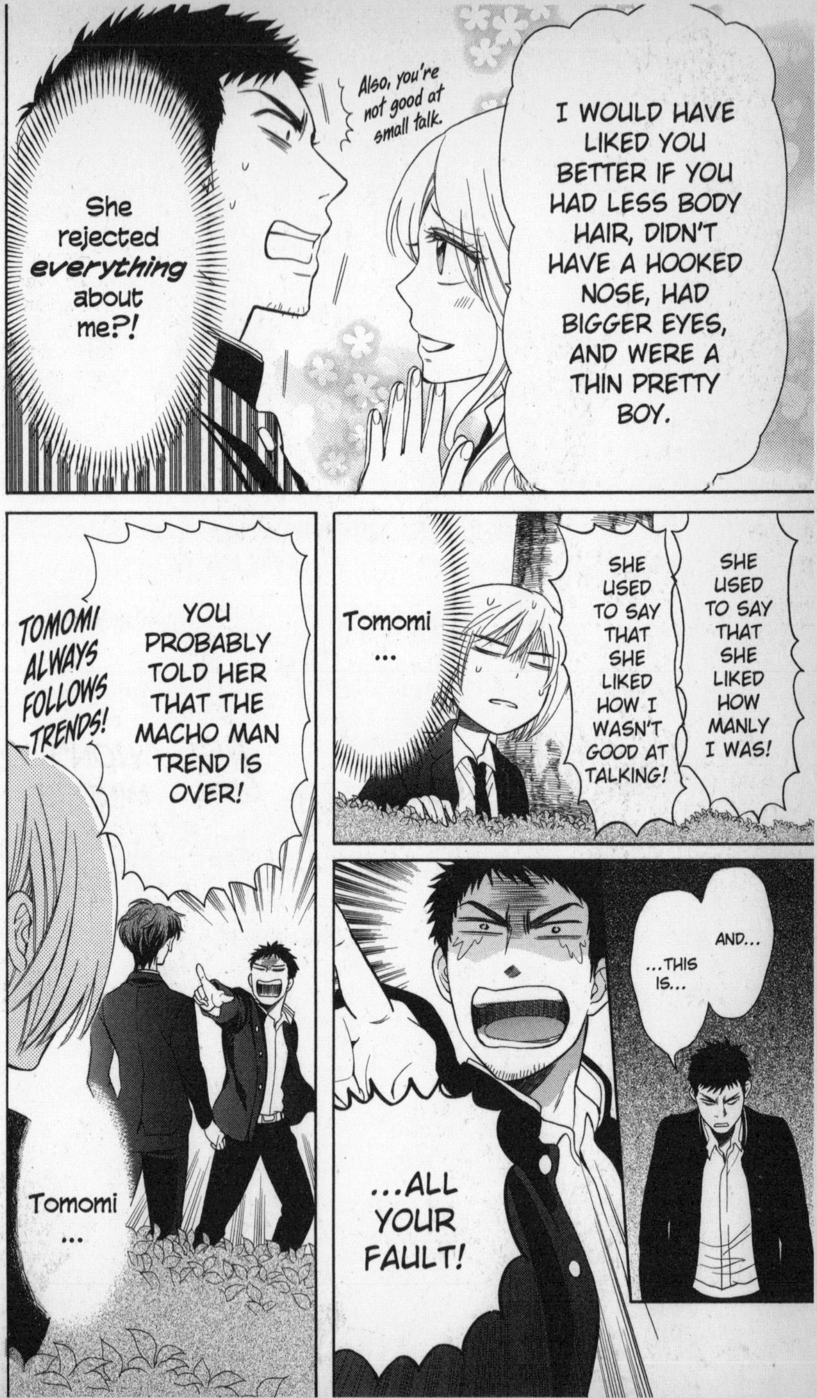
I WOULD HAVE LIKED YOU BETTER IF YOU HAD LESS BODY HAIR, DIDN'T HAVE A HOOKED NOSE, HAD BIGGER EYES, AND WERE A THIN PRETTY BOY.
Also, you're not good at small talk.
She rejected *everything* about me?!
SHE USED TO SAY THAT SHE LIKED HOW MANLY I WAS!
SHE USED TO SAY THAT SHE LIKED HOW I WASN'T GOOD AT TALKING!
Tomomi ...
AND...
...THIS IS...
...ALL YOUR FAULT!
YOU PROBABLY TOLD HER THAT THE MACHO MAN TREND IS OVER!
TOMOMI ALWAYS FOLLOWS TRENDS!
Tomomi ...

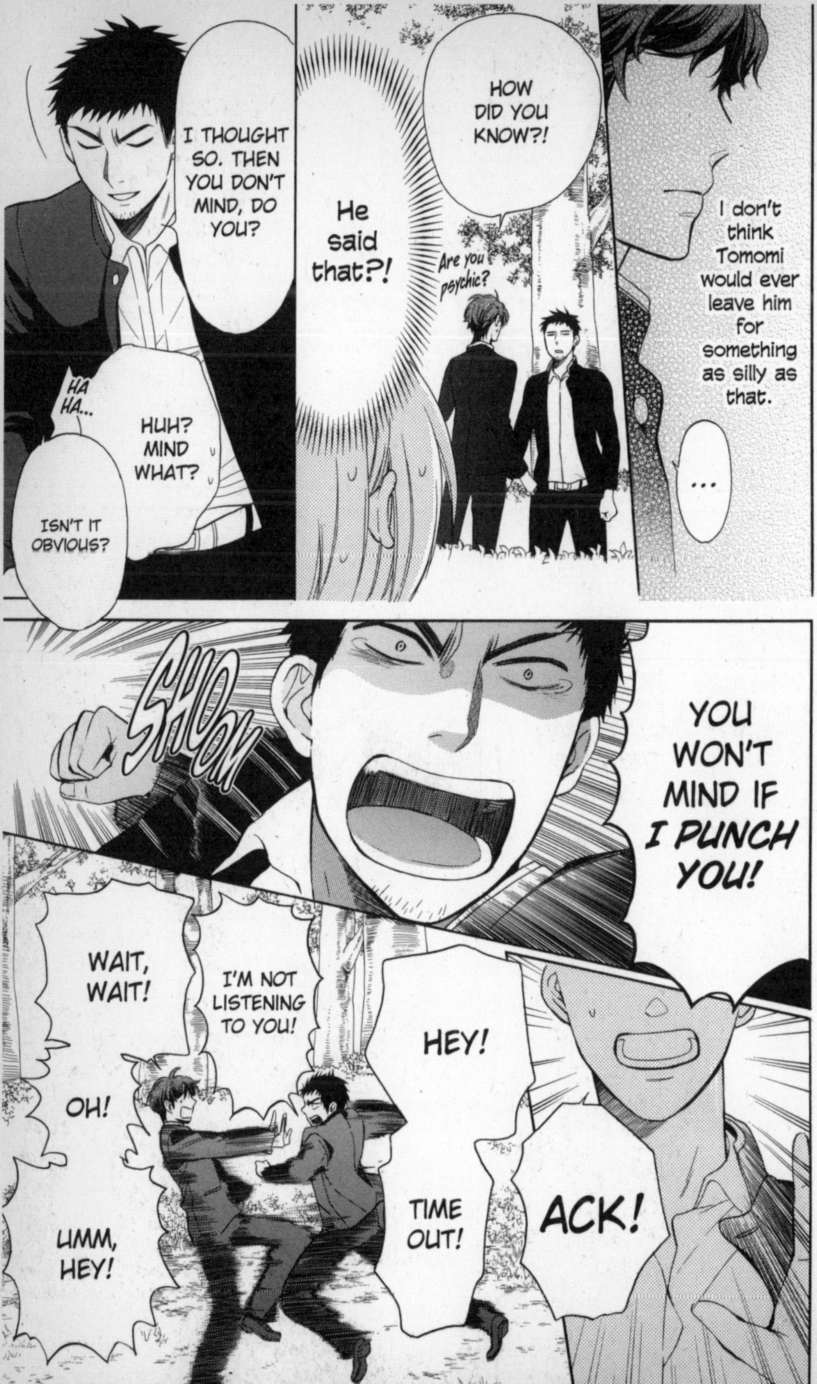
I don't think Tomomi would ever leave him for something as silly as that.
...
HOW DID YOU KNOW?!
Are you psychic?
He said that?!
I THOUGHT SO. THEN YOU DON'T MIND, DO YOU?
HUH? MIND WHAT?
HA HA...
ISN'T IT OBVIOUS?
YOU WON'T MIND IF *I PUNCH YOU!*
SHOOM
ACK!
HEY!
TIME OUT!
I'M NOT LISTENING TO YOU!
WAIT, WAIT!
OH!
UMM, HEY!

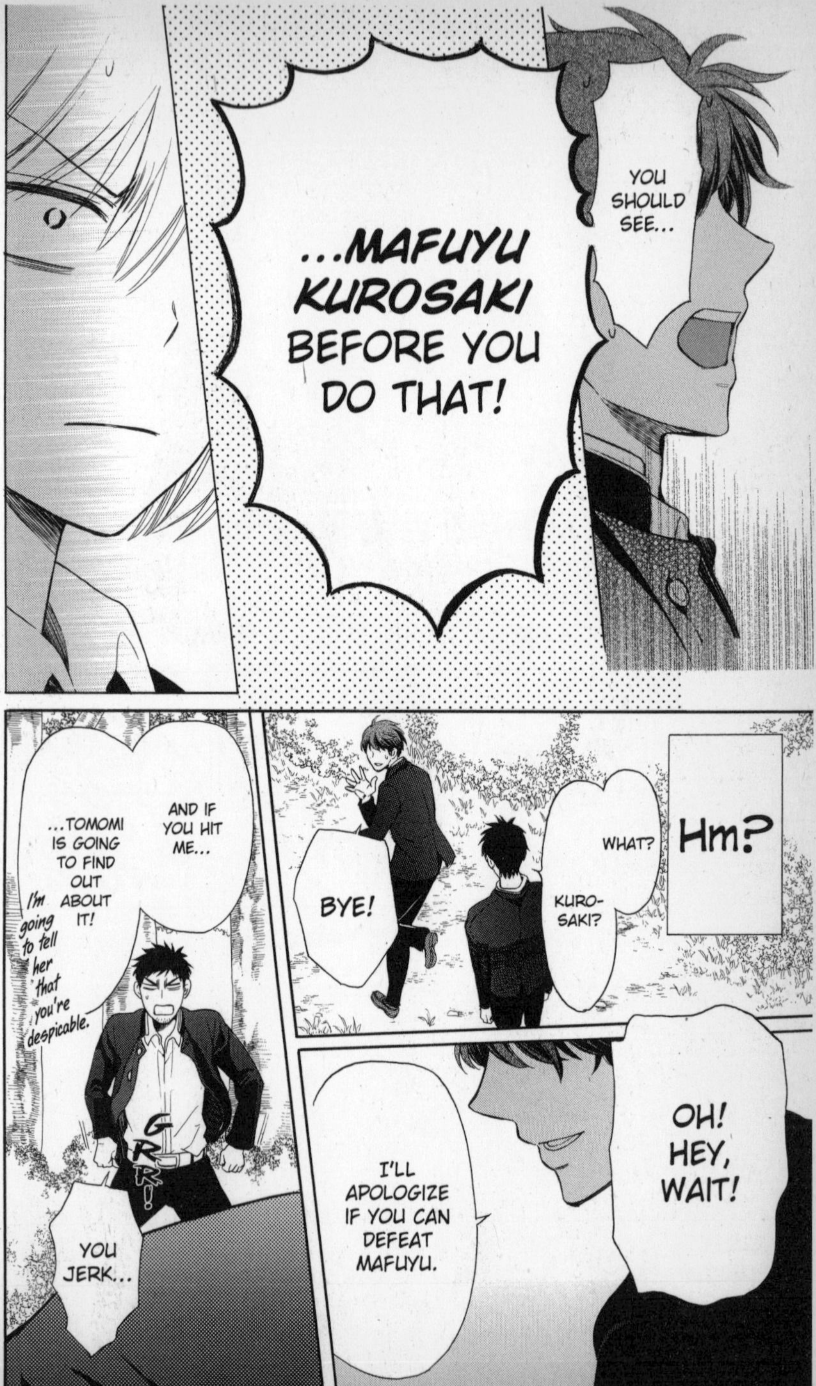
YOU SHOULD SEE...
...MAFUYU KUROSAKI BEFORE YOU DO THAT!
Hm?
WHAT? KURO-SAKI?
BYE!
OH! HEY, WAIT!
I'LL APOLOGIZE IF YOU CAN DEFEAT MAFUYU.
AND IF YOU HIT ME...
...TOMOMI IS GOING TO FIND OUT ABOUT IT!
I'm going to tell her that you're despicable.
GRR!
YOU JERK...

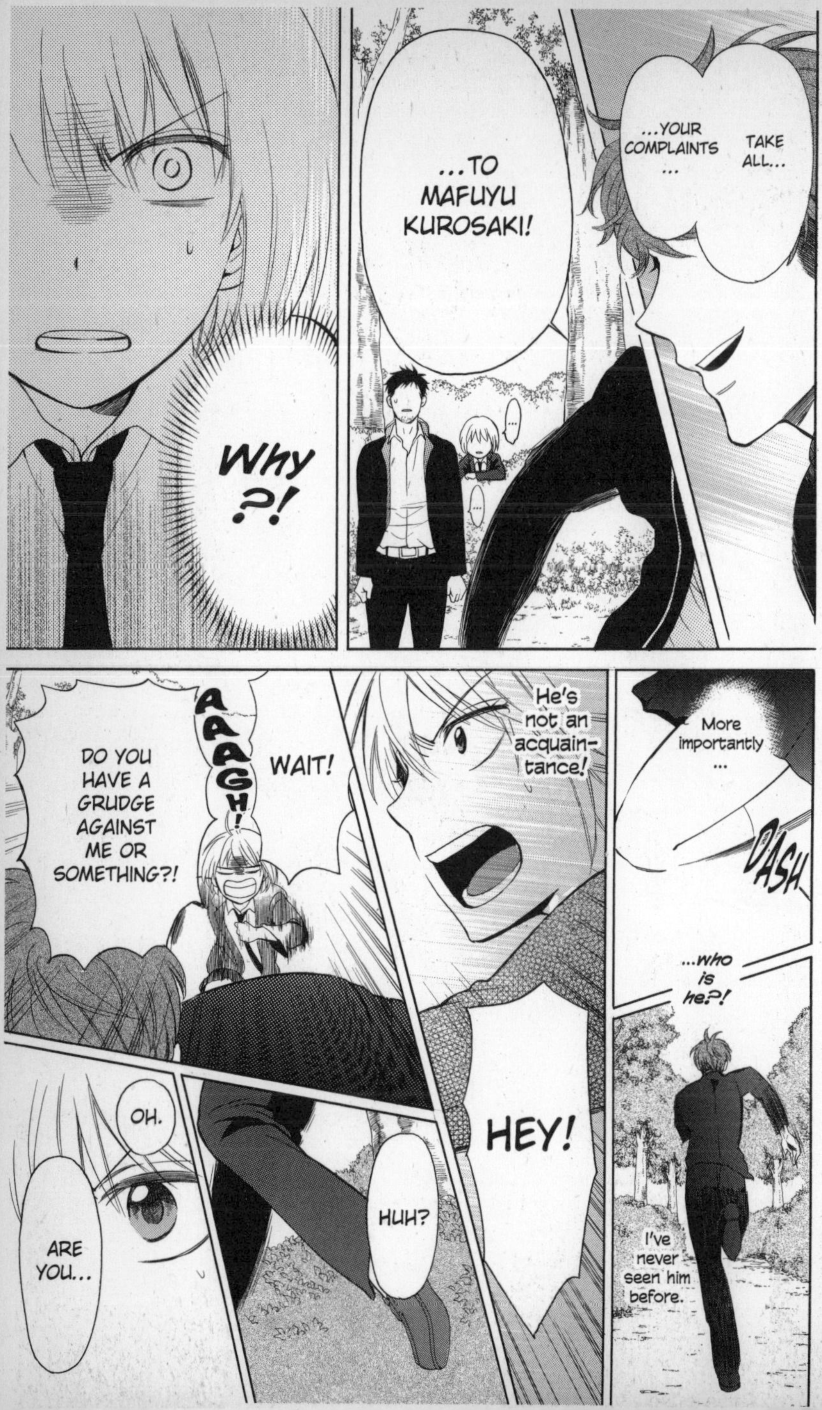
TAKE ALL...
...YOUR COMPLAINTS ...
...TO MAFUYU KUROSAKI!
...
...
Why?!
More importantly ...
DASH
...who is he?!
I've never seen him before.
He's not an acquaintance!
HEY!
WAIT!
AAAGH!
DO YOU HAVE A GRUDGE AGAINST ME OR SOMETHING?!
HUH?
OH.
ARE YOU...

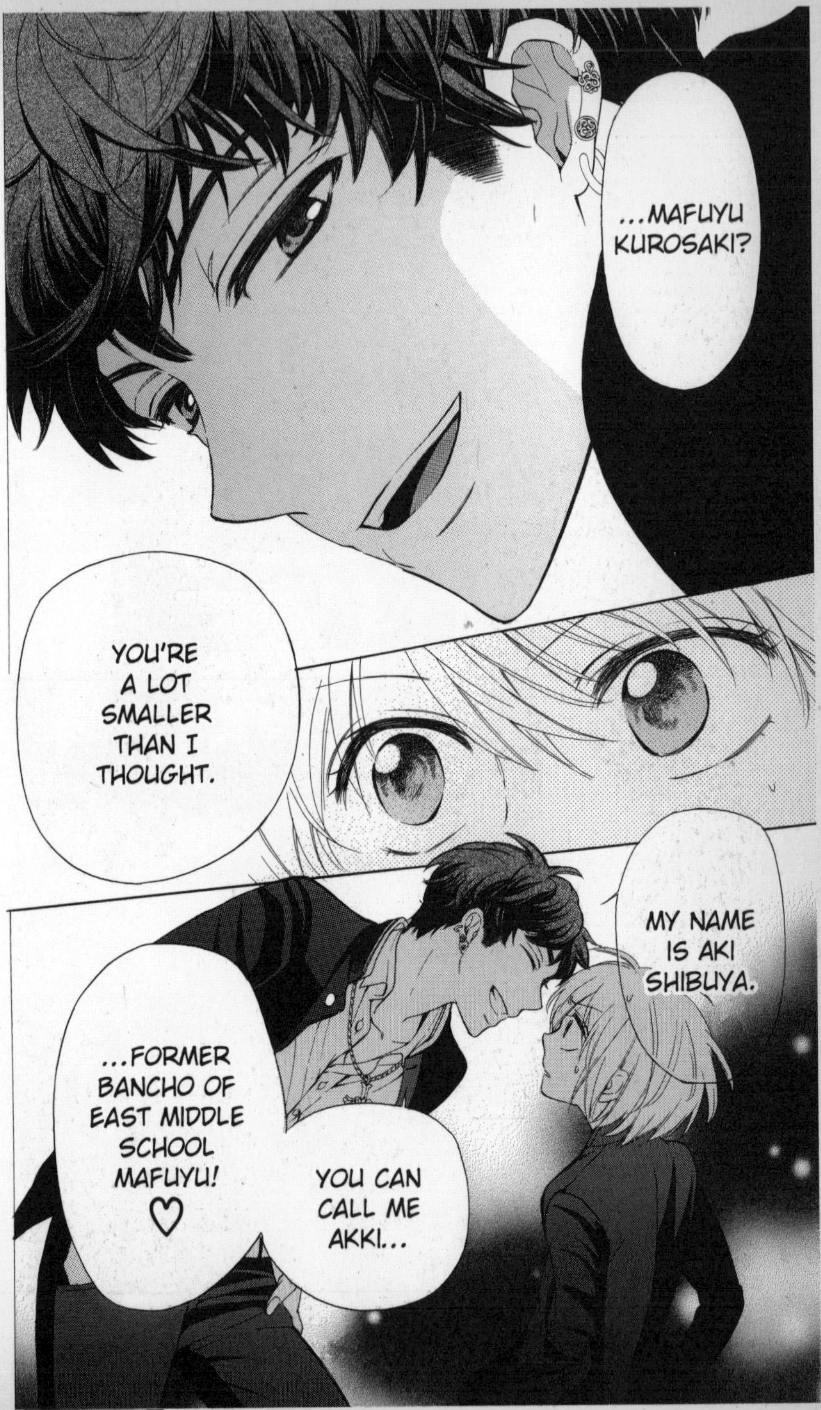
...MAFUYU KUROSAKI?
YOU'RE A LOT SMALLER THAN I THOUGHT.
MY NAME IS AKI SHIBUYA.
YOU CAN CALL ME AKKI...
...FORMER BANCHO OF EAST MIDDLE SCHOOL MAFUYU! ♡

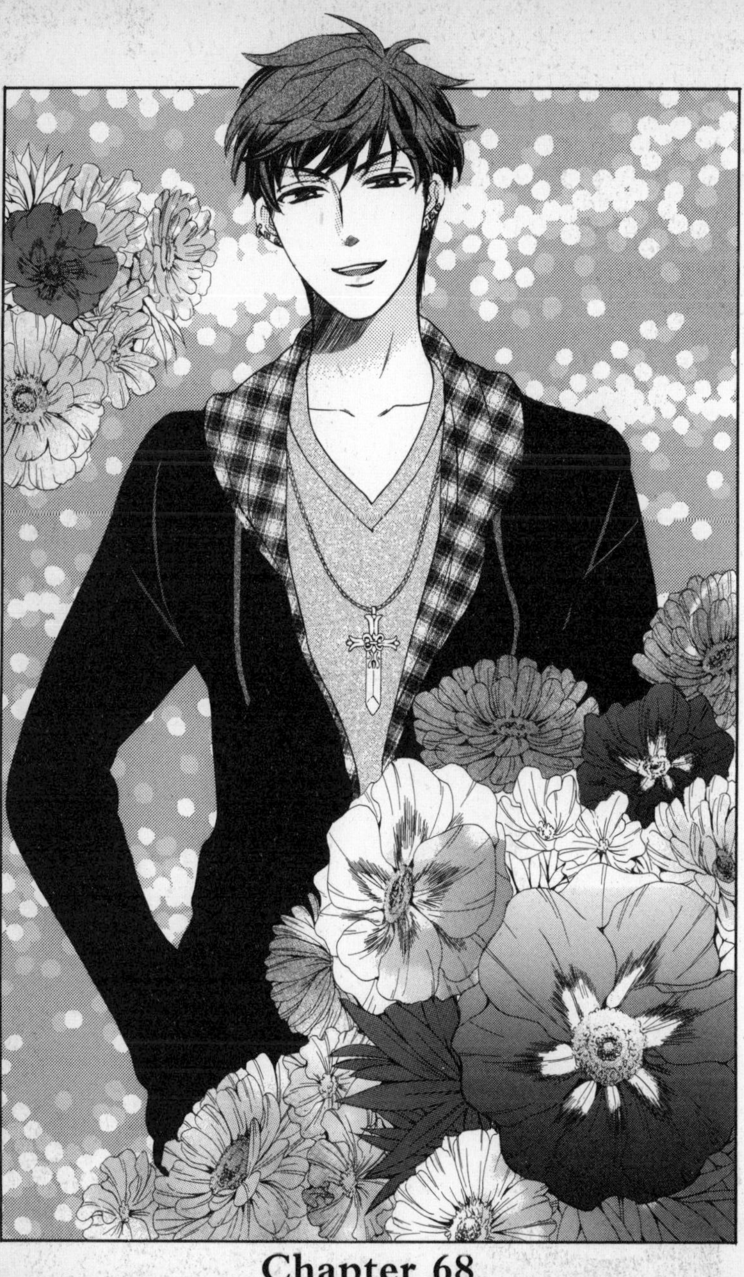

Chapter 68

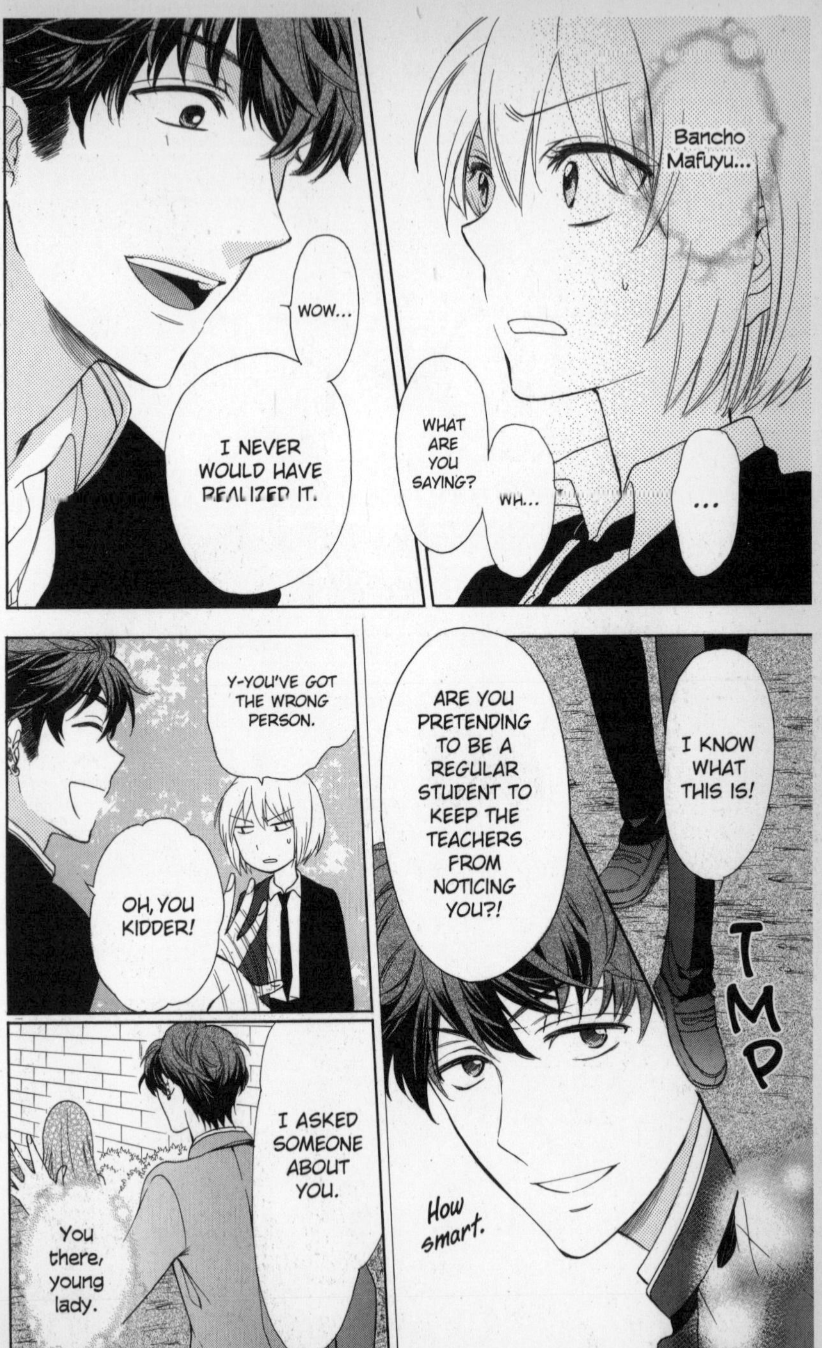
Bancho Mafuyu...
...
WH...
WHAT ARE YOU SAYING?
WOW...
I NEVER WOULD HAVE REALIZED IT.
I KNOW WHAT THIS IS!
TMP
ARE YOU PRETENDING TO BE A REGULAR STUDENT TO KEEP THE TEACHERS FROM NOTICING YOU?!
How smart.
Y-YOU'VE GOT THE WRONG PERSON.
OH, YOU KIDDER!
I ASKED SOMEONE ABOUT YOU.
You there, young lady.

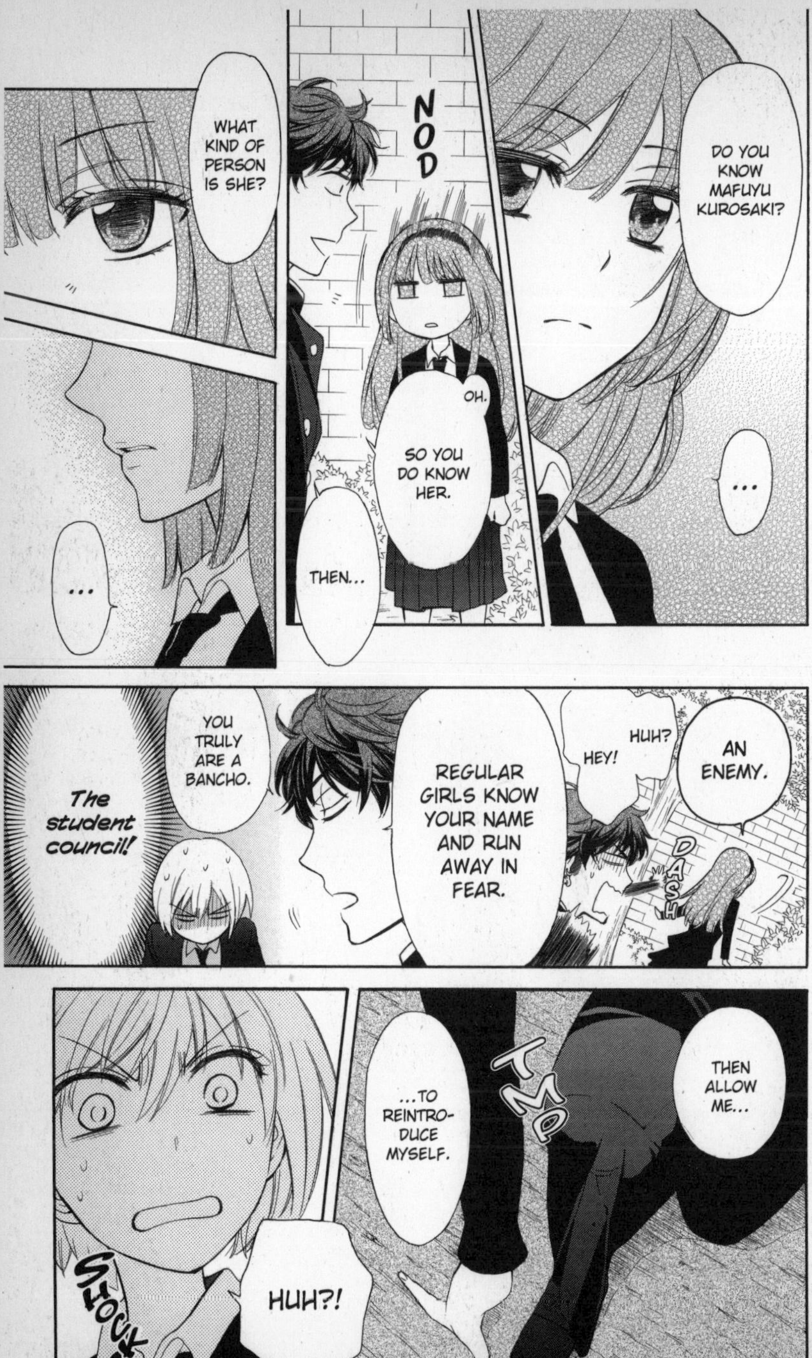
DO YOU KNOW MAFUYU KUROSAKI?
...
NOD
OH.
SO YOU DO KNOW HER.
THEN...
WHAT KIND OF PERSON IS SHE?
...
AN ENEMY.
HUH?
HEY!
DASH
REGULAR GIRLS KNOW YOUR NAME AND RUN AWAY IN FEAR.
YOU TRULY ARE A BANCHO.
The student council!
THEN ALLOW ME...
TMP
...TO REINTRODUCE MYSELF.
HUH?!
SHOCK

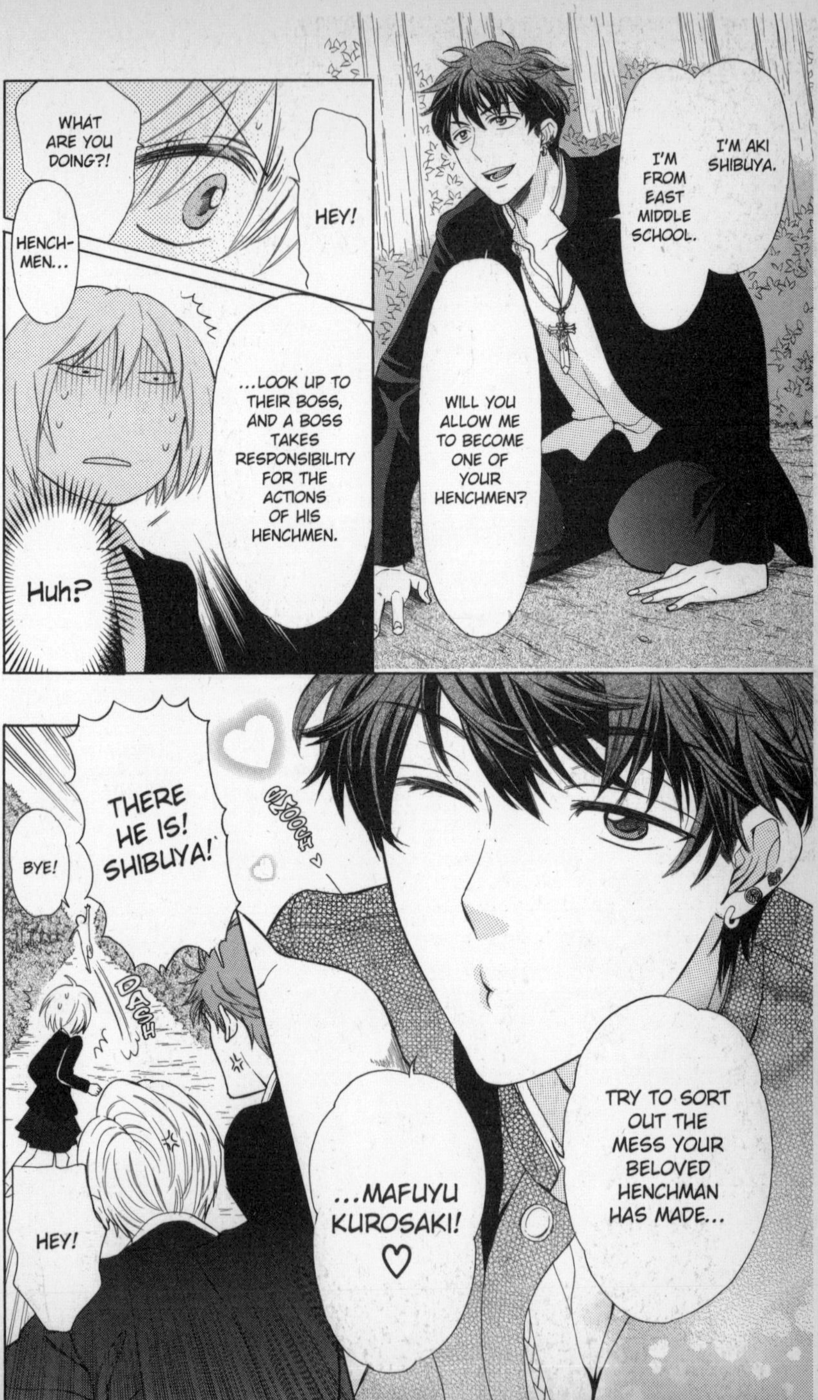
I'M AKI SHIBUYA.
I'M FROM EAST MIDDLE SCHOOL.
WILL YOU ALLOW ME TO BECOME ONE OF YOUR HENCHMEN?
HEY!
WHAT ARE YOU DOING?!
HENCH-MEN...
...LOOK UP TO THEIR BOSS, AND A BOSS TAKES RESPONSIBILITY FOR THE ACTIONS OF HIS HENCHMEN.
Huh?
TRY TO SORT OUT THE MESS YOUR BELOVED HENCHMAN HAS MADE...
...MAFUYU KUROSAKI! ♡
SMOOCH ♡
THERE HE IS! SHIBUYA!
BYE!
DASH
HEY!

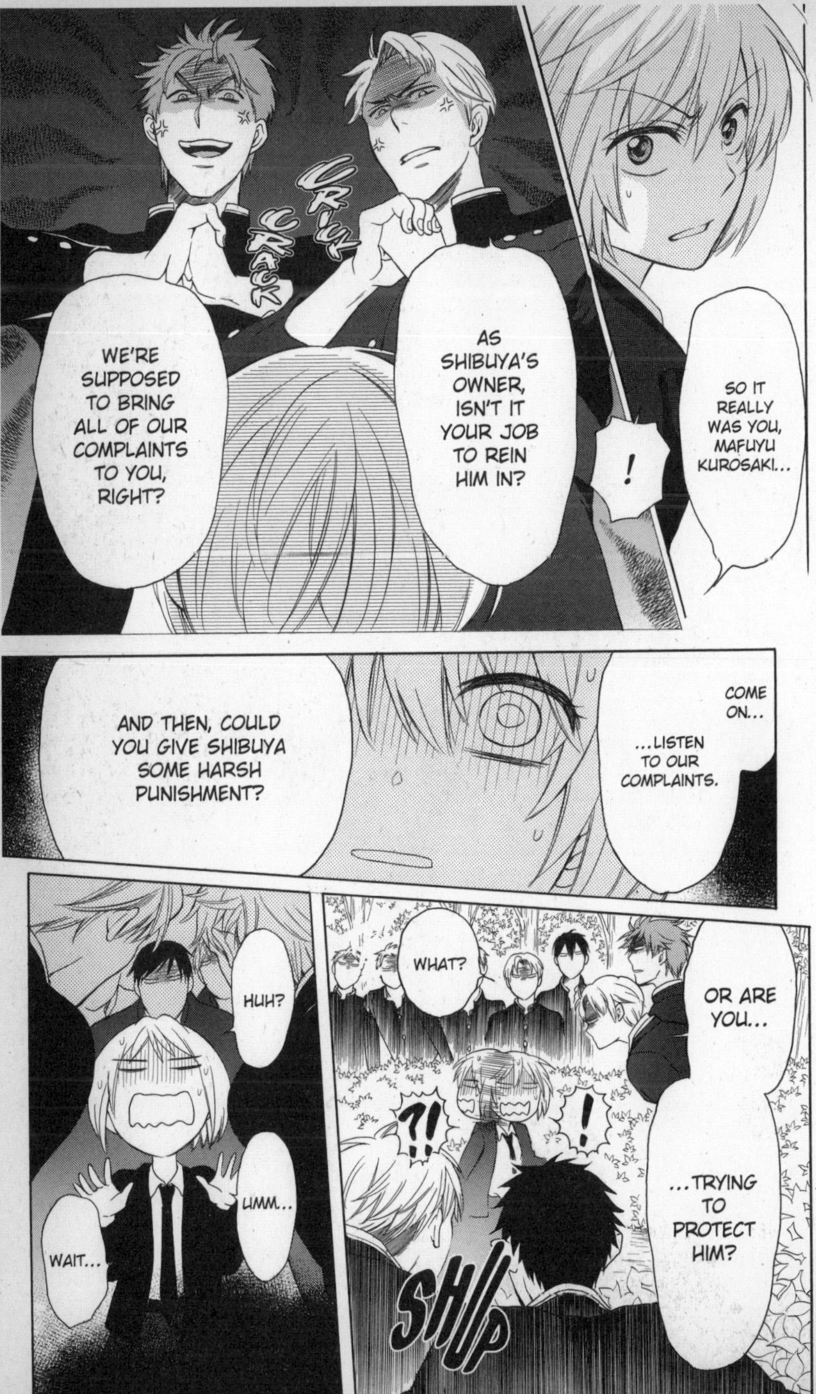
SO IT REALLY WAS YOU, MAFUYU KUROSAKI...
!
CRACK
AS SHIBUYA'S OWNER, ISN'T IT YOUR JOB TO REIN HIM IN?
WE'RE SUPPOSED TO BRING ALL OF OUR COMPLAINTS TO YOU, RIGHT?
COME ON...
...LISTEN TO OUR COMPLAINTS.
AND THEN, COULD YOU GIVE SHIBUYA SOME HARSH PUNISHMENT?
OR ARE YOU...
...TRYING TO PROTECT HIM?
WHAT?
!
?!
HUH?
UMM...
WAIT...

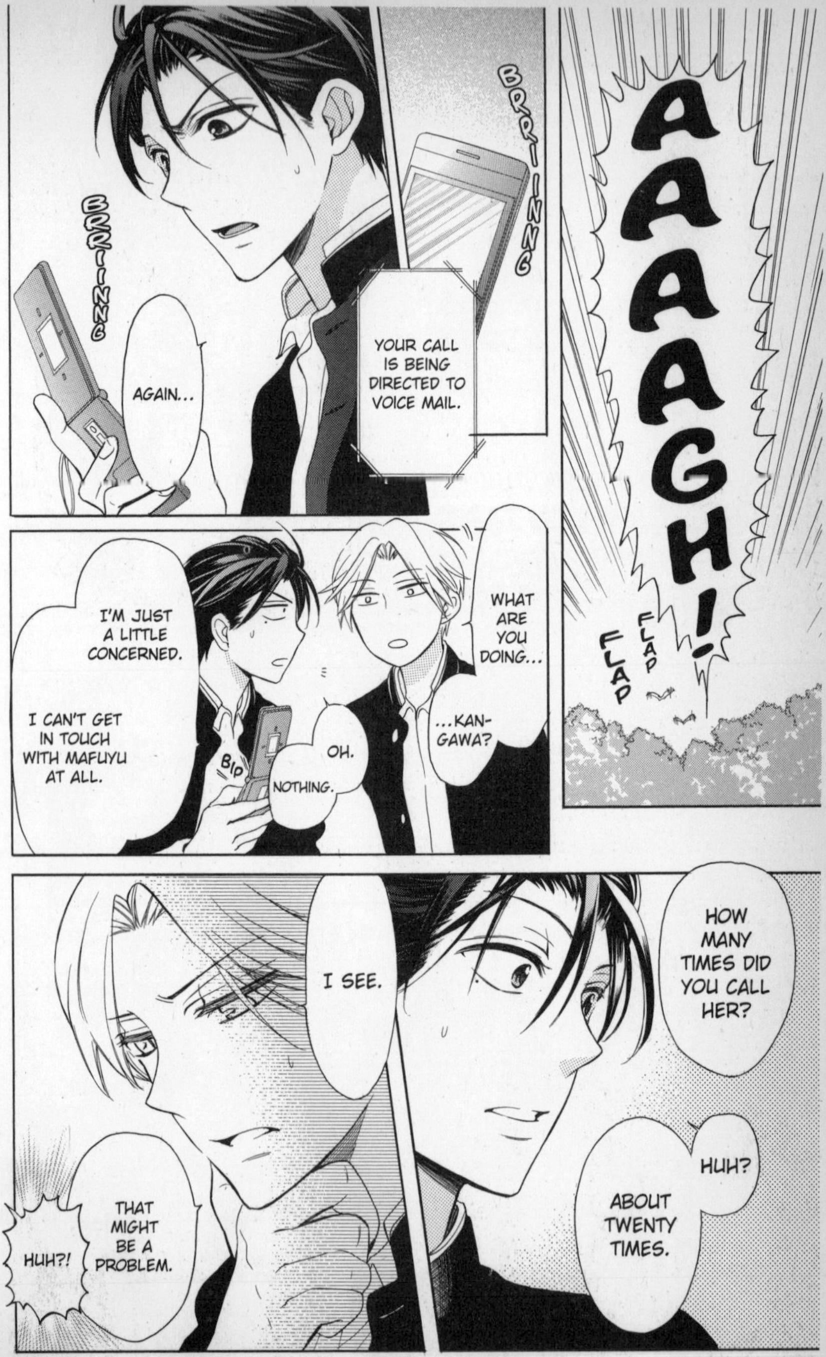
AAAAGH!
FLAP FLAP
BRRIIING
BRRIIING
YOUR CALL IS BEING DIRECTED TO VOICE MAIL.
AGAIN...
WHAT ARE YOU DOING...
...KAN-GAWA?
OH.
NOTHING.
BIP
I'M JUST A LITTLE CONCERNED.
I CAN'T GET IN TOUCH WITH MAFUYU AT ALL.
HOW MANY TIMES DID YOU CALL HER?
HUH?
ABOUT TWENTY TIMES.
I SEE.
THAT MIGHT BE A PROBLEM.
HUH?!

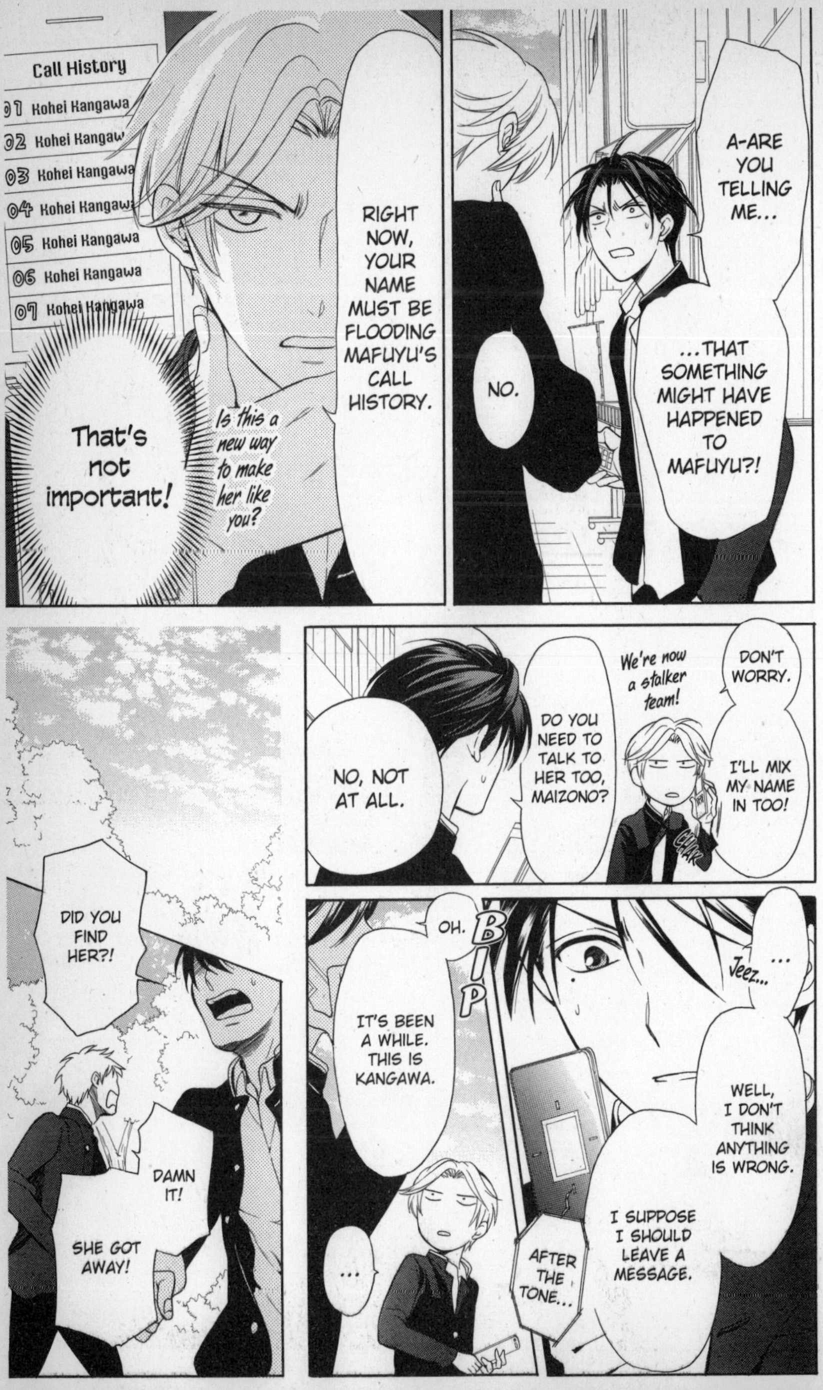
A-ARE YOU TELLING ME...
...THAT SOMETHING MIGHT HAVE HAPPENED TO MAFUYU?!
NO.
RIGHT NOW, YOUR NAME MUST BE FLOODING MAFUYU'S CALL HISTORY.
Is this a new way to make her like you?
That's not important!
Call History
01 Kohei Kangawa
02 Kohei Kangaw
03 Kohei Kangawa
04 Kohei Kangaw
05 Kohei Kangawa
06 Kohei Kangawa
07 Kohei Kangawa
DON'T WORRY.
I'LL MIX MY NAME IN TOO!
We're now a stalker team!
DO YOU NEED TO TALK TO HER TOO, MAIZONO?
NO, NOT AT ALL.
...
Jeez...
WELL, I DON'T THINK ANYTHING IS WRONG.
I SUPPOSE I SHOULD LEAVE A MESSAGE.
BIP
OH.
IT'S BEEN A WHILE. THIS IS KANGAWA.
AFTER THE TONE...
...
DID YOU FIND HER?!
DAMN IT!
SHE GOT AWAY!

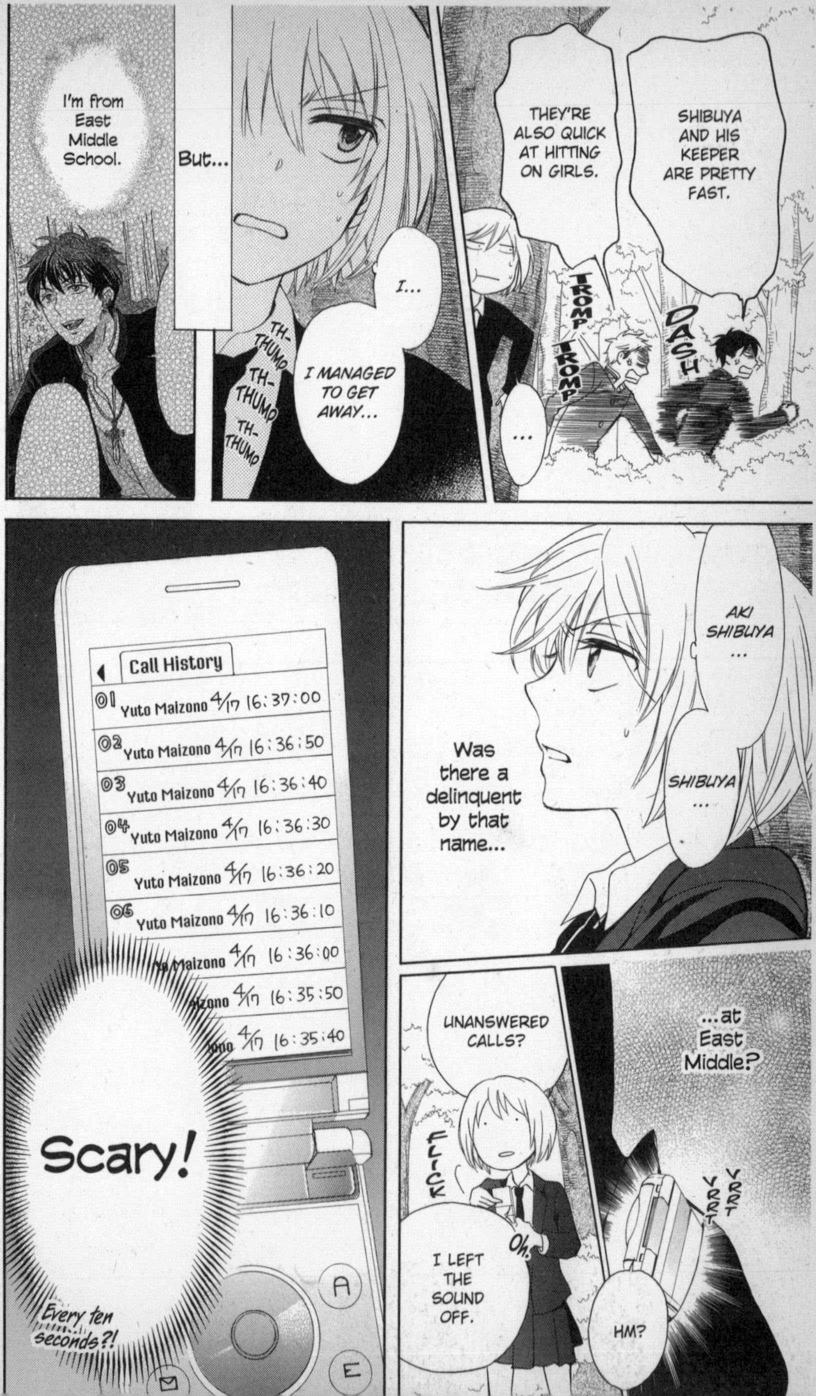
SHIBUYA AND HIS KEEPER ARE PRETTY FAST.
THEY'RE ALSO QUICK AT HITTING ON GIRLS.
DASH
TROMP TROMP
...
I...
I MANAGED TO GET AWAY...
TH-THUMP TH-THUMP TH-THUMP
But...
I'm from East Middle School.
AKI SHIBUYA...
SHIBUYA...
Was there a delinquent by that name...
...at East Middle?
VRRT VRRT
HM?
UNANSWERED CALLS?
FLICK
Oh.
I LEFT THE SOUND OFF.
Call History
01 Yuto Maizono 4/17 16:37:00
02 Yuto Maizono 4/17 16:36:50
03 Yuto Maizono 4/17 16:36:40
04 Yuto Maizono 4/17 16:36:30
05 Yuto Maizono 4/17 16:36:20
06 Yuto Maizono 4/17 16:36:10
Maizono 4/17 16:36:00
izono 4/17 16:35:50
4/17 16:35:40
Scary!
Every ten seconds?!

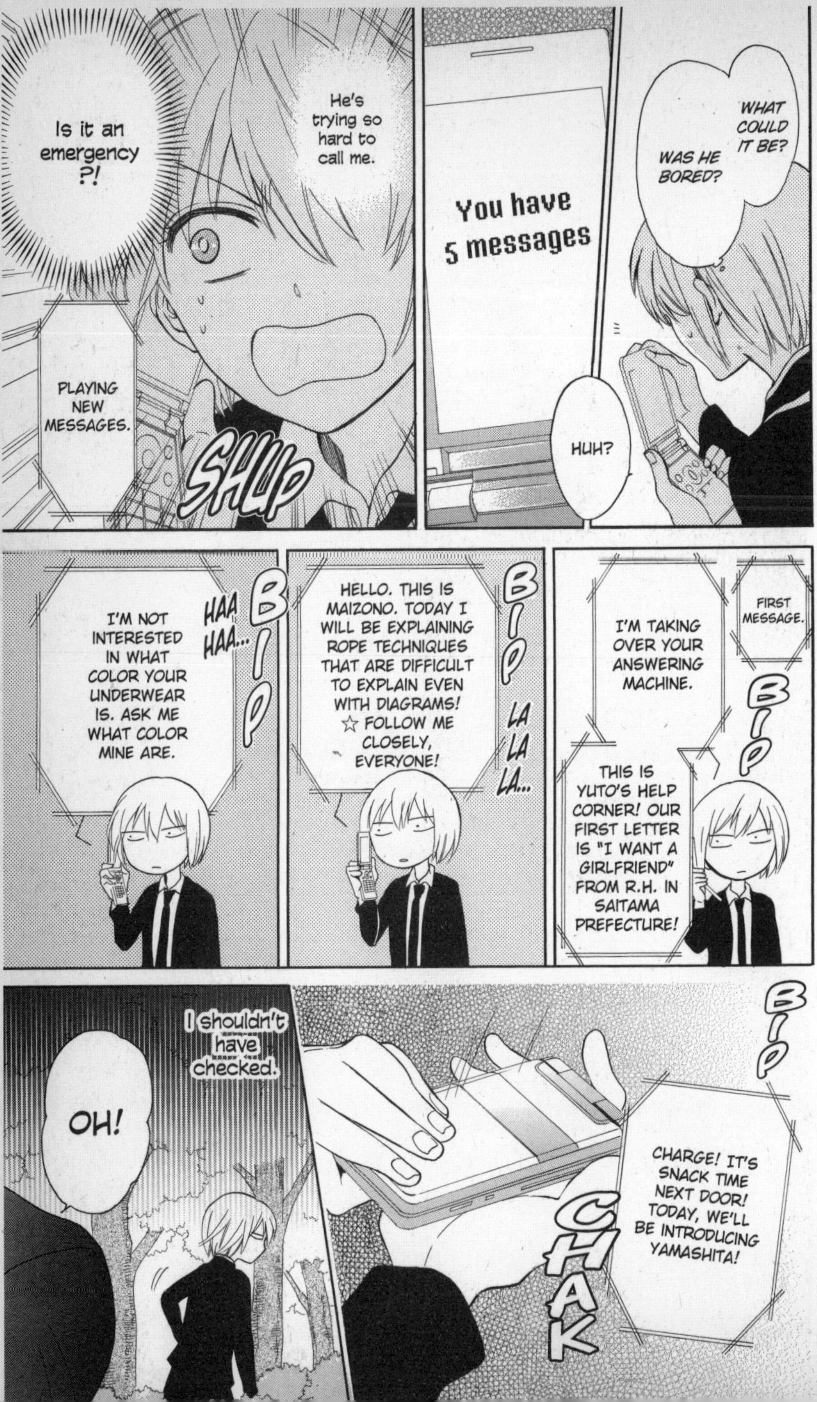
WHAT COULD IT BE?
WAS HE BORED?
HUH?
You have 5 messages
He's trying so hard to call me.
Is it an emergency ?!
PLAYING NEW MESSAGES.
SHUP
FIRST MESSAGE.
BIP
I'M TAKING OVER YOUR ANSWERING MACHINE.
THIS IS YUTO'S HELP CORNER! OUR FIRST LETTER IS "I WANT A GIRLFRIEND" FROM R.H. IN SAITAMA PREFECTURE!
BIP
HELLO. THIS IS MAIZONO. TODAY I WILL BE EXPLAINING ROPE TECHNIQUES THAT ARE DIFFICULT TO EXPLAIN EVEN WITH DIAGRAMS! ☆ FOLLOW ME CLOSELY, EVERYONE!
LA LA LA...
BIP
HAA HAA...
I'M NOT INTERESTED IN WHAT COLOR YOUR UNDERWEAR IS. ASK ME WHAT COLOR MINE ARE.
BIP
CHARGE! IT'S SNACK TIME NEXT DOOR! TODAY, WE'LL BE INTRODUCING YAMASHITA!
CHAK
I shouldn't have checked.
OH!

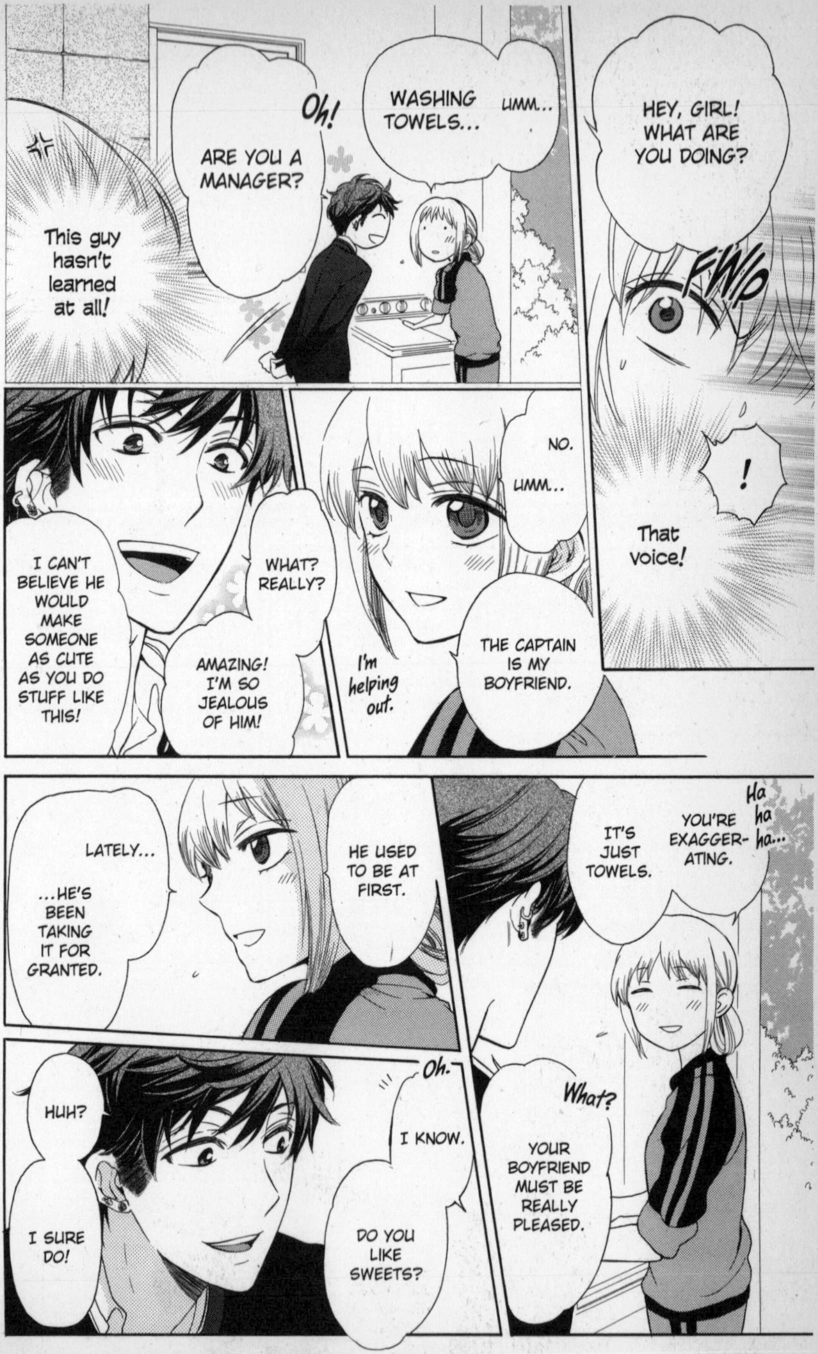
HEY, GIRL! WHAT ARE YOU DOING?
FWIP
!
That voice!
UMM...
WASHING TOWELS...
Oh!
ARE YOU A MANAGER?
This guy hasn't learned at all!
NO.
UMM...
THE CAPTAIN IS MY BOYFRIEND.
I'm helping out.
WHAT? REALLY?
AMAZING! I'M SO JEALOUS OF HIM!
I CAN'T BELIEVE HE WOULD MAKE SOMEONE AS CUTE AS YOU DO STUFF LIKE THIS!
Ha ha ha...
YOU'RE EXAGGER-ATING.
IT'S JUST TOWELS.
What?
YOUR BOYFRIEND MUST BE REALLY PLEASED.
HE USED TO BE AT FIRST.
LATELY...
...HE'S BEEN TAKING IT FOR GRANTED.
Oh.
I KNOW.
DO YOU LIKE SWEETS?
HUH?
I SURE DO!

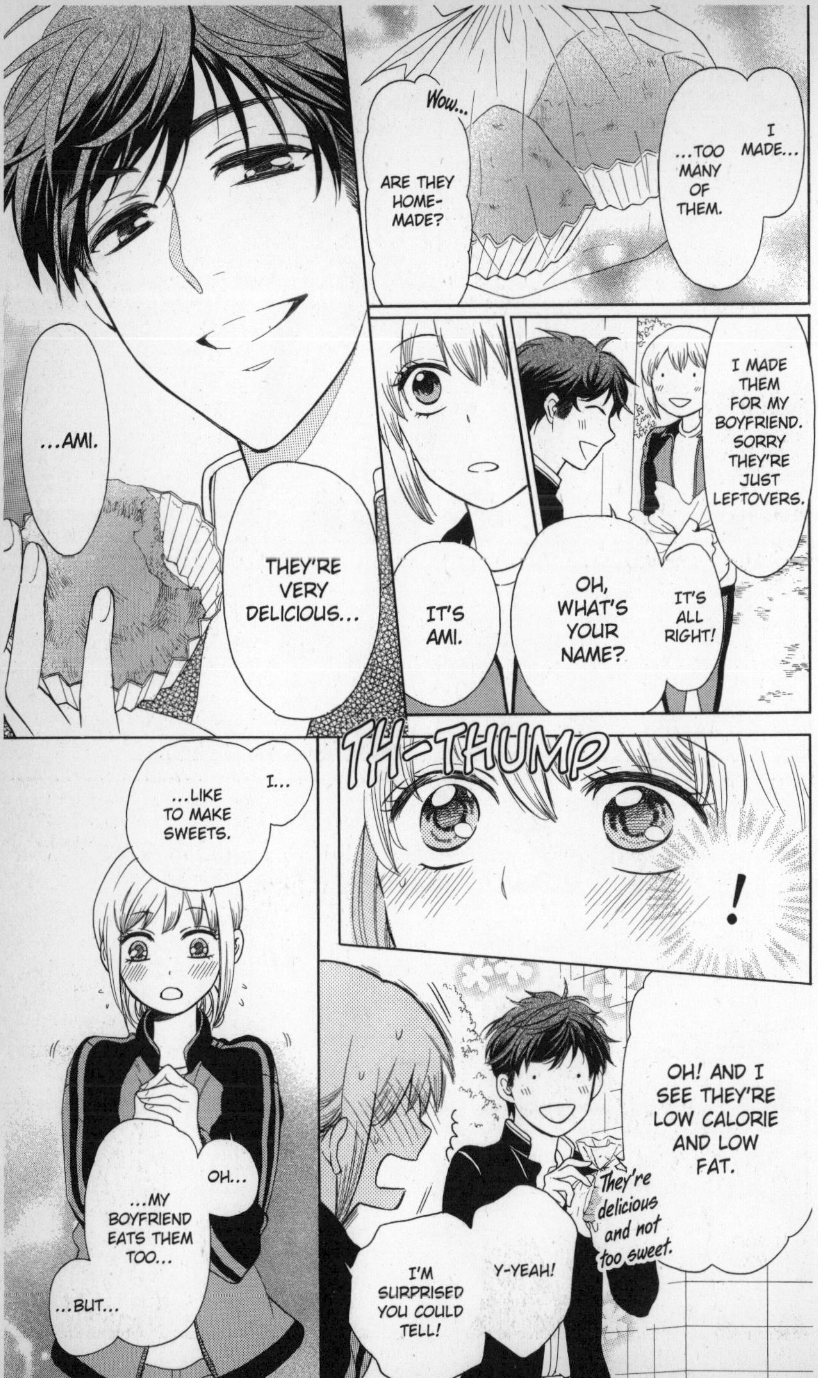
I MADE...
...TOO MANY OF THEM.
Wow...
ARE THEY HOME-MADE?
I MADE THEM FOR MY BOYFRIEND. SORRY THEY'RE JUST LEFTOVERS.
IT'S ALL RIGHT!
OH, WHAT'S YOUR NAME?
IT'S AMI.
THEY'RE VERY DELICIOUS...
...AMI.
TH-THUMP
!
OH! AND I SEE THEY'RE LOW CALORIE AND LOW FAT.
They're delicious and not too sweet.
Y-YEAH!
I'M SURPRISED YOU COULD TELL!
I...
...LIKE TO MAKE SWEETS.
OH...
...MY BOYFRIEND EATS THEM TOO...
...BUT...

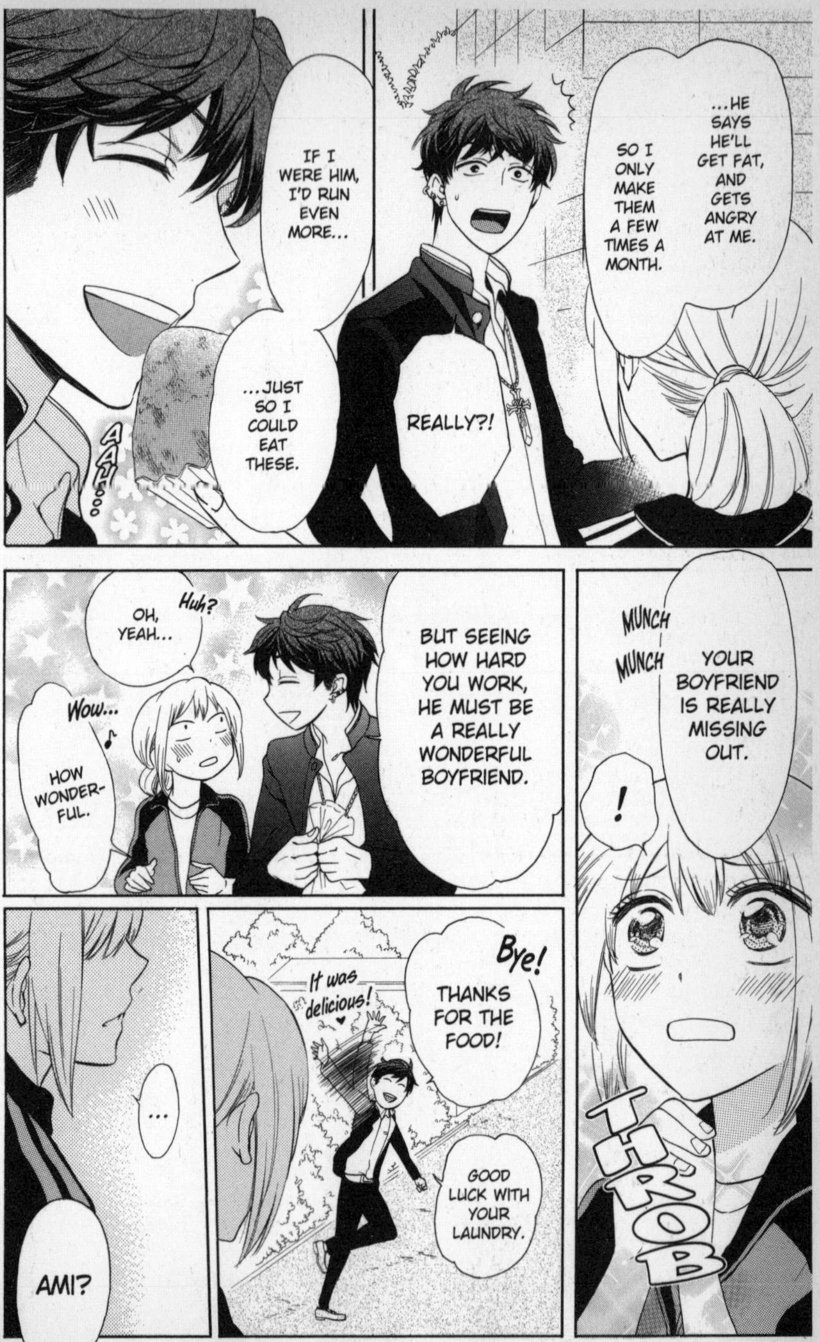
...HE SAYS HE'LL GET FAT, AND GETS ANGRY AT ME.
SO I ONLY MAKE THEM A FEW TIMES A MONTH.
REALLY?!
IF I WERE HIM, I'D RUN EVEN MORE...
...JUST SO I COULD EAT THESE.
AAH...
MUNCH MUNCH
YOUR BOYFRIEND IS REALLY MISSING OUT.
!
THROB
BUT SEEING HOW HARD YOU WORK, HE MUST BE A REALLY WONDERFUL BOYFRIEND.
Huh?
OH, YEAH...
Wow...
HOW WONDER-FUL.
Bye!
THANKS FOR THE FOOD!
It was delicious!
GOOD LUCK WITH YOUR LAUNDRY.
...
AMI?

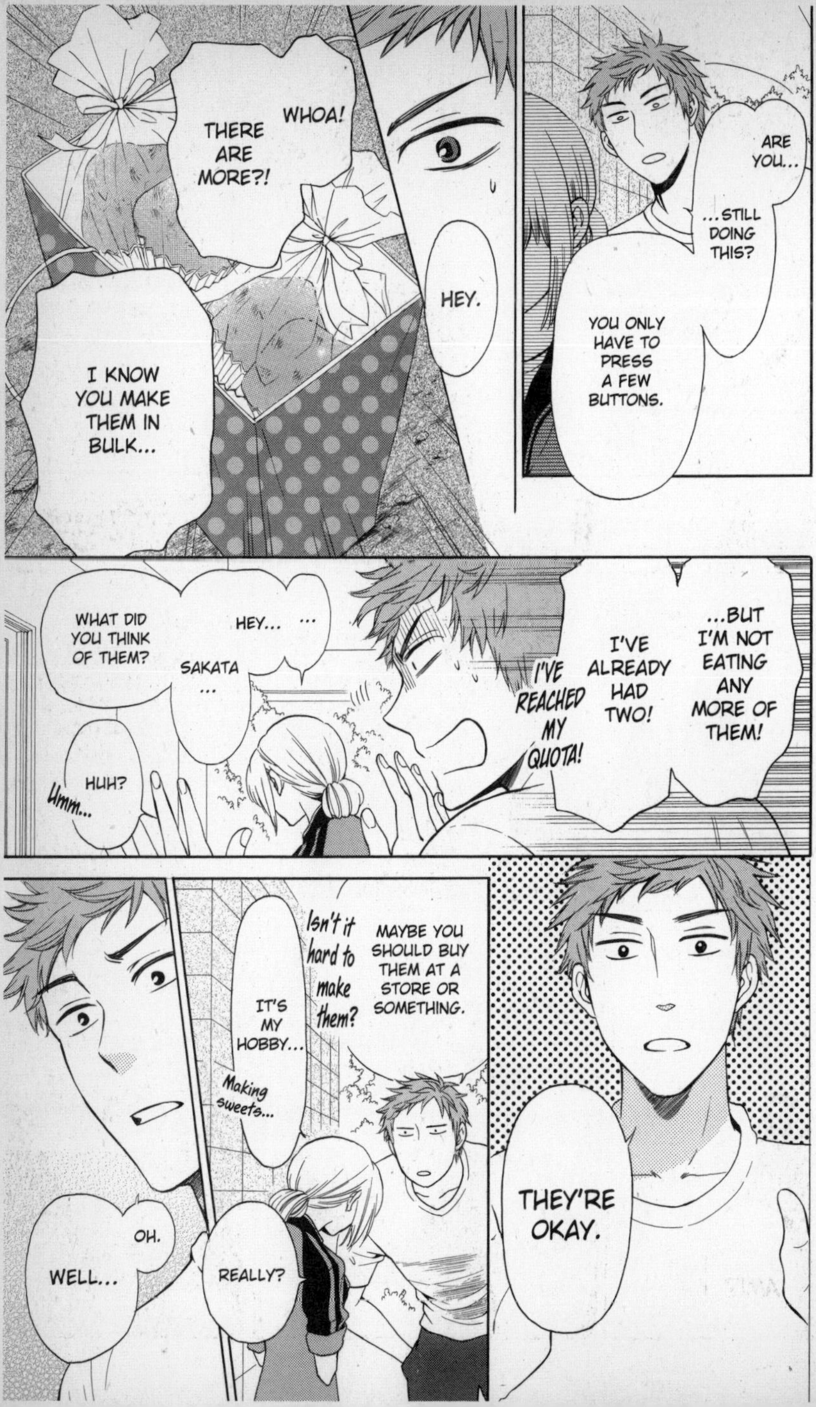
ARE YOU...
...STILL DOING THIS?
YOU ONLY HAVE TO PRESS A FEW BUTTONS.
HEY.
WHOA!
THERE ARE MORE?!
I KNOW YOU MAKE THEM IN BULK...
...BUT I'M NOT EATING ANY MORE OF THEM!
I'VE ALREADY HAD TWO!
I'VE REACHED MY QUOTA!
HEY... ...
SAKATA ...
WHAT DID YOU THINK OF THEM?
HUH?
Umm...
THEY'RE OKAY.
MAYBE YOU SHOULD BUY THEM AT A STORE OR SOMETHING.
Isn't it hard to make them?
IT'S MY HOBBY...
Making sweets...
REALLY?
OH.
WELL...

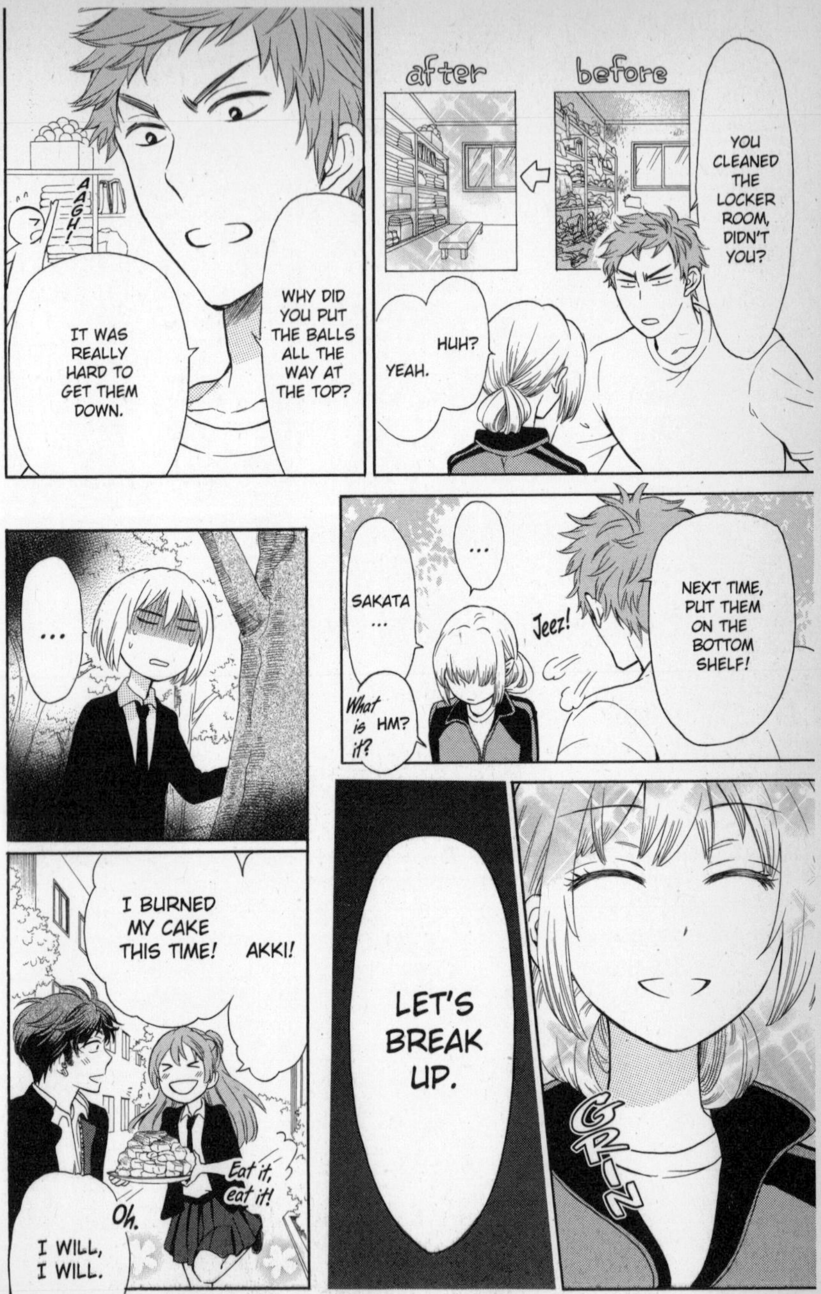
YOU CLEANED THE LOCKER ROOM, DIDN'T YOU?
before
after
HUH? YEAH.
WHY DID YOU PUT THE BALLS ALL THE WAY AT THE TOP?
AAGH!
IT WAS REALLY HARD TO GET THEM DOWN.
NEXT TIME, PUT THEM ON THE BOTTOM SHELF!
Jeez!
...
SAKATA ...
HM? What is it?
...
GRIN
LET'S BREAK UP.
AKKI!
I BURNED MY CAKE THIS TIME!
Eat it, eat it!
Oh.
I WILL, I WILL.

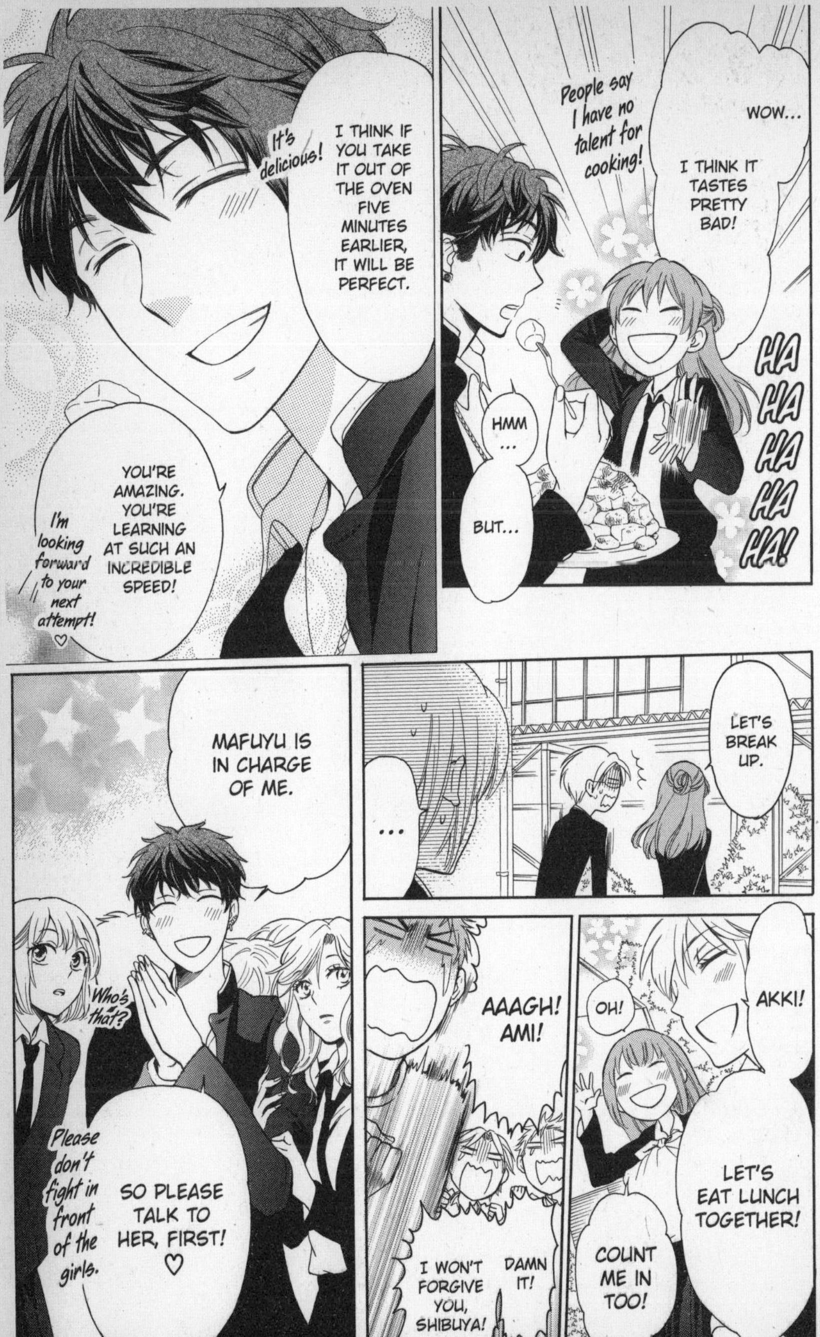
WOW...
I THINK IT TASTES PRETTY BAD!
People say I have no talent for cooking!
HA HA HA HA HA!
HMM...
BUT...
I THINK IF YOU TAKE IT OUT OF THE OVEN FIVE MINUTES EARLIER, IT WILL BE PERFECT.
It's delicious!
YOU'RE AMAZING. YOU'RE LEARNING AT SUCH AN INCREDIBLE SPEED!
I'm looking forward to your next attempt! ♡
LET'S BREAK UP.
...
AKKI!
OH!
LET'S EAT LUNCH TOGETHER!
COUNT ME IN TOO!
AAAGH! AMI!
DAMN IT!
I WON'T FORGIVE YOU, SHIBUYA!
MAFUYU IS IN CHARGE OF ME.
Who's that?
SO PLEASE TALK TO HER, FIRST! ♡
Please don't fight in front of the girls.

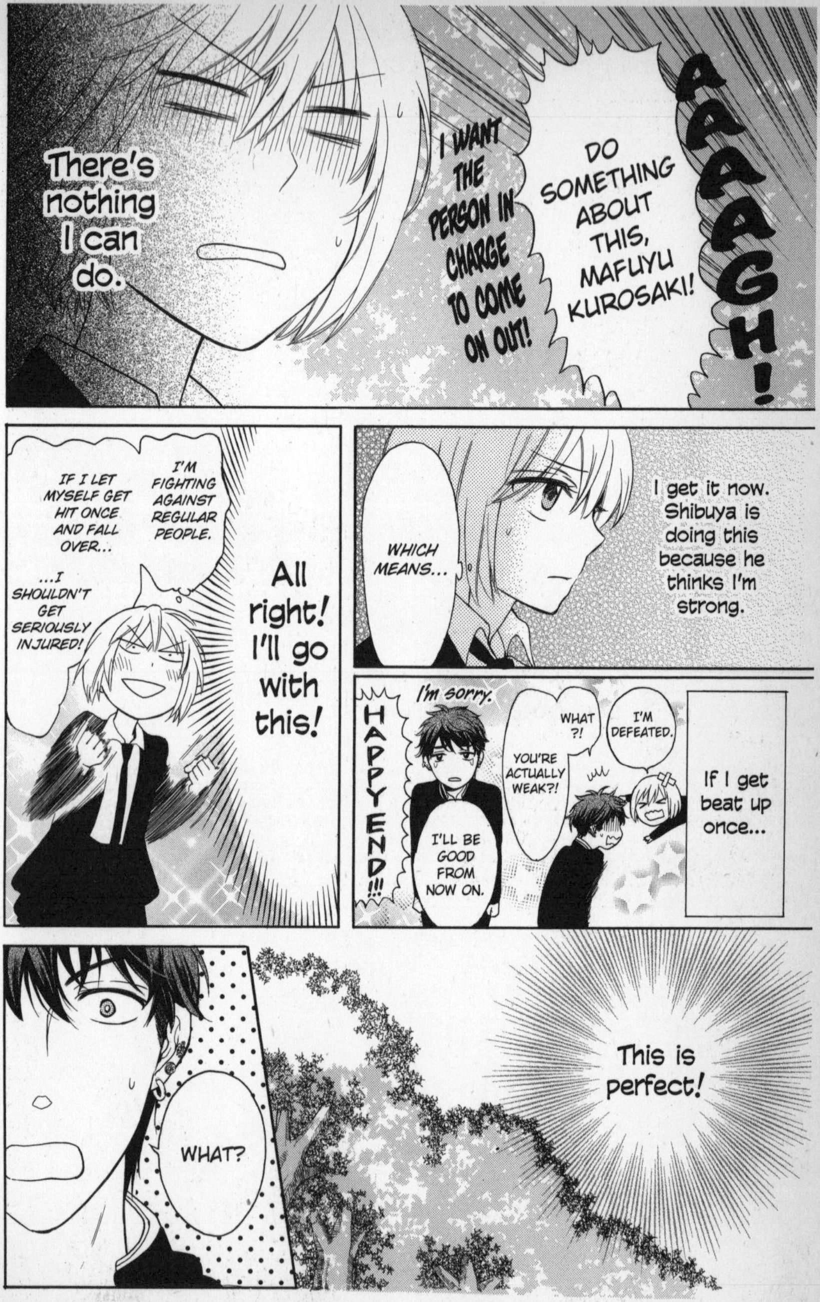
AAAAGH!
DO SOMETHING ABOUT THIS, MAFUYU KUROSAKI!
I WANT THE PERSON IN CHARGE TO COME ON OUT!
There's nothing I can do.
I get it now. Shibuya is doing this because he thinks I'm strong.
WHICH MEANS...
If I get beat up once...
I'M DEFEATED.
WHAT?!
YOU'RE ACTUALLY WEAK?!
I'm sorry.
HAPPY END!!!
I'LL BE GOOD FROM NOW ON.
All right! I'll go with this!
I'M FIGHTING AGAINST REGULAR PEOPLE.
IF I LET MYSELF GET HIT ONCE AND FALL OVER...
...I SHOULDN'T GET SERIOUSLY INJURED!
This is perfect!
WHAT?

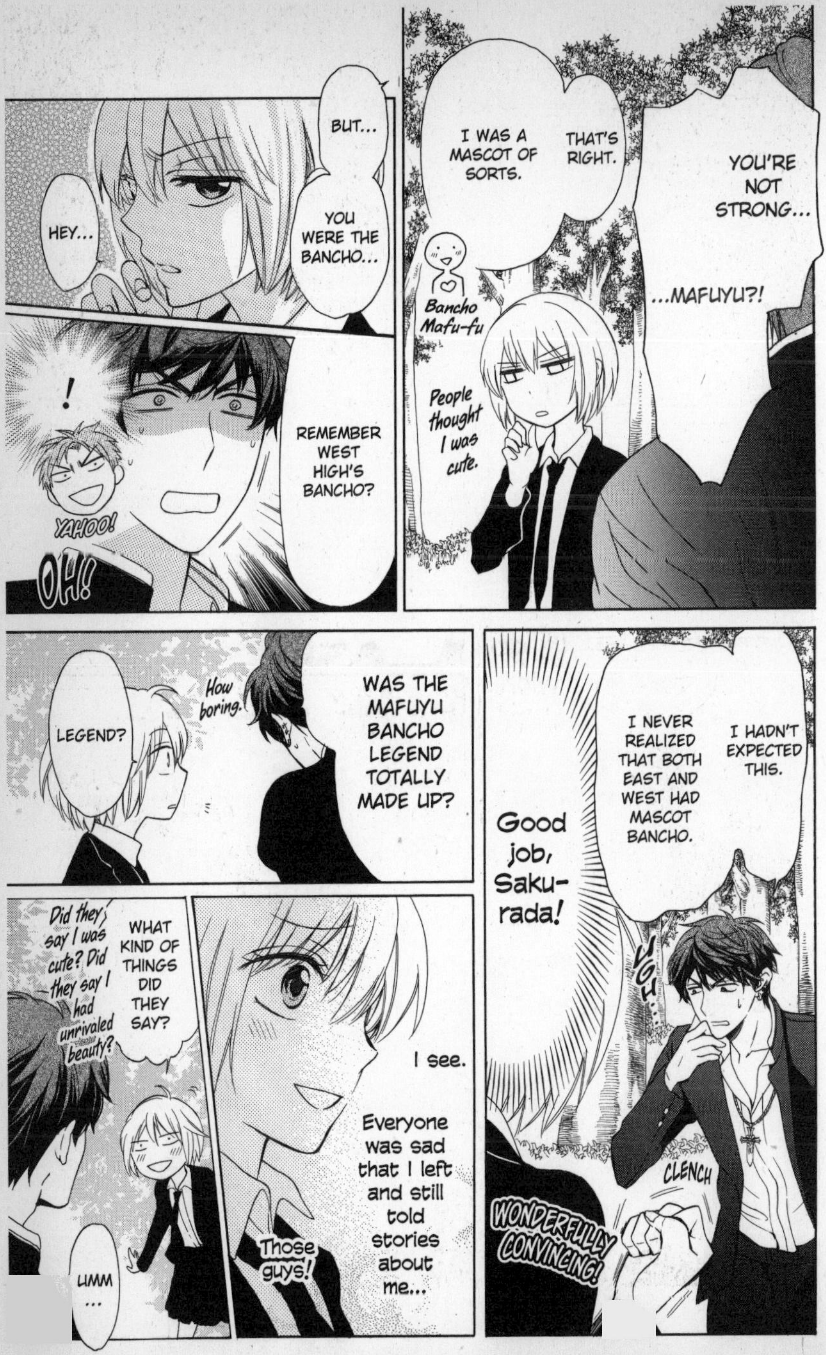

YOU'RE NOT STRONG...
...MAFUYU?!
THAT'S RIGHT.
I WAS A MASCOT OF SORTS.
Bancho Mafu-fu
People thought I was cute.
BUT...
YOU WERE THE BANCHO...
HEY...
REMEMBER WEST HIGH'S BANCHO?
!
YAHOO!
OH!
I HADN'T EXPECTED THIS.
I NEVER REALIZED THAT BOTH EAST AND WEST HAD MASCOT BANCHO.
Good job, Saku-rada!
UGH...
CLENCH
WONDERFULLY CONVINCING!
WAS THE MAFUYU BANCHO LEGEND TOTALLY MADE UP?
How boring.
LEGEND?
I see.
Everyone was sad that I left and still told stories about me...
Those guys!
WHAT KIND OF THINGS DID THEY SAY?
Did they say I was cute? Did they say I had unrivaled beauty?
UMM...

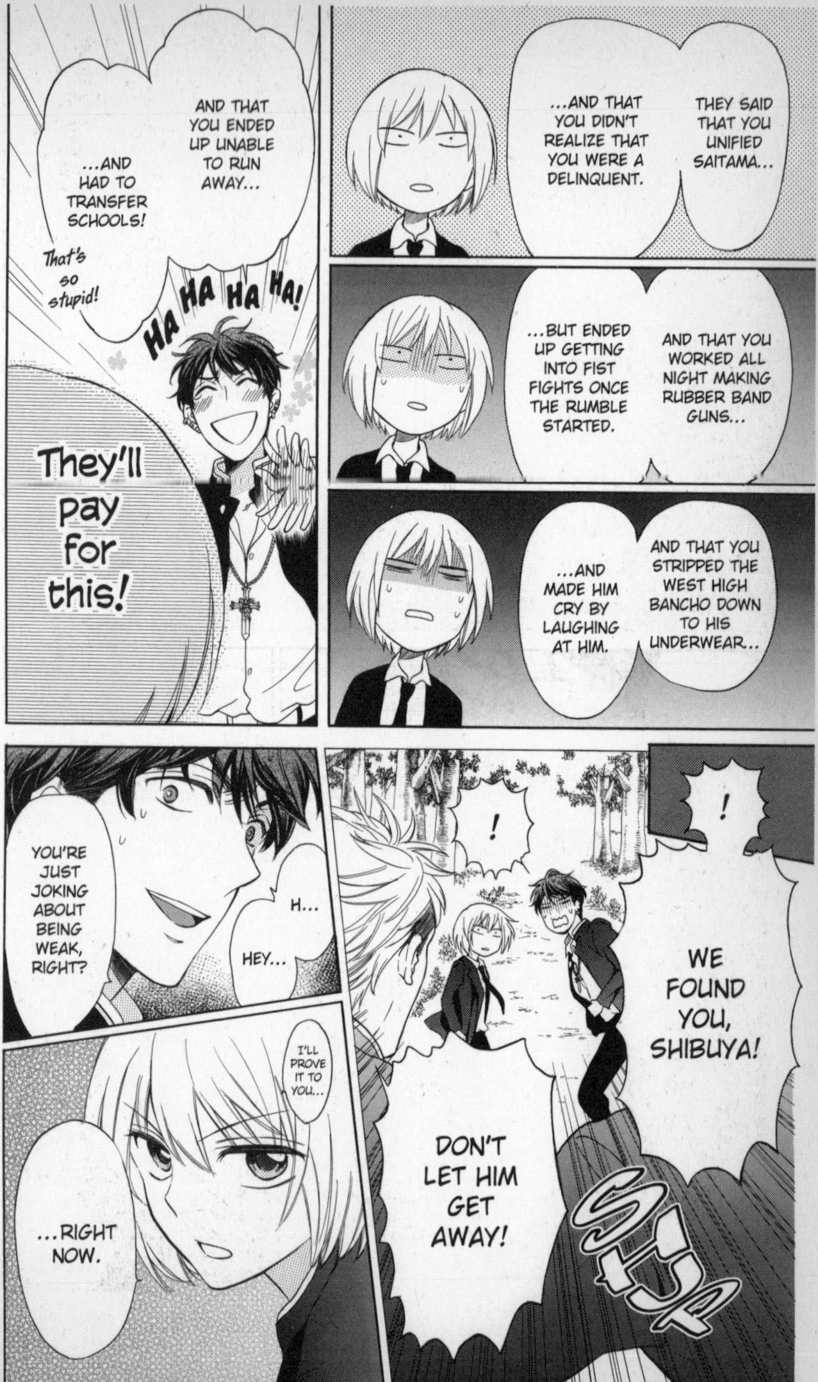
THEY SAID THAT YOU UNIFIED SAITAMA...
...AND THAT YOU DIDN'T REALIZE THAT YOU WERE A DELINQUENT.
AND THAT YOU WORKED ALL NIGHT MAKING RUBBER BAND GUNS...
...BUT ENDED UP GETTING INTO FIST FIGHTS ONCE THE RUMBLE STARTED.
AND THAT YOU STRIPPED THE WEST HIGH BANCHO DOWN TO HIS UNDERWEAR...
...AND MADE HIM CRY BY LAUGHING AT HIM.
AND THAT YOU ENDED UP UNABLE TO RUN AWAY...
...AND HAD TO TRANSFER SCHOOLS!
HA HA HA HA HA!
That's so stupid!
They'll pay for this!
!
!
WE FOUND YOU, SHIBUYA!
DON'T LET HIM GET AWAY!
H... HEY...
YOU'RE JUST JOKING ABOUT BEING WEAK, RIGHT?
I'LL PROVE IT TO YOU...
...RIGHT NOW.

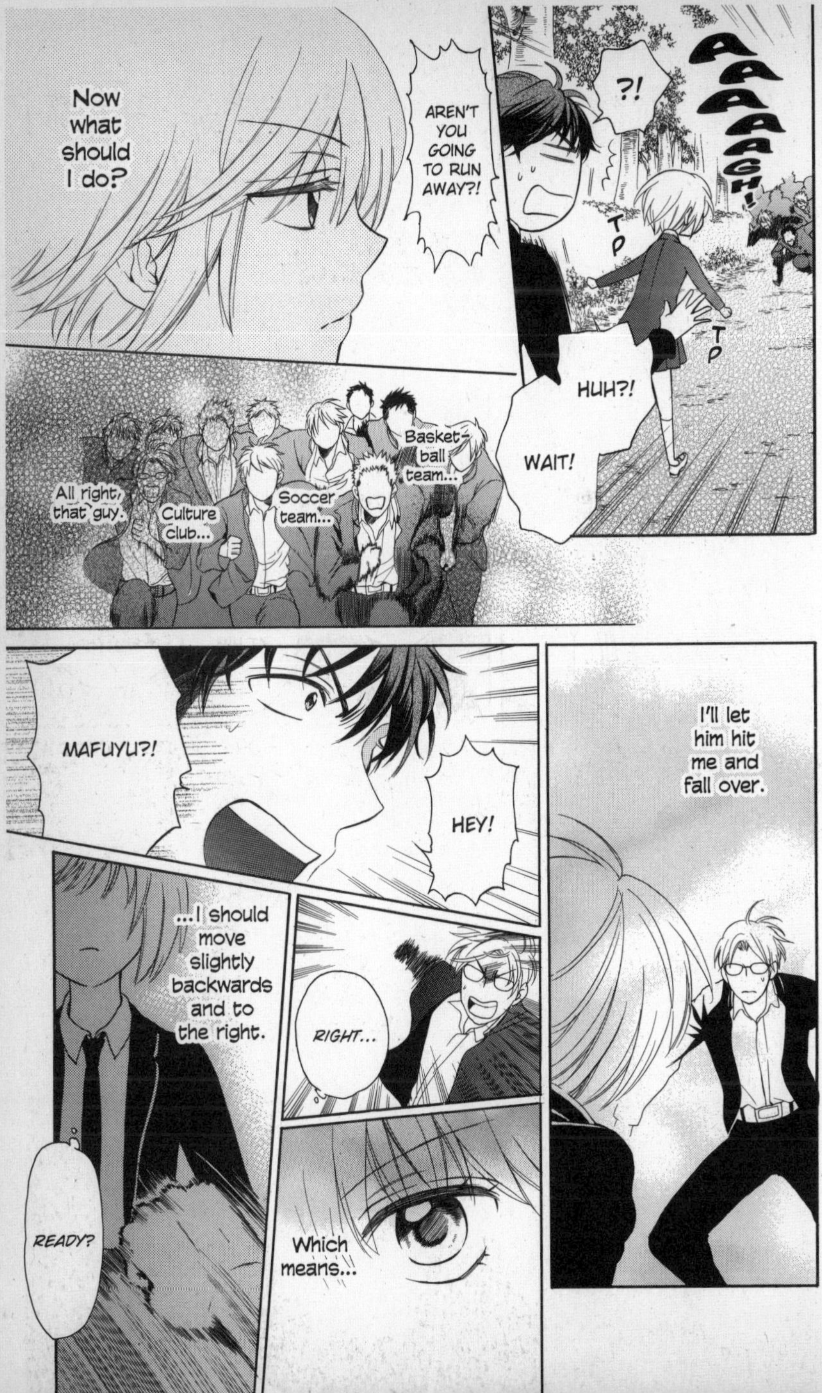
AAAAAGH!
?!
TP
TP
HUH?!
WAIT!
AREN'T YOU GOING TO RUN AWAY?!
Now what should I do?
Basket-ball team...
Soccer team...
Culture club...
All right, that guy.
I'll let him hit me and fall over.
HEY!
MAFUYU?!
RIGHT...
Which means...
...I should move slightly backwards and to the right.
READY?

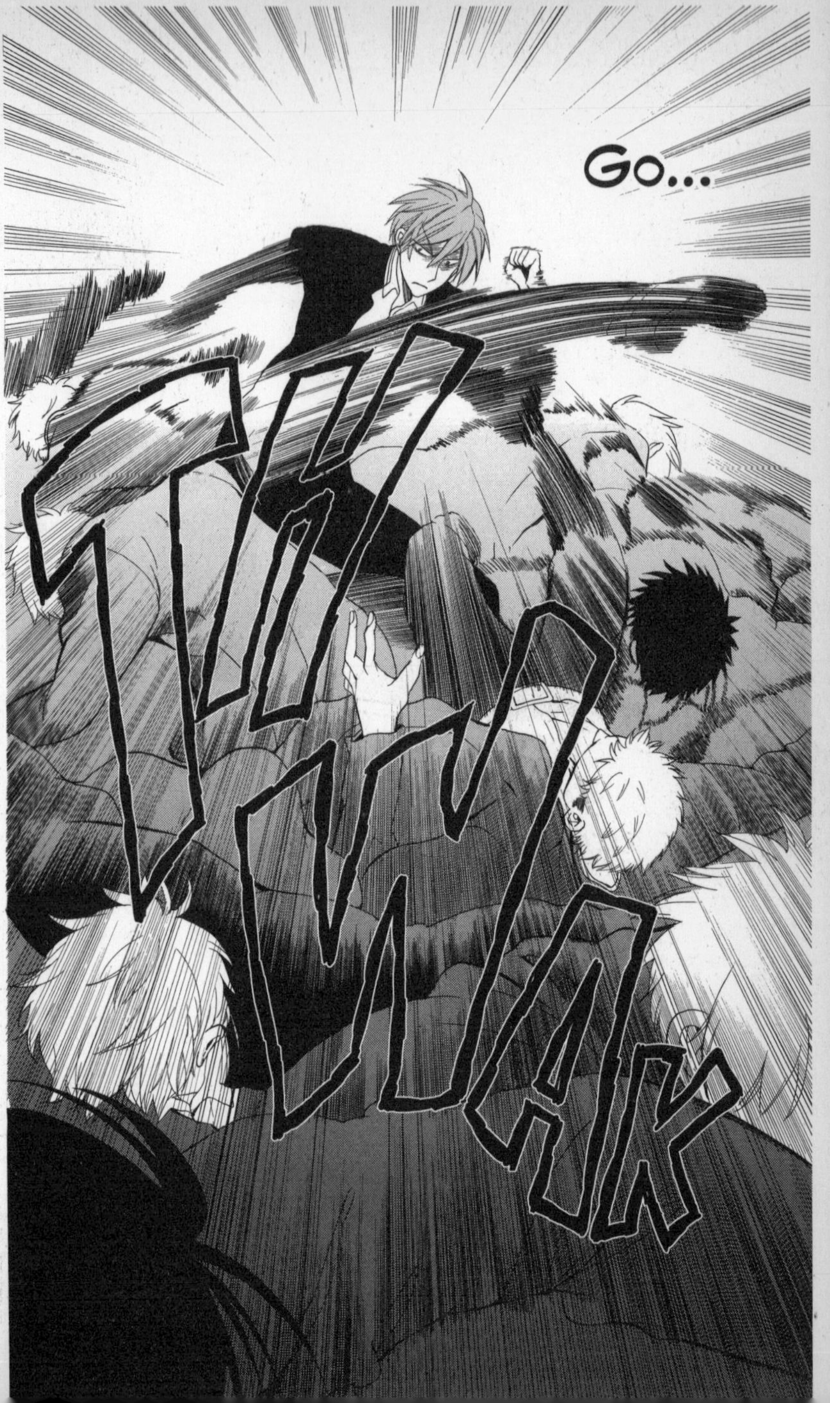
Go...
THWACK

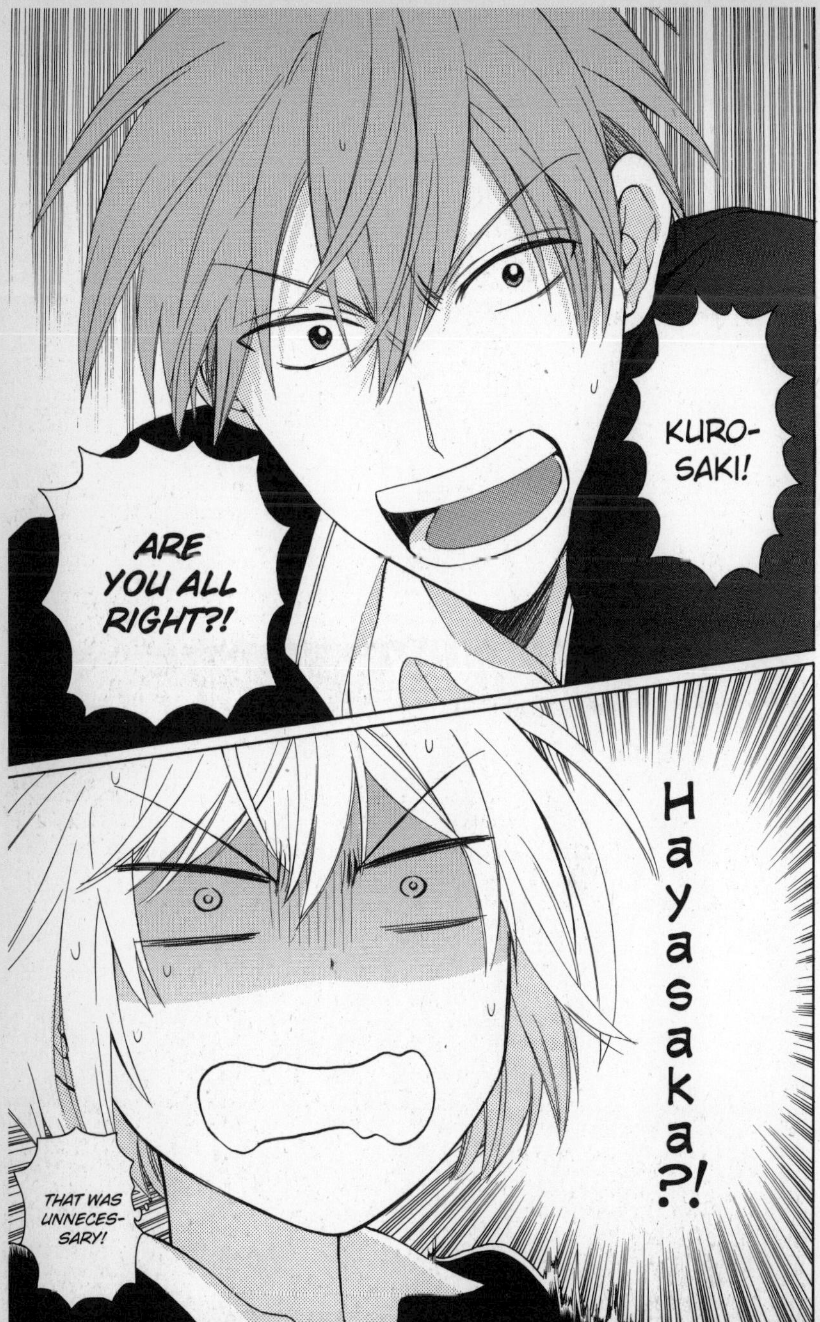
KURO-SAKI!
ARE YOU ALL RIGHT?!
Hayasaka?!
THAT WAS UNNECES-SARY!

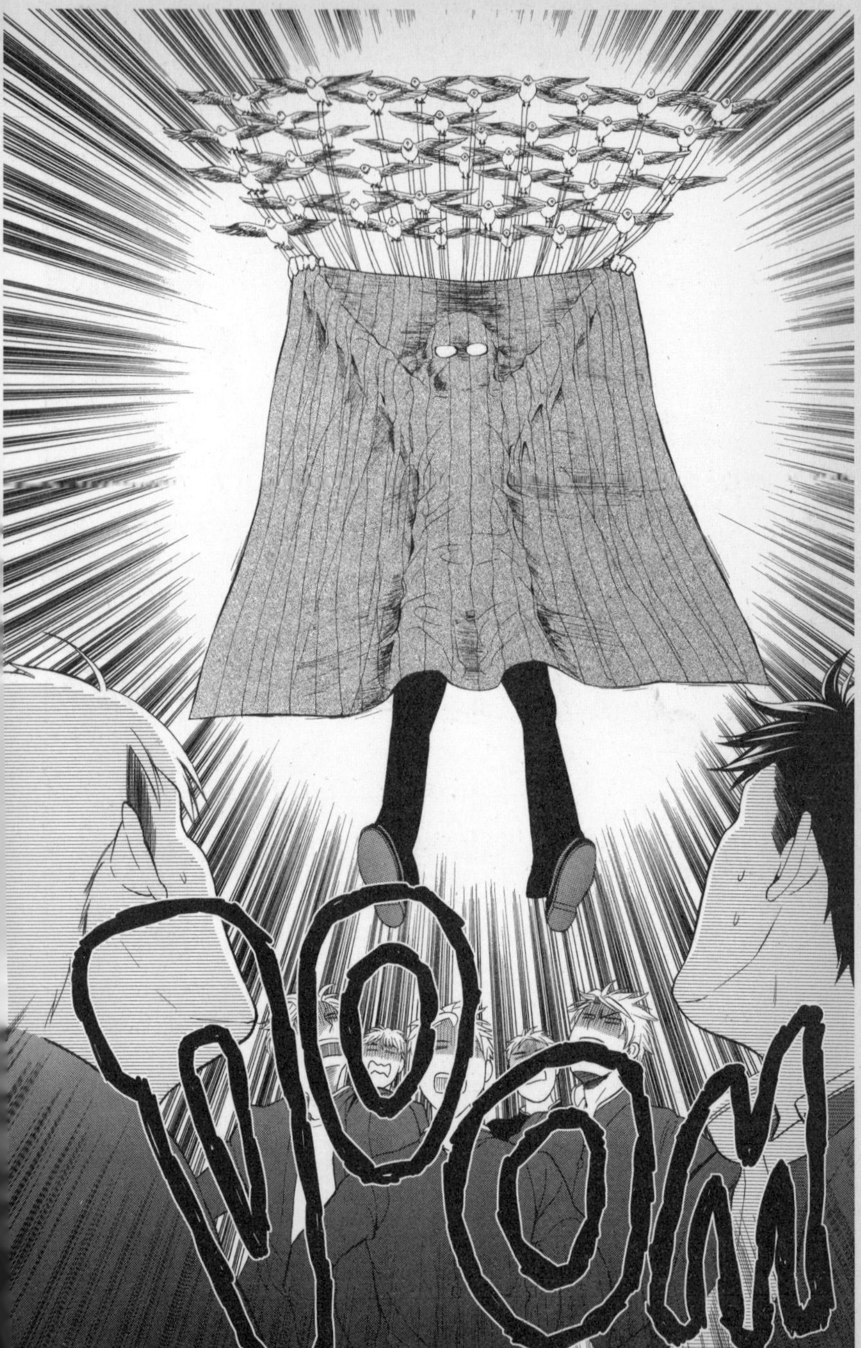
VOOM

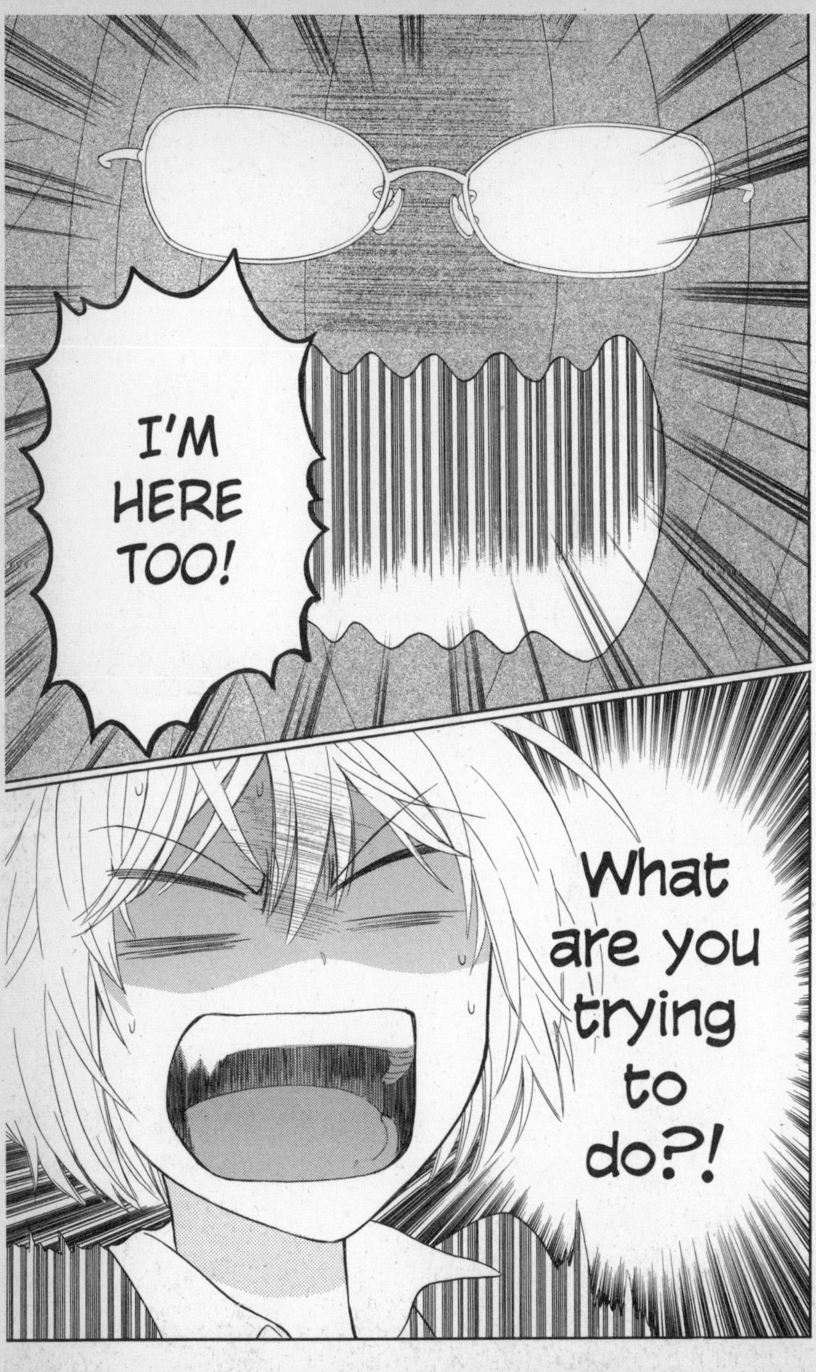
I'M HERE TOO!
What are you trying to do?!

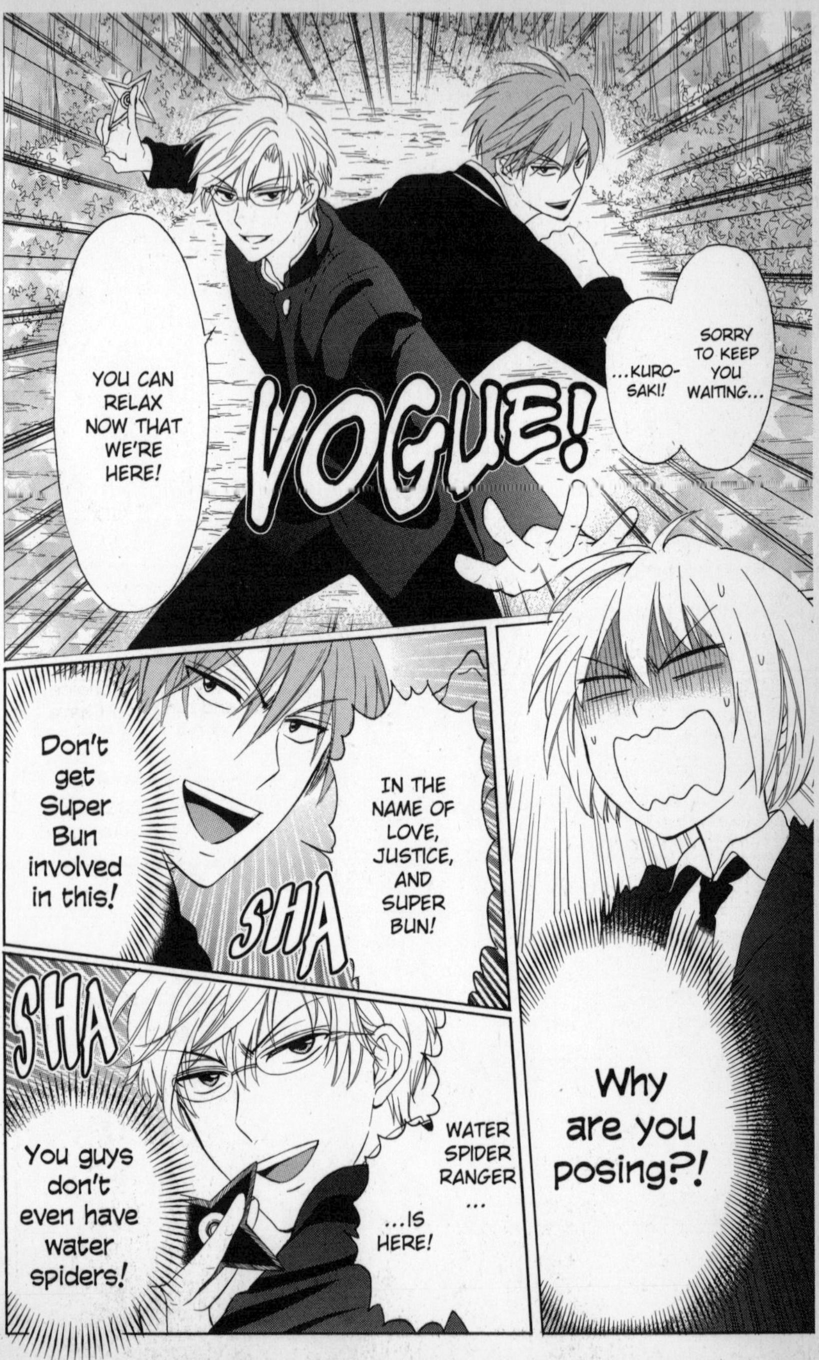
SORRY TO KEEP YOU WAITING...
...KURO-SAKI!
VOGUE!
YOU CAN RELAX NOW THAT WE'RE HERE!
Why are you posing?!
IN THE NAME OF LOVE, JUSTICE, AND SUPER BUN!
SHA
Don't get Super Bun involved in this!
WATER SPIDER RANGER ...
...IS HERE!
SHA
You guys don't even have water spiders!

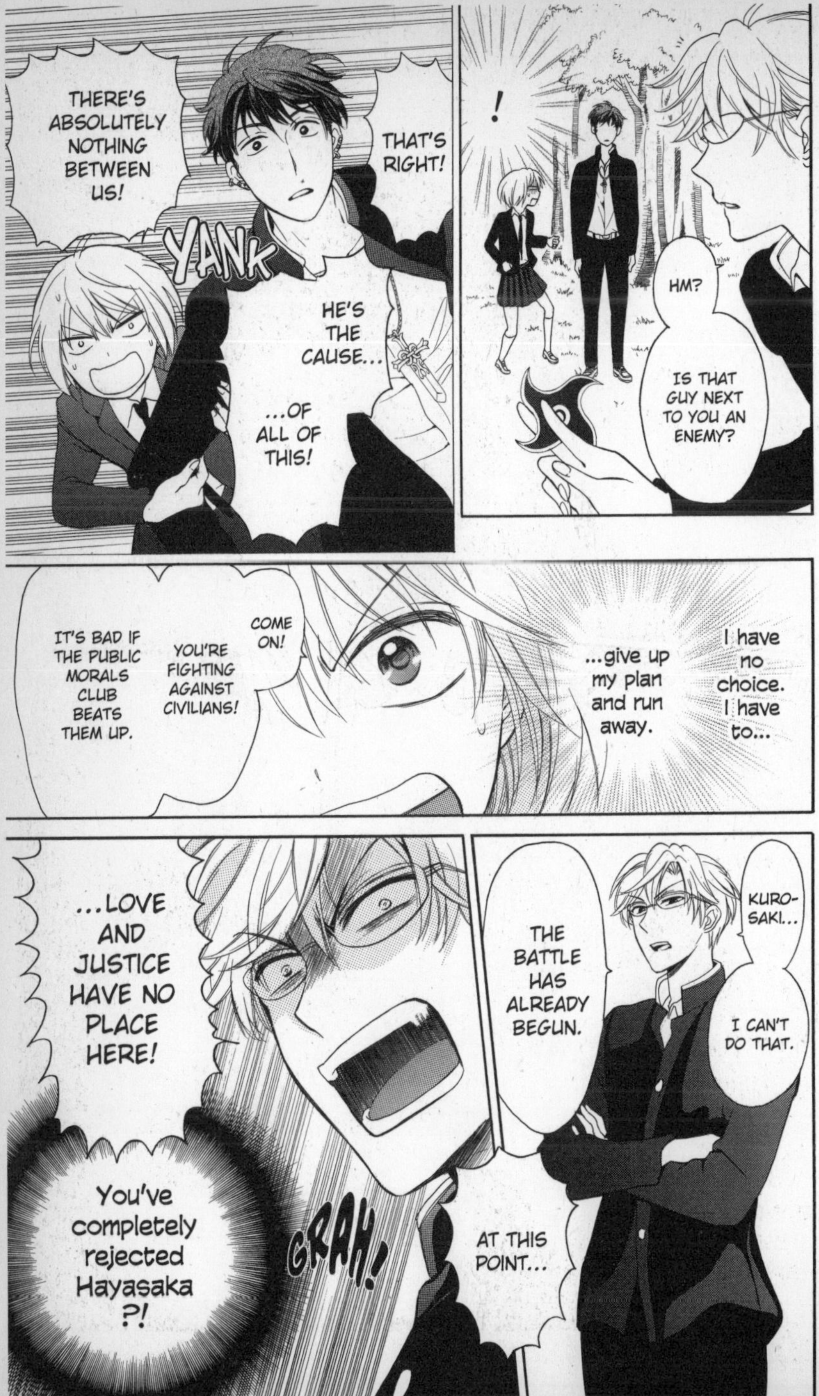
!
HM?
IS THAT GUY NEXT TO YOU AN ENEMY?
THAT'S RIGHT!
THERE'S ABSOLUTELY NOTHING BETWEEN US!
YANK
HE'S THE CAUSE...
...OF ALL OF THIS!
I have no choice. I have to...
...give up my plan and run away.
COME ON!
YOU'RE FIGHTING AGAINST CIVILIANS!
IT'S BAD IF THE PUBLIC MORALS CLUB BEATS THEM UP.
KURO-SAKI...
I CAN'T DO THAT.
AT THIS POINT...
THE BATTLE HAS ALREADY BEGUN.
...LOVE AND JUSTICE HAVE NO PLACE HERE!
GRAH!
You've completely rejected Hayasaka?!

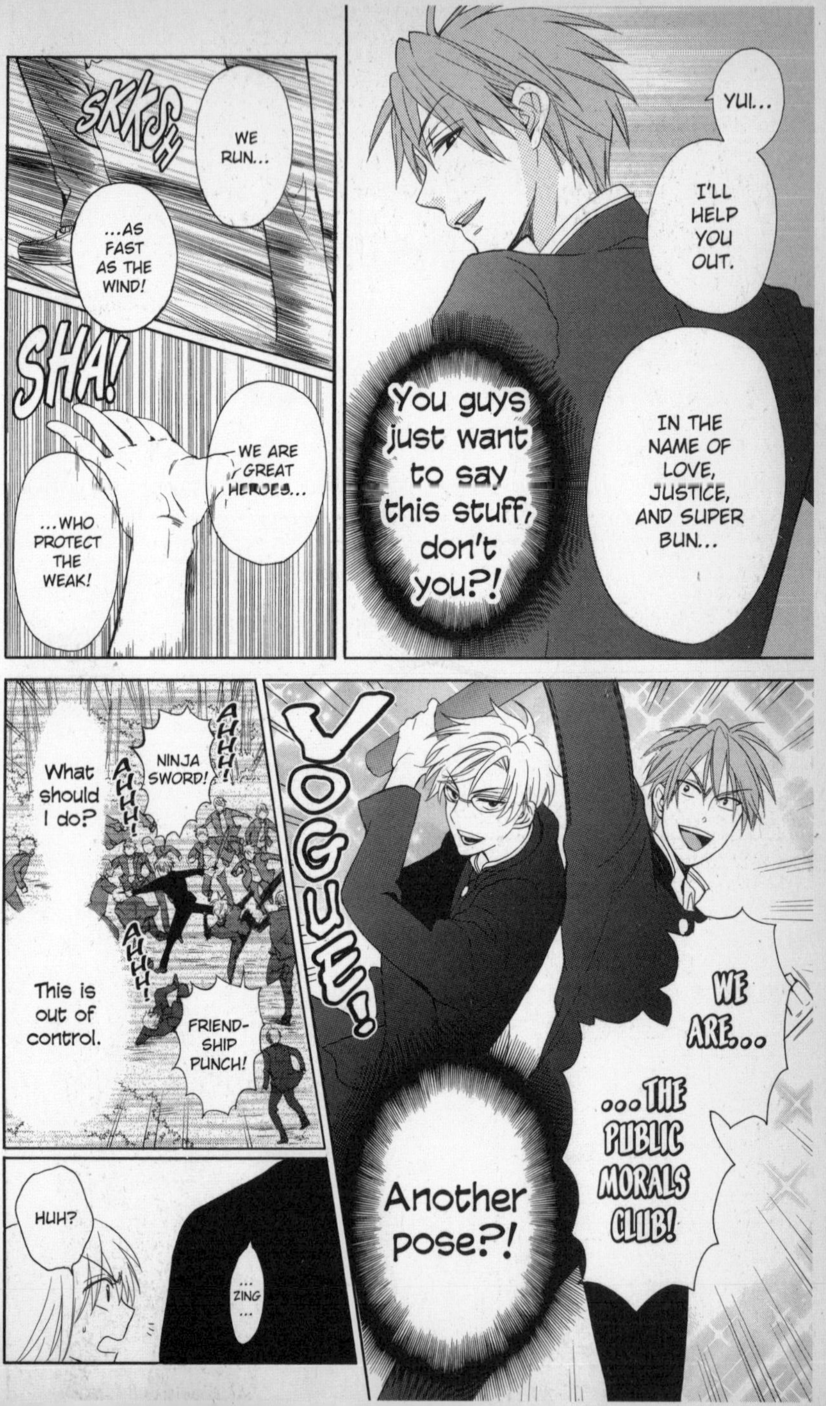

YUI...
I'LL HELP YOU OUT.
IN THE NAME OF LOVE, JUSTICE, AND SUPER BUN...
You guys just want to say this stuff, don't you?!
SKKSH
WE RUN...
...AS FAST AS THE WIND!
SHA!
WE ARE GREAT HEROES...
...WHO PROTECT THE WEAK!
WE ARE...
...THE PUBLIC MORALS CLUB!
VOGUE!
Another pose?!
AHHHH!
NINJA SWORD!
AHHHH!
What should I do?
AHHHH!
FRIENDSHIP PUNCH!
This is out of control.
...ZING...
HUH?

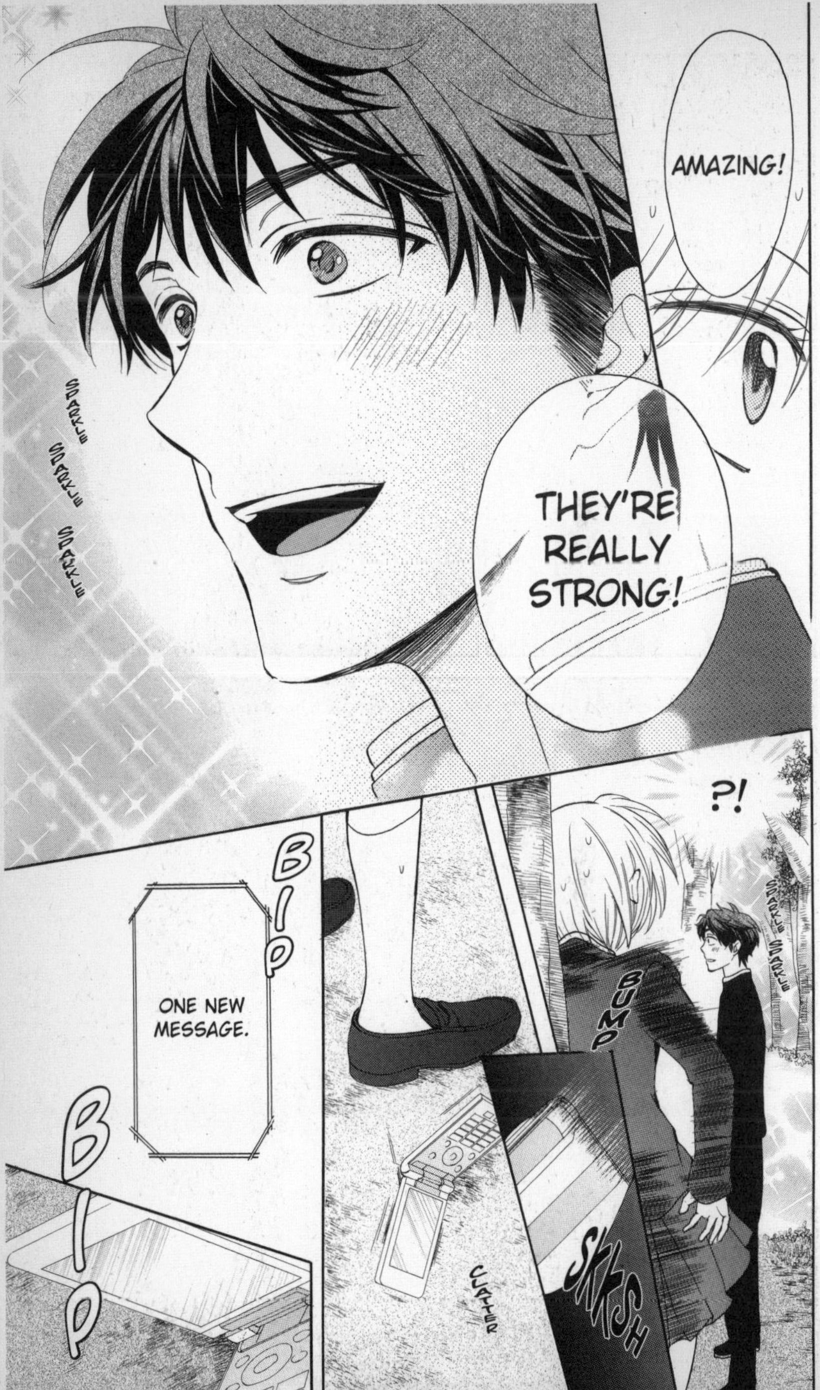
AMAZING!
THEY'RE REALLY STRONG!
SPARKLE SPARKLE SPARKLE
?!
SPARKLE SPARKLE
BUMP
SKSH
CLATTER
BIP BIP
ONE NEW MESSAGE.
BIP BIP

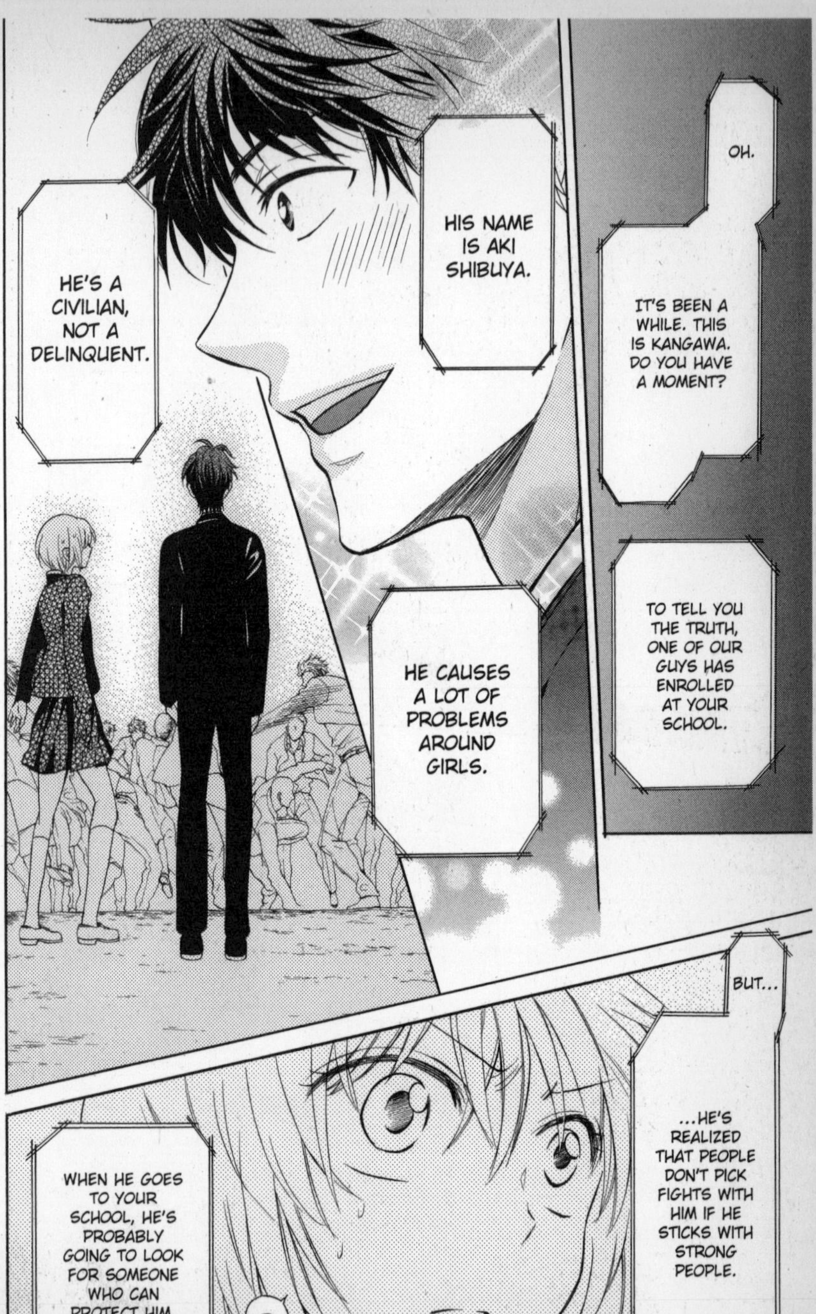
OH.
IT'S BEEN A WHILE. THIS IS KANGAWA. DO YOU HAVE A MOMENT?
TO TELL YOU THE TRUTH, ONE OF OUR GUYS HAS ENROLLED AT YOUR SCHOOL.
HIS NAME IS AKI SHIBUYA.
HE CAUSES A LOT OF PROBLEMS AROUND GIRLS.
HE'S A CIVILIAN, NOT A DELINQUENT.
BUT...
...HE'S REALIZED THAT PEOPLE DON'T PICK FIGHTS WITH HIM IF HE STICKS WITH STRONG PEOPLE.
WHEN HE GOES TO YOUR SCHOOL, HE'S PROBABLY GOING TO LOOK FOR SOMEONE WHO CAN PROTECT HIM.
?

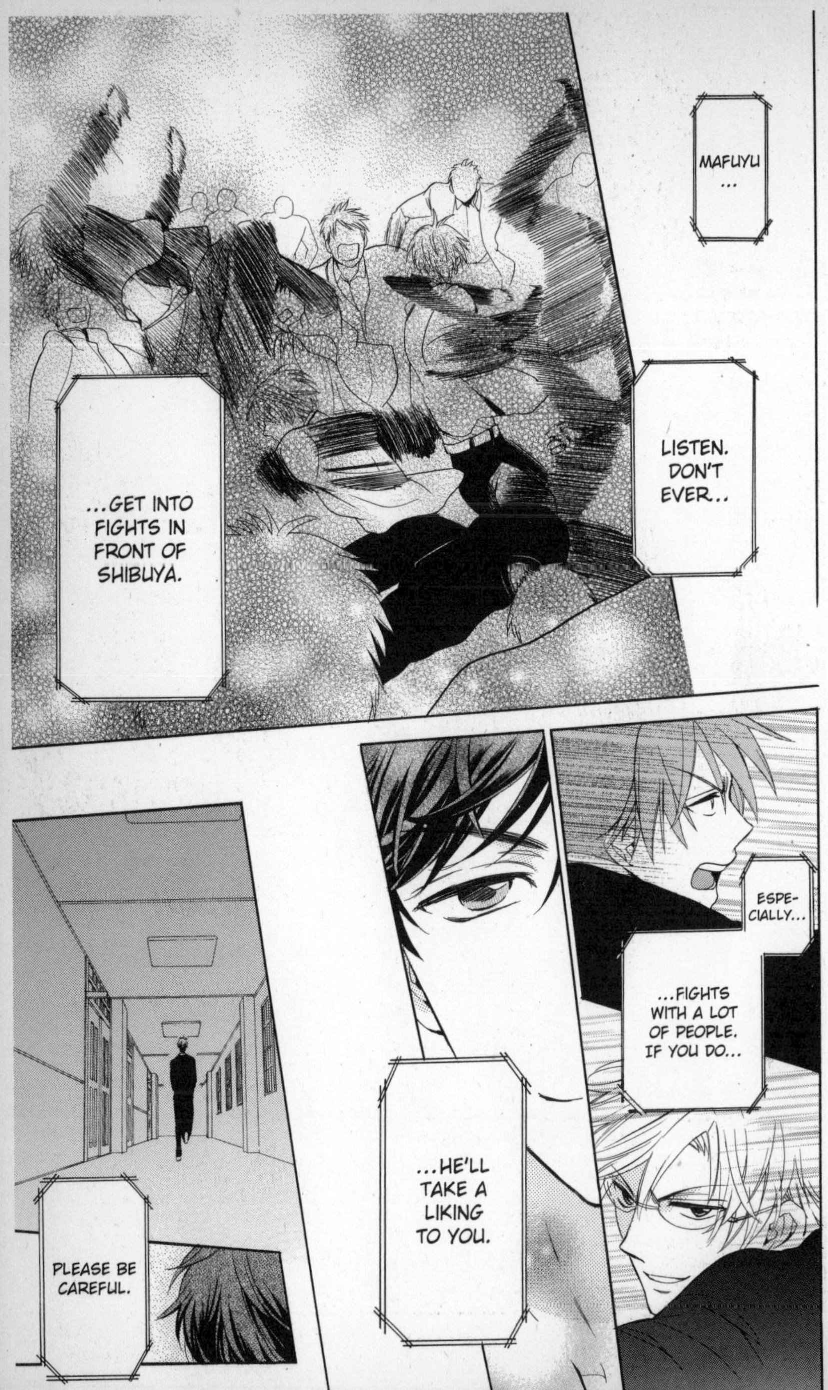
MAFUYU ...
LISTEN. DON'T EVER...
...GET INTO FIGHTS IN FRONT OF SHIBUYA.
ESPE-CIALLY...
...FIGHTS WITH A LOT OF PEOPLE. IF YOU DO...
...HE'LL TAKE A LIKING TO YOU.
PLEASE BE CAREFUL.

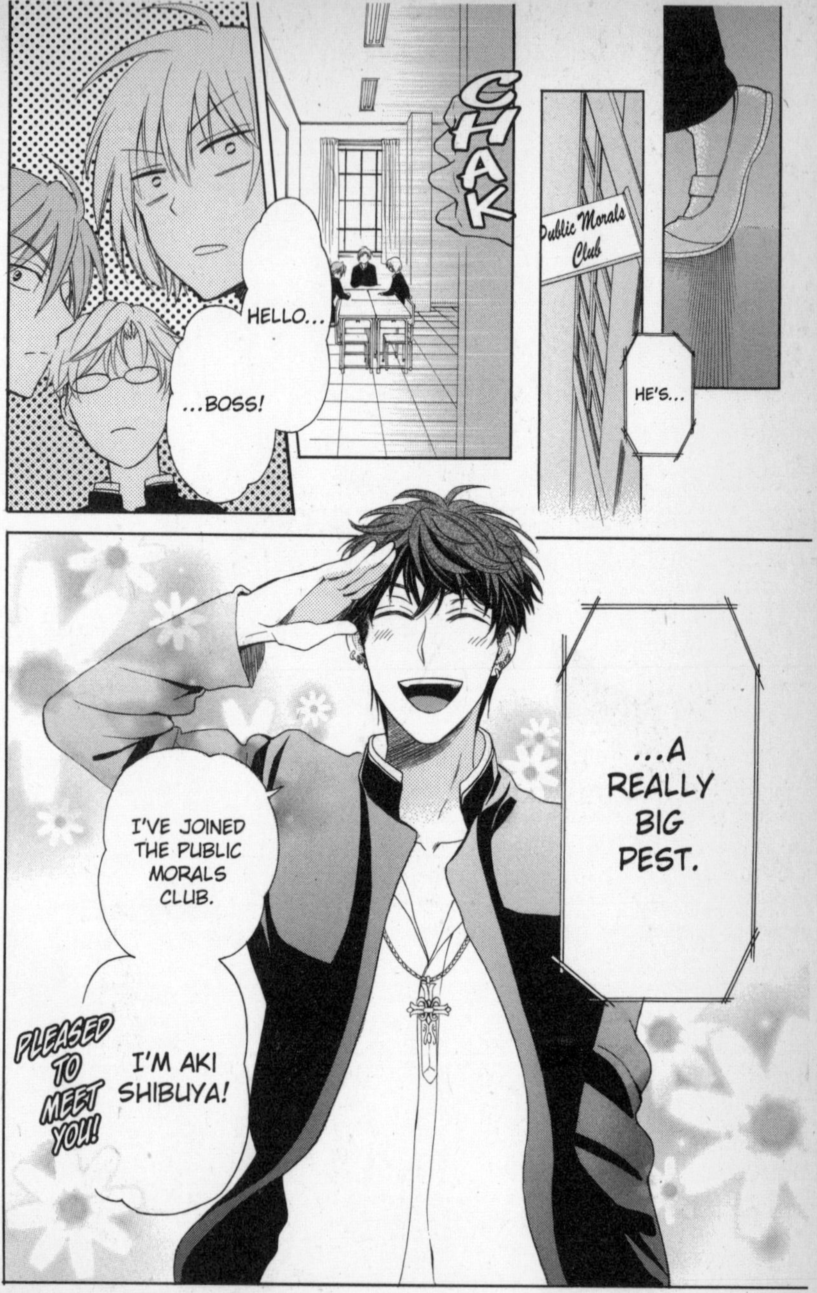
Public Morals Club
HE'S...
CHAK
HELLO...
...BOSS!
...A REALLY BIG PEST.
I'VE JOINED THE PUBLIC MORALS CLUB.
I'M AKI SHIBUYA!
PLEASED TO MEET YOU!

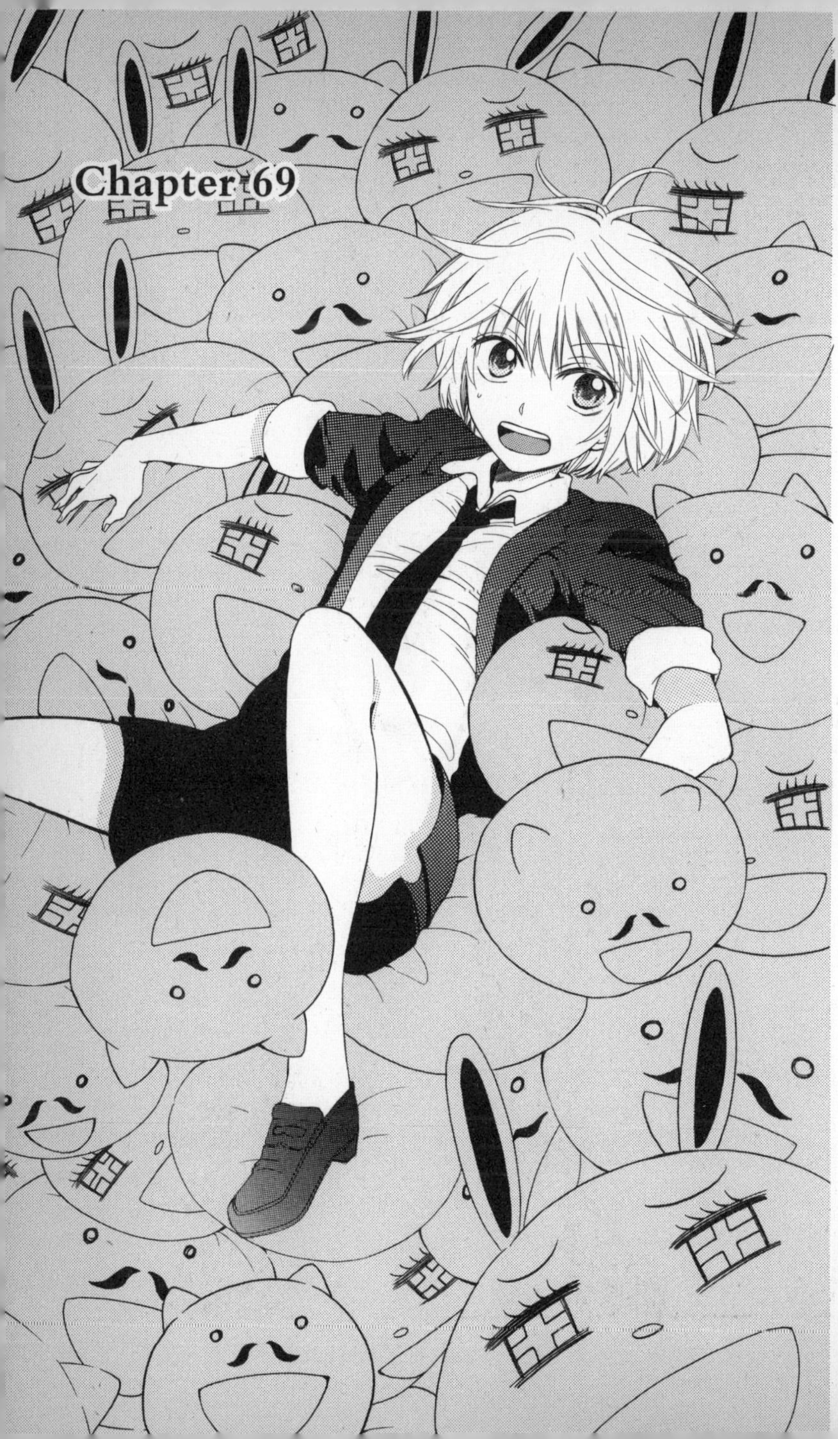
Chapter 69

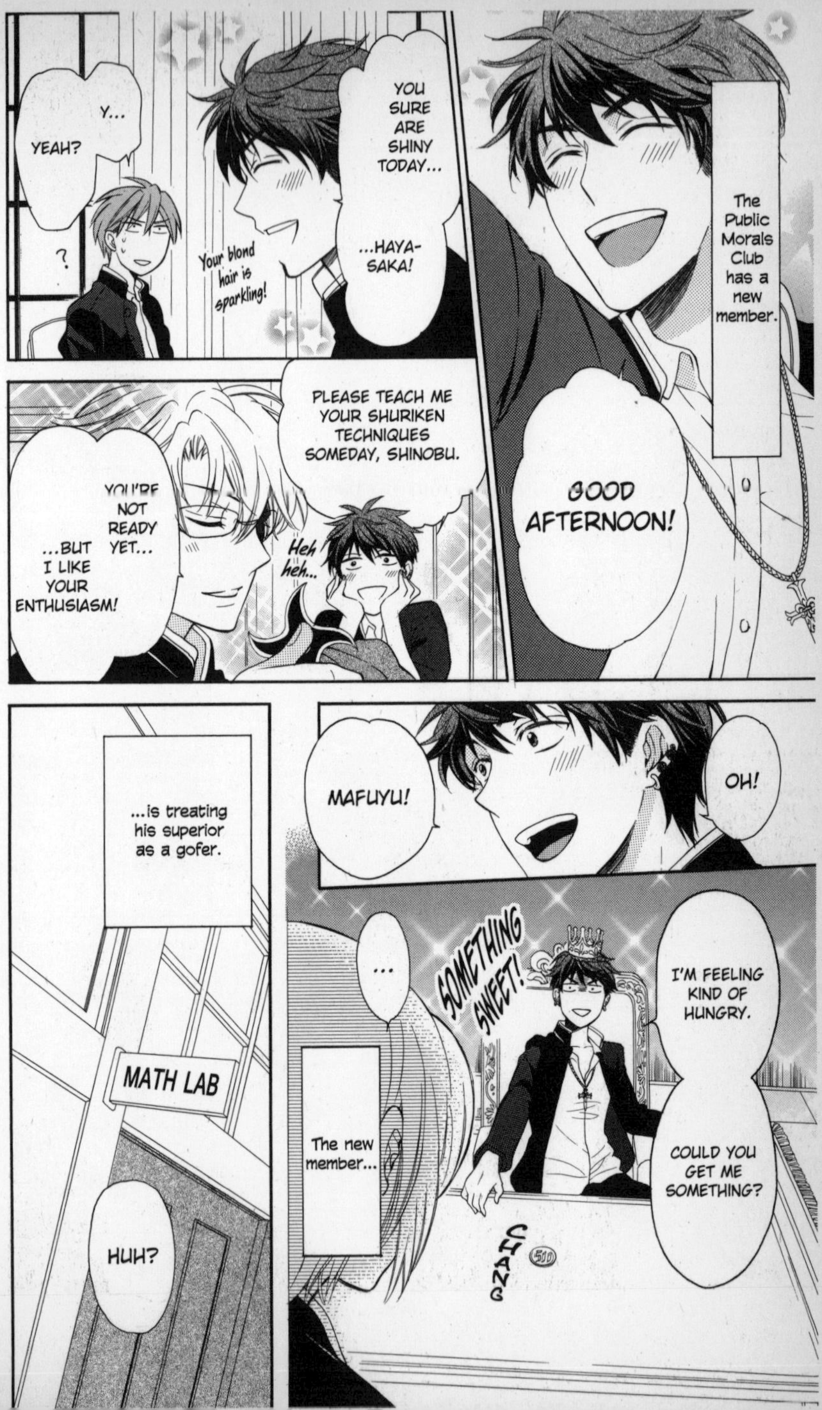
The Public Morals Club has a new member.
GOOD AFTERNOON!
YOU SURE ARE SHINY TODAY...
...HAYA-SAKA!
Your blond hair is sparkling!
Y...
YEAH?
?
PLEASE TEACH ME YOUR SHURIKEN TECHNIQUES SOMEDAY, SHINOBU.
Heh heh...
YOU'RE NOT READY YET...
...BUT I LIKE YOUR ENTHUSIASM!
OH!
MAFUYU!
I'M FEELING KIND OF HUNGRY.
SOMETHING SWEET!
COULD YOU GET ME SOMETHING?
...
The new member...
CHANG
510
...is treating his superior as a gofer.
MATH LAB
HUH?

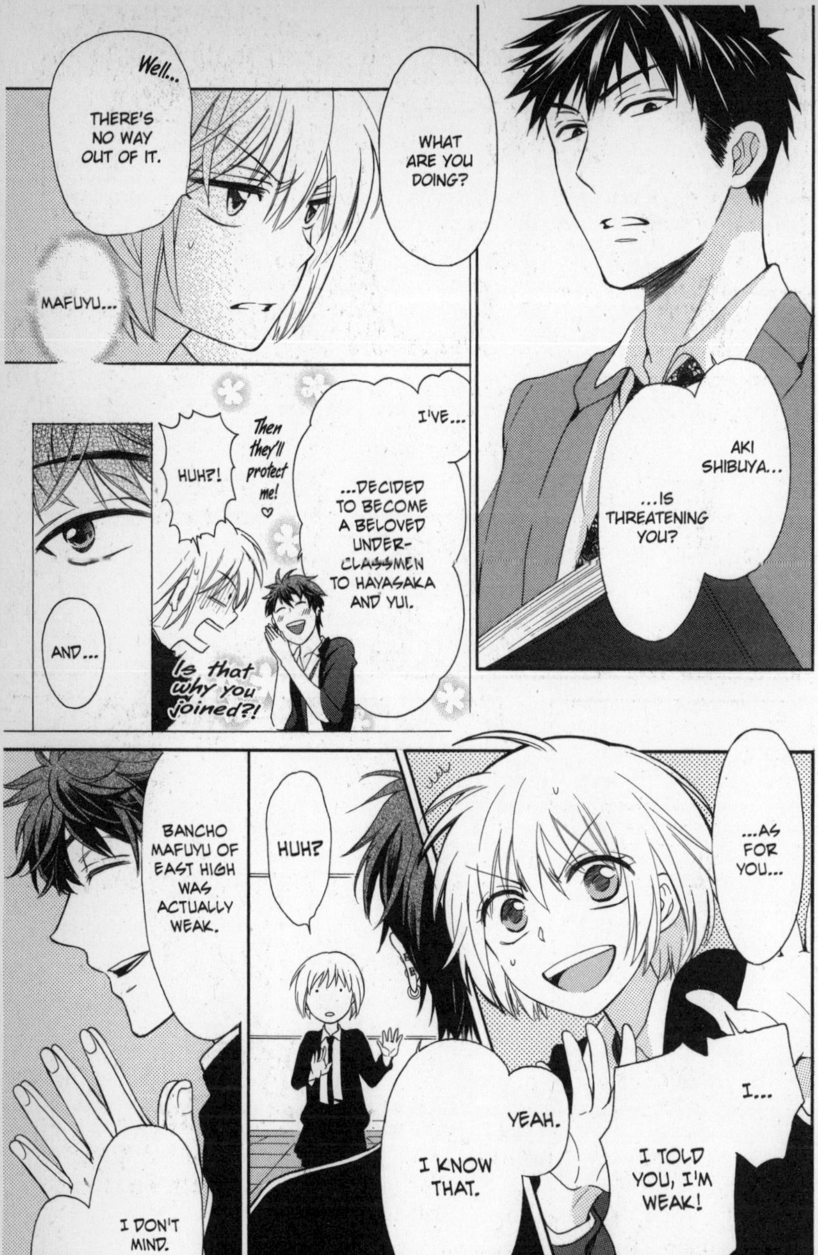
WHAT ARE YOU DOING?
AKI SHIBUYA...
...IS THREATENING YOU?
Well...
THERE'S NO WAY OUT OF IT.
MAFUYU...
I'VE...
...DECIDED TO BECOME A BELOVED UNDER-CLASSMEN TO HAYASAKA AND YUI.
HUH?!
Then they'll protect me! ♡
Is that why you joined?!
AND...
...AS FOR YOU...
I...
I TOLD YOU, I'M WEAK!
YEAH.
I KNOW THAT.
HUH?
BANCHO MAFUYU OF EAST HIGH WAS ACTUALLY WEAK.
I DON'T MIND.
BUT...

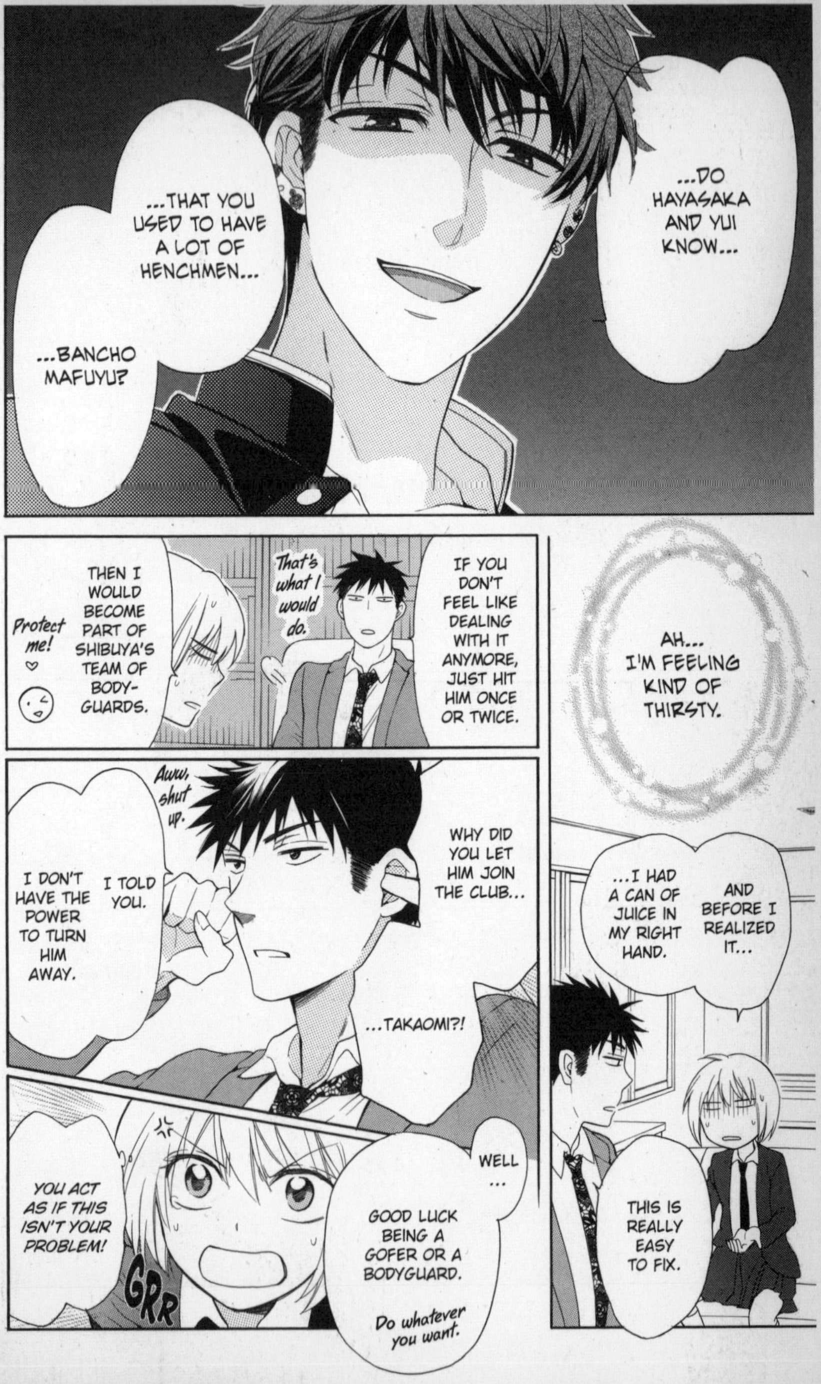
...DO HAYASAKA AND YUI KNOW...
...THAT YOU USED TO HAVE A LOT OF HENCHMEN...
...BANCHO MAFUYU?
AH... I'M FEELING KIND OF THIRSTY.
AND BEFORE I REALIZED IT...
...I HAD A CAN OF JUICE IN MY RIGHT HAND.
THIS IS REALLY EASY TO FIX.
IF YOU DON'T FEEL LIKE DEALING WITH IT ANYMORE, JUST HIT HIM ONCE OR TWICE.
That's what I would do.
THEN I WOULD BECOME PART OF SHIBUYA'S TEAM OF BODY-GUARDS.
Protect me! ♡
WHY DID YOU LET HIM JOIN THE CLUB...
...TAKAOMI?!
Aww, shut up.
I TOLD YOU.
I DON'T HAVE THE POWER TO TURN HIM AWAY.
WELL...
GOOD LUCK BEING A GOFER OR A BODYGUARD.
Do whatever you want.
YOU ACT AS IF THIS ISN'T YOUR PROBLEM!
GRR

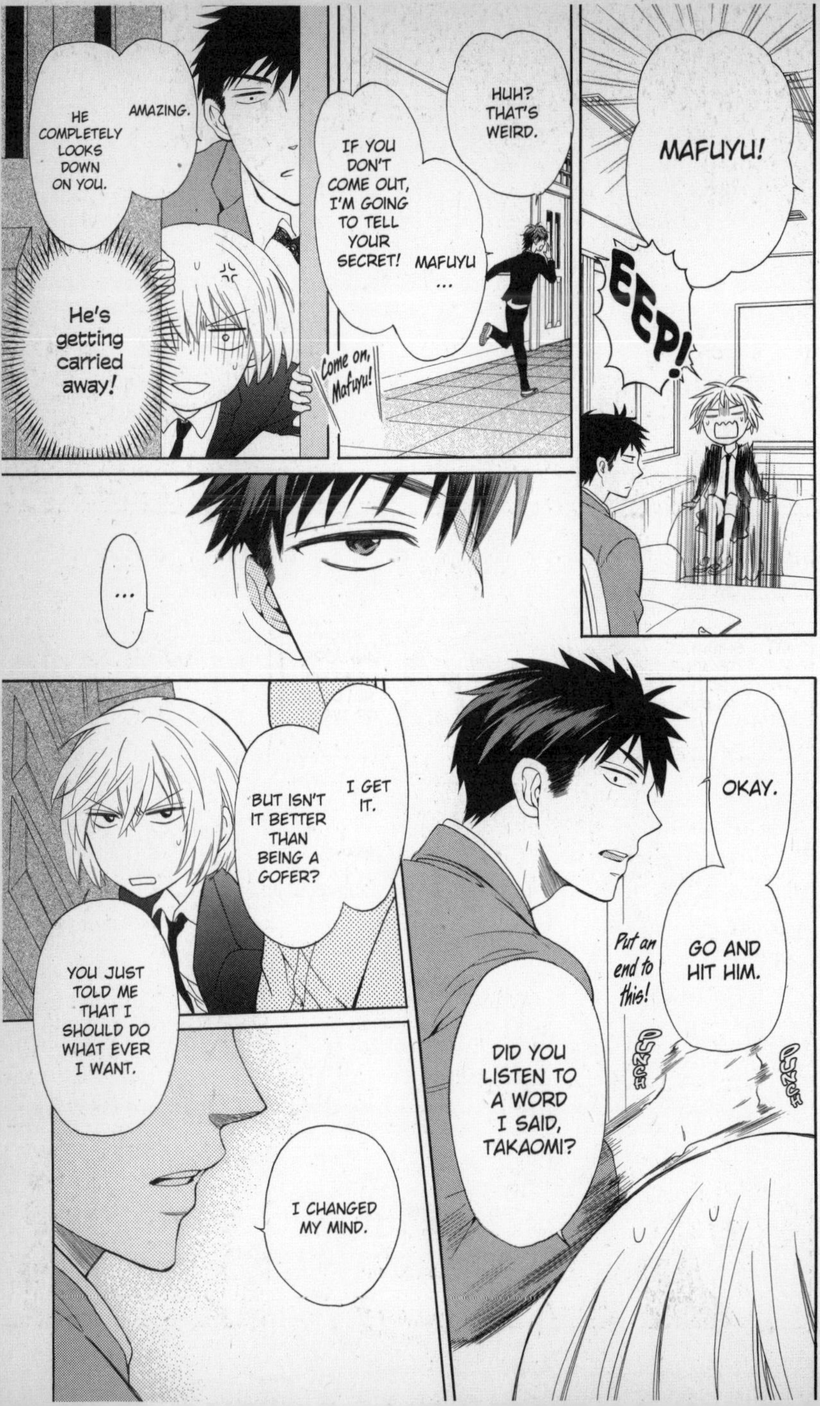
MAFUYU!
EEP!
HUH? THAT'S WEIRD.
IF YOU DON'T COME OUT, I'M GOING TO TELL YOUR SECRET!
MAFUYU ...
Come on, Mafuyu!
AMAZING.
HE COMPLETELY LOOKS DOWN ON YOU.
He's getting carried away!
...
OKAY.
GO AND HIT HIM.
Put an end to this!
PUNCH
PUNCH
I GET IT.
BUT ISN'T IT BETTER THAN BEING A GOFER?
YOU JUST TOLD ME THAT I SHOULD DO WHAT EVER I WANT.
DID YOU LISTEN TO A WORD I SAID, TAKAOMI?
I CHANGED MY MIND.

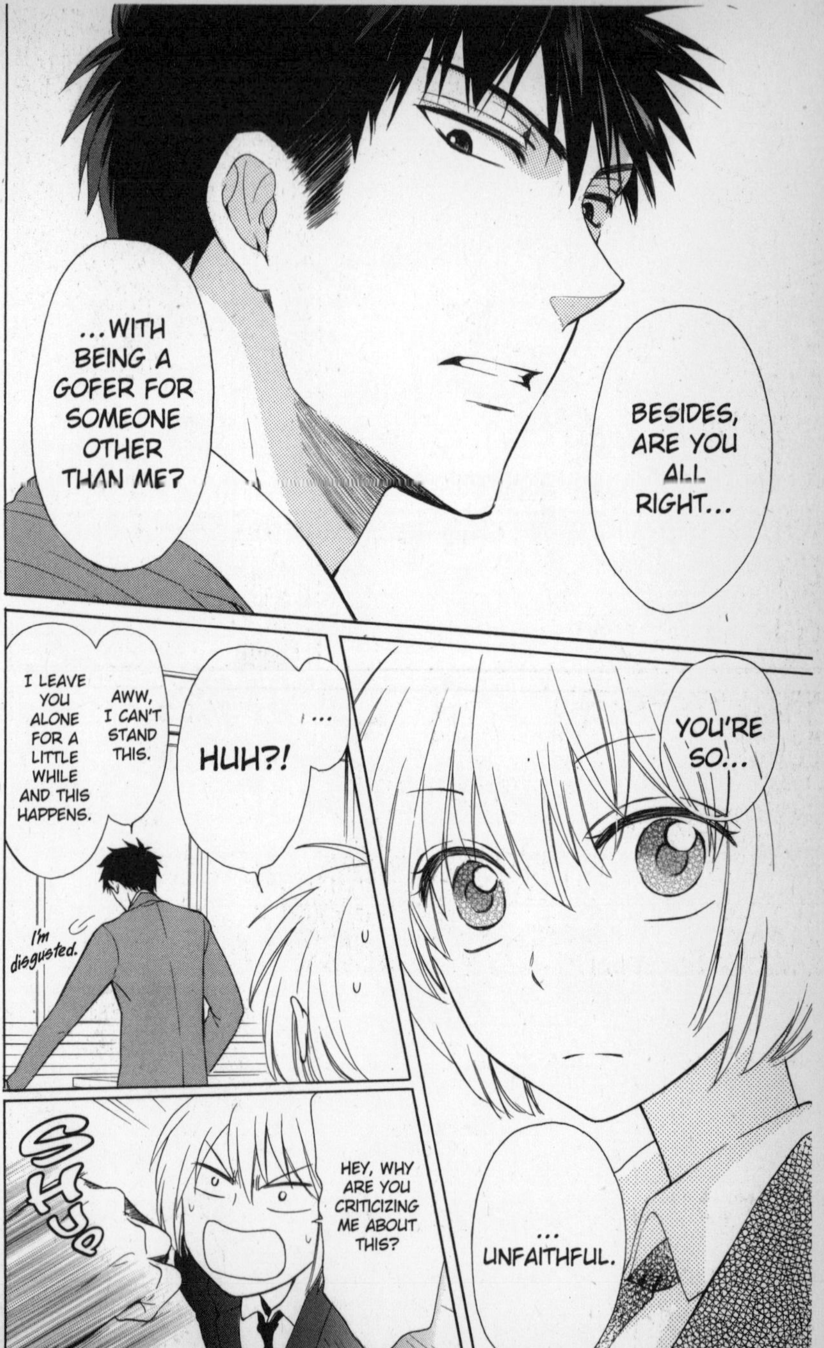
BESIDES, ARE YOU ALL RIGHT...
...WITH BEING A GOFER FOR SOMEONE OTHER THAN ME?
YOU'RE SO...
... UNFAITHFUL.
...
HUH?!
AWW, I CAN'T STAND THIS.
I LEAVE YOU ALONE FOR A LITTLE WHILE AND THIS HAPPENS.
I'm disgusted.
HEY, WHY ARE YOU CRITICIZING ME ABOUT THIS?

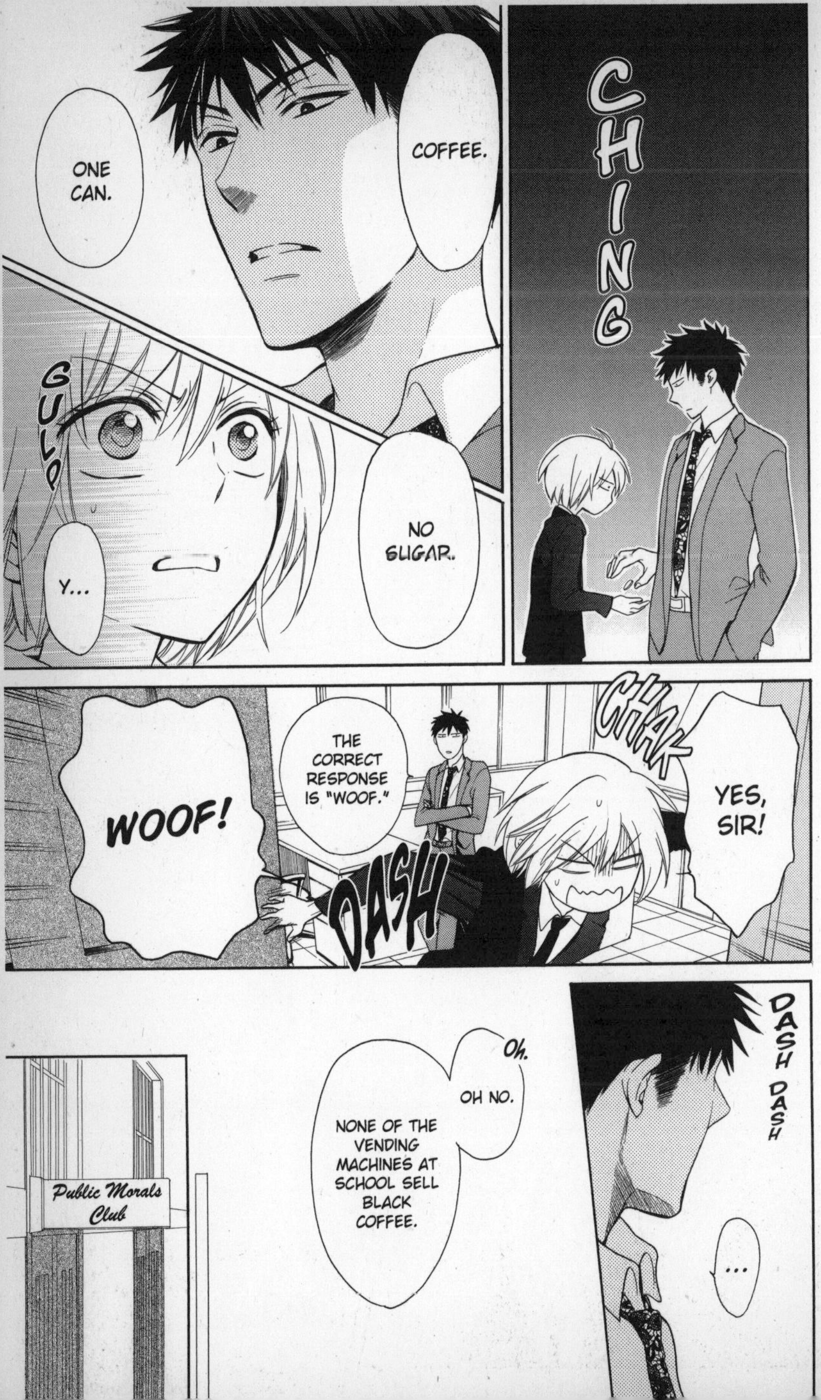
CHING
COFFEE.
ONE CAN.
NO SUGAR.
GULP
Y...
YES, SIR!
CHAK
THE CORRECT RESPONSE IS "WOOF."
DASH
WOOF!
DASH DASH DASH
...
Oh.
OH NO.
NONE OF THE VENDING MACHINES AT SCHOOL SELL BLACK COFFEE.
Public Morals Club

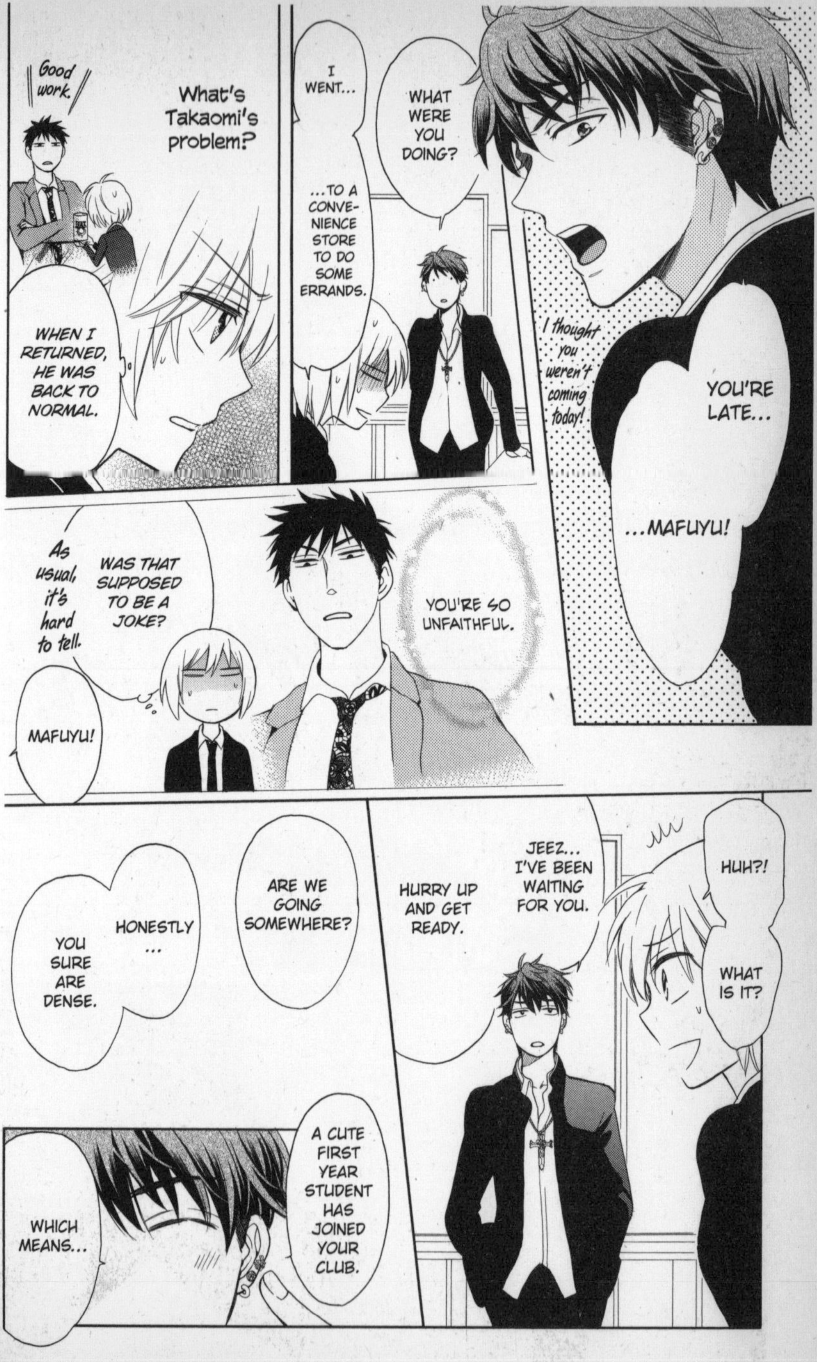
YOU'RE LATE...
...MAFUYU!
I thought you weren't coming today!
WHAT WERE YOU DOING?
I WENT...
...TO A CONVENIENCE STORE TO DO SOME ERRANDS.
What's Takaomi's problem?
Good work.
WHEN I RETURNED, HE WAS BACK TO NORMAL.
YOU'RE SO UNFAITHFUL.
WAS THAT SUPPOSED TO BE A JOKE?
As usual, it's hard to tell.
MAFUYU!
HUH?!
WHAT IS IT?
JEEZ... I'VE BEEN WAITING FOR YOU.
HURRY UP AND GET READY.
ARE WE GOING SOMEWHERE?
HONESTLY...
YOU SURE ARE DENSE.
A CUTE FIRST YEAR STUDENT HAS JOINED YOUR CLUB.
WHICH MEANS...

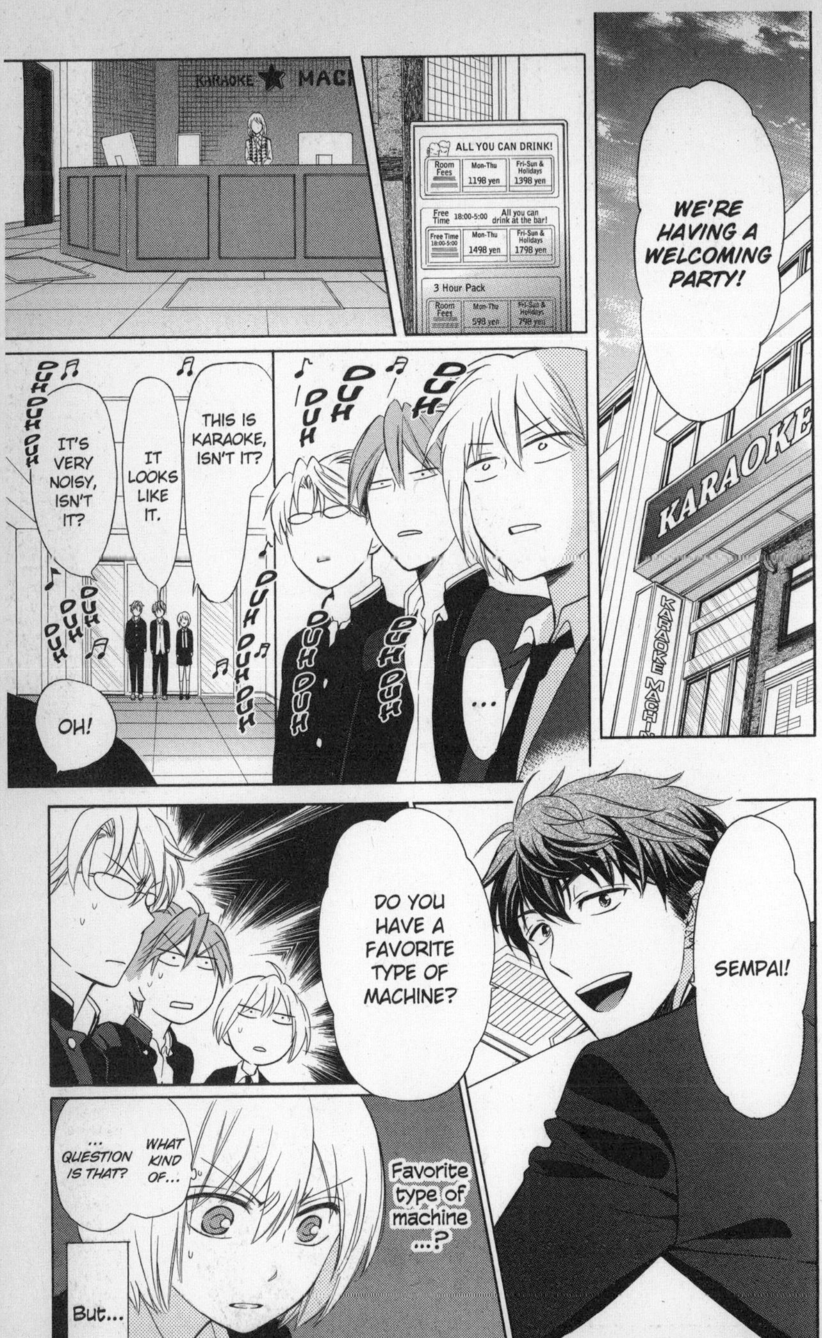
WE'RE HAVING A WELCOMING PARTY!
KARAOKE
KARAOKE
KARAOKE MACHIN
ALL YOU CAN DRINK!
Room Fees
Mon-Thu 1198 yen
Fri-Sun & Holidays 1398 yen
Free Time 18:00-5:00
All you can drink at the bar!
Free Time 18:00-5:00
Mon-Thu 1498 yen
Fri-Sun & Holidays 1798 yen
3 Hour Pack
Room Fees
Mon-Thu 598 yen
Fri-Sun & Holidays 798 yen
KARAOKE ★ MACH
...
DUH DUH DUH
DUH DUH
DUH DUH
DUH DUH DUH DUH
THIS IS KARAOKE, ISN'T IT?
IT LOOKS LIKE IT.
IT'S VERY NOISY, ISN'T IT?
DUH DUH DUH
DUH DUH DUH
OH!
SEMPAI!
DO YOU HAVE A FAVORITE TYPE OF MACHINE?
Favorite type of machine ...?
WHAT KIND OF...
... QUESTION IS THAT?
But...

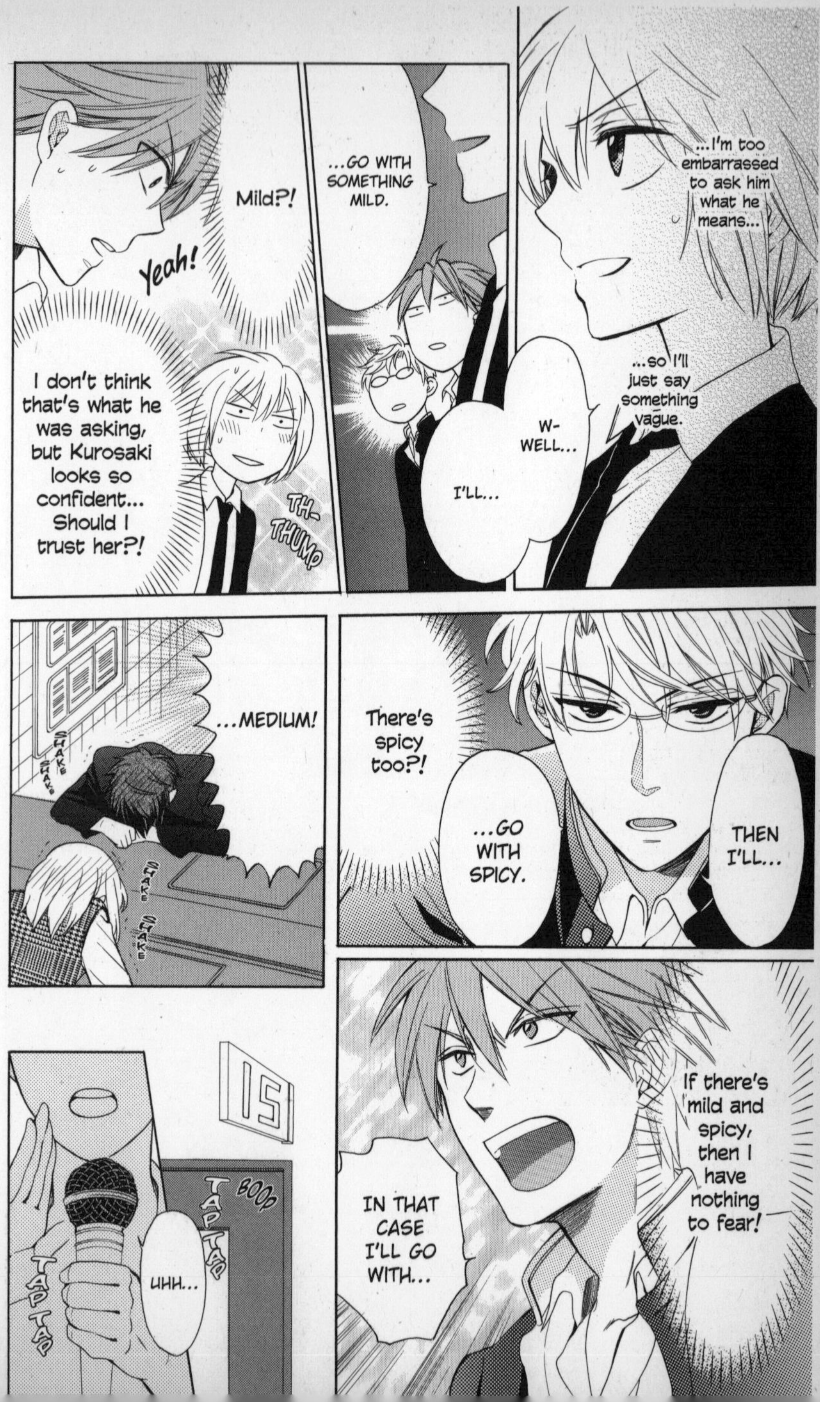
...I'm too embarrassed to ask him what he means...
...so I'll just say something vague.
W-WELL...
I'LL...
...GO WITH SOMETHING MILD.
Mild?!
Yeah!
I don't think that's what he was asking, but Kurosaki looks so confident... Should I trust her?!
TH-THUMP
THEN I'LL...
...GO WITH SPICY.
There's spicy too?!
...MEDIUM!
SHAKE SHAKE
SHAKE SHAKE
If there's mild and spicy, then I have nothing to fear!
IN THAT CASE I'LL GO WITH...
15
BOOP
TAP TAP
UHH...
TAP TAP

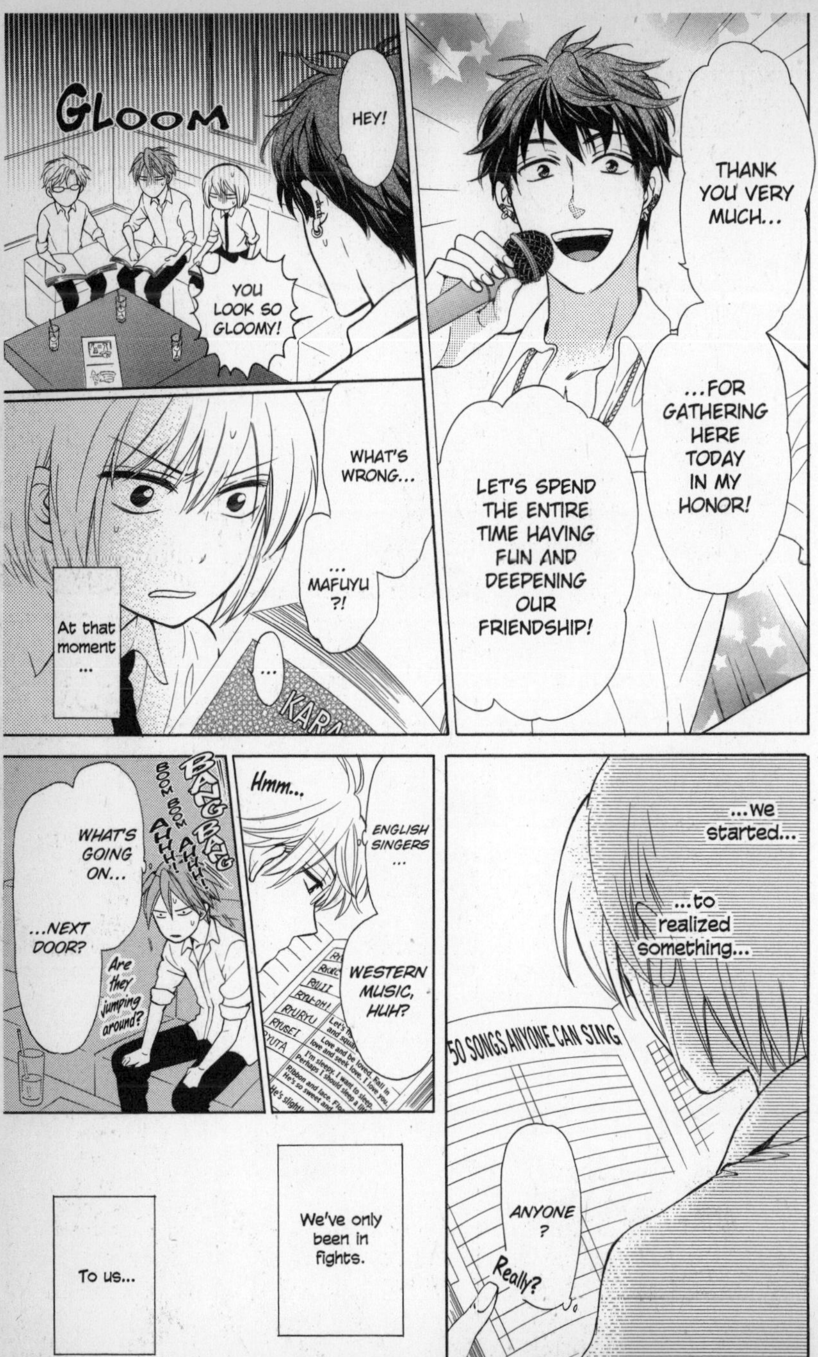
THANK YOU VERY MUCH...
...FOR GATHERING HERE TODAY IN MY HONOR!
LET'S SPEND THE ENTIRE TIME HAVING FUN AND DEEPENING OUR FRIENDSHIP!
HEY!
GLOOM
YOU LOOK SO GLOOMY!
WHAT'S WRONG...
...MAFUYU?!
...
At that moment...
...we started...
...to realized something...
50 SONGS ANYONE CAN SING
ANYONE?
Really?
Hmm...
ENGLISH SINGERS...
WESTERN MUSIC, HUH?
WHAT'S GOING ON...
...NEXT DOOR?
BANG BANG
BOOM BOOM
AHHH! AHHH!
Are they jumping around?
We've only been in fights.
To us...

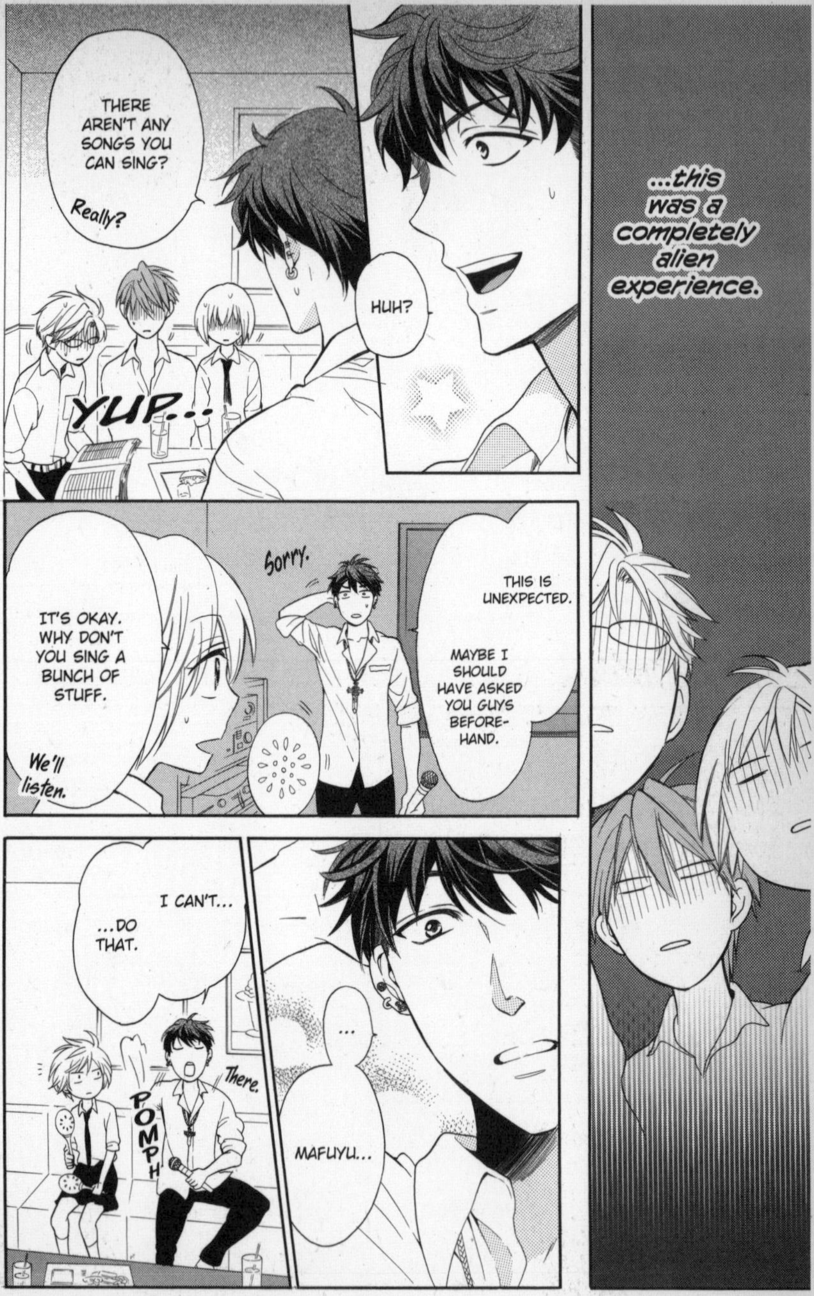
...this was a completely alien experience.
HUH?
THERE AREN'T ANY SONGS YOU CAN SING?
Really?
YUP...
THIS IS UNEXPECTED.
MAYBE I SHOULD HAVE ASKED YOU GUYS BEFORE-HAND.
Sorry.
IT'S OKAY. WHY DON'T YOU SING A BUNCH OF STUFF.
We'll listen.
...
MAFUYU...
I CAN'T...
...DO THAT.
There.
POMPH

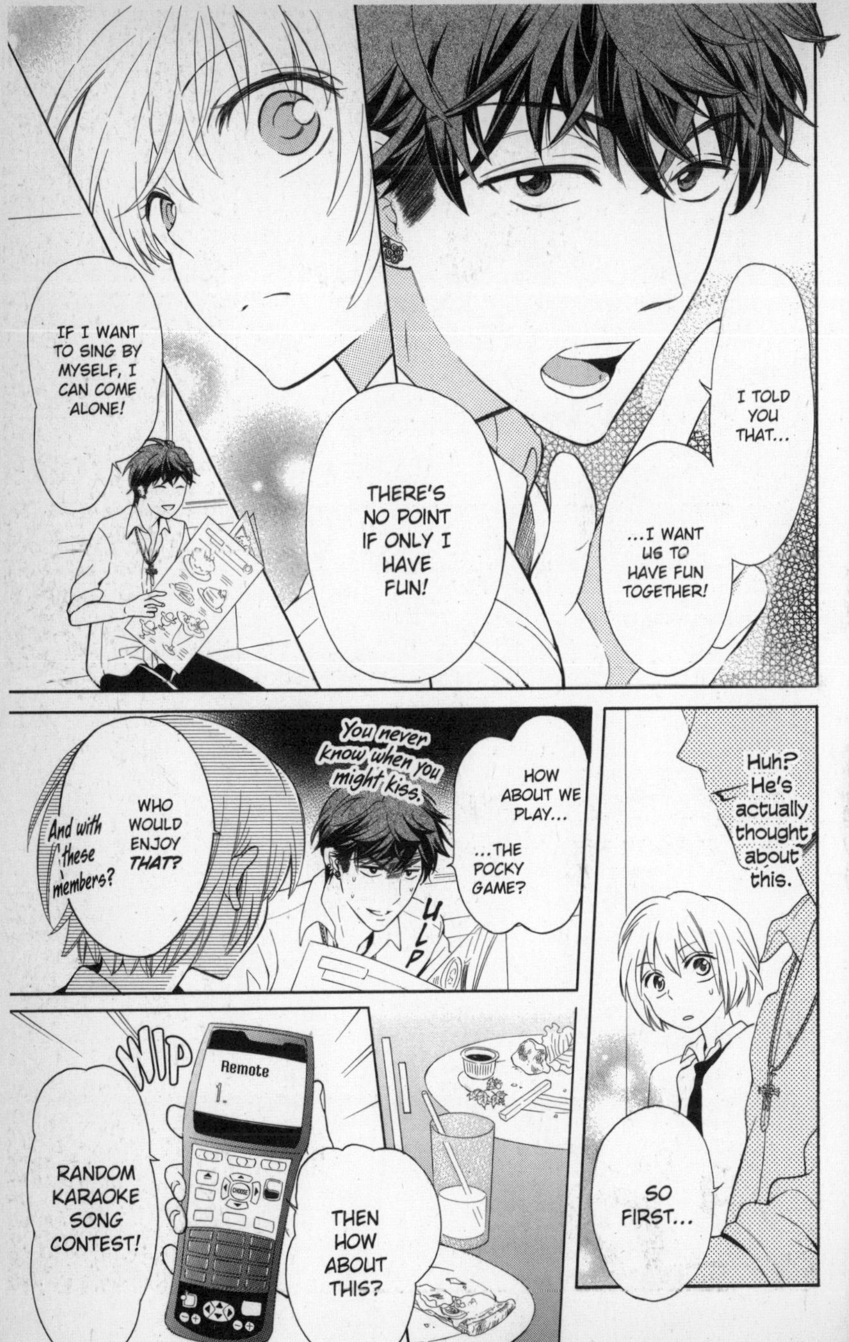
I TOLD YOU THAT...
...I WANT US TO HAVE FUN TOGETHER!
THERE'S NO POINT IF ONLY I HAVE FUN!
IF I WANT TO SING BY MYSELF, I CAN COME ALONE!
Huh? He's actually thought about this.
HOW ABOUT WE PLAY...
...THE POCKY GAME?
You never know when you might kiss.
ULP
WHO WOULD ENJOY *THAT?*
And with these members?
SO FIRST...
THEN HOW ABOUT THIS?
WIP
Remote
1.
RANDOM KARAOKE SONG CONTEST!

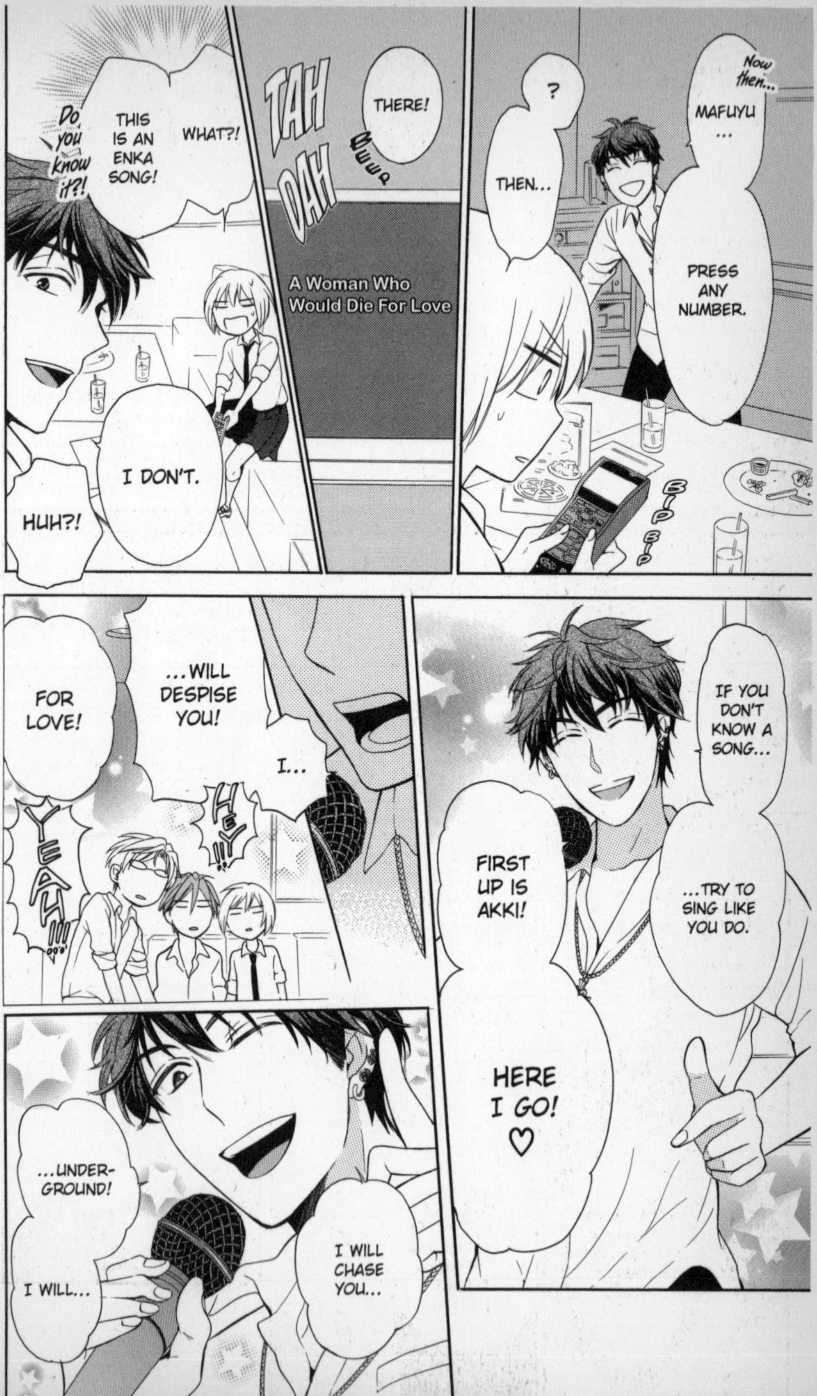
Now then...
MAFUYU...
PRESS ANY NUMBER.
?
THEN...
BIP BIP
THERE!
TAH DAH
A Woman Who Would Die For Love
WHAT?!
THIS IS AN ENKA SONG!
Do you know it?!
I DON'T.
HUH?!
IF YOU DON'T KNOW A SONG...
...TRY TO SING LIKE YOU DO.
FIRST UP IS AKKI!
HERE I GO! ♡
I...
...WILL DESPISE YOU!
FOR LOVE!
HEY!!!
YEAH!!!
I WILL CHASE YOU...
...UNDER-GROUND!
I WILL...

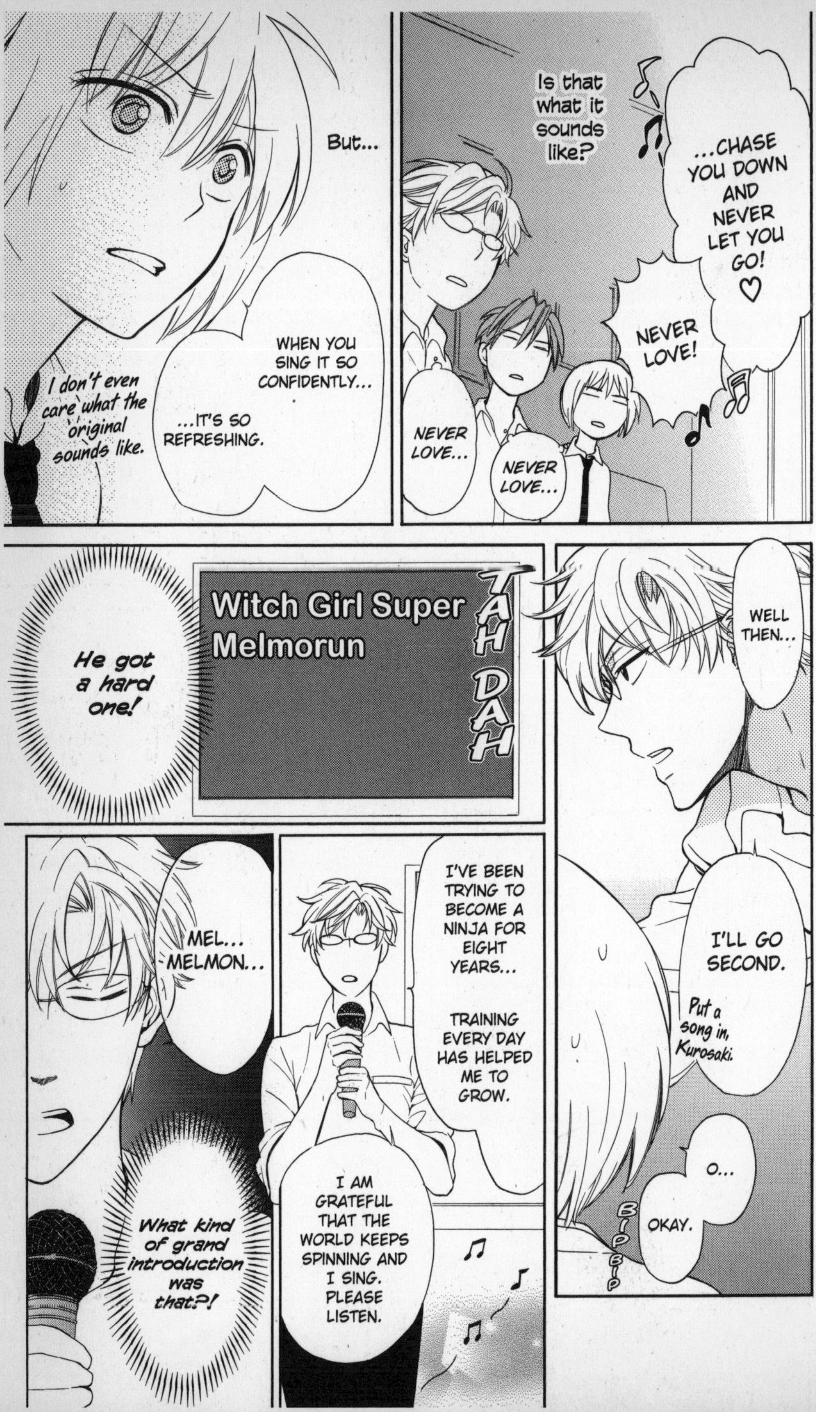
...CHASE YOU DOWN AND NEVER LET YOU GO! ♡
Is that what it sounds like?
NEVER LOVE!
NEVER LOVE...
NEVER LOVE...
But...
WHEN YOU SING IT SO CONFIDENTLY...
...IT'S SO REFRESHING.
I don't even care what the original sounds like.
WELL THEN...
I'LL GO SECOND.
Put a song in, Kurosaki.
O...
OKAY.
BIP BIP
TAH DAH
Witch Girl Super Melmorun
He got a hard one!
I'VE BEEN TRYING TO BECOME A NINJA FOR EIGHT YEARS...
TRAINING EVERY DAY HAS HELPED ME TO GROW.
I AM GRATEFUL THAT THE WORLD KEEPS SPINNING AND I SING. PLEASE LISTEN.
MEL... MELMON...
What kind of grand introduction was that?!

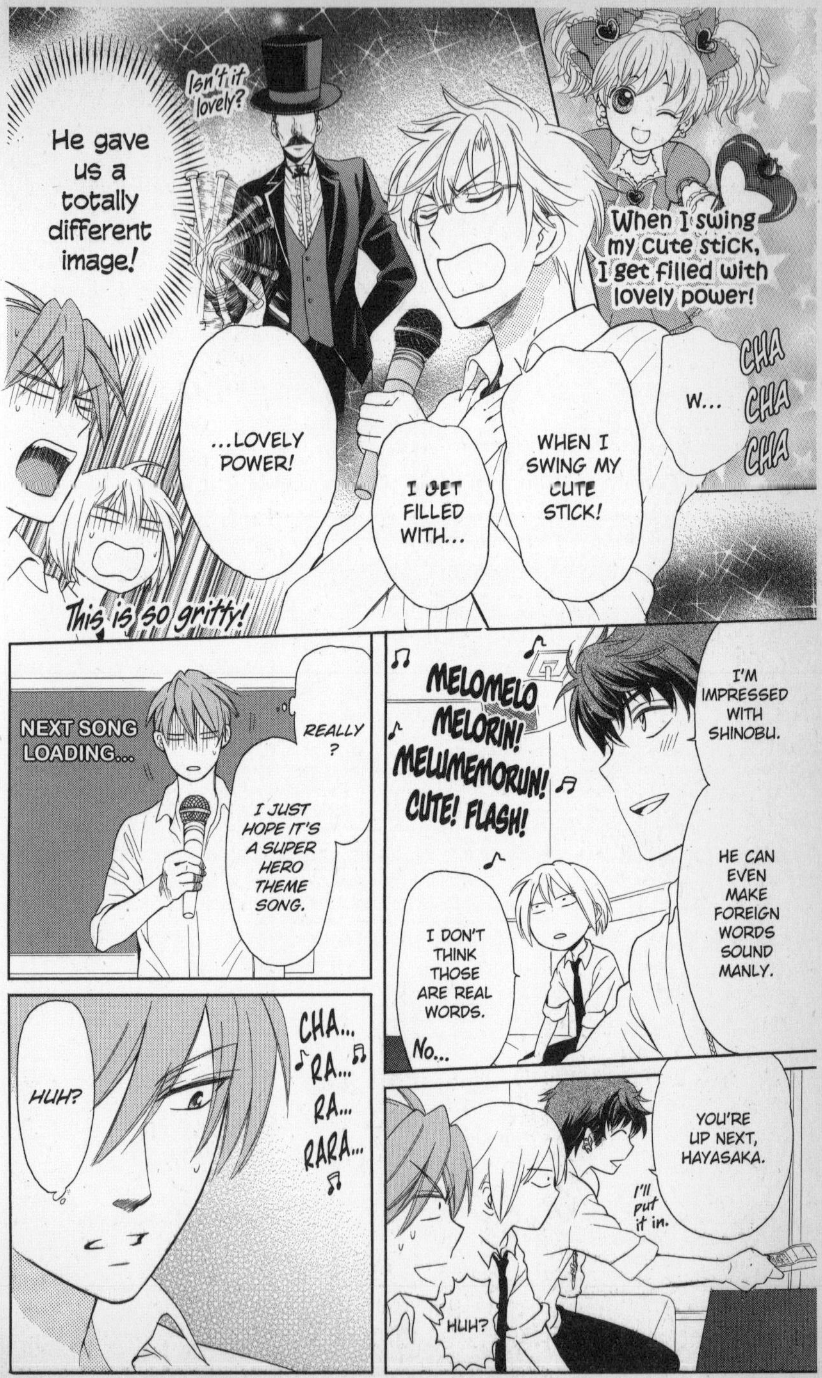
When I swing my cute stick, I get filled with lovely power!
CHA CHA CHA
W...
WHEN I SWING MY CUTE STICK!
I GET FILLED WITH...
...LOVELY POWER!
Isn't it lovely?
He gave us a totally different image!
This is so gritty!
I'M IMPRESSED WITH SHINOBU.
MELOMELO MELORIN! MELUMEMORUN! CUTE! FLASH!
HE CAN EVEN MAKE FOREIGN WORDS SOUND MANLY.
I DON'T THINK THOSE ARE REAL WORDS.
No...
REALLY?
NEXT SONG LOADING...
I JUST HOPE IT'S A SUPER HERO THEME SONG.
YOU'RE UP NEXT, HAYASAKA.
I'll put it in.
HUH?
CHA... RA... RA... RARA...
HUH?

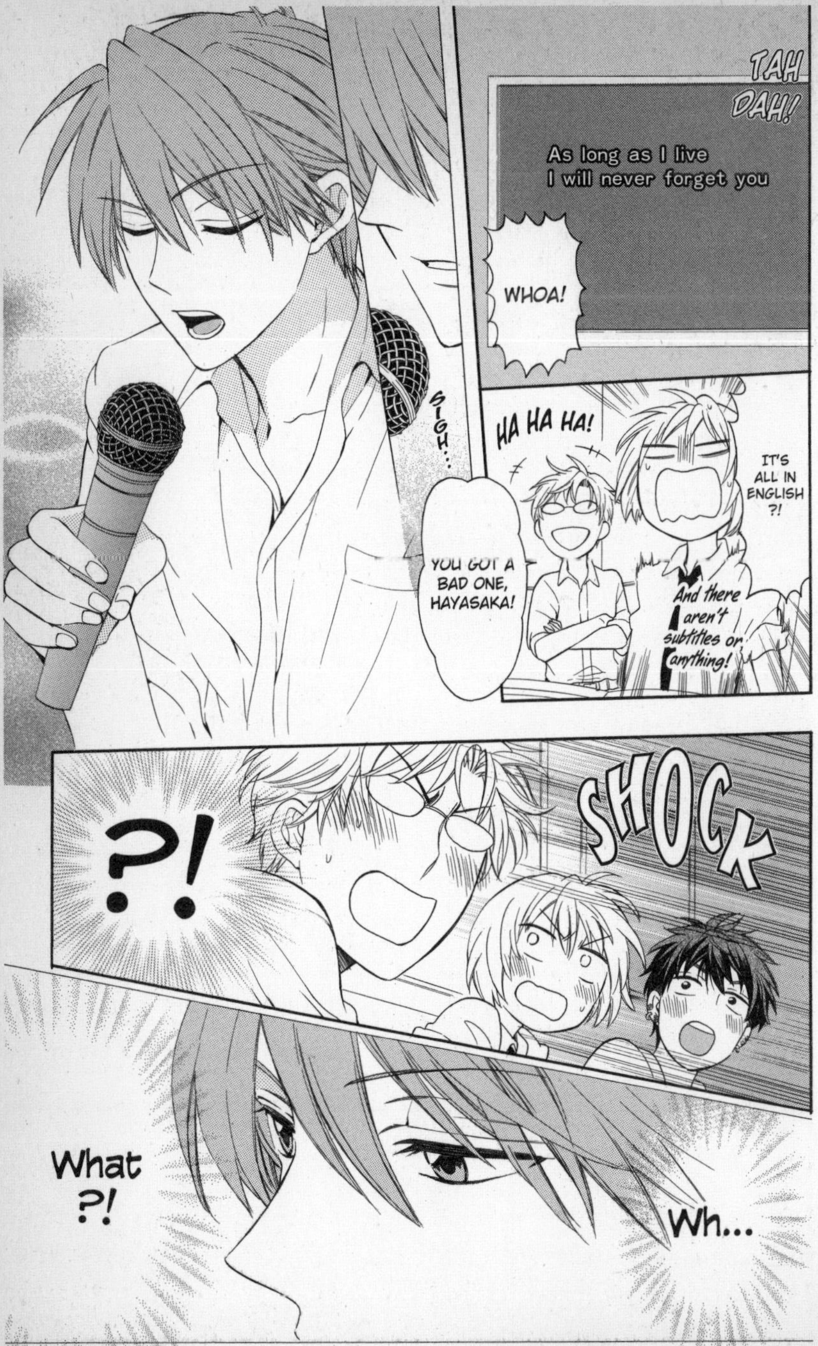
TAH DAH!
As long as I live
I will never forget you
WHOA!
HA HA HA!
IT'S ALL IN ENGLISH?!
And there aren't subtitles or anything!
YOU GOT A BAD ONE, HAYASAKA!
SIGH...
SHOCK
?!
Wh...
What?!

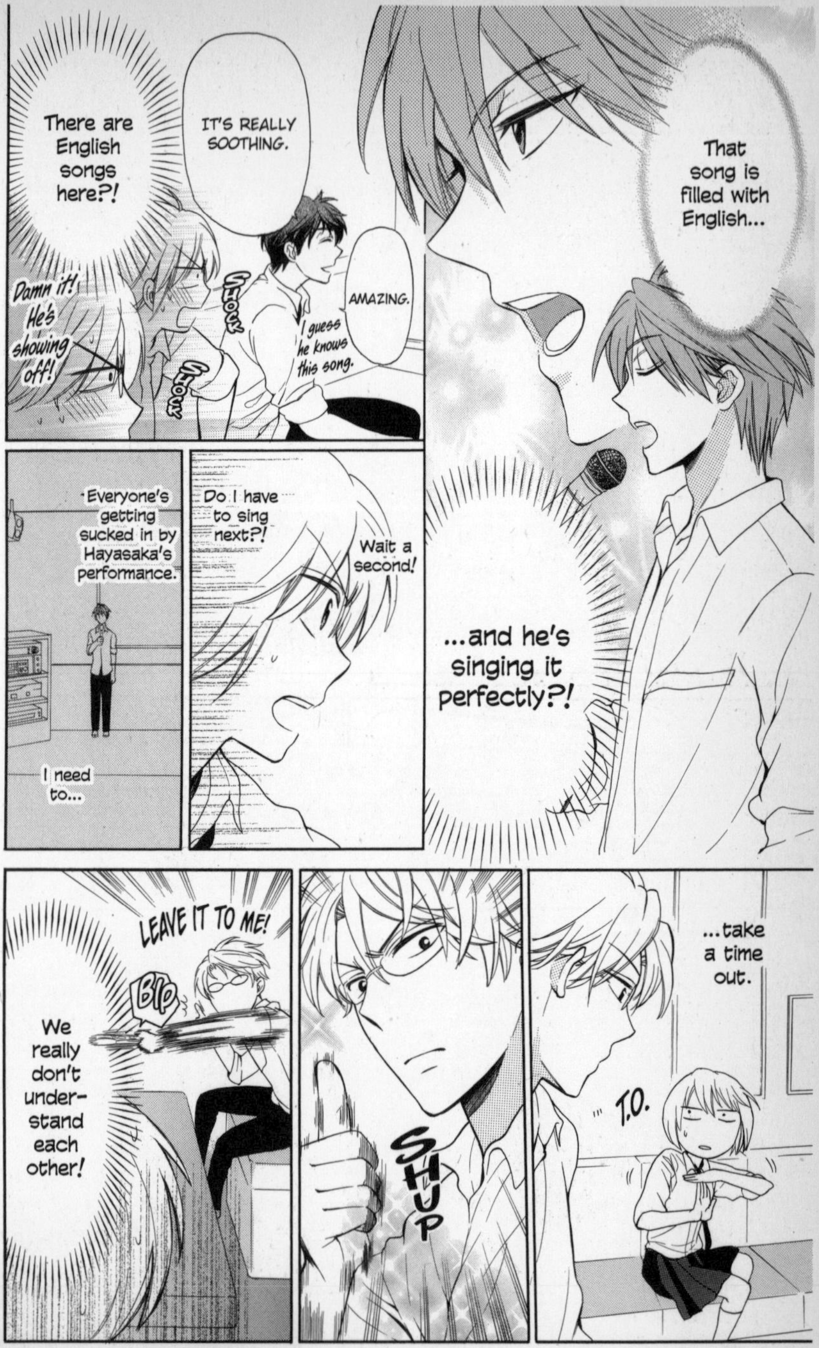
That song is filled with English...
...and he's singing it perfectly?!
IT'S REALLY SOOTHING.
There are English songs here?!
AMAZING.
I guess he knows this song.
SHOCK
SHOCK
Damn it! He's showing off!
Wait a second!
Do I have to sing next?!
Everyone's getting sucked in by Hayasaka's performance.
I need to...
...take a time out.
T.O.
SHUP
LEAVE IT TO ME!
BLIP
We really don't understand each other!

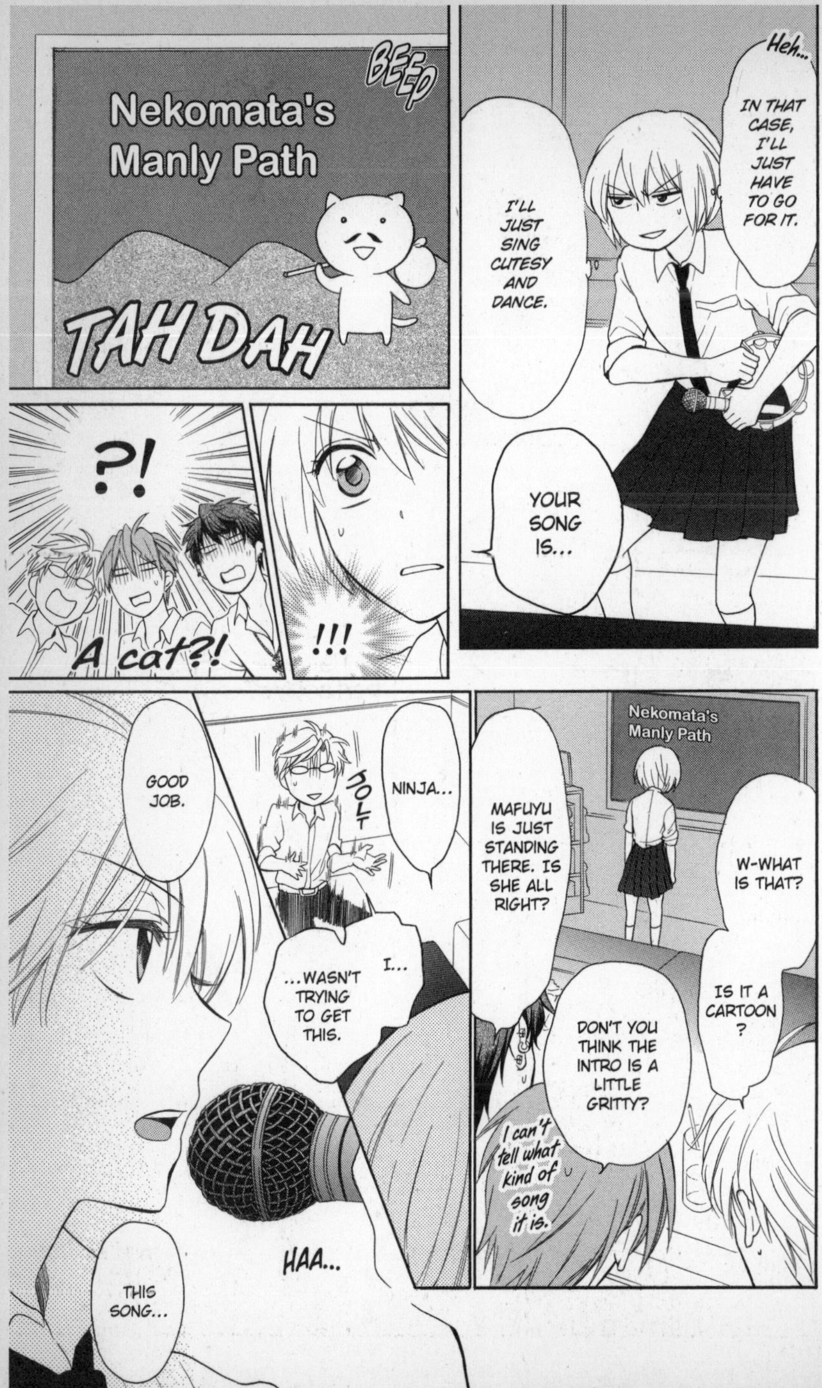
Heh...
IN THAT CASE, I'LL JUST HAVE TO GO FOR IT.
I'LL JUST SING CUTESY AND DANCE.
YOUR SONG IS...
BEEP
Nekomata's Manly Path
TAH DAH
!!!
?!
A cat?!
Nekomata's Manly Path
W-WHAT IS THAT?
MAFUYU IS JUST STANDING THERE. IS SHE ALL RIGHT?
IS IT A CARTOON?
DON'T YOU THINK THE INTRO IS A LITTLE GRITTY?
I can't tell what kind of song it is.
NINJA...
JOLT
GOOD JOB.
I...
...WASN'T TRYING TO GET THIS.
HAA...
THIS SONG...

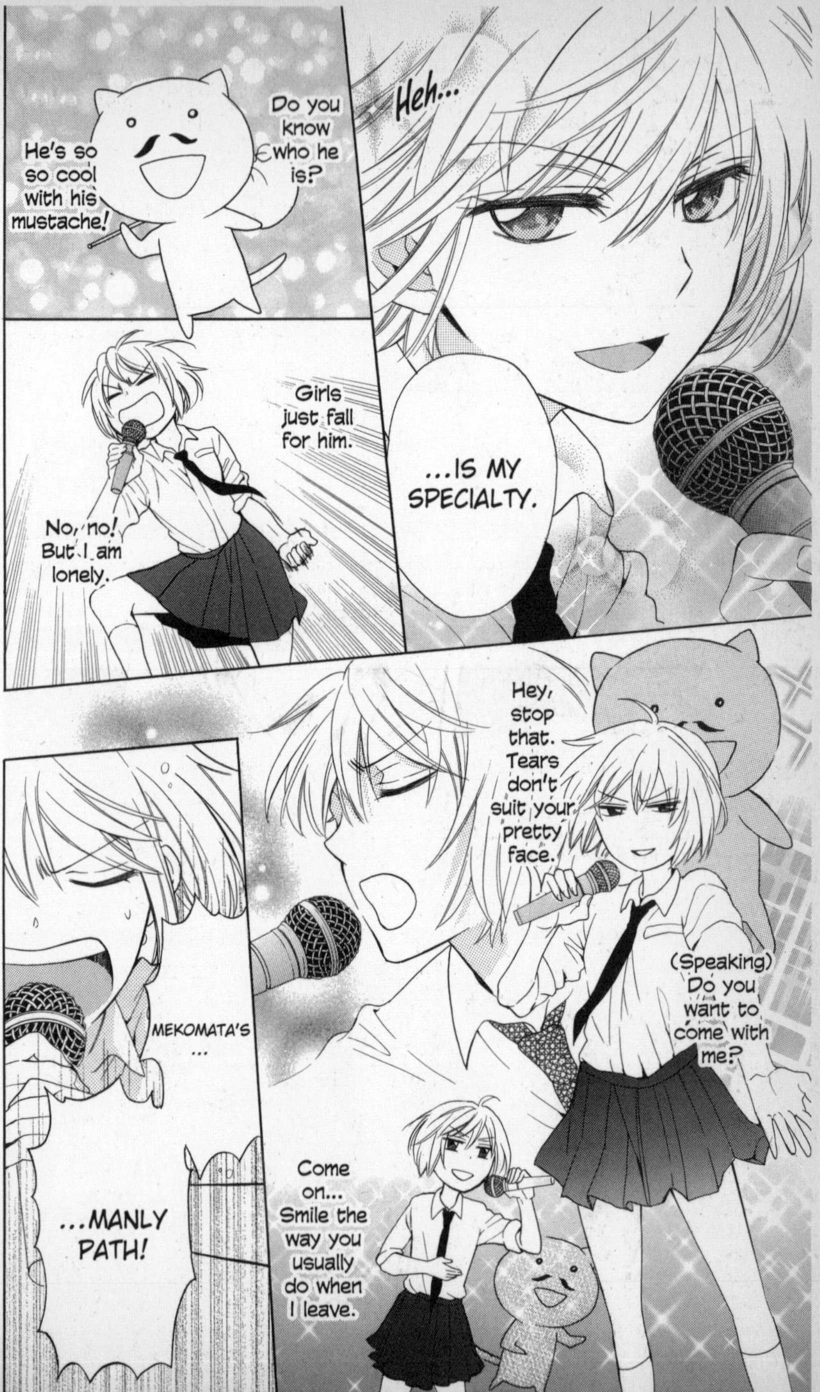
Heh...
...IS MY SPECIALTY.
Do you know who he is?
He's so so cool with his mustache!
Girls just fall for him.
No, no! But I am lonely.
Hey, stop that. Tears don't suit your pretty face.
(Speaking) Do you want to come with me?
Come on... Smile the way you usually do when I leave.
MEKOMATA'S ...
...MANLY PATH!

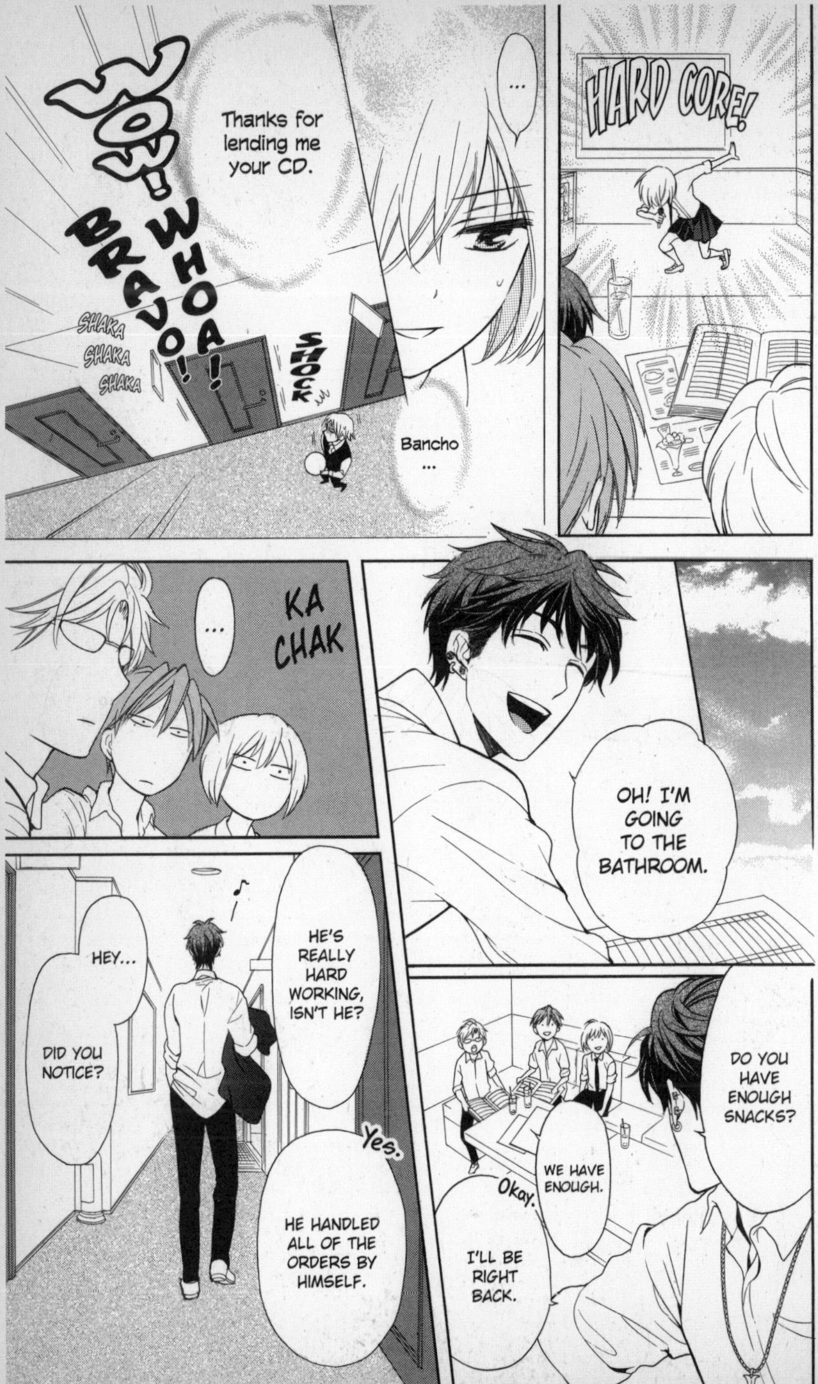
HARD CORE!
...
Thanks for lending me your CD.
Bancho ...
WOW! WHOA! BRAVO!
SHAKA SHAKA SHAKA
SHOCK
OH! I'M GOING TO THE BATHROOM.
...
KA CHAK
DO YOU HAVE ENOUGH SNACKS?
WE HAVE ENOUGH.
Okay.
I'LL BE RIGHT BACK.
HE'S REALLY HARD WORKING, ISN'T HE?
Yes.
HE HANDLED ALL OF THE ORDERS BY HIMSELF.
HEY...
DID YOU NOTICE?

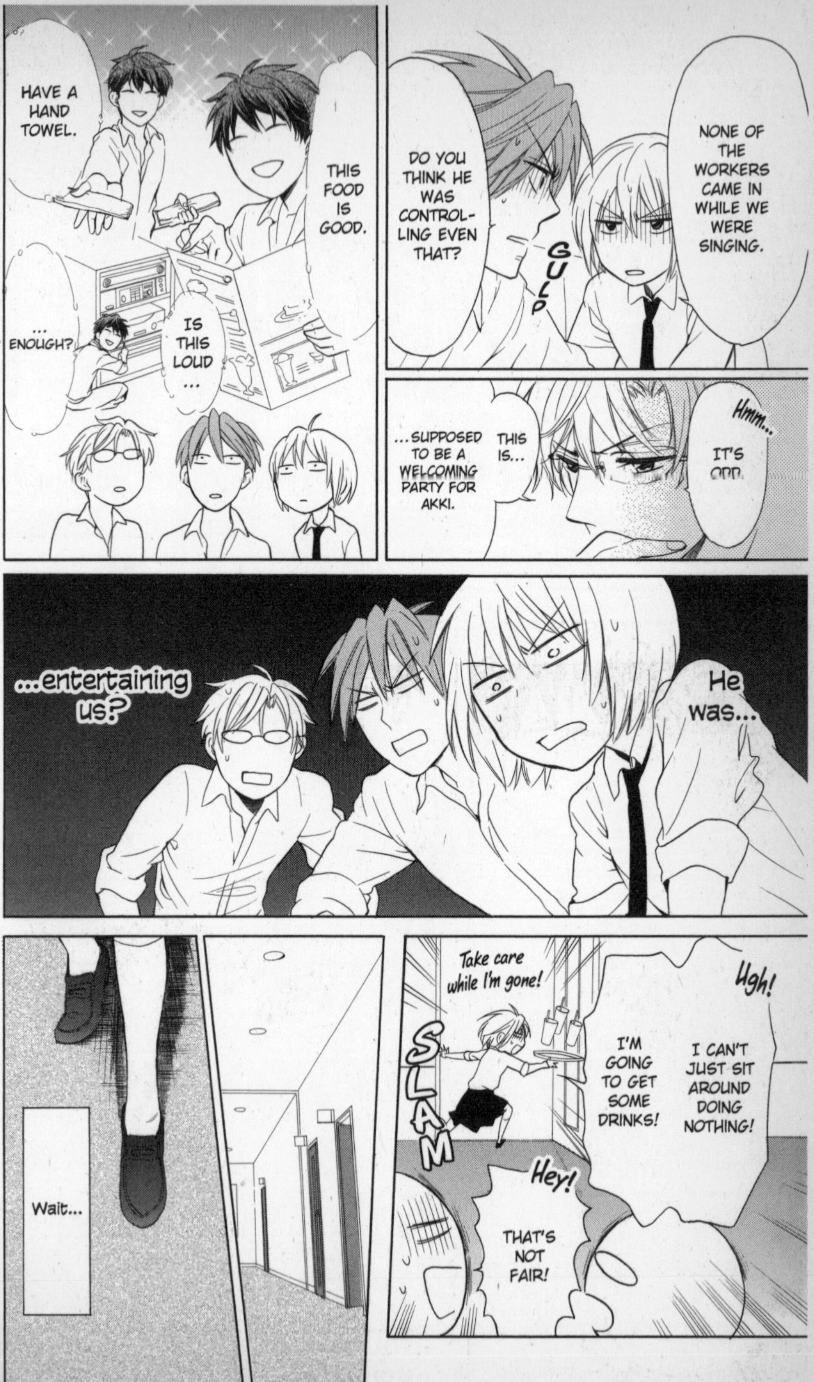
NONE OF THE WORKERS CAME IN WHILE WE WERE SINGING.
DO YOU THINK HE WAS CONTROLLING EVEN THAT?
GULP
Hmm...
IT'S ODD.
THIS IS...
...SUPPOSED TO BE A WELCOMING PARTY FOR AKKI.
THIS FOOD IS GOOD.
HAVE A HAND TOWEL.
IS THIS LOUD...
...ENOUGH?
He was...
...entertaining us?
Ugh!
I CAN'T JUST SIT AROUND DOING NOTHING!
I'M GOING TO GET SOME DRINKS!
Take care while I'm gone!
SLAM
Hey!
THAT'S NOT FAIR!
Wait...

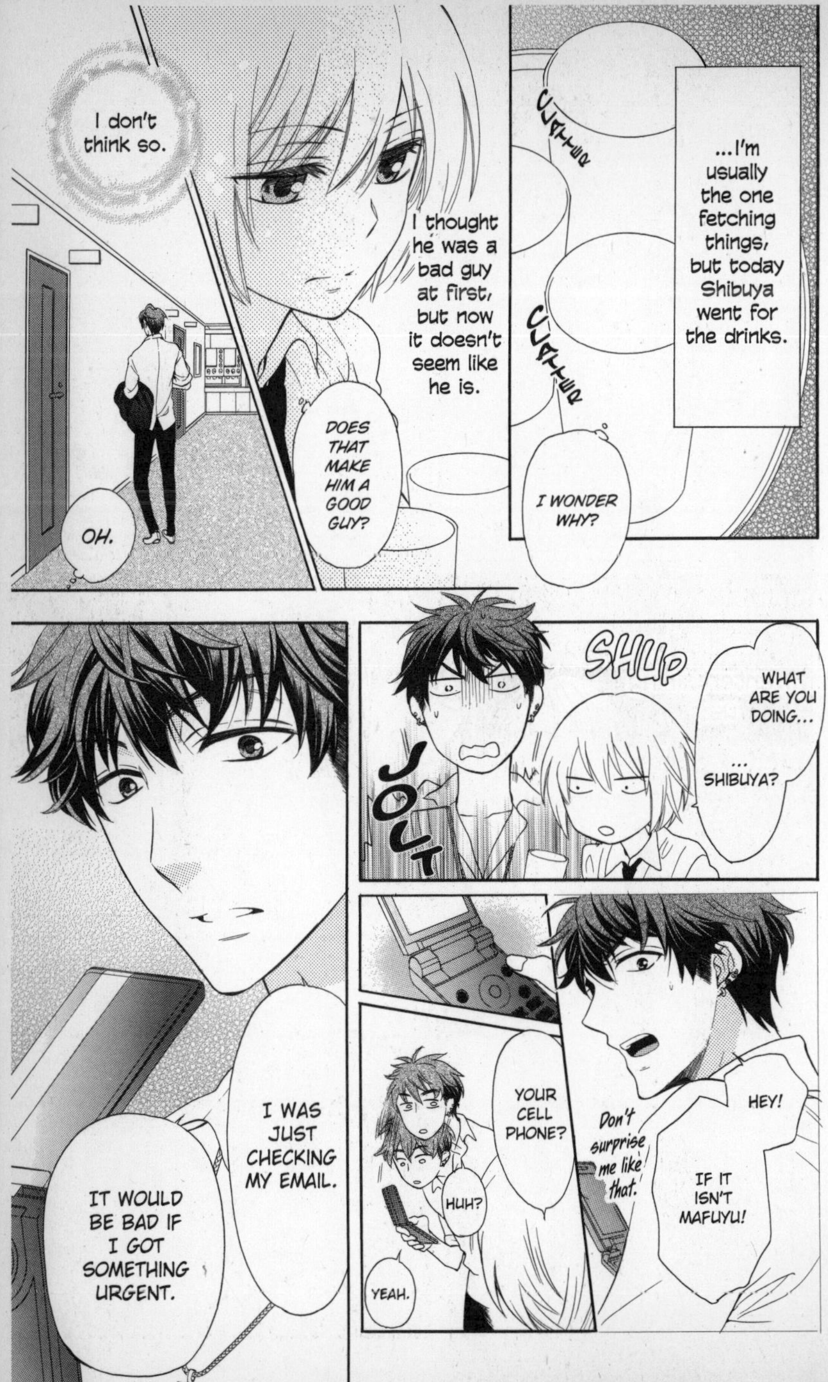
...I'm usually the one fetching things, but today Shibuya went for the drinks.
CLATTER
CLATTER
I WONDER WHY?
I thought he was a bad guy at first, but now it doesn't seem like he is.
DOES THAT MAKE HIM A GOOD GUY?
I don't think so.
OH.
WHAT ARE YOU DOING... ...SHIBUYA?
SHUP
JOLT
HEY!
IF IT ISN'T MAFUYU!
Don't surprise me like that.
YOUR CELL PHONE?
HUH?
YEAH.
I WAS JUST CHECKING MY EMAIL.
IT WOULD BE BAD IF I GOT SOMETHING URGENT.

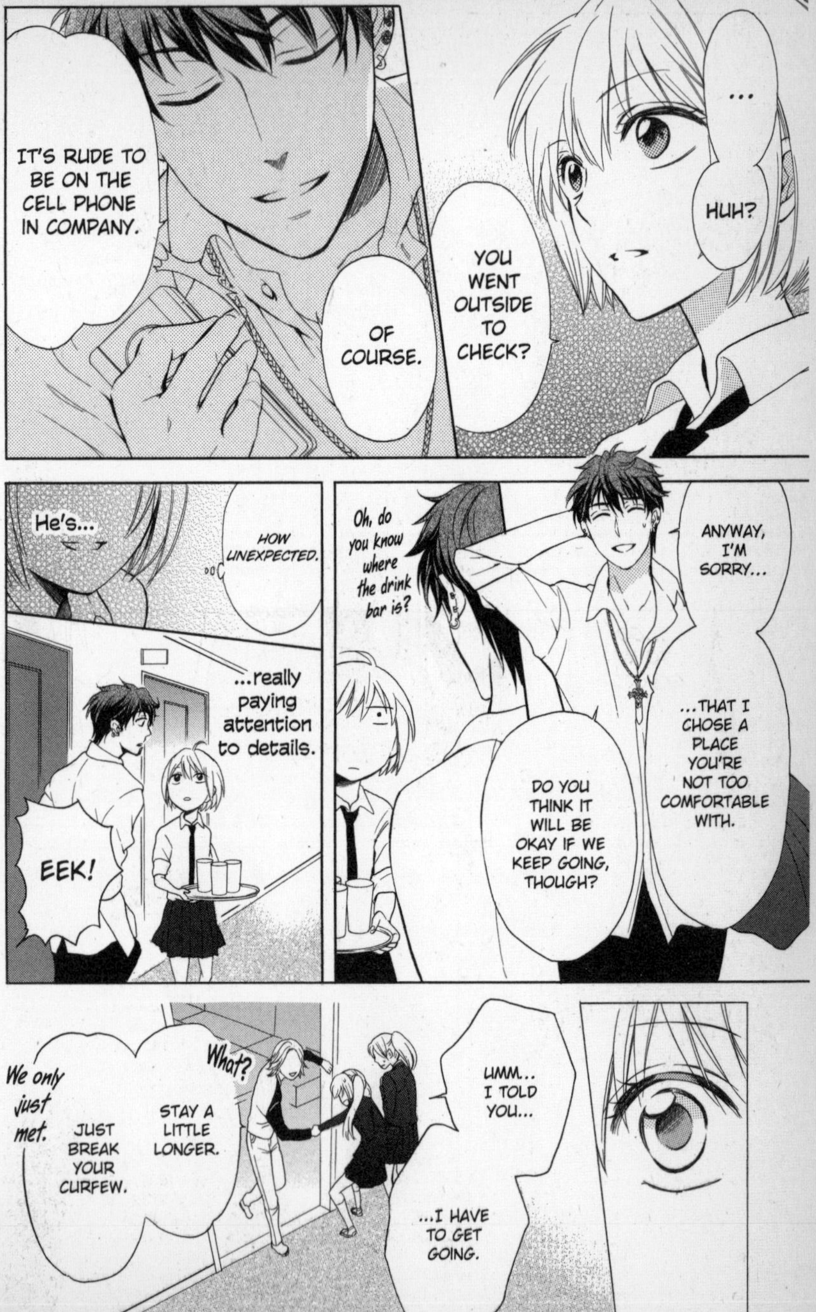
...
HUH?
YOU WENT OUTSIDE TO CHECK?
OF COURSE.
IT'S RUDE TO BE ON THE CELL PHONE IN COMPANY.
ANYWAY, I'M SORRY...
...THAT I CHOSE A PLACE YOU'RE NOT TOO COMFORTABLE WITH.
DO YOU THINK IT WILL BE OKAY IF WE KEEP GOING, THOUGH?
Oh, do you know where the drink bar is?
HOW UNEXPECTED.
He's...
...really paying attention to details.
EEK!
UMM... I TOLD YOU...
...I HAVE TO GET GOING.
What?
STAY A LITTLE LONGER.
JUST BREAK YOUR CURFEW.
We only just met.

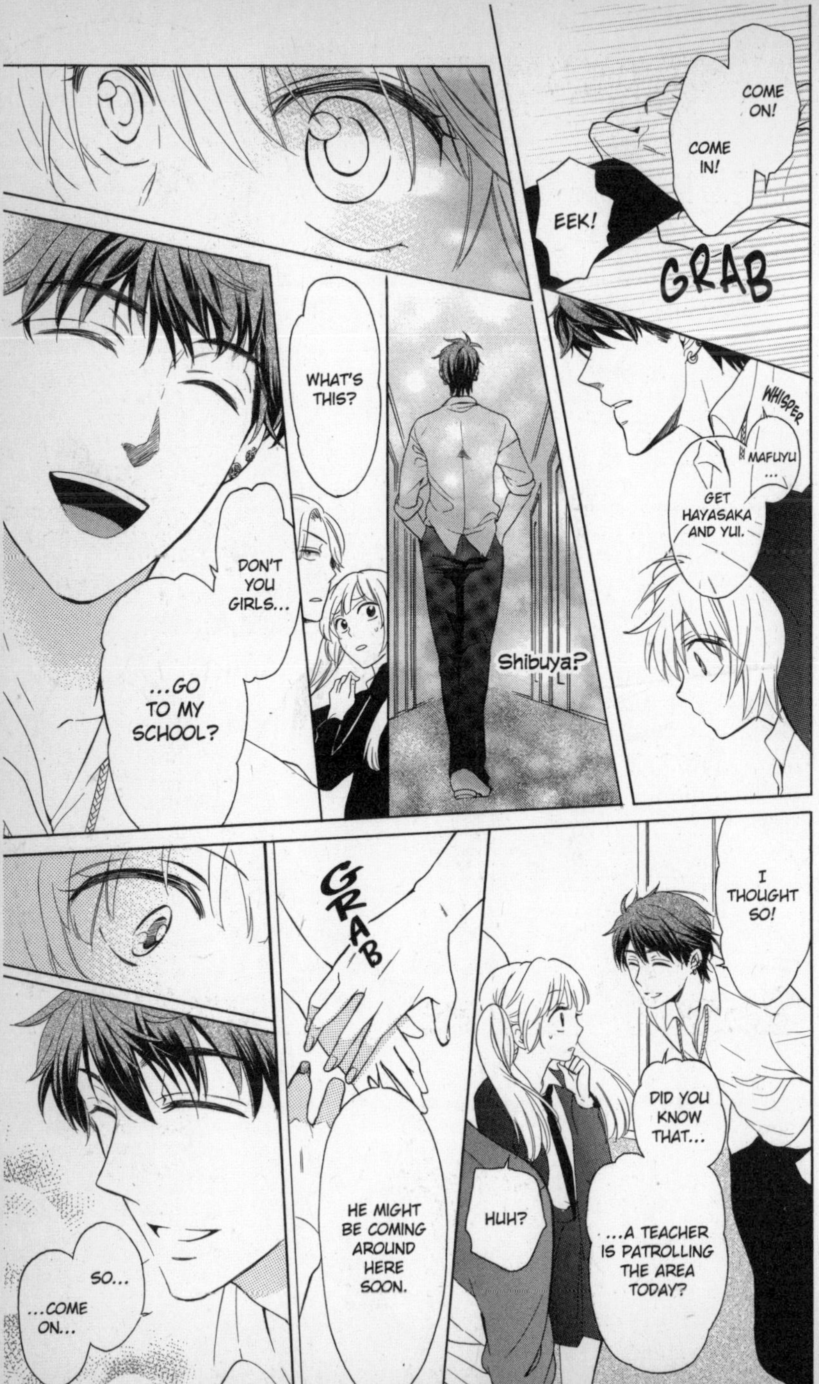
COME ON!
COME IN!
EEK!
GRAB
WHISPER
MAFUYU...
GET HAYASAKA AND YUI.
Shibuya?
WHAT'S THIS?
DON'T YOU GIRLS...
...GO TO MY SCHOOL?
I THOUGHT SO!
DID YOU KNOW THAT...
...A TEACHER IS PATROLLING THE AREA TODAY?
HUH?
GRAB
HE MIGHT BE COMING AROUND HERE SOON.
SO...
...COME ON...

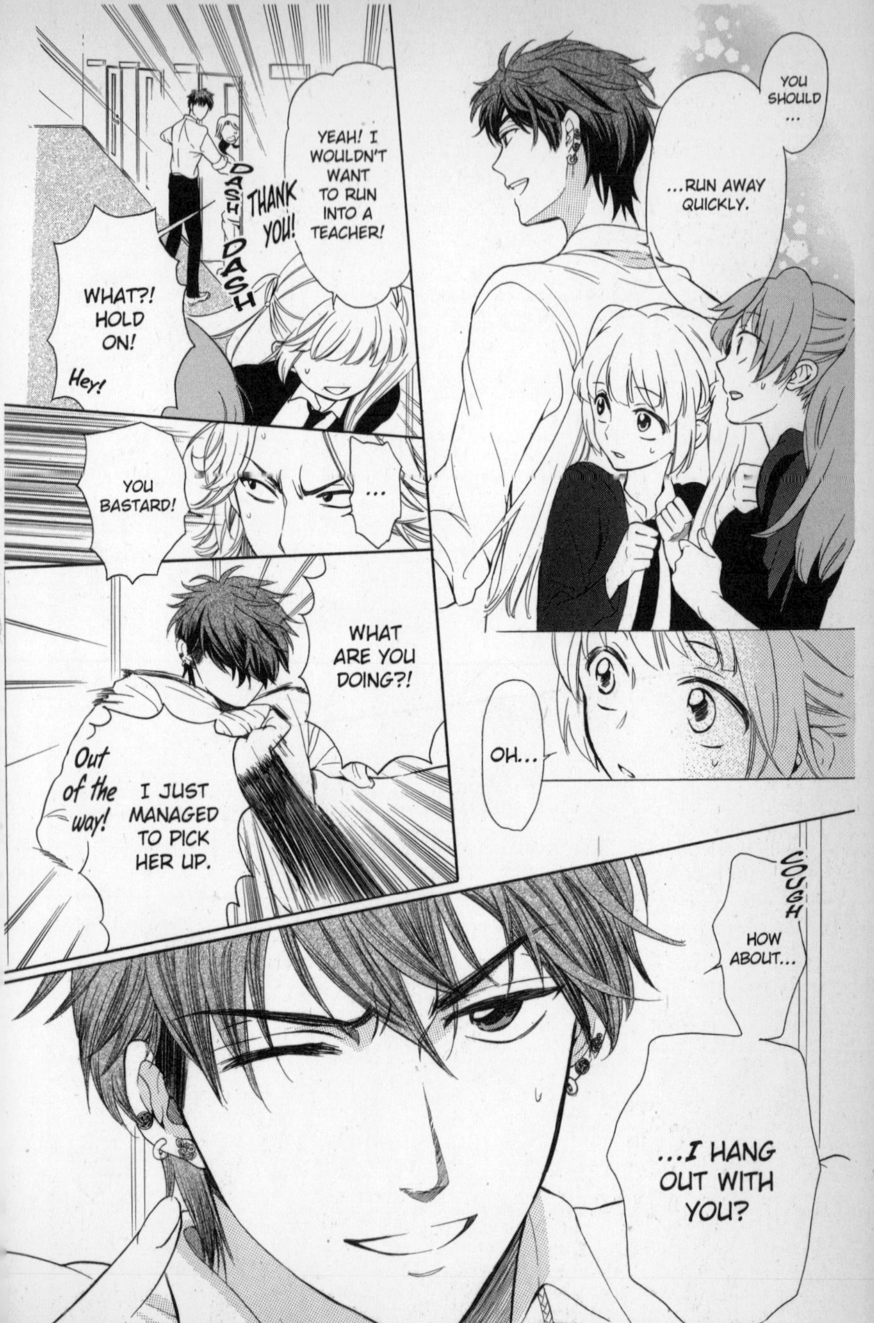
YOU SHOULD ...
...RUN AWAY QUICKLY.
YEAH! I WOULDN'T WANT TO RUN INTO A TEACHER!
THANK YOU!
DASH DASH
WHAT?! HOLD ON!
Hey!
YOU BASTARD!
...
WHAT ARE YOU DOING?!
Out of the way!
I JUST MANAGED TO PICK HER UP.
OH...
COUGH
HOW ABOUT...
...I HANG OUT WITH YOU?

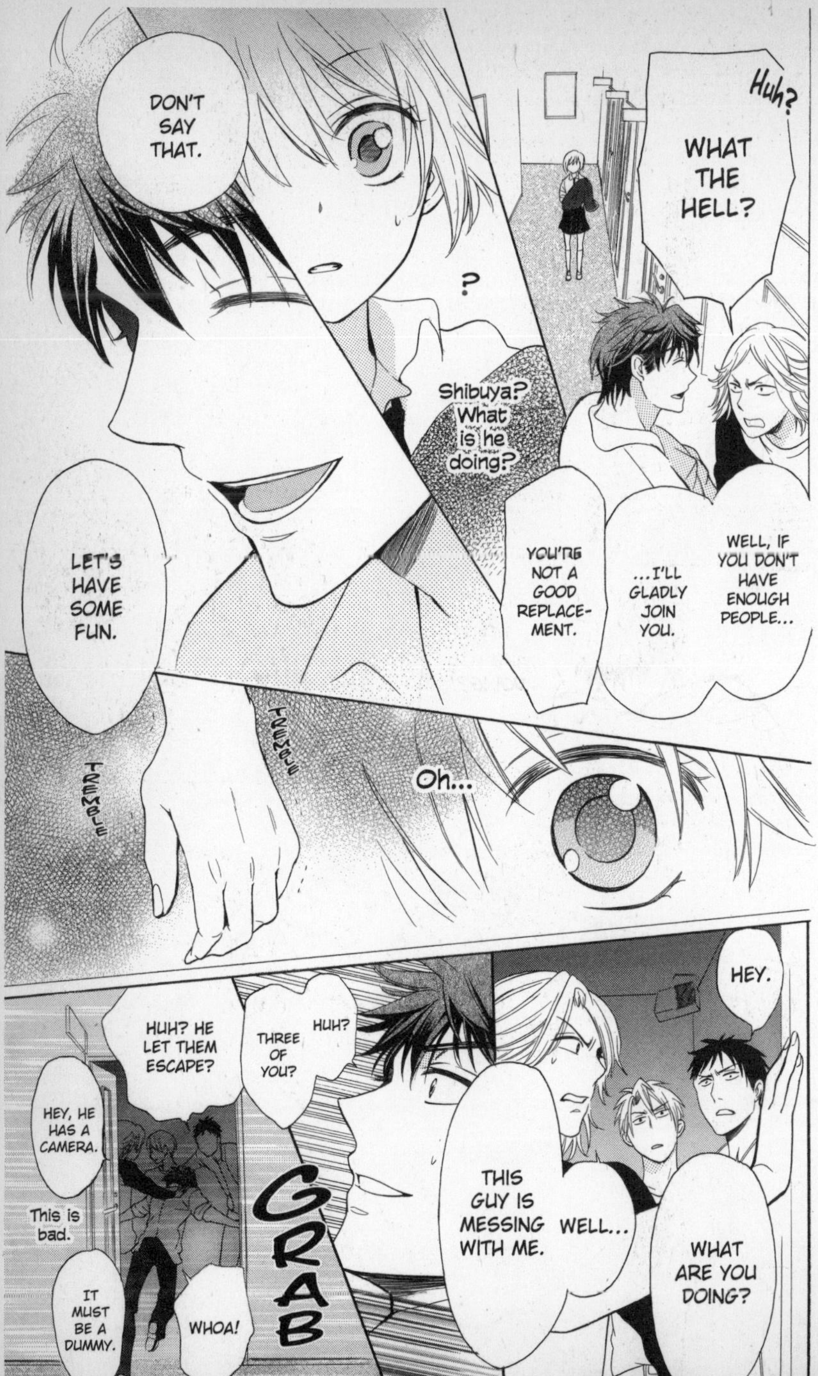
Huh?
WHAT THE HELL?
WELL, IF YOU DON'T HAVE ENOUGH PEOPLE...
...I'LL GLADLY JOIN YOU.
YOU'RE NOT A GOOD REPLACEMENT.
?
Shibuya? What is he doing?
DON'T SAY THAT.
LET'S HAVE SOME FUN.
Oh...
TREMBLE
TREMBLE
HEY.
WHAT ARE YOU DOING?
WELL...
THIS GUY IS MESSING WITH ME.
GRAB
HUH?
THREE OF YOU?
HUH? HE LET THEM ESCAPE?
HEY, HE HAS A CAMERA.
This is bad.
IT MUST BE A DUMMY.
WHOA!

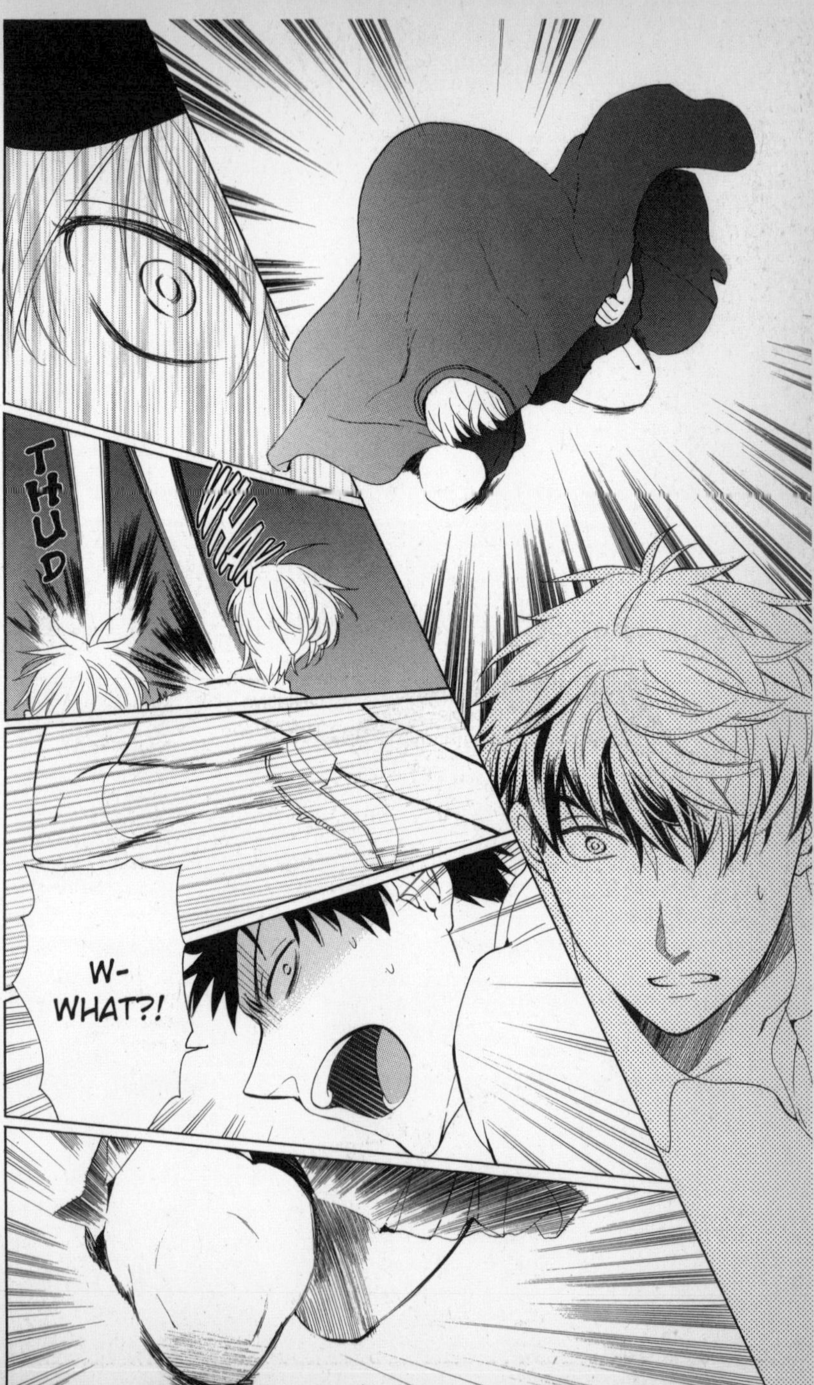
WHAK
THUD
W-
WHAT?!

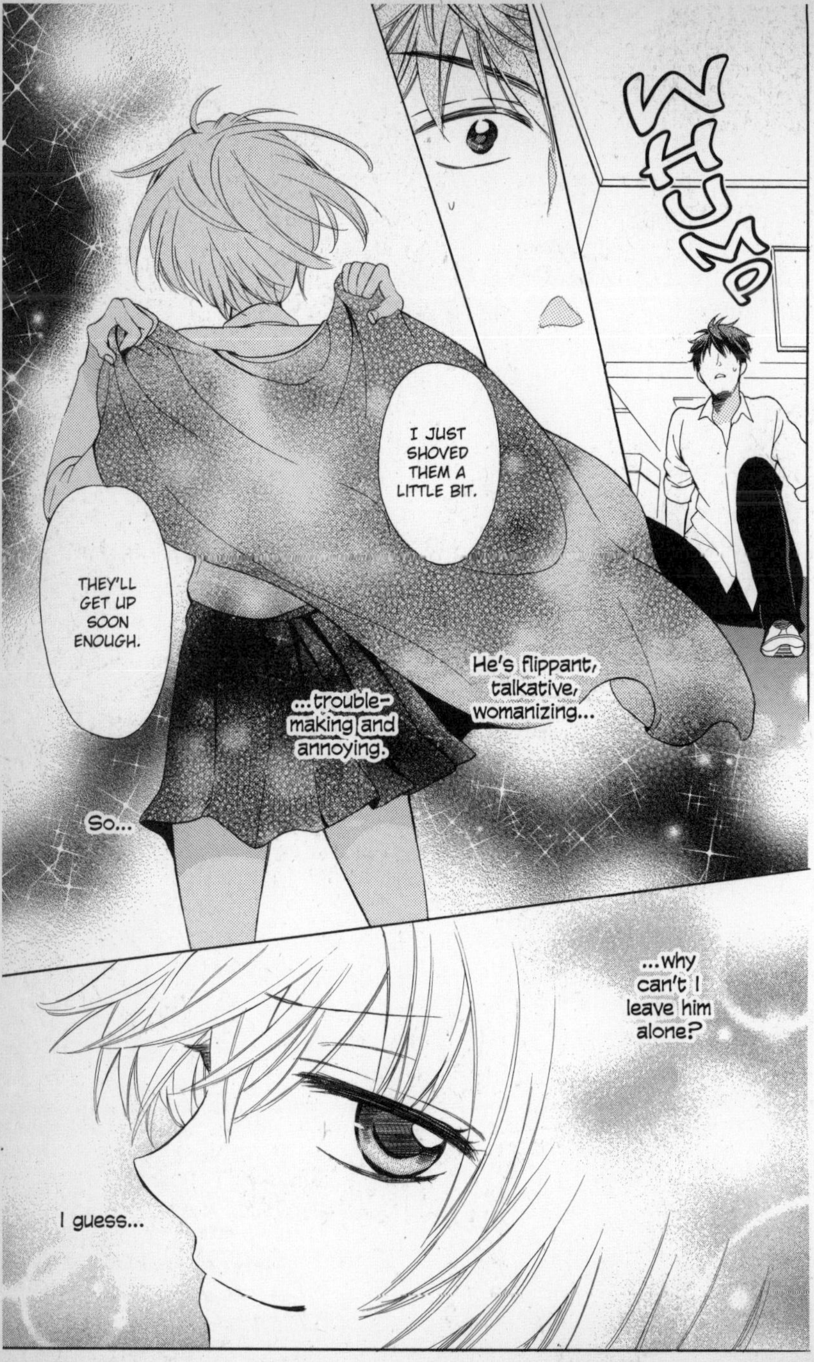
WHUMP
I JUST SHOVED THEM A LITTLE BIT.
THEY'LL GET UP SOON ENOUGH.
He's flippant, talkative, womanizing...
...trouble-making and annoying.
So...
...why can't I leave him alone?
I guess...

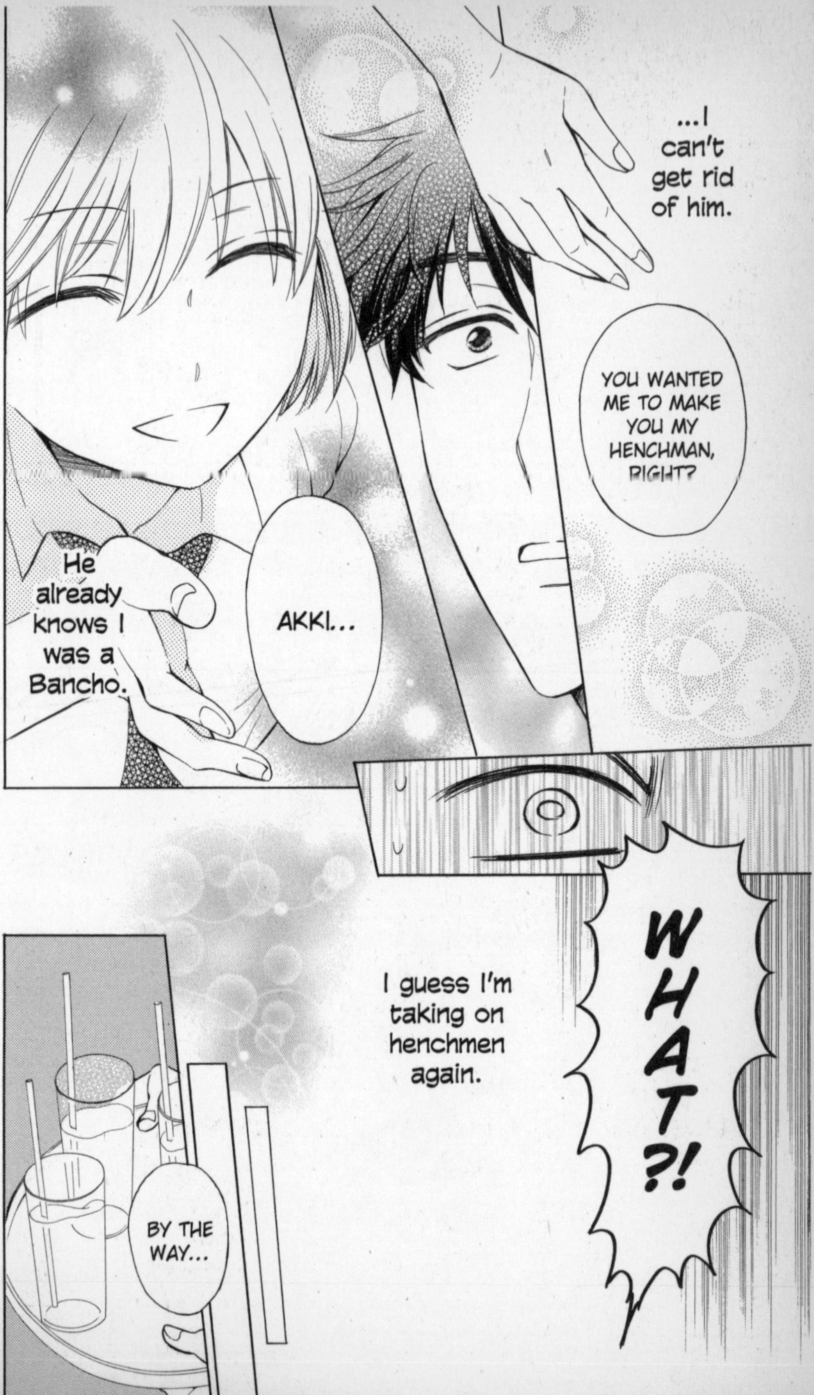
...I can't get rid of him.
YOU WANTED ME TO MAKE YOU MY HENCHMAN, RIGHT?
AKKI...
He already knows I was a Bancho.
WHAT?!
I guess I'm taking on henchmen again.
BY THE WAY...

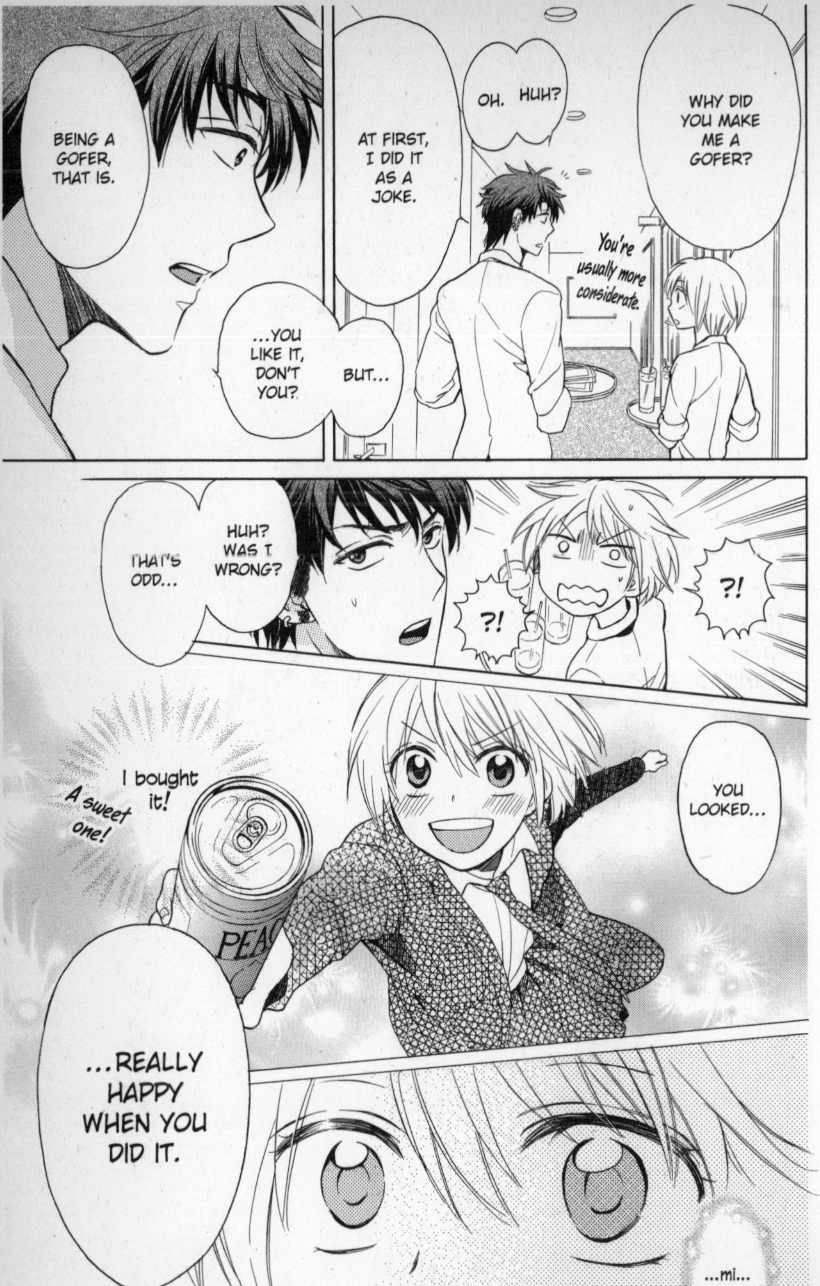

WHY DID YOU MAKE ME A GOFER?
OH. HUH?
You're usually more considerate.
AT FIRST, I DID IT AS A JOKE.
BUT...
...YOU LIKE IT, DON'T YOU?
BEING A GOFER, THAT IS.
?!
?!
HUH? WAS I WRONG?
THAT'S ODD...
YOU LOOKED...
I bought it!
A sweet one!
PEAC
...REALLY HAPPY WHEN YOU DID IT.
...mi...

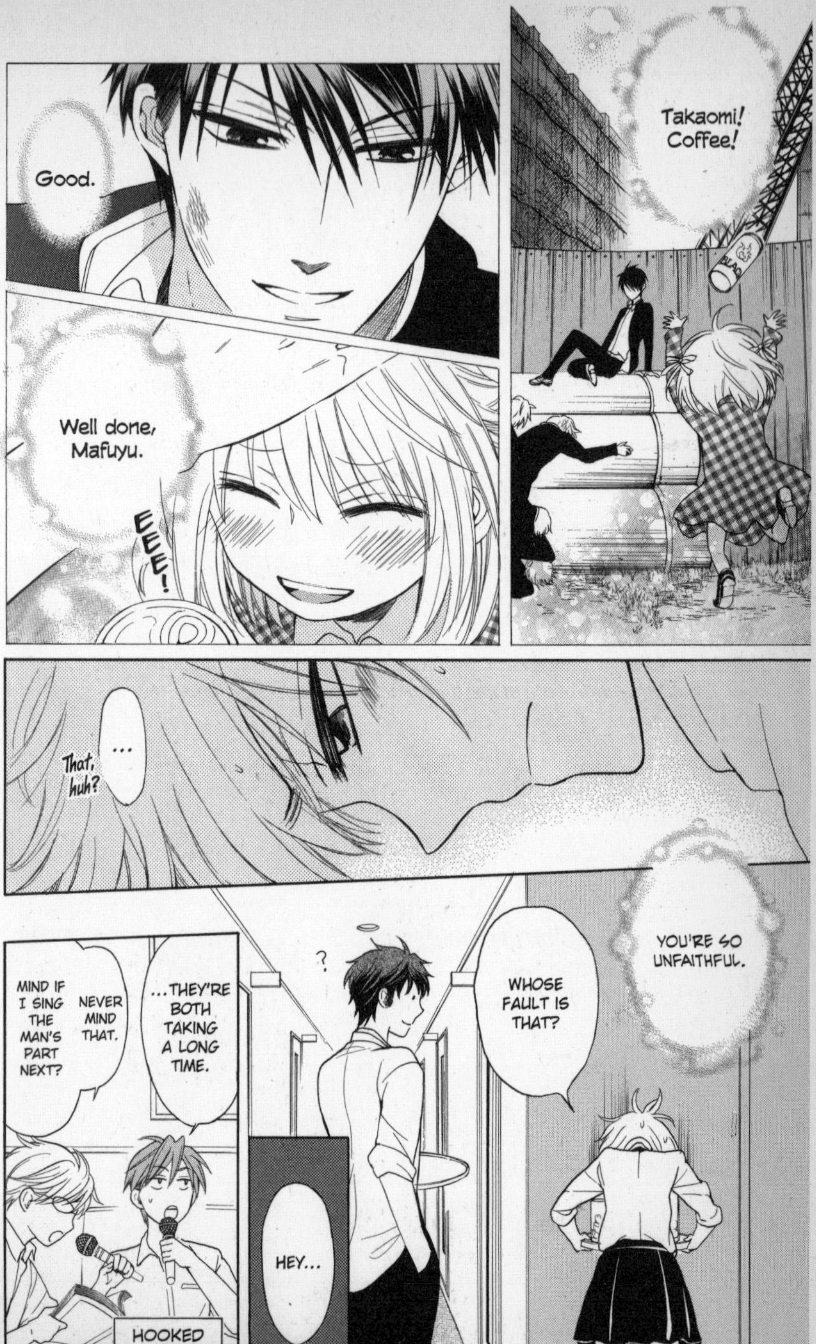
Takaomi! Coffee!
Good.
Well done, Mafuyu.
EEE!
That, huh?
...
YOU'RE SO UNFAITHFUL.
WHOSE FAULT IS THAT?
?
HEY...
...THEY'RE BOTH TAKING A LONG TIME.
NEVER MIND THAT.
MIND IF I SING THE MAN'S PART NEXT?
HOOKED ON DUETS

Thank you very much for buying volume 12! Just a little while ago I was happy that I completed volume 10, and now I'm at volume 12.

When I think about the plot points I should be getting to, I feel like I should pick up the pace. But if I get rid of the playful chapters, I won't have any fun.

I know! If I get rid of the main story... The main story... No, I can't do that.

There are only three more student council members left. We've finished over half of the story arc. I hope you'll continue to follow me in volume 13. I still have about two years' worth of material! The first year is too long! I've been taking my sweet time.

By the way, I've been keeping a blog of information on how I'm doing and about work. If you search for "Izumi Tsubaki Blog" you should find it. Check it out if you have the time.

Also, I was told that I have so many characters that the story has gotten confusing, so I made a character introduction page. Go to the next page!

AYABE FAMILY

CHARACTER RELATIONSHIPS

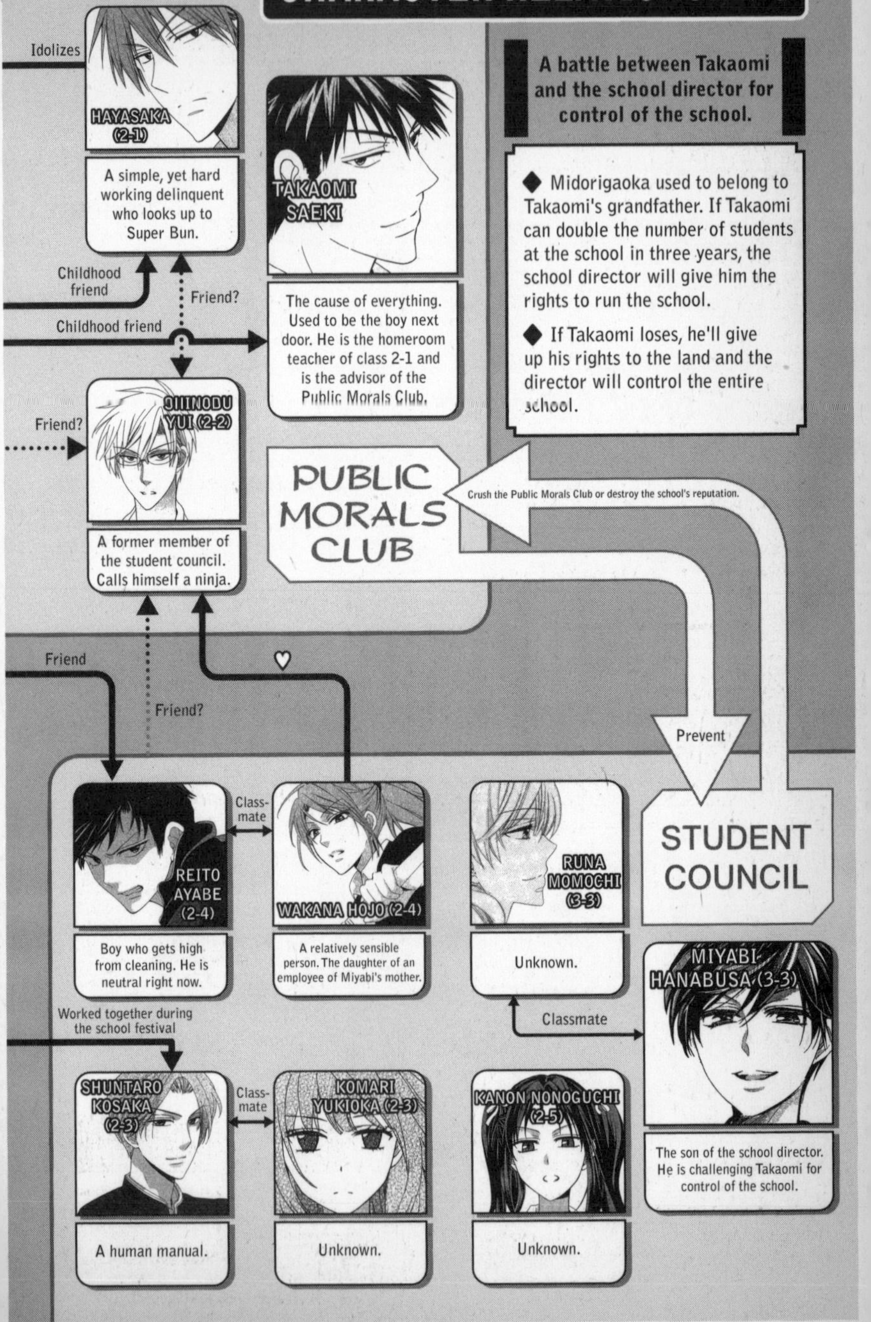

A battle between Takaomi and the school director for control of the school.
◆ Midorigaoka used to belong to Takaomi's grandfather. If Takaomi can double the number of students at the school in three years, the school director will give him the rights to run the school.
◆ If Takaomi loses, he'll give up his rights to the land and the director will control the entire school.
Idolizes
HAYASAKA (2-1)
A simple, yet hard working delinquent who looks up to Super Bun.
TAKAOMI SAEKI
The cause of everything. Used to be the boy next door. He is the homeroom teacher of class 2-1 and is the advisor of the Public Morals Club.
Childhood friend
Friend?
Childhood friend
Friend?
JIINODU YUI (2-2)
A former member of the student council. Calls himself a ninja.
PUBLIC MORALS CLUB
Crush the Public Morals Club or destroy the school's reputation.
Friend
♡
Friend?
Prevent
STUDENT COUNCIL
REITO AYABE (2-4)
Boy who gets high from cleaning. He is neutral right now.
Class-mate
WAKANA HOJO (2-4)
A relatively sensible person. The daughter of an employee of Miyabi's mother.
RUNA MOMOCHI (3-3)
Unknown.
Classmate
MIYABI HANABUSA (3-3)
The son of the school director. He is challenging Takaomi for control of the school.
Worked together during the school festival
SHUNTARO KOSAKA (2-3)
A human manual.
Class-mate
KOMARI YUKIOKA (2-3)
Unknown.
KANON NONOGUCHI (2-5)
Unknown.

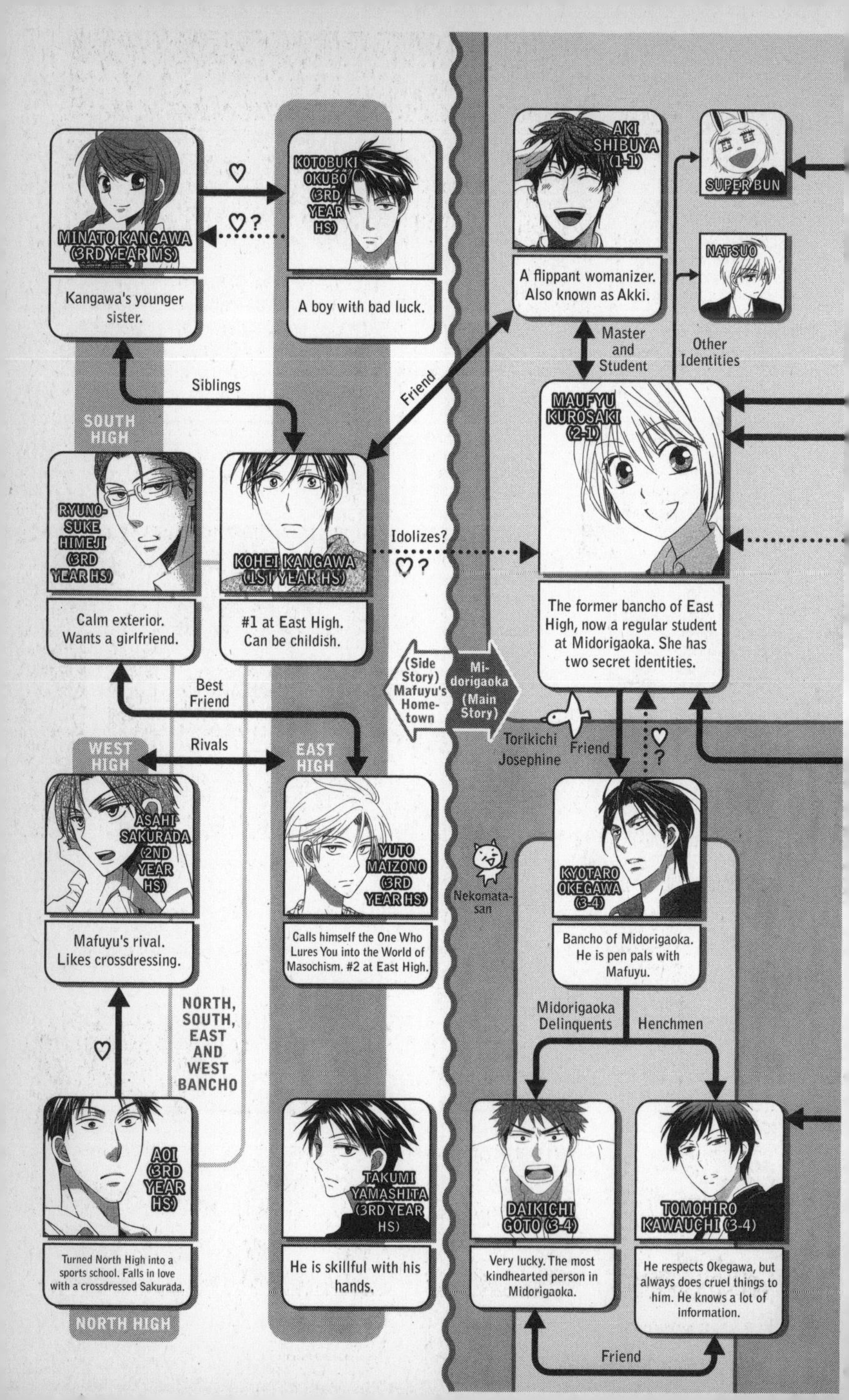

MINATO KANGAWA (3RD YEAR MS)
Kangawa's younger sister.
KOTOBUKI OKUBO (3RD YEAR HS)
A boy with bad luck.
♡
♡?
AKI SHIBUYA (1-1)
A flippant womanizer. Also known as Akki.
SUPER BUN
NATSUO
Other Identities
Master and Student
Siblings
Friend
SOUTH HIGH
MAUFYU KUROSAKI (2-1)
The former bancho of East High, now a regular student at Midorigaoka. She has two secret identities.
RYUNO-SUKE HIMEJI (3RD YEAR HS)
Calm exterior. Wants a girlfriend.
KOHEI KANGAWA (1ST YEAR HS)
#1 at East High. Can be childish.
Idolizes?
♡?
(Side Story) Mafuyu's Home-town
Mi-dorigaoka (Main Story)
Best Friend
Rivals
WEST HIGH
EAST HIGH
Torikichi Josephine
Friend
♡?
ASAHI SAKURADA (2ND YEAR HS)
Mafuyu's rival. Likes crossdressing.
YUTO MAIZONO (3RD YEAR HS)
Calls himself the One Who Lures You into the World of Masochism. #2 at East High.
Nekomata-san
KYOTARO OKEGAWA (3-4)
Bancho of Midorigaoka. He is pen pals with Mafuyu.
NORTH, SOUTH, EAST AND WEST BANCHO
Midorigaoka Delinquents
Henchmen
♡
AOI (3RD YEAR HS)
Turned North High into a sports school. Falls in love with a crossdressed Sakurada.
TAKUMI YAMASHITA (3RD YEAR HS)
He is skillful with his hands.
DAIKICHI GOTO (3-4)
Very lucky. The most kindhearted person in Midorigaoka.
TOMOHIRO KAWAUCHI (3-4)
He respects Okegawa, but always does cruel things to him. He knows a lot of information.
Friend
NORTH HIGH

BANCHO KANGAWA'S MANLINESS

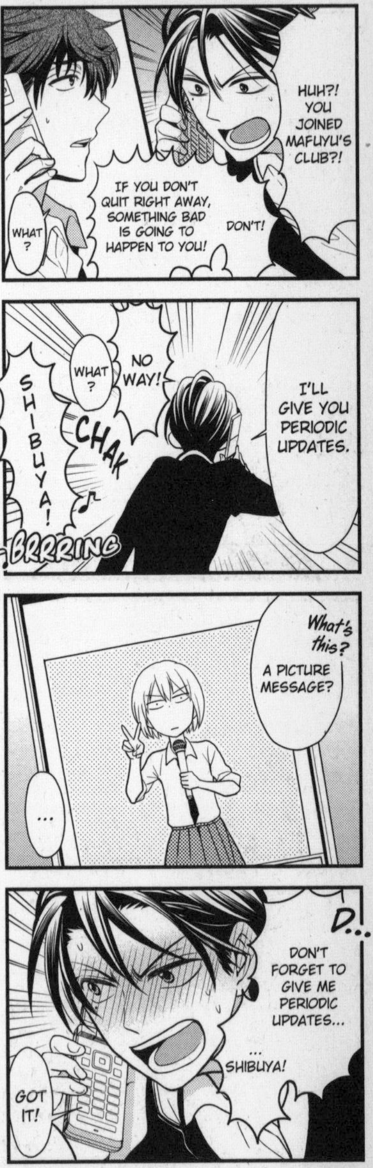
HUH?! YOU JOINED MAFUYU'S CLUB?!
DON'T!
IF YOU DON'T QUIT RIGHT AWAY, SOMETHING BAD IS GOING TO HAPPEN TO YOU!
WHAT?
I'LL GIVE YOU PERIODIC UPDATES.
NO WAY!
WHAT?
CHAK
SHIBUYA!
BRRRING
What's this?
A PICTURE MESSAGE?
...
D...
DON'T FORGET TO GIVE ME PERIODIC UPDATES...
... SHIBUYA!
GOT IT!

EMAIL FRIENDS

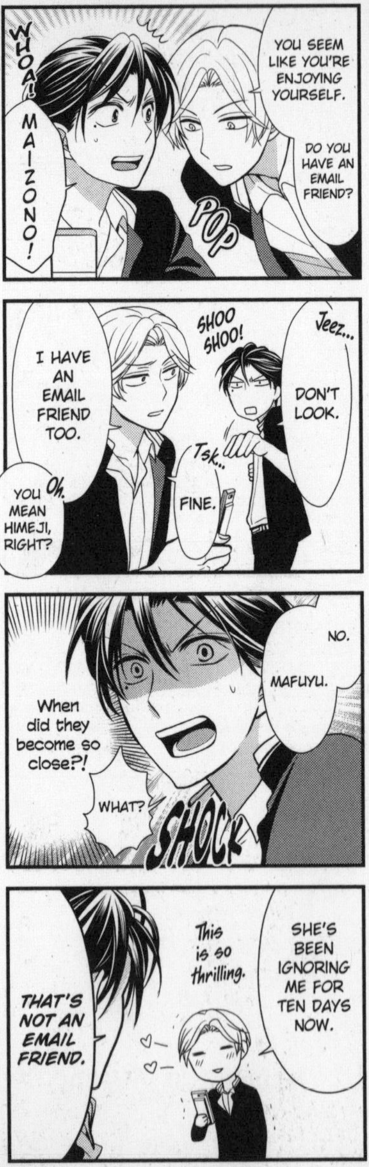
YOU SEEM LIKE YOU'RE ENJOYING YOURSELF.
DO YOU HAVE AN EMAIL FRIEND?
POP
WHOA! MAIZONO!
Jeez...
DON'T LOOK.
SHOO SHOO!
Tsk...
FINE.
I HAVE AN EMAIL FRIEND TOO.
Oh.
YOU MEAN HIMEJI, RIGHT?
NO.
MAFUYU.
When did they become so close?!
WHAT?
SHOCK
SHE'S BEEN IGNORING ME FOR TEN DAYS NOW.
This is so thrilling.
THAT'S NOT AN EMAIL FRIEND.

VALUE

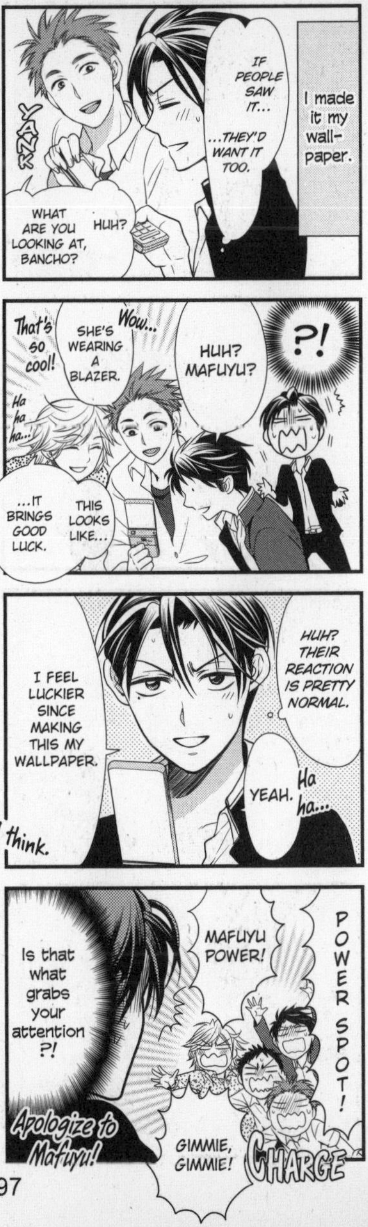
I made it my wallpaper.
IF PEOPLE SAW IT...
...THEY'D WANT IT TOO.
HUH?
WHAT ARE YOU LOOKING AT, BANCHO?
YANK
?!
HUH? MAFUYU?
Wow...
SHE'S WEARING A BLAZER.
That's so cool!
Ha ha ha...!
THIS LOOKS LIKE...
...IT BRINGS GOOD LUCK.
HUH? THEIR REACTION IS PRETTY NORMAL.
Ha ha...
YEAH.
I FEEL LUCKIER SINCE MAKING THIS MY WALLPAPER.
I think.
POWER SPOT!
MAFUYU POWER!
Is that what grabs your attention?!
CHARGE
GIMMIE, GIMMIE!
Apologize to Mafuyu!

WONDERFUL WALLPAPER

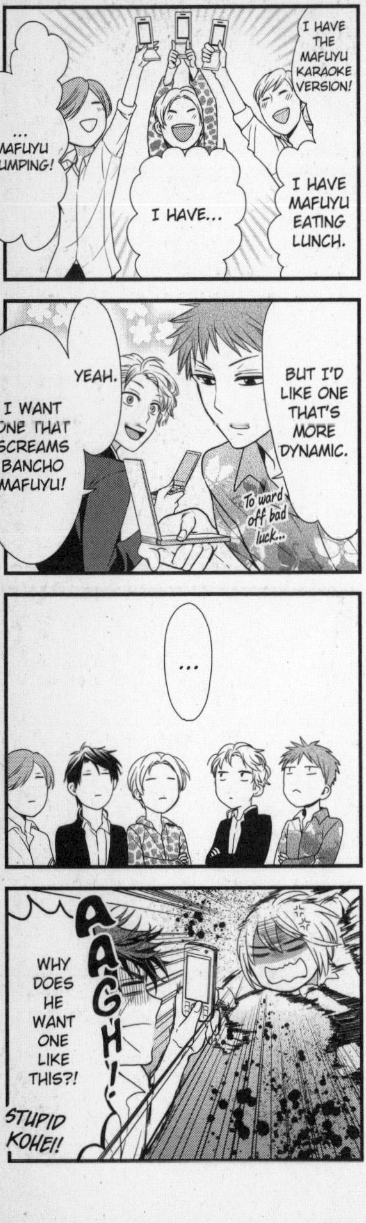
I HAVE THE MAFUYU KARAOKE VERSION!
I HAVE MAFUYU EATING LUNCH.
I HAVE...
... MAFUYU JUMPING!
BUT I'D LIKE ONE THAT'S MORE DYNAMIC.
To ward off bad luck...
YEAH.
I WANT ONE THAT SCREAMS BANCHO MAFUYU!
...
AAGH!
WHY DOES HE WANT ONE LIKE THIS?!
STUPID KOHEI!

MAFUYU OBSERVATION DIARY

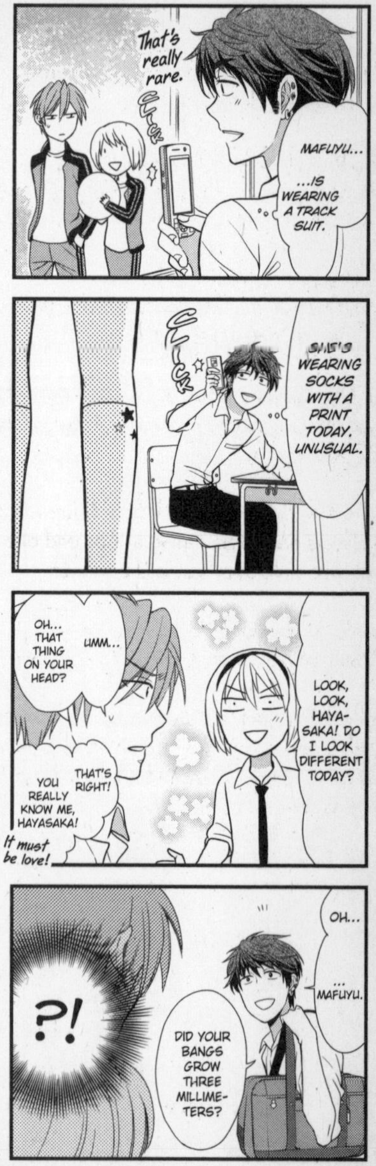
That's really rare.
CLICK
MAFUYU...
...IS WEARING A TRACK SUIT.
CLICK
SHE'S WEARING SOCKS WITH A PRINT TODAY. UNUSUAL.
LOOK, LOOK, HAYA-SAKA! DO I LOOK DIFFERENT TODAY?
UMM...
OH... THAT THING ON YOUR HEAD?
THAT'S RIGHT!
YOU REALLY KNOW ME, HAYASAKA!
It must be love!
OH...
...MAFUYU.
DID YOUR BANGS GROW THREE MILLIMETERS?
?!

BEYOND THE LENS

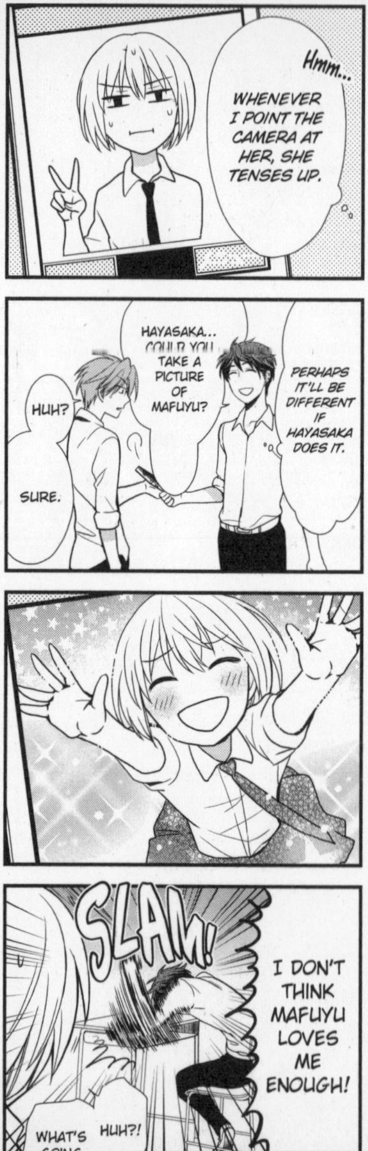
Hmm...
WHENEVER I POINT THE CAMERA AT HER, SHE TENSES UP.
PERHAPS IT'LL BE DIFFERENT IF HAYASAKA DOES IT.
HAYASAKA... COULD YOU TAKE A PICTURE OF MAFUYU?
HUH?
SURE.
SLAM!
I DON'T THINK MAFUYU LOVES ME ENOUGH!
HUH?!
WHAT'S GOING ON?

End Notes

Page 15, panel 3: fold up the bedding
Traditional Japanese beds (*futon*) are made up on the floor
and folded away during the day.

Page 54, panel 4: Suke, Kaku
Characters from the show *Mito Komon*, a samurai drama about
the fictional adventures of former vice shogun Tokugawa Mitsukuni.

Page 69, panel 4: Shogi kuzushi
A game similar to pickup sticks except shogi pieces
(think flattened marbles) are used.

Page 85, panel 1: He's a lord
Shinobu's wig is a hairstyle worn by lords during Japan's
feudal era.

Page 173, panel 5: The Pocky Game
Two players each start eating at one end of a Pocky stick. The
person who pulls away last is the winner.

Page 174, panel 3: Enka
A Japanese music genre known for its sentimental ballads.

Page 197, panel 4: Power spot
Power spots are thought to be places where a healing,
spiritual energy can be absorbed, including Mount Fuji
or certain shrines.

Izumi Tsubaki began drawing manga in her first year of high school. She was soon selected to be in the top ten of *Hana to Yume's* HMC (*Hana to Yume* Mangaka Course), and subsequently won *Hana to Yume's* Big Challenge contest. Her debut title, *Chijimete Distance* (Shrink the Distance), ran in 2002 in *Hana to Yume* magazine, issue 17. Her other works include *The Magic Touch* (*Oyayubi kara Romance*) and *Oresama Teacher*, which she is currently working on.

ORESAMA TEACHER
Vol. 12
Shojo Beat Edition

STORY AND ART BY
Izumi Tsubaki

English Translation & Adaptation/JN Productions
Touch-up Art & Lettering/Eric Erbes
Design/Yukiko Whitley
Editor/Pancha Diaz

ORESAMA TEACHER by Izumi Tsubaki © Izumi Tsubaki 2011
All rights reserved. First published in Japan in 2011 by HAKUSENSHA, Inc., Tokyo.
English language translation rights arranged with HAKUSENSHA, Inc., Tokyo.

Printed in Canada

Published by VIZ Media, LLC
P.O. Box 77010
San Francisco, CA 94107

10 9 8 7 6 5 4 3 2 1
First printing, January 2013

www.viz.com   www.shojobeat.com

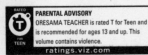

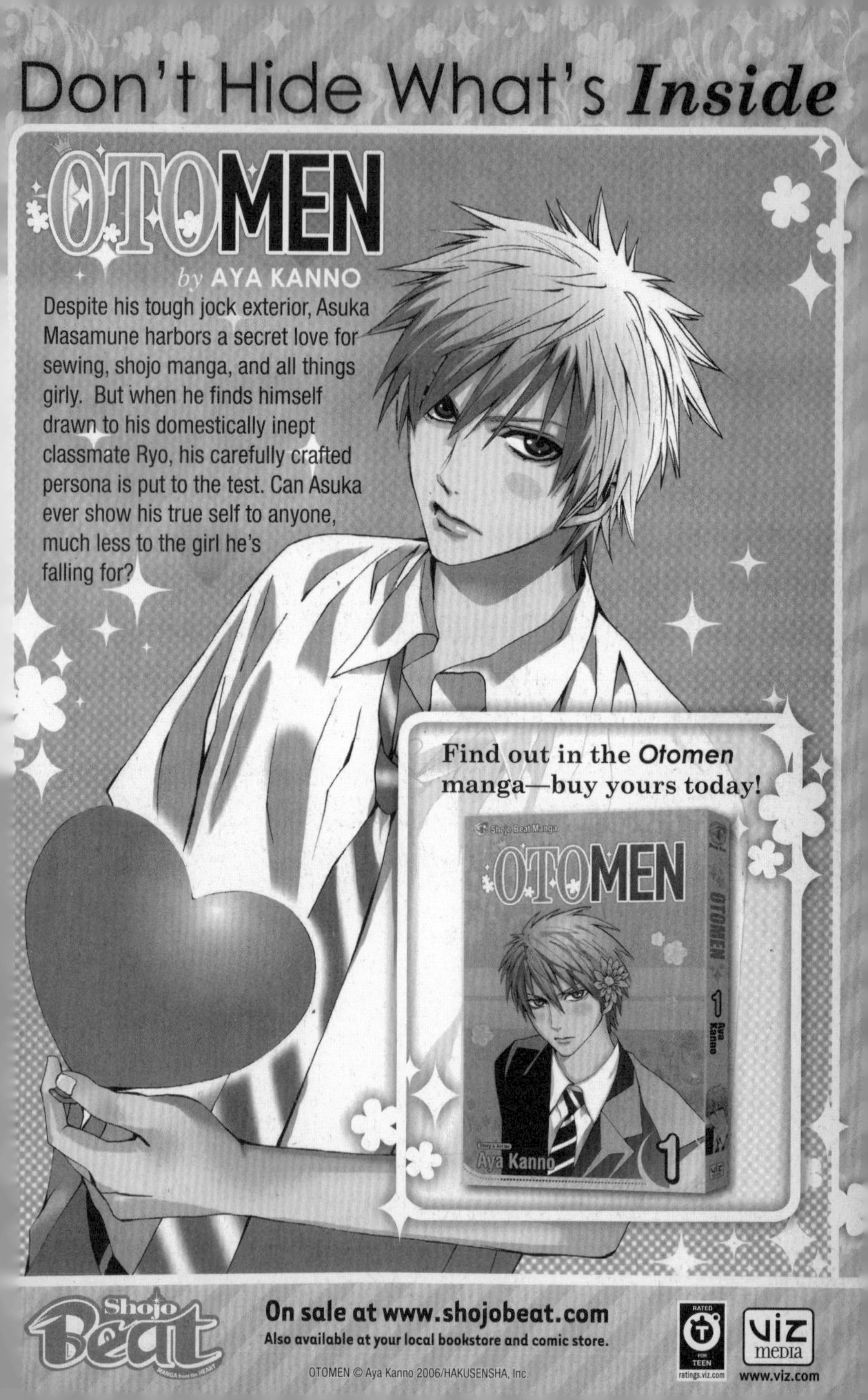
Don't Hide What's Inside
OTOMEN
by AYA KANNO
Despite his tough jock exterior, Asuka Masamune harbors a secret love for sewing, shojo manga, and all things girly. But when he finds himself drawn to his domestically inept classmate Ryo, his carefully crafted persona is put to the test. Can Asuka ever show his true self to anyone, much less to the girl he's falling for?
Find out in the Otomen manga—buy yours today!
Shojo Beat Manga
OTOMEN
Story & Art by
Aya Kanno
1
Shojo Beat
On sale at www.shojobeat.com
Also available at your local bookstore and comic store.
OTOMEN © Aya Kanno 2006/HAKUSENSHA, Inc.
RATED T FOR TEEN
ratings.viz.com
VIZ media
www.viz.com

A **Publisher's Weekly** bestseller!

What happens when the hottest boy in school

...is a girl?!?

Hana-Kimi
HISAYA NAKAJO
VOLUMES 1·2·3
Hana-Kimi
HISAYA NAKAJO
VOLUMES 4·5·6
Hana-Kimi
Story & Art by HISAYA NAKAJO
VOLUMES 7·8·9

Find out in these 3-in-1 collections of the hit shojo series!

Hana-Kimi

Story & Art by HISAYA NAKAJO

Mizuki Ashiya has such a crush on a track star named Izumi Sano that she moves from the U.S. to Japan to enroll in the all-male high school he goes to! Pretending to be a boy, Mizuki becomes Sano's roommate...

...but how can she keep such a big secret when she's so close to the guy she wants?

IN STORES NOW!

3-in-1 Vol. 1 ISBN: 978-1-4215-4224-9
3-in-1 Vol. 2 ISBN: 978-1-4215-4225-6
3-in-1 Vol. 3 ISBN: 978-1-4215-4229-4

Only **$14.99 US / $16.99 CAN** each!

RATED T+ FOR OLDER TEEN ratings.viz.com

Shojo Beat

VIZ media www.viz.com

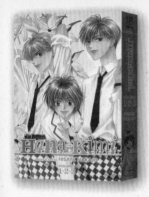

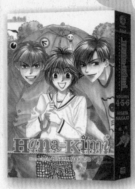

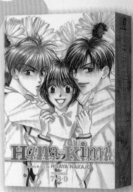

Surprise!

You may be reading the wrong way!

It's true: In keeping with the original Japanese comic format, this book reads from right to left—so action, sound effects, and word balloons are completely reversed. This preserves the orientation of the original artwork—plus, it's fun! Check out the diagram shown here to get the hang of things, and then turn to the other side of the book to get started!

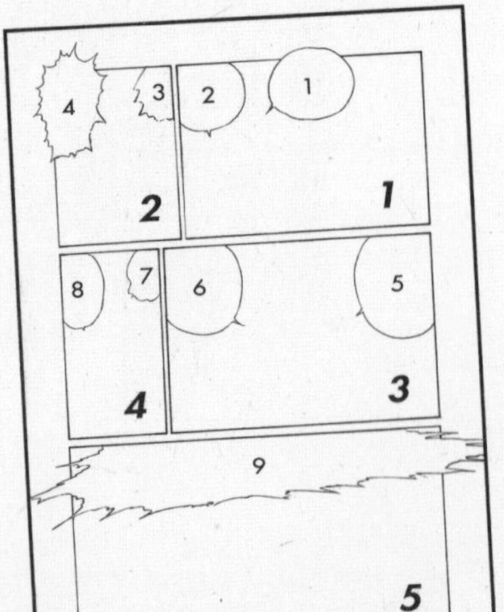

1
2
1
3
4
2
5
6
3
7
8
4
9
5
142

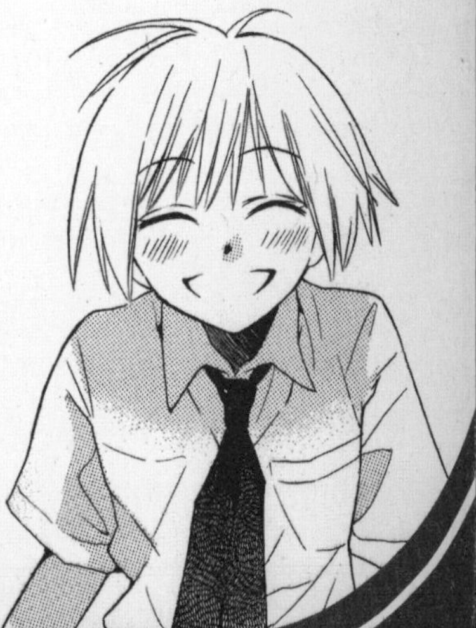

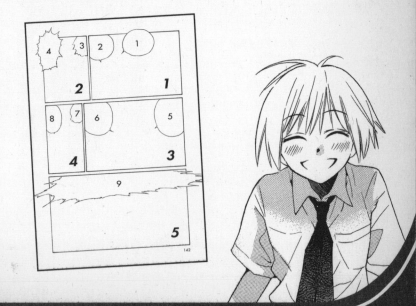